HELPING CHILDREN
LEARN TO READ

Consulting Editor
Jack Nelson
Rutgers University

HELPING CHILDREN LEARN TO READ

Patrick J. Finn
State University of New York at Buffalo

RANDOM HOUSE  NEW YORK

First Edition
987654321
Copyright © 1985 by Random House, Inc.

Library of Congress Cataloging in Publication Data

Finn, Patrick J.
    Helping children learn to read.
    Bibliography: p.
    Includes index.
    1. Reading (Elementary)   I. Title.
LB1573.F52   1985   372.4'1   84-24933
ISBN 0-394-32893-0

Manufactured in the United States of America

Book design by Celine Brandes/Photo Plus Art
Art by Amy Finn

To My Mother
Alverna Smerz Finn

PREFACE

Helping Children Learn to Read is a basic text on teaching reading. It presents a survey of traditional and current beliefs concerning the content of the reading program and methods of teaching reading. It presents examples of programs, materials, and methods used in classrooms and shows how they are used.

However, the current and traditional wisdom about these topics is not without its contradictions and controversies. One thing that sets textbooks of this kind apart is how they deal with these contradictions and controversies.

One way to cope with controversy is to avoid it. For example, several textbooks for basic courses in teaching reading present a traditional, behavioristic approach. These books explain to the reader what one teaches when he or she teaches reading and how one goes about teaching those things in terms of a respected, time-honored tradition. Challenges to this tradition are simply not mentioned.

On the other hand, there has been a great deal of interest in the recent past among educators in psycholinguistics, cognitive psychology, and the sociology of learning. New findings and new ways of thinking about language and learning have resulted in new ideas of what one teaches when he or she teaches reading and how one goes about teaching those things. There are textbooks for basic courses in teaching reading that reflect these trends only. Traditional notions that are not compatible with these trends are simply not given any serious consideration.

The kinds of textbooks discussed thus far have one thing in common. They present a *single* point of view. The reasoning behind this approach is the belief that undergraduates need to learn one way of teaching reading and that controversy should be avoided in the basic courses. It is soon enough to introduce controversy during advanced courses or even during graduate courses.

I believe this position is misguided for the following reasons:

1. The average adult knows there are competing ideas regarding reading curriculum and methods. One would hope that a college-level course in teaching reading would give a student enough information to discuss issues that regularly appear in letters to the editor of daily newspapers.
2. Beginning teachers are asked to make decisions and answer questions about what they are doing. We owe it to them to make them aware of the existence of controversy and the terms of the debate.
3. Every teacher has to decide what to do on Monday morning and has to learn how to do it. Teachers who are trained in a single approach are in a vulnerable position. Challenges to their Monday morning strategies are likely to lead to a defensive retreat into dogmatism.

4. Teachers who have learned how to fill up a teaching day are sometimes reluctant to examine their assumptions or entertain suggestions on how to improve their teaching programs. Students in graduate school often take the attitude that since they already teach reading, there is no point in considering what appear to be abstract and irrelevant issues.

The point is that one wants to produce reflective teachers who are willing to examine the assumptions their curriculum and methods are based on and to consider other points of view. One is not likely to produce such teachers if teaching reading is presented at the start as a set of cut-and-dried procedures. The best way of producing such teachers is to show them from the start that there is more than one way of teaching reading and to make them familiar with the assumptions involved in taking a particular approach.

A second way of coping with the controversies that surround teaching reading is to present the better-known points of view on matters of curriculum and method and to adopt the commonsense attitude that these points of view would not be widely accepted if they did not have some validity. One therefore finds textbooks in which various points of view on matters of content and methods are presented as evenhandedly as possible. In this approach, one takes the broad areas of concern for the reading teacher (for example, readiness, word recognition, or comprehension) and asks two questions:

1. What is the content of this area (the curriculum)?
2. What is the best way to teach this content?

Then one presents well-established points of view on these questions and offers some advice about what one should do as a teacher. The pattern is then repeated for each new area of concern.

What this pattern fails to take into account is that the points of view presented under various areas of concern often represent the same schools of thought. For example, the idea that learning to read may be thought of as an ordered set of small steps reappears in every area of concern for the teaching of reading. However, books of this type often fail to take notice of this continuity from topic to topic, or they take notice of it in an inconsistent manner.

In *Helping Children Learn to Read*, four ways of looking at and thinking about learning are presented in the first chapter in two pairs. The first pair represents two traditions or schools of thought that have a long history in the study of psychology. One school of thought concentrates on dividing learning into small steps to be presented to the learner one bit at a time, in a particular order. This school of thought has been characterized as "bottom-up" and as concentrating on the "outer" aspects of reading (letter-sound correspondences, and so on). Its adherents have a particular fascination with the relation between ease of learning and frequency. This is the time-honored empirical tradition.

The second school of thought concentrates on whole tasks and large concepts that the learner is expected to engage and apprehend. To master such wholes, the learner takes notice of parts and details. But each learner will find different parts and details troublesome, so a teacher cannot predict which bits will need to be taught to individuals. This school of thought has been characterized as "top-down" and as concentrating on the "inner" aspects of reading (the reader's insights into whole tasks and concepts). Its adherents have a particular fascination with the relationship between the ease of learning and the individual learner's internal condition—his or her level of cognitive development, emotional state, and so on. This is the time-honored rationalist tradition.

The second pair of ways of thinking about learning represents the contrast between viewing learning as a psychological (individual) process and as a sociological (group) process.

One view is that learning can be conceptualized as a thing that takes place inside a learner's head—an individual thing. It takes place as a result of the maturity of the learner's mind and the learner's interaction with the environment. The implication of this point of view is that it is the teacher's job to structure the environment to maximize each individual's potential to learn. This is a psychological view of learning.

A contrasting view is that learning can be conceptualized as a thing that takes place in society. This view concentrates on the social aspects of learning. The implication is that it is the teacher's job to create a community in the classroom where the thing to be learned is valued by the community and where members of the community who are lacking knowledge and skills have access to members of the community who possess knowledge and skills. This is a sociological view of learning.

In *Helping Children Learn to Read,* as each area is introduced, questions of curriculum and methods are addressed. Where it is relevant, these questions are related to the empirical and rationalist traditions and to the sociological and psychological views of the learning process.

Referring to these four traditions explicitly, consistently, and coherently ensures continuity from topic to topic; it gives the student guidance in deciding where his or her beliefs fit into the scheme of things; and it relates teaching decisions to underlying assumptions. One is less likely to see students claiming to adhere to both sides of an issue without the realization that there is a logical conflict in their thinking. On the other hand, it is likely to ensure against dogmatism. A person who is conscious of the assumptions that underlie a belief or an approach is not likely to think that one set of assumptions will apply equally well to every teaching goal in every area of the reading curriculum from grades 1 through 12. He or she is more likely to adopt those assumptions which best fit a particular teaching challenge and to adopt strategies compatible with those assumptions.

One final point: Empiricism, rationalism, and the psychological and sociological views of learning have their roots in philosophy, psychology, and sociology. When one introduces these points of view in a consistent way in a text on teaching reading, he or she runs the risk of overwhelming the student with concepts with which the student is not prepared to deal. In *Helping Children Learn to Read* I have endeavored to explain each concept that is introduced so that students (and teachers who are, after all, not philosophers, linguists, psychologists, and so on themselves) can understand them and see their relevance to the topic at hand.

ACKNOWLEDGMENTS

I would like to thank Professor Noel Entwistle and the Department of Education at the University of Edinburgh for their hospitality during my sabbatical year when this book took shape in my mind and the beginnings of it took shape on paper.

I would like to thank Mary Lyons for her assistance in library research and Rosemary Lonberger for tracking down materials and suggesting ideas for illustrations.

Mary Anne Doyle, Rosemary Lonberger, Mary Lyons, and Douglas Rogers were all students of mine who read drafts of early chapters and said they were good. I have great respect for all of them, and their approval was a great help.

Amy Finn did all the original line drawings. I think they are perfect.

All the original photographs of classroom settings were done by Carolyn King. The art work portrayed in these photographs was done by Jeannie Martino. I thank them for their excellent work and their cooperation on a very tight schedule.

My thanks also go to Rosemary Murray and the other teachers and students at College Learning Laboratory of the State University of New York College at Buffalo for their cooperation in obtaining these photographs

Nancy Myers typed the whole manuscript and did numerous revisions, and she did it cheerfully. Both her skill and cheerfulness made writing this book a whole lot easier.

I would also like to thank my colleagues who reviewed the manuscript and offered valuable suggestions: Dean Irene Athey, Rutgers University; Professor Jack Bagford, University of Iowa; Professor James V. Hoffman, University of Texas; Professor James E. Kerber, Ohio State University; Professor J. Kurth, North Texas State University; Dr. Genevieve Lopardo, Chicago State University; Professor Jana M. Mason, Center for the Study of Reading, Champaign, Illinois; Professor Imogene Ramsey, Eastern Kentucky University; Professor Wallace Ramsey, University of Missouri; Professor Richard L. Venezky, University of Delaware; and Professor Jerry Zutell, Ohio State University.

My daughters, Molly and Amy, have always offered me encouragement and support. But beyond that they have tended to the business of growing up and getting on with their lives in a way that has enabled me to tend to my business. For the past several years my chief business has been writing this book, and I thank them for their part in it.

My wife, Mary, and I have different interests, different fields of study, and different ways of thinking. We have talked a lot over a lot of years, and I don't honestly know any longer which of my ideas were originally her ideas. I couldn't have written this book without her. That is, however, one of the less important reasons that I bless the day I found her.

CONTENTS

1
FOUNDATIONS OF
TEACHING READING

1

THE FIRST TASK: DECIDING WHAT TO DO   2
What Is Reading?,   2
Where Do Trends in Methods Come From?,   2

BASIC DIFFERENCES IN THE STUDY OF LANGUAGE AND LEARNING   4
The Starting Point: Philosophy,   4
Counting, Measuring, Recording, Describing: The Empiricist
   Tradition,   4
The Study of the Mind: The Rationalist Tradition,   5
Contrasts in the Two Traditions,   5

EVENTS LEADING TO THE CURRENT SCENE   6
The Study of Language and Psychology Without Reference to
   the Mind,   6
The Impact of Empirical Assumptions on Education,   10
Psycholinguistics,   11
Cognitive Psychology: Mental Development and Language
   Development,   13
Some Shortcomings of Behaviorism, Psycholinguistics, and
   Cognitive Psychology,   15

LANGUAGE LEARNING AS A SOCIAL PROCESS   15
Language as Part of the Social System,   15
Language and Cognition as Part of Social Development,   16
Differences among Societies,   19
A Sociological Perspective on Learning,   21

TWO ASPECTS OF READING INSTRUCTION: CONTRASTING VIEWS   22
Empiricist Versus Rationalist Perspectives,   22
Psychological Versus Sociological Perspectives,   22
The Interdependence of These Perspectives,   22

SUMMARY   22

FOR FURTHER READING AND DISCUSSION   24

REFERENCES   25

2
READING READINESS   27

HOW THE CONCEPT OF READING READINESS ARISES   28

A TRADITIONAL CONCEPT   29
Assumptions Underlying Readiness Tasks,   29
Challenging the Assumptions Underlying Task A,   30

CONCEPTS OF READING READINESS IN PUBLISHED TESTS   30
Auditory Discrimination and Memory, Visual Discrimination and
    Memory,   30
Alphabet Knowledge,   31
Word Learning Tasks,   34
Oral Language Comprehension,   35
Readiness Tasks Reflect Assumptions About Reading,   36

THE USEFULNESS OF PUBLISHED READINESS TESTS   37
Predicting Who Will Learn to Read,   37
Selecting Students for Reading Instruction,   39
Diagnosis,   41
Unexamined Assumptions and Unwarranted Practices,   43

THE CONCEPT OF READINESS IN AN UP-TO-DATE CLASSROOM   44
To Test Readiness, Teach Reading,   44
Two Widely Divergent Methods,   44

THE CONCEPT OF READINESS AS A PREREADING CURRICULUM   48
Traditional Reading Readiness Skills,   48
Concepts Related to Print and Reading,   49
Understanding the Vocabulary of Reading Instruction,   50
Concepts Related to Storybooks,   51

LANGUAGE DEVELOPMENT AND READING READINESS   51
Reading Skill and Language Development,   51
Assessing Language Development,   53
Selecting and Diagnosing on the Basis of Language
    Development,   54

SCHOOL READINESS AND READING READINESS   **55**
Readiness for Instruction,   55
Assessing School Readiness,   55
Selecting and Diagnosing on the Basis of School Readiness,   56

SUMMARY   **57**

FOR FURTHER READING AND DISCUSSION   **58**

REFERENCES   **60**

3
TEACHING WORD RECOGNITION   63

DEFINING WORD RECOGNITION   **64**
The Beginning Reader's "Concept of Word,"   64
Learning Word Meaning Versus Word Learning Recognition,   64

APPROACHES USING THE WHOLE WORD METHOD   **65**
Paired-Associate Learning,   65
Language Experience,   65
Key Vocabulary,   65
Whole Words in the Environment,   67
Basal Readers,   70

SELECTING WORDS FOR THE WHOLE WORD METHOD   **71**
Criteria When Whole Word Is the Sole Method,   71
Criteria after Other Methods Are Introduced,   74

SOME PRINCIPLES FOR TEACHING WHOLE WORDS   **75**
Presenting Words in Context,   75
Pupils' Attention,   76
Attention to Appropriate Stimulus,   77
Use of Picture Clues,   78
Practice,   79

WHY USE THE WHOLE WORD APPROACH?   **80**

A CONTRASTING VIEW: THE LINGUISTIC APPROACH   **81**
Consistent Spelling-Sound Relationships,   81
Minimal Differences Between Words Taught,   81

SUMMARY   82

FOR FURTHER READING AND DISCUSSION   84

REFERENCES   84

4
PHONICS   87

DEFINITIONS   88

MORE PHONICS OR LESS PHONICS?   88

DECIDING WHAT TO TEACH   89
A Compromise Between Simplicity and Truth,   89
Some Generalizations Are Interesting But Not Very Useful,   89
Some Principles for Making Decisions,   90

SOME COMMON GENERALIZATIONS   90
Definition of "Consonants" and "Vowels,"   90
Sounds Represented by Single Consonant Letters,   91
Sounds Represented by Consonant Letters Together in
  a Syllable,   93
Spelling Clues to Vowel Sounds in One-Syllable Words,   94
Spelling Clues to Vowel Sounds in Two-Syllable Words,   96
Generalizations for Applying Stress (Accent),   99

KNOWING PHONICS AND KNOWING WHAT TO TEACH   100
Examples of Generalizations of Questionable Utility,   100
Examples of Fine Points,   101

SUMMARY   102

FOR FURTHER READING AND DISCUSSION   103

REFERENCES   104

5
ANALYSIS OF WORD STRUCTURE AS CLUES TO WORD RECOGNITION

ANALYSIS OF WORD STRUCTURE AS CLUES TO WORD RECOGNITION   107

DEFINITIONS   108
Morphemes,   108
Two Kinds of Suffixes,   109

TEACHING STRUCTURAL ANALYSIS   110
Purpose,   111
Timing,   112

SOME LESSONS FOR BEGINNING READERS   113
Compound Words,   113
Words with Inflectional Suffixes,   114
Words with Derivational Suffixes,   116
Words with Prefixes,   117

WORDS WITH INFLECTIONAL SUFFIXES: TWO ADDITIONAL PROBLEMS   118
Spelling Changes,   118
Changes in Pronunciation and Accent,   119

EMPIRICISM AND RATIONALISM IN CONSIDERING WORD STRUCTURE   119

SUMMARY   120

FOR FURTHER READING AND DISCUSSION   121

REFERENCES   123

6
CONTEXT

CONTEXT   125

DEFINING THE USE OF CONTEXT   126

USE OF CONTEXT CLUES BY EXPERIENCED READERS   126

TEACHING THE USE OF CONTEXT CLUES   127
Physical Context,   127
Picture Context,   128

Linguistic Context,   128
Teaching the Use of Context When the Need Arises,   130

THE ULTIMATE GOAL: INTEGRATING CLUES TO WORD RECOGNITION   131

SUMMARY   132

FOR FURTHER READING AND DISCUSSION   133

REFERENCES   134

7

TEACHING WORD RECOGNITION SKILLS   135

HOW IS WORD RECOGNITION TAUGHT?   136
Typical Lesson: First-Grade Phonics-Emphasis Basal
    Reader,   136
Typical Lesson: First-Grade Eclectic Basal Reader,   136
Differences Between the Lessons,   138

HOW ARE WORD RECOGNITION SKILLS LEARNED AND USED?   140
If Taught Phonics, Must Children Use It?,   140
If Taught Context, Must Children Use It?,   141

WHICH IS THE BEST APPROACH?   141
Straw Man Arguments,   141
What Is Happening in Real Classrooms?,   142
Research Findings,   143
The Role of the Teacher,   143

TEACHING AND LEARNING BY DEDUCTIVE AND INDUCTIVE METHODS   144
Differences and Similarities,   144
Tradition Associated with the Methods,   145
Which Is Better: Inductive or Deductive Teaching?,   147

ADVICE TO THE BEGINNING TEACHER   149

SUMMARY   150

FOR FURTHER READING AND DISCUSSION   152

REFERENCES   153

8
READING COMPREHENSION   155

WHAT DOES READING COMPREHENSION MEAN?   **156**

**CONCEPTS DERIVED FROM PSYCHOLOGICAL AND LINGUISTIC
EXPERIMENTATION**   **156**
 Comprehension Depends on Knowledge of Language,   156
 Comprehension Depends on Knowledge of the World,   158
 Comprehension Depends on the Reader's "Schema,"   160
 Comprehension Is Demonstrated by Evidence of Psycholinguistic
  Processes,   163
 Definitions of Reading Comprehension,   165

**CONCEPTS DERIVED FROM THEORIES OF EDUCATIONAL
MEASUREMENT**   **166**
 Theory of Independent Subskills,   166
 Theory of Hierarchically Related Subskills,   169
 The Usefulness of a Subskills Approach,   172

THE SPECIAL PLACE OF VOCABULARY KNOWLEDGE   **173**
 The Aptitude Interpretation,   173
 The Instrumental Interpretation,   173
 Knowledge of the World Interpretation,   174

**IS READING COMPREHENSION DIFFERENT FROM GENERAL
LANGUAGE COMPREHENSION?**   **174**
 Is Reading Comprehension Unrelated to Listening
  Comprehension?,   176
 Is Reading Comprehension Decoding plus Oral Language
  Comprehension?,   176
 Are Reading Comprehension Skills Different from Oral Language
  Comprehension Skills?,   177
 Teaching Comprehension Skills,   180

SUMMARY   **180**

FOR FURTHER READING AND DISCUSSION   **182**

REFERENCES   **183**

9
TEACHING READING COMPREHENSION   187

DEFINITIONS: COMPREHENSION INSTRUCTION   188

ASSUMPTIONS ABOUT TEACHING AND LEARNING COMPREHENSION   189
Comprehension Can Be Taught Directly,   189
Comprehension Can Be Taught Indirectly,   190

THE DIRECTED READING LESSON   196
The Preparation Stage,   197
The Question/Discussion Stage,   199
The Skills Development Stage,   206

TEACHING NEW VOCABULARY   207
The Complexities of Word Meaning,   207
What Does It Mean to Know a Word?,   207
Teaching Words Related Through the "Semantic
    Network,"   210
Teaching Words Having the Same Morphemes,   211

COMPREHENSION, FLUENCY, RATE OF READING, AND FLEXIBILITY   212
Fluency,   212
Rate of Reading,   213
Flexibility,   216
Increasing Rate and Flexibility: Two Different Goals,   217

TEACHING COMPREHENSION AS READING TO LEARN   218
Teaching Reading in the Content Areas,   218
Teaching Study Skills,   219
The Reading Teacher's Responsibility,   221

SUMMARY   221

FOR FURTHER READING AND DISCUSSION   224

REFERENCES   225

10
INDIVIDUAL DIFFERENCES

229

INTELLIGENCE   230
Measuring Intelligence,   230
The Use of IQ Test Scores in Teaching Strategies,   233
The Use of IQ Test Scores for Labeling People,   235
The Use of IQ Test Scores to Explain Reading Failure,   236
The Use of IQ Test Scores to Evaluate Progress,   237

VISUAL ACUITY: THE TEACHER'S ROLE   237
Symptoms of Vision Problems,   238
Visual Problems and Reading,   238
Referrals and Follow-Up,   239

AUDITORY ACUITY: THE TEACHER'S ROLE   239
Symptoms of Hearing Loss,   239
Hearing Loss and Reading,   240
Referrals and Follow-Up,   240

NEUROLOGICAL AND EMOTIONAL FACTORS   240
Symptoms of Neurological and Emotional Problems,   240
Referrals and Follow-Up,   241
Getting and Giving the Proper Advice,   241

CULTURAL AND ECONOMIC FACTORS   242
Economic Status and Language Use,   242
Societal Characteristics Shared by the Economically
    Disadvantaged,   245
The Language of the School,   249
Deprivation Theory,   249

SUMMARY   252

FOR FURTHER READING AND DISCUSSION   256

REFERENCES   257

11
ORGANIZATION FOR INSTRUCTION AND READING PROGRAMS

261

REASONS FOR GROUPING   262
Activities That Require Small Groups,   262
Student Characteristics,   262

ORGANIZATION FOR INSTRUCTION WITHIN THE CLASSROOM   264
Three-Group Plan Using Basal Reader,   264
Individualized Instruction: Holistic Approach,   268
Individualized Instruction: Atomistic Approaches,   270

ORGANIZATION PROBLEMS   280
Learning How a Program Works,   280
The Danger of Busywork,   281
The Quality of Teacher-Student Interaction,   282
Threats to the Teacher's Leadership Role,   283
Advice to the Beginning Teacher,   284

SCHOOLWIDE ARRANGEMENTS TO NARROW INDIVIDUAL DIFFERENCES   285
Classroom Assignment Strategies,   285
Advantages of Narrowing the Range of Achievement,   286
Problems,   286

COMPETING IDEALS: OBLITERATING VERSUS ACCENTUATING DIFFERENCES IN ACHIEVEMENT   287

SUMMARY   288

FOR FURTHER READING AND DISCUSSION   291

REFERENCES   292

12
ASSESSMENT OF READING ACHIEVEMENT AND TEACHING READING 293

CHARACTERISTICS ALL TESTS MUST POSSESS   **294**
Validity,   294
Reliability,   295

ASSESSMENT METHODS DETERMINED BY PURPOSE   **296**

STANDARDIZED READING ACHIEVEMENT TESTS   **297**
Characteristics of Standardized Reading Achievement
   Tests,   297
Individually Administered Tests,   299

FORMATIVE EVALUATION   **300**
The Informal Reading Inventory,   300
Standardized Individual Diagnostic Tests,   317
Standardized Group Diagnostic Tests,   318
Criterion-Referenced Testing,   318
Standardized Achievement Tests and Formative Evaluation,   320

SUMMARY   **321**

FOR FURTHER READING AND DISCUSSION   **323**

REFERENCES   **324**

CHAPTER 1

FOUNDATIONS OF TEACHING READING
THE STUDY OF LANGUAGE, THINKING, AND LEARNING

THE FIRST TASK: DECIDING WHAT TO DO

What Is Reading?
Where Do Trends in Methods Come From?

BASIC DIFFERENCES IN THE STUDY OF
LANGUAGE AND LEARNING

The Starting Point: Philosophy
Counting, Measuring, Recording, Describing:
   The Empiricist Tradition
The Study of the Mind: The Rationalist
   Tradition
Contrasts in the Two Traditions

EVENTS LEADING TO THE CURRENT SCENE

The Study of Language and Psychology
   Without Reference to the Mind

STRUCTURAL LINGUISTICS
COMMUNICATION THEORY
BEHAVIORISM

The Impact of Empirical Assumptions on
   Education

PERMISSIVENESS
ATTITUDE TOWARD DIALECT
LINGUISTIC READERS

Psycholinguistics

AS AN EMPIRICAL SCIENCE
AS A RATIONALIST SCIENCE

Cognitive Psychology: Mental Development and
   Language Development

PIAGET ON MENTAL DEVELOPMENT
LANGUAGE DEVELOPMENT AS PART OF
   COGNITIVE DEVELOPMENT

Some Shortcomings of Behaviorism,
   Psycholinguistics, and Cognitive Psychology

LANGUAGE LEARNING AS A SOCIAL PROCESS

Language as Part of the Social System
Language and Cognition as Part of Social
   Development

DEVELOPMENT OF MEANING
ROLE OF EGOCENTRIC SPEECH
THEORY OF INSTRUCTION
LEARNING: CONCRETE TO ABSTRACT, OR
   ABSTRACT TO CONCRETE?

Differences among Societies

COGNITIVE PROCESSES
HABITS OF LANGUAGE

A Sociological Perspective on Learning

TWO ASPECTS OF READING INSTRUCTION:
CONTRASTING VIEWS

Empiricist Versus Rationalist Perspectives
Psychological Versus Sociological Perspectives
The Interdependence of These Perspectives

SUMMARY

FOR FURTHER READING AND DISCUSSION

REFERENCES

FIRST TASK: DECIDING WHAT TO DO

What Is Reading?

Nearly every text on reading proposes a definition of reading. The common elements in all these definitions are that reading involves print, language, and comprehension. Learning to read is perceiving print and processing that perception in such a way as to lead to comprehension. One will also find agreement that the print to be read is related to language and that the meaning to be comprehended is related to language. What textbook definitions of reading may not specify or what they may not agree upon is how print is related to language and how language is related to meaning. How one views these relationships will naturally affect how one views the task of the reader. It will affect one's view of what a reader needs to learn and how one teaches those things.

The present broad division among reading educators is one of emphasis—that is, between those who concentrate on the relationship between print and language and those who concentrate on the relationship between language and meaning. One might say that the former reading educators and theorists concentrate on the outer aspects of reading, the things that can be observed in the environment—printed letters and words and language sounds—whereas the latter group concentrate on the inner aspect of reading, the meaning—the relationships that exist in the mind and cannot be observed.

This division has a very long history in philosophy, linguistics, and psychology. Many of the issues that have developed in reading education are a result of the struggle between these two points of view. As a matter of fact, many of the controversies that arise in teaching reading originate in philosophy, linguistics, and psychology.

Where Do Trends in Methods Come From?

Reading is a particular instance of using language; learning to read is a particular instance of learning in general. As a result, the teaching of reading is affected by developments and trends in the study of linguistics and psychology.

Halliday (1975) says the study of language has gone upward within language from phonology to syntax to semantics, and outward to the study of language as part of cognition and finally to the study of language as part of the total communication system within society—what Halliday (1978) calls the "social semiotic" (see Figure 1.1). One expects any day to find the publication of social semiotic reading programs that have, when examined, a great deal in common with psycholinguistic reading programs, which in turn have a great deal in common with the linguistic reading programs that preceded them. A cynic might conclude that reading teachers have continued to do the same thing over the years, but that we change the name of what we do to keep up with trends in related academic disciplines. But in fact there are substantial differences among these approaches that grow out of a long history of philosophy, linguistics, psychology, and lately, sociology.

The fact that reading programs have so much in common is evidence that each of the theories involved is, in itself, insufficient for guiding us in how to teach reading; several theories are necessary and relevant to decisions we make as reading teachers. Our job is to sort out what is necessary from each of these warring camps and to sort out the relevant from the irrelevant. The alternative, which has occurred too often, is that reading experts adopt a single theory as doctrine and reading teachers are forced to smuggle in that

FIGURE 1.1
EMPHASIS IN THE STUDY OF LANGUAGE IN THE LAST HALF-CENTURY.

1930   **Typical concerns of phonologists**

Position of speech organs during speech production
Order of appearance of speech sound in language development
Melody and rhythm of language (stress, pitch, juncture, cadence)
Identification of speech sounds, meaningful combinations of sounds (morphemes and words)

Typical concerns of grammarians (syntax)

Word categories (nouns, verbs, etc.)
Word structure (plural, past tense)
Relationships between words and phrases (nouns and modifiers, subject-verb-object, etc.)

Typical concerns of semanticists

Meanings of words in an intellectual sense (denotive)
Meanings of words in an emotional sense (connotive)
Meanings expressed between words (In "Mary learns Latin," *learns* expresses an action and
  Mary is the learner—the agent. In "Mary knows Latin," *knows* expresses a state or condi-
  tion and Mary is the person in that state or condition.

Typical concerns of cognitive psychologists who study language

In what way does language development depend on physical maturity and general intellectual development and learning?
In what way does language development and use affect general intellectual development
  and learning?

Typical concerns of a person who studies language *use* in society

What jobs can be done with language (give orders, express affection, ask for information,
  etc.)?
How is language use related to the kind of job being done, the context, the relationship between speakers?
What is the relationship between culture, thought, language development, and the use of
1980   language?

---

which is obviously needed but ignored or pro-hibited by the reigning doctrine.

There have been periods in America when the whole-word approach to reading was the accepted practice. There were undoubtedly countless surreptitious phonics lessons being conducted across the breadth of this country. In a period when oral reading was roundly condemned by experts, there were undoubt-edly numerous clandestine oral reading ses-sions being conducted complete with a "look-out" watching the hallway for approaching authorities.

It is important that reading teachers be able to make intelligent choices concerning methods and curriculum in light of progress in such fields as linguistics, psychology, and so-ciology. It is equally important that reading teachers individually and collectively be able to ward off unfounded attacks from within and outside education. Such attacks come from overly enthusiastic supporters of particular methods, from angry opponents of particular methods, and from linguists, psychologists, and sociologists who misunderstand what the reading teacher is trying to accomplish.

BASIC DIFFERENCES IN THE STUDY OF LANGUAGE AND LEARNING

The Starting Point: Philosophy

Reading programs that emphasize phonics and decoding—a *bottom-up* model in today's jargon—are descendants of a philosophical tradition, *empiricism,* that can be traced back to such worthies as John Locke and David Hume. Reading programs that deemphasize phonics and decoding and emphasize "reading for meaning"—a *top-down* model in today's jargon—are descendants of an equally respected tradition, *rationalism,* that can be traced back to such notables as Leibniz and Kant. Of course, Locke, Hume, Leibniz, and Kant never addressed the question of how to teach reading; but the traditions they represent—empiricism and rationalism—have a direct bearing on what one thinks about the nature of the human mind, language, and learning. And these in turn have a direct bearing on questions of how to teach reading.

It is perhaps going too far to say that when a teacher claims a program has too much emphasis on phonics, he or she is striking a blow for Leibniz. But, as a matter of fact, that teacher is acting on assumptions regarding the nature of human learning that can be traced to Leibniz and the debate between rationalists and empiricists. The major division between these spheres of influence rests on the question of whether or not it is profitable to study the human mind.

Counting, Measuring, Recording, Describing: The Empiricist Tradition

One group of social scientists believes it is not possible to study the human mind because the workings of the human mind are hidden from us. We can only know and study what we can perceive with our senses. For this group, explanations of human behavior are typically stated in terms of mechanical principles external to human beings—that is, explanations that do not refer to the mind, but that rely on the relationship of human behavior to events in the environment. This perspective leads to a particular kind of study. Empiricists are preoccupied with describing the environment, with gathering data, with measurement. They are interested in the frequency, intensity, and contiguity of events—that is, in measuring how often events occur, how perceptible they are, and what other events occur at the same (or nearly the same) time or place.

In the last century, this kind of activity on the part of social scientists led them to become interested in and envious of the tremendous progress in the physical sciences. They believed the social sciences were essentially the same as the physical sciences. The only difference was that the social sciences had not advanced their measurement devices to the point where they could describe their data in terms of mathematical formulas as the physical scientists had. This intensified their interest in measurement and also had an effect on the things they studied. For example, linguists of this school in the nineteenth century were preoccupied with the most physical, observable aspect of language—sound—and the science of phonology.

The Study of the Mind: The Rationalist Tradition

The other half of this division are people who believe that the human mind can be studied and indeed must be studied if one is to make progress in the fields of psychology, language, and education. People in this camp believe the human organism is not simply assaulted by sensations and that the effect of sensations cannot be predicted in terms of their frequency, intensity, and contiguity, but that the human mind is capable of and prone to selecting sensations and organizing them. A psychologist might state this idea as follows: Internal cognition is prior to external sensation. Whereas empiricists talk about sensation and *perception,* rationalists talk about sensations and *apperception*—directed attention to external sensation.

These notions lead people in this camp to be less interested in describing the environment to which humans react and more interested in building theories of how the human mind acts and reacts. This means attempting to describe the workings of the mind, which of course cannot be seen. But rationalists do not deny the physical environment and events that take place in it. Therefore, rationalist theories of language tend to incorporate the mental and physical aspects of language.

One of the earliest psychologists was Wilhelm Wundt (1832–1920). He was a rationalist who believed there were inner and outer psychological events. He believed humans are able to focus attention, to select, structure, and direct experiences from within. His study of human behavior included the study of cognitive or mental events. On the other hand, he believed it was also the legitimate concern of psychologists to study outer events—sensory motor events. Therefore, he was interested in associations, and in the frequency, intensity, and contiguity of events—the kinds of things that usually interest empiricists. Wundt took the same point of view in studying language: That is, language is an outer event—production and perception of sound—but it is also an inner event—the train of thought.

Contrasts in the Two Traditions

When one studies language as an inner *and* outer event, questions of how the two are related immediately emerge. Is thought simply inner language, or are language and thought separate? In producing language, does one produce a series of sounds that add up to words and eventually to a sentence, or does one start with an undifferentiated thought (a sentence) and divide that thought into words and words into sounds and utter them one at a time? In receiving language, does one process sounds as they are heard, add the sounds into words, and add the words to sentences, or does one assume that what is perceived is a sentence and organize what is heard and predict what will be heard in an aggressive search for meaning?

These questions reveal an important difference between the empiricist and rationalist traditions. Empiricists strive to break events down into their smallest parts and to explain events by describing the relationships between their parts. This is an *atomistic* approach. Rationalists tend to focus on wholes—large events—and to describe parts in terms of how they relate to the whole. This is a *holistic* approach. Rationalists look at empirical data, but tend toward holistic interpretations rather than atomistic ones.

Empiricists tend to study reading and teaching reading in terms of the outer aspects of the process—the relationship of print to sound, the perception of letters and words, and the frequency of words, letters and so on. Rationalists tend to study reading and the teaching of reading in terms of the inner aspects of language—the meaning—and in terms of the reader's mind, interest, previous knowledge, and ability to direct attention and organize stimuli rather than passively accept them as they come.

One aspect of the difference between the study and teaching of reading by empiricists and rationalists is that empiricists concentrate on the parts of a process in order to understand the whole, whereas rationalists concentrate on the whole of a process in order to understand the parts. These differences in approach are at the center of the current debate between adherents of the top-down (or cognitive) and bottom-up (or perceptual) models of reading (see Figure 1.2).

It is very useful to refer to empiricism and rationalism as "spheres of influence" rather than as "philosophies" because the history of science, like the history of all human endeavors, is not orderly and compartmentalized (Blumenthal, 1970). There are traditions associated with these spheres of influence, however, that enable us to see where a particular way of looking at language, learning, or the teaching of reading fits into one sphere or the other. The reading teacher's job of deciding and defending is much easier when conflicting advice and opinions can be put into perspective. For that reason issues that arise in the teaching of reading as a result of adopting an empiricist or rationalist point of view will be discussed in every chapter in this book.

EVENTS LEADING TO THE CURRENT SCENE

The Study of Language and Psychology Without Reference to the Mind

By the middle of this century, the most prominent linguist in the United States was Leonard Bloomfield (1887–1949). Bloomfield was a follower of the Swiss linguist Ferdinand de Saussure (1857–1913). Saussure is credited as being the founder of modern linguistics (Lyons, 1968). He was opposed to constructing theories; he emphasized data collection and argued that language can and should be studied without reference to its history. Bloomfield held these empiricist views and also had another interst that characterized the empiricist tradition in the social sciences: He wanted the study of language to be as "scientific" as the study of physics. These principles, applied to the study of language, led to what became known as *structural linguistics*.

STRUCTURAL LINGUISTICS

Structural linguistics is an attempt to describe language as data without reference to meaning. One goes about doing this by collecting a lot of data—transcriptions of language produced by people—and then looking at such things as frequency, intensity, and contiguity, all the classical concerns of the empiricists. This endeavor was taken to the limit by such linguists as Kenneth Pike, who attempted to write grammars of languages of preliterate peoples who had had little contact with Western civilization. Theoretically, a linguist applying the principles of structural linguistics could write a grammar of a language he or she did not know.

But it is hard to imagine writing a grammar of a language one does not know. Suppose an anthropologist who did not know English arrived in New York City and wanted to write a grammar of the people. According to the methods of structural linguists, he or she would first collect a lot of data—or copy down in a phonetic notation the speech he or she heard. Suppose the anthropologist had a transcription system that was able to capture

FIGURE 1.2
SOME CHARACTERISTICS OF EMPIRICISM AND RATIONALISM.

Empiricism	Rationalism
Focuses on outer aspects of language	Focuses on inner aspects of language
Focuses on how separate parts contribute to whole	Focuses on whole and how parts relate within wholes
Views language as perceived in parts that are added up to wholes (bottom-up)	Views language as perceived in wholes that are analyzed into parts (top-down)
Views the mind as a comparatively passive receiver of stimuli that attends to the most frequent or most intense stimuli	Views the mind as an active seeker and organizer of stimuli that will attend to stimuli because it is meaningful or fits into a perceived organization
In reading, focuses on perception of letters and words, relationship of print to sound, frequency of words as indicators of ease of learning; brings the atomistic and mechanical aspects of reading together finally to consider meaning	In reading, focuses on meanings and on wholes; analyzes wholes to consider perception of words and letters and the relationship of print to sound finally to consider mechanical relationships of parts
Atomistic	Holistic
Mechanistic	Organic

the sounds and the melody (pitch, rhythm, stress, and juncture) of the language and that this system was good enough to enable him or her to divide the recorded speech into words, phrases, and sentences.

Imagine what rules (grammar) the researcher would be able to formulate about the structure of English. He or she might make observations like the following: The word *the* is very frequent in this language; it never appears at the end of a sentence, and it frequently appears at the beginning of a phrase. He or she might observe that the syllables we represent in written English as *ing*, *est*, and *er* appear often at the end of words. He or she might surmise that *of*, *in*, and *on* are a class of words because of their frequency and the position at which they occur in phrases. When the anthropologist had a great amount of data, he or she could compile many facts about the

structure of English and write a description of this language in terms of these observations. Such a description of a language is a grammar of the language. Notice that there is no mention of the meaning of the language, only a description of the physical data.

Other linguists applied the principles of structural linguistics to describing English syntax. Subjects and predicates were defined in terms of their positions in sentences. Nouns were described as words that follow *noun determiners*—that is, words that fit into the slots "a _____," "the _____," and "my _____." Adjectives were described as words that fit into the slots "more _____," and "most _____," or "_____er," and "_____est." Words such as *because, if,* and *when* came to be called "clause markers." Linguists went to great lengths to describe the syntax of English without referring to meaning.

COMMUNICATION THEORY

A second science of language appeared about this time and was connected particularly with World War II. This science was called *communication theory* (Miller, 1951; Cherry, 1957). The United States government was very interested in making telephone, radio, and radar communication as perfect as possible. This effort was motivated by wartime applications, and a great deal of money and talent—in the form of drafted psychologists and linguists—went into the effort.

When one receives messages (in Morse code, for example) on the radio receiver, there is sometimes noise in the channel. The essence of communication theory is that if the operator does not hear a particular letter code, he or she does not need to simply guess about the identity of the letter. If the operator has received *th__*, for instance, he or she knows that the likelihood that the missing letter is a vowel is rather high, and the likelihood that it is an *r* is much greater than any other consonant letter.

An interesting thing about communication theory is that predictions are based on recording thousands of words of messages and simply figuring out from observed messages the statistical probabilities of a letter appearing after a particular letter, after two particular letters, three particular letters, and so on. It is *not* based on knowledge of English spelling or what we know about the order of words in sentences from our knowledge of English grammar. These latter approaches would rely on what the message sender and receiver know—a mental phenomenon—and communication theory is an empirical science. In Figure 1.3, one of the people is relying on empiricist assumptions and the other is relying on rationalist assumptions—although they may not be conscious of their assumptions or of how their assumptions differ.

♦ If you think about the following questions about the persons in Figure 1.3, you may gain considerable insight into the differences between these spheres of influence:

1. Which is more ''scientific'' in the way that physics is scientific?

FIGURE 1.3
A SCIENTIST AND A PRACTITIONER TACKLE A COMMUNICATION PROBLEM.

We fed 100,000 words of messages sent to and from ships at sea into a computer and calculated the number of times each letter is preceded and followed by every letter; the number of times each two letter combination is preceded and followed by every letter; and so on for three and four letter combinations.

When a ship's radio operator receives a message and certain letters not received clearly, he simply types the surrounding letters into a computer and the computer tells him what letters could possibly have occurred and which letter most probably occurred. The operator can then make a judgment based on statistical probabilities about what the letter in doubt is.

I've been a ship's radio operator for ten years. I speak English. I am a reasonably good speller, but I don't know many spelling ''rules.''

When I receive a message and certain letters are not received clearly, I almost always know what the letter is. I don't know how, exactly. I just know that it must be a certain letter because I recognize the word it is in. I usually recognize the word because I know the meaning of the sentence, or I get the gist of the whole message.

2. *Which relies on what the operator "knows"?*
3. *Which relies on counting, recording, measuring?*
4. *Which is a holistic or top-down approach?*
5. *Which is an atomistic or bottom-up approach?*
6. *Do you see how these two approaches may have some relevance to the process of reading and to teaching reading?*

The effect of communication theory on the current reading scene is particularly interesting because the psycholinguistic model of reading proposed by Smith (1971) draws on communication theory. Smith, like Goodman (1967; 1970), believes that *prediction* of what appears in a text is an essential part of the reading process. But Smith and Goodman are rationalists, and so they refer to the reader's knowledge of language and the meaning of the passage in their model. This is an example of the way empiricists and rationalists may describe the same outcomes and come to the same conclusions using different methods of studying and thinking about language.

BEHAVIORISM

Empiricism had always dominated the study of psychology in America, and by the 1950s a particularly pure form of empiricism had emerged. The study of psychology was the study of observable behavior and the events in the environment that shaped behavior. Learning was defined as the association between some event in the environment (the stimulus) and an observable action on the part of the learner (the response). This branch of psychology is known as behaviorism, and the learning theory it explores is known as stimulus-response theory.

Behaviorism reflects the classic concerns of the empiricist tradition. Behaviorists are interested in observation, measurement, and recording observable events and behaviors. They strive to analyze their data into its most elemental parts. They are interested in the frequency, intensity, and contiguity of stimuli and responses. Much of the experimentation in behaviorist psychology has been done on animals—pigeons, cats, and rats. Applying learning theory derived from the study of animals to human learning reflects another aspect of the empiricist tradition: that one can describe human behavior as animal behavior without ascribing any special significance to the human mind.

Classical Stimulus-Response Theory. Classical stimulus-response theory proposes that if an animal (a child in the case of reading) is rewarded for making a response to a stimulus, the animal is likely to make that response again in the presence of the stimulus. For example, one might present a monkey with a red lever; if the monkey presses the lever (the desired response), it is given food (the reinforcement). After a few trials, the monkey will press the red lever every time it is presented. The monkey has *learned* through classic stimulus-response "conditioning." Figure 1.4 shows a typical application of classical stimulus-response learning theory in reading instruction.

Operant Conditioning. Probably the best-known behaviorist psychologist is B. F. Skinner. He introduced the idea that there are two kinds of responses—those with a known stimulus, which he called "respondents," and those that have no observable stimulus, which he called "operants." Skinner observed that organisms emit some behaviors (operants) for which there are no observable stimuli and that by rewarding some operants and not rewarding others, the psychologist can shape behavior.

To demonstrate the truth of this assumption, Skinner and others have taught animals (pigeons, for example) very complex combi-

Child: Father.
Teacher: Good. That's
          another point for
          you.

FIGURE 1.4
**A CLASSICAL BEHAVIORIST STIMULUS-RESPONSE-
REINFORCEMENT APPLICATION TO READING INSTRUCTION.**

nations of behaviors by rewarding certain operants with food. The technique is called *operant conditioning*. A parent who praises a three-year-old for "reading" when the child awkwardly turns a page in a book is shaping the child's behavior by rewarding reading-like behaviors and ignoring other book-related behaviors. This may be regarded as a form of operant conditioning.

The Impact of Empirical Assumptions on Education

PERMISSIVENESS

Several aspects of structural linguistics have had a very real effect on education. Structural linguistics is purely descriptive; it is nonprescriptive and nonjudgmental. When transcribing data, a linguist does not ask whether it is considered correct to say such and such; he or she writes down what is said, and it becomes part of the data. Going back to the earlier example, the linguist who is collecting data on a New York City street would copy down *ain't* and *you wasn't* and be interested only in identifying the frequency (how often it was uttered) and distribution (whether it appeared in certain parts of phrases and sentences and not others). The linguist might observe that *ain't* is rare and may even observe that it is a word found in the data from some subjects and not others. He or she might guess that there is a dialect difference involved but would not make any judgment about whether or not the word was correct.

This is where the notion that modern linguistics is permissive (not concerned with standards) originated. It is a misunderstanding. Linguists of the Bloomfield-Pike variety were not talking about English usage as it traditionally concerned the schools. They were not talking about dialect differences in terms of whether political and economic advantages are attached to particular dialects, let alone whether it is the business of the schools to teach some standard dialect. They were talking about studying language as a natural phenomenon—as a physicist or chemist studies matter.

ATTITUDE TOWARD DIALECT

The notion of studying language from a nonjudgmental, nonprescriptive point of view had far-reaching effects. Books such as Hall's *Leave Your Language Alone!* (1950) were published expressing the point of view that one dialect is as good as another, and that therefore one should not attempt to switch dialects or to switch anyone else's dialect (one's students', for example). Whether dialect differences play a part in learning to read became a central issue in this debate.

The matter of dialect differences became a politically charged issue in the decades that followed the heyday of structuralism. Attitudes of "middle America," and particularly of the schools, toward black English became a concern in the civil rights struggle. These issues will reappear in Chapter 10, where student characteristics that affect learning to read are discussed.

LINGUISTIC READERS

Bloomfield was not only a leader in linguistics, he was directly interested in the teaching of reading. In keeping with his empiricist point of view, he saw teaching reading as teaching word recognition and letter-sound relationships—that is, the outer aspects of

reading. He acknowledged that the goal of reading was comprehension of meaning, but asserted that children comprehend language before they come to school, yet they do not know how to read. As an empiricist, he was also interested in frequency and contiguity of events.

His system (presented in *Let's Read*, Bloomfield and Barnhart, 1961), is based on the principle of teaching the most frequent and most consistent letter-sound relationships first. This direct attention to the reading process by a linguist resulted in a teaching method called *the linguistic method* and in textbooks based on this method called *linguistic readers*.

Psycholinguistics

AS AN EMPIRICAL SCIENCE

It is perfectly natural that when the principles and methodologies of psychology and linguistics had so much in common, they should get together. Two conferences were held to explore the common interests of psychologists and linguists, the first at Cornell in 1951 and the second at Indiana University in 1953. Out of these meetings grew great hope that through joint efforts, and by applying the empiricist principles of structural linguistics, behavioral psychology, and communication theory, there would soon be tremendous technological breakthroughs in such things as machine translation of language and speech-to-print typewriters.

The term *psycholinguistics* was popularized as a description of the joint study of language by psychologists and linguists. It was an unfortunate time to coin such a word, because a revolution was about to take place in the study of linguistics and psychology. Ten years later, the term was still used to describe the study of language by psychologists and linguists, but both fields had come under a rival sphere of influence—rationalism. The suddenness of this turnabout and the fact that the same term—*psycholinguistics*—was used to refer to this field before and after the revolution has led to considerable confusion.

AS A RATIONALIST SCIENCE

In the late 1950s, a revolution in linguistics and psychology was caused by the work of a single individual, Noam Chomsky. Chomsky attacked the basic premise of structural linguistics. He showed that one cannot assign structure to a great many English sentences without reference to the meaning of the sentence. He further asserted that even in the many sentences where structures can be assigned in terms of frequency, position, stress, juncture, and so on (the physical characteristics of language attended to by the empiricist tradition), it is thoroughly wrongheaded to refuse to recognize an obvious fact: that sentences have meaning, and as speakers of a language, linguists know the meaning. Chomsky was asserting the time-honored rationalist position—that the mind exists and that it can and should be studied.

Chomsky (1965) proposed a *generative transformational grammar* that was a counterproposal to the grammars proposed by structural linguists. The main feature of this grammar is that every sentence has a deep structure (a structure in the mind of the speaker), as well as a surface structure (a physical manifestation of speech sounds). Transformational grammar is an attempt to describe the relationship between the two.

Reaction Against Excessive Empiricism. It is impossible to describe Chomsky's impact on the study of language from a psychologist's point of view without reference to B. F. Skinner's book *Verbal Behavior* (1957). Skinner was among the best-known behaviorist psychologists. Indeed, the term "Skinnerian" is synonymous with "behaviorist." *Verbal Behavior* was the most thorough and literal application of behaviorism to language.

Chomsky's review in 1959 of Skinner's book is one of the few book reviews that has been more widely read, and is more influential, than the book it reviews. Chomsky very effectively criticized this purely behaviorist-empiricist approach to the study of language. One might say that Chomsky held this approach up to ridicule. The effectiveness of this review is indicated, perhaps, by the fact that Skinner has never responded to it.

An unfortunate result of this episode was that, although the issue was whether behaviorism was a useful theory to explain language, many people felt that behaviorism had been discredited in general. There was a reaction against stimulus-response theory in all aspects of learning, and a reaction against all traditional empiricist concerns in the study of language. Stimulus-response theory is useful in teaching many aspects of reading, such as letter and word recognition, letter and sound relationships, and some aspects of vocabulary development. The application of behaviorist principles to teaching reading will be discussed repeatedly throughout this book.

Nativism. When one admits mind into the study of language, the question arises as to where the properties of the mind that account for language come from. The traditional answer of rationalists, and it is Chomsky's answer, is that human beings are born with the capacity to learn and to use language. We are genetically endowed with this capacity. It is a capacity that developed in our evolutionary history.

The idea that language is natural rather than learned has a long history. Herodotus, a Greek historian of the fifth century B.C., is supposed to have written of an Egyptian king who isolated a child from birth in order to find out what language he would speak. The king wanted to know what the "natural" language of human beings was. At the end of the nineteenth century, according to Blumenthal (1970), language authorities commonly believed that a child raised in isolation would develop a language as rich as that of his or her parents.

Of course the environment must have some effect, or children would not learn French in a French-speaking community and English in an English-speaking community. Like Wundt, contemporary rationalists acknowledge that language is both an inner and an outer phenomenon. The inner aspects are thought to be genetically endowed, and the outer aspects susceptible to influence from the environment. But perhaps as a reaction to behaviorism, and particularly because Skinner's behavioristic explanation of language in *Verbal Behavior* was so thoroughly discredited by Chomsky, psycholinguists tended to play down the effect of the environment on language. The term "language acquisition" was coined to avoid the word "learning."

Psycholinguists, following Chomsky, assume the nativist position and study how children acquire rules of language—how the genetically programmed mechanism for language develops. They are preoccupied with changes going on in the child's development of language that reflect changes going on in the mind. They acknowledge that the child must be exposed to language, but for the most part they consider language in the environment as given. They do not argue that all children are exposed to the same amount and kind of language, but they believe that a minimal amount of language is necessary and sufficient for normal language development. They tend not to study what effect language in the child's environment has on the child's language development. It is not their question.

The Mind as Active Organizer of Input. One tenet of psycholinguistics that has important implications for education is that in human learning, input is never into a static system; input is into a system that is active, excited, and organized. This is a rationalist view, as opposed to the behaviorist view that the mind passively awaits inputs to which it responds. Questions of how students learn to recognize words and letters and how they comprehend language center on whether the mind is an active, interested seeker and organizer of stimuli or a passive receiver. Focusing on one view or the other will have a great effect on the kinds of decisions one makes as a reading teacher.

Cognitive Psychology: Mental Development and Language Development

The questions that have occupied psychologists and linguists since Chomsky are rationalist questions. The rationalist questions that are relevant to teaching reading and to choices reading teachers must make have to do with how language is related to other aspect of the mind—thinking, knowing, and perceiving—in short, how language is related to *cognition*. Among educators, probably the best-known cognitive psychologist is Piaget.

PIAGET ON MENTAL DEVELOPMENT

The three prominent characteristics of Piaget's theory are that cognitive growth proceeds in stages, that there are radical shifts in a child's cognitive capacity as it passes from one stage to another, and that development depends on the maturity of the child and its interaction with its environment. For example, Piaget has shown that children learn the concept known as "conservation of volume" in an all-or-none fashion. Children at the early "preoperational stage" do not have the concept that a quantity of liquid keeps the same volume regardless of changes in its shape. If water is poured from a short, wide vessel to a tall, narrow vessel, the child will assert that there is now more water (presumably because the water level is higher in the narrow vessel), even though it saw the water poured with no water added in the operation.

From Piaget's point of view, conservation of volume comes about from an interaction between the child's biological maturation and its experiences in the environment. At first the child does not have the concept of conservation of volume; it seems to think that changing the shape can affect volume without adding or subtracting quantity. With maturation and experience with the environment, the concept of conservation of volume emerges in a fairly sudden fashion.

This is not a stimulus-response theory or an operant conditioning theory. It is a theory of the unfolding of a genetically preprogrammed cognitive development wherein the child acts on its environment, explores it, and manipulates it. The concepts the child builds from this interaction are dependent on the child's maturity level. The child does not pass from one stage to another because it is rewarded for a new response to old experiences, but because, at a higher level of maturation, the old responses become inconsistent with the way the child now sees the world. There has been a mental reorganization.

LANGUAGE DEVELOPMENT AS PART OF COGNITIVE DEVELOPMENT

Piaget views changes in language behavior as symptoms of changes in the child's mental development. His interest in language is always as an appendage to his main interest, the growth of cognition. His book, *The Language and Thought of the Child* (1955), describes the child's use of language during the "preoperational stage" (roughly ages 2 to 7). Piaget claims that in the first part of the preoperational stage, the child's language is egocentric most of the time—that is, the child's speech is directly mostly at itself. The child does not mean to communicate with others through speech.

According to Piaget, thought arises within the child as cognitive capacity matures; eventually thought becomes "inner speech," and eventually inner speech becomes audible speech. But when audible speech appears, the child is still egocentric. It does not yet see others as separate from itself; therefore, this audible speech is not directed at others as separate individuals.

By the end of the preoperational stage, the child's audible speech is almost entirely "socialized speech." It is directed at others whom the child is finally aware of as being separate from itself. But this change from egocentric to socialized speech is seen as a natural outcome of a change in the child's view of the world, which in turn depends in part on maturation and in part on interaction with others, particularly other children. The child's interactions with others help it to notice that others have a different perspective on the world. This realization comes into conflict with the child's egocentric view of the world. Thus, maturation plus interaction leads to a change in mental organization, and this in turn leads to an observable change in the use of language.

Since language plays an important part in interactions between people, one might ask what role language has in leading the child to notice that others have a different perspective. This question is asked by others who are preoccupied with the role of social interaction in the development of both thought and language. But Piaget is a psychologist who is interested primarily in cognitive development and who has a strong belief in maturation as the essential factor in cognitive development. The question of the role of language in this process is simply not addressed.

Educators who claim to be interpreters of Piaget have criticized some Piaget-inspired nursery school programs for attempting to accelerate children's cognitive development, and for placing too much emphasis on language (Brainerd, 1978). For those not conversant with Piaget's writing, these may seem to be startling criticisms of nursery school programs. Is it not the business of schools to accelerate cognitive development and to emphasize language development? But the fact is that Piaget's emphasis on maturation and his treating language as an outcome rather than a cause of development make these criticisms quite consistent with his views.

Some Shortcomings of Behaviorism, Psycholinguistics, and Cognitive Psychology

Piaget's theory of cognitive development and the psycholinguistic theories of language development are both strongly nativist theories. Certain capacities are genetically endowed and arise with maturation. The environment has a role in both cases, but the contribution of the environment to the growth of language and cognition is deemphasized. Children are assumed to have the necessary and sufficient experience with environment and exposure to language to facilitate cognitive development and language acquisition. How differences in a child's environment affect cognitive and language development are not nativists' questions. However, these are important questions to educators, and so to

some extent Piagetian psychology and psycholinguistics are not useful to education because they do not ask the questions to which educators seek answers.

We have seen in this discussion how behaviorists ask relevant questions: How is behavior explained in terms of the environment? How is learning affected by manipulating the environment? But psycholinguists and cognitive psychologists say behaviorists have the wrong slant on things. Language and learning are about the mind. The mind has genetically endowed properties, and if one does not recognize these properties, the resulting explanations of learning are either wrong or incomplete. These cognitive psychologists and linguists, however, fail to explore the questions relevant to education: How do changes in the environment affect learning?

The situation seems to be that educator's questions are asked by people with only a partially satisfactory point of view and that people with complementary points of view do not study some questions essential to educators. Fortunately, there are psychologists and linguists who are both rationalists and nativists, but whose emphasis is on the role of social interaction in both cognitive and language development. It is to this group that we turn now.

LANGUAGE LEARNING AS A SOCIAL PROCESS

Language as Part of the Social System

Halliday (1975) has pointed out that the study of language development during the 1970s moved away from the "sterile debate" of whether language and language learning are genetically endowed and ready-made, or environmentally fashioned and evolving. There has been a shift from the study of language development as an isolated phenomenon to the study of language development as part of cognitive development and dependent on cognitive development.

Halliday feels that neither language itself nor the learning of language by a child can be understood except in reference to some broader system. Just as Piaget and his followers have studied language development as part of the cognitive system, Halliday has studied language as part of the social system. Halliday believes that *culture* can be defined as a system of meanings. A child must construct this system of meanings for itself. The process takes place in the mind; it is a cognitive process, but it takes place through social interaction.

Halliday (1977) has identified functions that are present in all human societies and that are accomplished through language. For example, to express one's needs so that others will take care of them is something individuals do in all cultures. It is a function that Halliday has identified as the *instrumental* function. To establish contact and express togetherness with others is another thing individuals do in all cultures. Halliday identifies this as the *interactional* function. Halliday identifies several such functions that he believes are part of the meaning systems of all cultures.

Through interactions with their parents and others, children learn that these meanings are possible and that these meanings can be communicated through cries, looks, gestures, and so on. At some point, children learn that particular vocalizations are understood by those around them as expressing particular functions. At the point that meanings become attached to vocalizations, language emerges. These vocalizations may not be words of the mother tongue; often they are not even imitations of words of the mother tongue. At a

later stage, children adopt the vocalizations those around them use to serve these functions, and learning the mother tongue ensues. There is little discontinuity when children abandon their unique vocalizations and adopt those of the adults around them because the functions language serves are derived from the culture and are the same for the adults as for the children who are learning their language.

The importance of Halliday in this discussion is that he places the child's major discoveries about the world and about language in social interaction. His emphasis in describing language acquisition is not on the child as an individual, but on the child as part of society.

Language and Cognition as Part of Social Development

Vygotsky (1896–1934) was a Russian psychologist and educator. He first became influential in America when his book, *Thought and Language,* was published in English in 1962. More recently, another collection of his essays has been published as a book entitled *Mind in Society* (1978). Vygotsky's thinking on the development of language and cognition was guided by two principles: (1) that the study of psychology is the study of process in motion—the study of change; and (2) that human beings live in society and society undergoes changes throughout its history. Changes in society produce changes in the characteristics of human cognition.

Vygotsky was a rationalist and a nativist, like Chomsky and Piaget. Vygotsky believed that the *range* of possibilities for cognitive development is predetermined by the genetic endowment of humankind; however, the *actual* cognitive development of an individual is determined in part by that individual's interaction with other human beings in society. Vygotsky's preoccupation with the role of social interaction can be seen in his discussion of how meaning develops for a child, and the relationships among inner speech, egocentric speech, and social speech.

DEVELOPMENT OF MEANING

According to Vygotsky, meaning is always developed in society—in interaction with other persons—and later becomes internalized. The act of pointing is an example. Extending one's finger may be a random or a meaningless act; but if one extends one's finger *at* something and intends to direct the attention of others toward the object, the act has meaning. Such meaning can arise only in interaction with others.

Vygotsky suggests that this meaning arises when a child tries unsuccessfully to grasp an object and the act is *interpreted by others* as the child's directing their attention. Soon the child associates the gesture with the resulting behavior of others, and the gesture takes on meaning. The crucial elements of this example are that meaning is not created in a child's mind and then conveyed to others; meaning arises in social interaction and then becomes established in the child's mind. This is a central tenet of Vygotsky's cognitive theory: that interpersonal (social) processes become intrapersonal (mental) processes.

THE ROLE OF EGOCENTRIC SPEECH

Vygotsky believed that from its onset speech is social—it is used primarily to communicate with other individuals. Only after the social character of speech is well established does egocentric speech arise. The function of egocentric speech is to transfer social, collaborative behavior inward. In other words, the child begins to converse with itself as it has done with others. Vygotsky showed that one can induce egocentric speech by introduc-

ing problems or complications into some task a child is performing. For example, if a child is painting and some of the paints are taken away without the child's noticing, egocentric speech will emerge when the child goes to use a missing color. Vygotsky claims that the child uses egocentric speech to solve problems as it has solved problems by talking to others.

Eventually egocentric speech becomes inner speech, which serves for logical thinking. Once again Vygotsky places the origins of thought in social interaction. Egocentric speech is a transition from social, collective activity to individual activity. The origin of what Vygotsky calls "the higher psychological processes" (language and thought) are found first in social interactions and later become individual mental processes. The path of the higher psychological processes is always from society (outside the individual) to inside the individual.

THEORY OF INSTRUCTION

Vygotsky's theory of development and his theory of instruction stem from the idea that a person can solve more difficult problems and employ more difficult concepts in collaboration with others than he or she can alone. Piaget assesses development in terms of the kinds of problems a child can solve alone. Piaget asserts that until the child matures to the stage where the solution to a particular problem is possible, there is no point in trying to teach the child to solve the problem. Vygotsky, on the contrary, assesses development in terms of the kinds of problems a child can solve in collaboration with others. He calls the difference between what the child can do alone and what it can do in collaboration with others the "zone of proximal development." It is within this zone that new concepts are developing for the child through social interactions. These concepts have not yet been internalized, and therefore the child cannot cope with them alone.

Vygotsky defines learning as interaction with others in solving problems or dealing with concepts one is not capable of solving or dealing with alone. His notion of instruction is to identify the child's zone of proximal development and to present problems and tasks to the child which it can work through in collaboration with peers or teachers. When the child is then capable of solving this set of problems by itself, the child has reached a new level of development, and the zone of proximal development will also have changed; the child will have moved to a higher level.

The implications of these aspects of Vygotsky's thinking are that the curriculum should be preplanned and hierarchical. One cannot determine a pupil's real development and zone of proximal development unless one has an idea of what is to be learned and in what order it is to be learned. Both peers and adults are important in the social interactions where learning occurs, but whereas Piaget favors peer interaction to facilitate discovery, Vygotsky emphasizes the importance of the "experienced learner." This, together with the idea that school learning is systematic, emphasizes the teacher's role in the process.

Vygotsky's notion of the zone of proximal development may appear to some to be identical to the concept of reading readiness. It is not necessarily. This will be discussed further in Chapter 2. The zone of proximal development is very similar to the notions of "independent" and "instructional" reading levels, which will be discussed in Chapter 12.

LEARNING: CONCRETE TO ABSTRACT, OR ABSTRACT TO CONCRETE?

Vygotsky differentiates between school and nonschool learning in that the former is systematic and deliberately concentrates on the zone of proximal development. He also differentiates between spontaneous and scientific concepts. *Spontaneous* concepts are those a child will learn in social interactions outside of school—such as the meaning of the words *brother* and *sister*. *Scientific* concepts are those that are learned in school and that may be learned first on a fairly abstract plane. A student may use the word *exploitation* in recitation or in a classroom discussion long before he or she has a precise meaning for the word or understands the nuances of it. Given his attitude toward the role of social interaction in learning, it follows that Vygotsky is not at all put off by the superficial use of abstract terms in the initial stages of learning. This is simply one more case of meaning being created and developed in social interaction before it is internalized by the individual.

Vygotsky believes there is an interaction between learning scientific concepts in school and learning spontaneous concepts outside school. He agrees with most other educators that scientific concepts can, and should, be built upon spontaneous concepts. To use the previous example, the student's eventual learning of the precise meaning of *exploitation* will depend on everyday experiences with people who are stronger or weaker or who have more or less authority. But Vygotsky claims the reverse is also true. The students' understanding and categorization of everyday dealings with people who are stronger or weaker or who have more or less authority will be affected by their having a precise understanding of the word *exploitation*. This notion of two-way interaction between formation of scientific concepts and spontaneous concepts is relevant to many aspects of teaching reading, such as word recognition, comprehension, and vocabulary development.

Differences among Societies

COGNITIVE PROCESSES

Vygotsky believed that differences in society would produce differences in cognitive development. He suggested an investigation among the Soviet people of Central Asia at a time when this section of the Soviet Union was coming under collective farming and there was a concentrated effort to eliminate widespread illiteracy. What Vygotsky wanted to know was whether collectivization and literacy would change the way the people thought. The investigation was carried out by Luria and published many years later (Luria, 1976).

Luria asked questions and presented problems to groups of people in this remote area of the USSR. For example, he would ask: "How would you explain a car to someone who had never seen one?" Illiterate peasants from remote villages gave such answers as "Everyone knows what a car is," or "If you get in a car and go for a drive, you'll find out," or "If a person hasn't seen a thing, he won't be able to understand it. And that's that." But a man who worked on a collective farm and had had a ten-week school course responded: "A car is a thing that moves fast, uses electricity, water, and air. It covers great distances, so it makes difficult work easier."

The point of this investigation is to show that if society changes—in particular if literacy and collective farming (and its attendant need to plan and work collectively) are introduced into a culture of individual farms run by illiterate peasants—the way the people think will change. An interesting aspect of this study is that the people were asked to solve problems where the "given information" was contrary to known facts. For example, the fact may be that the journey from Center Town to North Town is six hours. The interviewer would

pose a problem like this: "From South Town to Center Town is three hours on foot, and from Center Town to North Town is three hours. How long would it take to get from South Town to North Town?" With illiterate peasants, such exchanges as the following occurred:

RESPONDENT: "No it's six hours from Center Town to North Town. You can't get there in three hours."
INTERVIEWER: "All right, but try to solve the problem. Even if it's wrong, try to figure it out."
RESPONDENT: "No. How can I solve a problem if it isn't so?"

Peasants with schooling or experience on collective farms, on the other hand, solved such problems readily.

This is particularly interesting because the same kinds of problems were presented to adolescents by Piaget to determine whether they had reached the formal operational stage. According to Piaget, if you give a person a problem based on a hypothesis contrary to fact, that person will be able to solve the problem in terms of the hypothesis only if he or she has reached the highest stage of cognitive development—the formal operational stage. The important contrast between Piaget and Luria is that Piaget claims development to this highest stage cannot be rushed. The child will not reach this stage until it has matured sufficiently—but Piaget also implies that everyone, in all societies, *will* reach this stage. Luria has shown that adults in a culture may not demonstrate certain cognitive capacities, but that if changes take place in society, these capacities may suddenly become manifest.

Other psychologists (Cole and Scribner, 1974, for example) have made observations similar to Luria's in cross-cultural research but have placed a different interpretation on them.

They believe that all levels of cognitive development appear in all cultures, but that habitual ways of dealing with problems and habitual ways of expressing oneself in language are determined by aspects of society and culture. These psychologists would say that the peasant in the above example was capable of solving the problem but would not do so because in his culture one has little experience with accepting a premise that is contrary to fact.

HABITS OF LANGUAGE

Basil Bernstein (1971, 1973, and 1975) believes that different characteristics of groups in society result in differences in the way people habitually express themselves in language. He refers to these different modes of expression as *language codes*. He describes two codes, elaborated and restricted; he claims these codes are associated with social class membership.

Origins of Codes. The group characteristics that produce the differences in codes are bound up with feelings of solidarity within groups. Group solidarity is determined by such things as attitudes toward nonconformity and authority, feelings of power or of powerlessness, and the amount of opportunity for dealing with people outside the group.

For example, where conformity is expected, where opinions are dictated by group consensus, there is little occasion to express unique and individually held beliefs or opinions. Communication is often possible by alluding to shared opinions and beliefs. In such circumstances, there is a reduced need for explicit, detailed language. On the other hand, where nonconformity is tolerated, there are occasions where one must express unique, individually held thoughts, beliefs, and opinions, and these are likely to be challenged by others. In such situations, language must be

explicit and detailed—intended to convey meaning not shared by the other party in the dialog.

Bernstein argues that group characteristics which encourage the use of the restricted code are found among the lower socioeconomic classes, whereas group characteristics that demand frequent use of the elaborated code are found among the middle and upper socioeconomic classes. Therefore, Bernstein links the habitual use of codes with socioeconomic class. This idea has not met universal favor; the idea as well as its critics are discussed further in Chapters 10 and 11.

Characteristics of Codes. Levitas (1974), in summarizing Bernstein, defines the *restricted* code as one which arises where the experiences of the participants are so closely shared that the need to verbalize communication is reduced. Speech structure is simplified; nonverbal means of communication gain importance; circumstances and manner of speech assume importance over content; and meanings tend to be descriptive and narrative, rather than analytical or abstract. Such language is implicit and relies on context to convey meaning. Such language may be referred to as implicit, context-dependent language. An *elaborated* code arises where participants are conscious of their separateness from others, of their own individuality. Speech structures are complex; the importance of nonverbal means of communication is reduced; content is more important than circumstances or manner of speech; and analytical and abstract meanings are more likely. Such language is explicit and does not rely on context to convey meaning. Such language may be referred to as explicit, context-independent language.

Language Codes and Teaching Reading. The characteristics of the elaborated code are the characteristics of the language of the school. Children who have had a great deal of experience with the elaborated code have an advantage in school from the start. Their exposure to the language of the school is a matter of further development of a mode of communication with which they have experience. For children who have not had much experience with the elaborated code, exposure to the language of the school is a matter of discontinuity, of culture shock.

The discontinuity of codes is even more exaggerated as the medium of language changes in the school from oral language to writing. In the language of schoolbooks there can be no (or minimal) reliance on nonverbal means of communication or on circumstances or manner of speech. The author does not know the reader. The author usually presumes that the meaning he or she intends to convey is not already known to the reader. The language is generally more complex, detailed, analytical, and abstract. Therefore, there is great continuity in experience with the elaborated code and the written language of schoolbooks, whereas there is discontinuity between experience with the restricted code and the written language of schoolbooks.

If one accepts the notion that social group characteristics have a bearing on language use and that language use has a bearing on school success and particularly success in dealing with written school language, it follows that part of the attention of the reading teacher should focus on the characteristics of the classroom as a society. The teacher should ask whether the social group characteristics of the classroom provide an incentive to engage in elaborated code, or whether the social group characteristics of the classroom encourage habitual use of restricted code.

• The terms *elaborated code* and *restricted code* are not used in later discussions of this topic in this book. Instead, the terms *explicit, context-independent language* (for elaborated code) and *implicit, context-dependent language* (for restricted code) are used.

The word *code* was used by Bernstein in his early work when his interest centered on such matters as word choices, sentence length, and use of adverbs—that is, how meanings are "coded" for transmission. The words *elaborated* and *restricted* were first used to describe such matters as word choice: When using explicit, context-independent language, one tends to use a wide range of words; that is, one tends to use an elaborated set of words. When using implicit, context-dependent language, one tends to use a narrower range of words, a restricted set of words.

However, the words *elaborated, restricted,* and *code* are not good words to describe the characteristics of language use that were discussed later by Bernstein and that are discussed in this chapter and taken up in later chapters. Furthermore, the words *elaborated* and *restricted* are value-laden for most people and should be avoided, since questions of whether one code is superior to the other divert attention from the relationship between habits of language use and learning to read.

A Sociological Perspective on Learning

Halliday's views on language development, Vygotsky's and Luria's views on the development of language and cognition, and Bernstein's views on the habitual use of implicit, context-dependent versus explicit, context-independent language have all been influential in bringing about an interest in the sociological aspects of learning. All this intellectual activity has focused the attention of educators on the society of the classroom and its effects on learning, particularly on language development and learning language skills such as reading.

One finds people addressing the question of whether a child is "ready" to learn to read in terms of how well the child functions in the society of the classroom. This is discussed in

Chapter 2. One finds people addressing the question of whether large-group, small-group, or individual instruction is preferable in terms of the sociological characteristics of groups of different sizes and whether these characteristics of groups are conducive to learning. This is addressed throughout the book, particularly in Chapter 11. Among those who accept the fact that experience with explicit, context-independent language is desirable for school learning, one finds interest in the question of whether the social environment of the classroom promotes or discourages the use of explicit, context-independent language. This issue is addressed in Chapters 10 and 11.

TWO ASPECTS OF READING INSTRUCTION: CONTRASTING VIEWS

Empiricist Versus Rationalist Perspectives

Empiricist assumptions have been contrasted with rationalist assumptions in this chapter. Empiricists tend to concentrate on the outer aspects of reading and to begin with the parts and work toward the whole (referred to as a "bottom-up" approach in current terminology). Rationalists tend to concentrate on the inner aspects of reading and deal with the parts only as they relate to the whole (referred to as a "top-down" approach in current terminology).

Psychological Versus Sociological Perspectives

A second contrasting pair of perspectives has been introduced in this chapter—the psychological point of view (emphasis on the

learner as an individual) and the sociological point of view (emphasis on the learner as a member of a social group). When teachers take a psychological perspective, they concentrate on imparting knowledge and skills to individuals; if every child is working to capacity, the classroom is functioning well. When teachers take a sociological perspective, they concentrate on creating a classroom society that will provide incentive and opportunity for learning; if the classroom is functioning properly, each student is working up to capacity.

The Interdependence of These Perspectives

The contrast between empiricism and rationalism comes into play when one considers what one should teach, where one should start, and what one's objectives are. In short, these perspectives have important implications for matters of curriculum. The contrast between the psychological and sociological perspectives comes into play when one considers how to teach. These perspectives have important implications in matters of methodology. However, since matters of curriculum and methodology are interdependent, these pairs of perspectives are also interdependent. One of the themes that will be developed throughout this book is that empiricism tends to be more compatible with a psychological approach to learning, and rationalism tends to be more compatible with a sociological approach.

SUMMARY

Reading is a language enterprise; therefore, teachers of reading are influenced by trends in linguistics. Learning to read is a learning enterprise; therefore, teachers of reading are influenced by trends in psychology. A single philosophical division profoundly affects the study of linguistics and psychology—that is, the division between empiricism and rationalism. Empiricists concentrate on the study of observable events and behaviors and attempt to explain language and learning in terms of these events and behaviors. Rationalists study language and learning as functions of the mind that cannot be observed but can be known.

Scientists in the empiricist tradition tend to break down observations into their smallest parts and to build theories of whole processes from observations about their parts. Scientists in the rationalist tradition tend to create theories of how the mind operates and explain smaller behaviors and events in terms of theories of whole processes. By the middle of this century, both linguistics and psychology were highly empirical sciences. The study of psychology was the study of behaviorism, and the study of linguistics was the study of structural linguistics. By the 1960s, however, a great shift had taken place. The study of psychology became the study of cognitive psychology, and the study of linguistics became the study of transformational grammar. The study of language acquisition and language performance from the point of view of psychology *and* linguistics became known as psycholinguistics (a term used in this book to refer to the period dating from Chomsky).

Psycholinguists believe that humans are genetically endowed with the capacity for language and that the human mind has a genetically determined capacity to organize input. Such theories are referred to as nativistic. Piaget, the best-known cognitive psychologist, is a nativist in that he believes all cognitive development proceeds in stages, and these stages are determined by maturation in the individual. Piaget views language as part of cognitive development.

Behaviorists concentrate on external events, and their theory and technology are useful in teaching outer aspects of reading, such as sound-letter relationships. But since they avoid consideration of mental events, behaviorist theories do not address inner aspects of reading, such as comprehension. Both psycholinguists and cognitive psychologists such as Piaget are mentalists, but they are also nativists. Their explanations of cognitive and language development emphasize the natural unfolding of genetically predetermined processes. Such explanations are not very useful to teachers.

In the last decade, the study of language and cognitive development from a sociological point of view has come into prominence. Since schools and teachers are part of a child's social environment, such studies are very useful to teachers because they investigate social interaction and their effect on cognitive development and language learning. Vygotsky's work is particularly useful, since he disagrees with Piaget's contention that one cannot speed up development. Vygotsky believes that a child can always operate on a higher cognitive plane in cooperation with others than it is capable of doing by itself, and that such experience facilitates development. Luria has shown that changes in social experience, including schooling of previously unschooled people, results in their demonstrating advanced levels of cognitive development.

Bernstein has argued that characteristics of groups within society lead to differences in the language habitually used by individuals within groups. He refers to these as restricted and elaborated codes. For example, where a high degree of conformity is demanded, there is limited occasion to express unique, privately held opinions or to try to persuade others to adopt those opinions; therefore, the need for using explicit language is reduced and implicit, context-dependent language becomes habitual. Where nonconformity is tolerated, there are an increased number of occasions for using language that is explicit and that does not rely on shared meanings, and many experiences with explicit, context-independent language are provided. The typical language of the school, and particularly the written language encountered in the school, is explicit, context-independent language. Children who do not have experience with explicit, context-independent language are at a disadvantage in their school experience—particularly in dealing with written language.

This chapter has contrasted the empiricist and rationalist perspectives on one hand, and the psychological and sociological perspectives on the other. Empiricist and rationalist perspectives are particularly relevant to questions of what one should teach and where one should start. These are questions of curriculum. The psychological and sociological perspectives are particularly relevant to questions of how one teaches. These are questions of method. However, since method and curriculum are intimately related, these perspectives tend to merge. A theme that will be developed in this book is that the empirical and psychological perspectives frequently appear together and that the rationalist and sociological perspectives frequently appear together.

Each of the points of view developed in this chapter (philosophic, linguistic, psychological, and sociological) has a potential effect on teaching reading. For example, there are those who view reading as essentially a task of perceiving symbols and attaching sounds to them, and there are those who view reading as essentially a task of understanding the author's meaning, with letter-sound relationships incidental to the task. Whichever view one adopts as a reading teacher, on this point or on many other such points, will have an effect on what one does as a teacher—on what one teaches and how one teaches.

FOR FURTHER READING AND DISCUSSION

In looking at textbooks on teaching reading, one often finds that one of the perspectives discussed in this chapter is quite clearly represented. The first two books on the following list seem to reflect a clearly empiricist point of view, whereas the second two appear to reflect a rationalist point of view.

Get one book from each category and compare them. What evidence do you find that these books represent the empiricist or rationalist points of view? Do you agree that the books have been properly categorized? To what extent do you find the other point of view represented in each book? Do you think it is possible to present a program of teaching reading and stay strictly within one category?

Which of these books seems to emphasize a psychological perspective? Which of these books seems to emphasize a sociological perspective?

1. Lapp, Diane, and James Flood. *Teaching Reading to Every Child.* New York: Macmillan, 1978.
2. Otto, W., R. Rude, and D. L. Spiegel. *How to Teach Reading.* Reading, MA: Addison-Wesley, 1979.

3. Lee, D. M., and J. B. Rubin. *Children and Language.* Belmont, CA: Wadsworth, 1979.

4. Stauffer, R. G. *The Language Experience Approach to the Teaching of Reading.* New York: Harper & Row, 1980.

REFERENCES

Bernstein, Basil. *Class, Codes and Control: Theoretical Studies Towards a Sociology of Language,* Vol. 1. London: Routledge and Kegan Paul, 1971.

————. *Class, Codes and Control: Applied Studies Toward a Sociology of Language,* Vol. 2. London: Routledge and Kegan Paul, 1973.

————. *Class, Codes and Control: Towards a Theory of Educational Transmission,* Vol. 3. London: Routledge and Kegan Paul, 1975.

Bloomfield, L., and C. Barnhart. *Let's Read: A Linguistic Approach.* Detroit: Wayne State University Press, 1961.

Blumenthal, A. L. *Language and Psychology: Historical Aspects of Psycholinguistics.* New York: Wiley, 1970.

Brainerd, C. J. *Piaget's Theory of Intelligence.* Englewood Cliffs, NJ: Prentice-Hall, 1978.

Cherry, C. *On Human Communication: A Review, A Survey, A Criticism.* Cambridge, MA: MIT Press, 1957.

Chomsky, N. Review of *Verbal Behavior,* by B. F. Skinner. *Language,* 35 (1959): 26–58.

————. *Aspects of the Theory of Syntax.* Cambridge, MA: MIT Press, 1965.

Cole, M., and S. Scribner. *Culture and Thought.* New York: Wiley, 1974.

Goodman, K. S. Reading: A psycholinguistic guessing game. *Journal of the Reading Specialist,* 4 (1967): 126–35.

————. Comprehension-centered reading. *Claremont Reading Conference Yearbook,* 34 (1970): 125–35.

Hall, R. A. *Leave Your Language Alone!* Ithaca, NY: Linguistica, 1950.

Halliday, M. A. K. *Learning How to Mean.* New York: Elsevier, 1975.

————. *Explorations in the Functions of Language.* New York: Elsevier, 1977.

————. *Language as a Social Semiotic.* London: Edward Arnold, 1978.

Levitas, M. *Marxism and the Sociology of Education.* London: Routledge and Kegan Paul, 1974.

Luria, A. R. *Cognitive Development: Its Cultural and Social Foundations.* Cambridge, MA: Harvard University Press, 1976.

Lyons, J. *Introduction to Theoretical Linguistics.* Cambridge, MA: Cambridge University Press, 1968.

Miller, G. A. *Language and Communication,* New York: McGraw-Hill, 1951.

Piaget, J. *The Language and Thought of the Child.* New York: World, 1955.

Skinner, B. F. *Verbal Behavior.* New York: Appleton, 1957.

Smith, F. *Understanding Reading: A Psycholinguistic Analysis of Reading and Learning to Read.* New York: Holt, Rinehart and Winston, 1971.

Vygotsky, L. S. *Thought and Language.* Cambridge, MA: MIT Press, 1962.

————. *Mind in Society.* Cambridge, MA: Harvard University Press, 1978.

CHAPTER
2
READING READINESS

HOW THE CONCEPT OF READING READINESS ARISES

A TRADITIONAL CONCEPT

Assumptions Underlying Readiness Tasks
Challenging the Assumptions Underlying Task A

CONCEPTS OF READING READINESS IN PUBLISHED TESTS

Auditory Discrimination and Memory, Visual Discrimination and Memory
Alphabet Knowledge
Word Learning Tasks
Oral Language Comprehension
Readiness Tasks Reflect Assumptions About Reading

READING AS AN ATOMISTIC ENTERPRISE
READING AS A HOLISTIC ENTERPRISE

THE USEFULNESS OF PUBLISHED READINESS TESTS

Predicting Who Will Learn to Read

PUBLISHERS' CLAIMS
RESEARCH FINDINGS
WHY PREDICT SUCCESS?

Selecting Students for Reading Instruction

PREDICTING INDIVIDUAL SUCCESS ON THE BASIS OF CORRELATIONS
EFFECTS OF WITHHOLDING INSTRUCTION

Diagnosis

THE MEANING OF TEST NAMES
THE MEANING OF INCORRECT RESPONSES
FINDING THE REASONS FOR INCORRECT RESPONSES
THE RELEVANCE OF INDIVIDUAL TASKS TO READING INSTRUCTION

Unexamined Assumptions and Unwarranted Practices

GROUPING CHILDREN WHO FAIL A TASK
GROUPING CHILDREN WHO FAIL THE TEST

THE CONCEPT OF READINESS IN AN UP-TO-DATE CLASSROOM

To Test Readiness, Teach Reading
Two Widely Divergent Methods

THE LANGUAGE EXPERIENCE APPROACH
THE PHONIC-LINGUISTIC SYSTEM

THE CONCEPT OF READINESS AS A PREREADING CURRICULUM

Traditional Reading Readiness Skills
Concepts Related to Print and Reading
Understanding the Vocabulary of Reading Instruction
Concepts Related to Storybooks

LANGUAGE DEVELOPMENT AND READING READINESS

Reading Skill and Language Development
Assessing Language Development

AN ATOMISTIC APPROACH
A HOLISTIC APPROACH

Selecting and Diagnosing on the Basis of
Language Development

SCHOOL READINESS AND READING READINESS

Readiness for Instruction
Assessing School Readiness

AN ATOMISTIC APPROACH
A HOLISTIC APPROACH

Selecting and Diagnosing on the Basis of
School Readiness

SUMMARY

FOR FURTHER READING AND DISCUSSION

REFERENCES

HOW THE CONCEPT OF READING READINESS ARISES

Imagine the problems that would confront a committee that has been appointed by the minister of education in an emerging Third World nation where only 5 percent of the population is literate. The committee has been charged with two tasks: to teach an additional 20 percent of the adult population to read in the next five years, and to start a reading program in the newly formed public primary schools aimed at universal literacy for the next generation.

How would the committee members choose the adult population for the literacy program so as to maximize the chances of success in attaining 25 percent adult literacy? What qualities would they look for in candidates for the program? Would they be interested in the candidates' performance in perception, their psychological characteristics, their knowledge, their problem-solving ability, their personality traits, their social characteristics, and/or their socioeconomic status?

How would they decide when to teach children to read in the primary school? At

what age? Would they consider any or all of the characteristics that were considered in deciding which adults to include in the literacy program. Would they begin to teach some of the children at an earlier age than the others? How would they decide which children would learn at an earlier age?

As soon as we start to think about these problems, we realize that the committee needs more facts about the situation: What is the point of making an additional 20 percent of the adult population literate? Is it to supply teachers for the primary school, to supply workers for modern business offices or for high-technology industry, or to facilitate democratic government?

What may be the social and political outcomes of a successful literacy program? Are there advantaged and disadvantaged groups in the country? What are the implications if a disproportionately large number of adults are selected for reading instruction from an already powerful group? What are the implications of starting to teach reading to some children at an earlier age than others? Will early reading instruction turn into social, political, or economic advantage for the individuals who receive it?

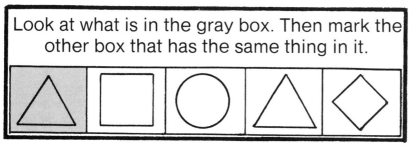

FIGURE 2.1
TASK A.

♦ Before you continue reading, you might stop and think about these questions and discuss them with your classmates. You may be surprised to find the number of issues that arise and just how complicated the process is of determining who is ready to learn to read. In such a discussion, it is likely that you will touch on many of the issues and practices presented in this chapter.

A TRADITIONAL CONCEPT

Assumptions Underlying Readiness Tasks

People have many characteristics. Some of them are obviously irrelevant to success in learning to read, such as color of hair, and some of them are obviously related, such as adequate eyesight. However, a great many characteristics are *possibly* relevant to success in learning to read, but may not be relevant or may not always be relevant. As a result, a great deal of research has been done to answer the question of what characteristics are relevant to learning to read.

One suggested characteristic is a child's ability to match forms in tasks such as marking the two shapes in the row that are identi-

cal, as in task A (Figure 2.1). This is one task of many that is supposed to test a child's ability to make judgments about visual similarities and differences in shapes and symbols. This ability is referred to as *visual discrimination.*

Using this example task as a test of visual discrimination, one can examine the reasoning that goes into reading readiness research. What would make anyone think success on such a task would be an indication of success in learning to read? The reasoning goes something like this: If a person is going to learn to read, he or she is going to have to be able to distinguish one letter from another and to distinguish one word from another. A child who does not recognize a difference between *bad* and *dad* is likely to have trouble learning to read. But since the alphabet is probably a very strange set of symbols to prereaders and since the difference between *bad* and *dad* may be quite subtle for someone not familiar with the alphabet, it might be wise to first identify children who can see that (in the example above) the two triangles are alike, whereas the circle, square, and diamond are each unique in the set. People who are able to make these kinds of visual discriminations are better prospects for learning to read than people who cannot make these kinds of discriminations.

Challenging the Assumptions Underlying Task A

The reasoning above contains a whole series of assumptions that seem to be valid—but they may not be. For example, if a child is asked to tell which of the two shapes in the example are alike and he or she does not do it, the assumption is made that the child cannot discriminate likenesses and differences in shapes. If one were to stop and think about that, one would see that there are several reasons why a child might not identify the triangle. Maybe the child does not know what *same* means in this context. Maybe the child knows what *same* means but sees that the diamond is like the triangle and is confused or afraid there is a trick in the question. Or perhaps the child simply just doesn't want to answer.

Another premise that ought to be examined is that if a child is successful on this task, he or she is ready to learn to read. This appears to be an assumption that is easy to test. One might give children a test with items like task A (Figure 2.1) and then try to teach the children to read. As a matter of fact, researchers have done just that and have discovered that success at performing tasks like task A is not a very good way of predicting who will be successful in learning to read and who will not (MacGinitie, 1969).

There are other assumptions hidden in the reasoning that ability to perform correctly tasks like task A will identify children who are ready to learn to read. Making these kinds of assumptions explicit and testing their validity is one of the major concerns of educational research. Some characteristics of children that have been suggested as indicators of readiness and the assumptions that lie behind specifying these skills as indicators will be examined in the following sections.

CONCEPTS OF READING READINESS IN PUBLISHED TESTS

In this section we will present a variety of items that are found on reading readiness tests and examine the assumptions underlying them. Items will be presented in four broad categories according to the assumptions that appear to underlie them.

Auditory Discrimination and Memory, Visual Discrimination and Memory

One assumption underlying reading readiness test items is that to learn to read is to learn a set of specific skills that—when put together—make up the act of reading. When one thinks of reading as putting together symbols and sounds so that a person can say words when he or she sees them, two kinds of skills appear to be necessary for learning to read—auditory skills and visual skills. In order to match sound to symbol, one would expect that a person can tell one symbol from another and can distinguish one speech sound from another. Therefore tests of auditory and visual discrimination are frequently included in reading readiness tests.

A typical item designed to test auditory discrimination would ask the student to match pictures of things that begin with the same sound. The correct response to task B (Figure 2.2) would be to mark the picture of the rope as the teacher says the names of the pictures and asks which starts with the same sound as *road*. Another example of a test of auditory discrimination would be to identify pictures of things whose names rhyme. The correct response to task C (Figure 2.3) would be to mark the picture of the jet as the teacher says the names of the pictures and asks which ends with the same sound as *net*.

FIGURE 2.2
TASK B.

FIGURE 2.3
TASK C.

In addition to task A, other items like task D (Figure 2.4) are designed to test visual discrimination. The task is to identify the identical shapes. Some tests add another element to visual discrimination tasks by having the student copy a figure rather than match it to an identical one. Such a task asks the student to make the second drawing look just like the first one, as in task E (Figure 2.5). Notice that these tasks do not involve printing. They involve oral language, pictures, and shapes (but not letters).

Alphabet Knowledge

A second set of reading readiness tasks *do* involve printed letters and words. The assumption underlying these tasks is that in order to find out whether a child is ready to learn to read, one should see if the child has the knowledge and skills that one teaches in the beginning stages of reading instruction.

Examples of such items are tasks in which the student draws a line through the identical letters in task F (Figure 2.6) or the identical

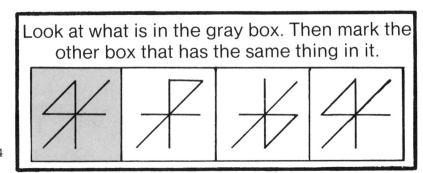

FIGURE 2.4
TASK D.

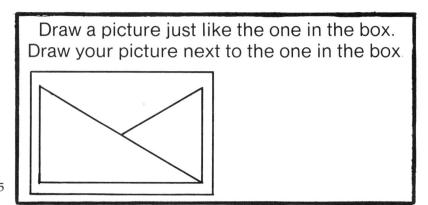

FIGURE 2.5
TASK E.

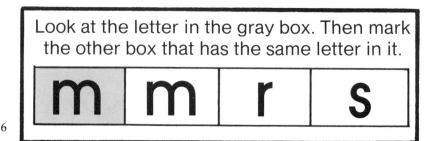

FIGURE 2.6
TASK F.

words in task G (Figure 2.7). Another visual discrimination task that involves actual letters asks the student to copy words, as in task H (Figure 2.8).

Although tasks F, G, and H use letters and words, the student would not necessarily need to know the names of the letters or recognize the words to perform satisfactorily. Task I

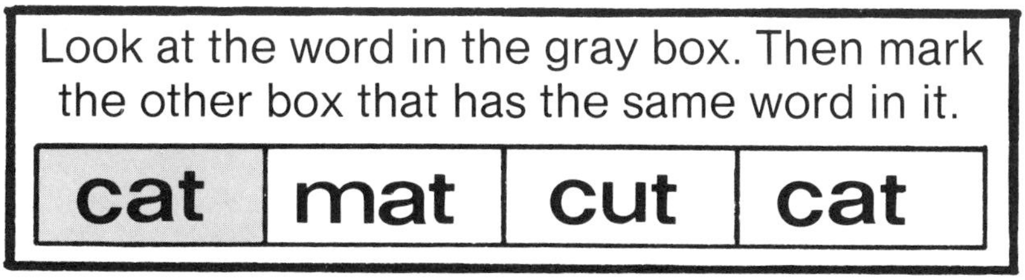

Look at the word in the gray box. Then mark the other box that has the same word in it.

cat	mat	cut	cat

FIGURE 2.7
TASK G.

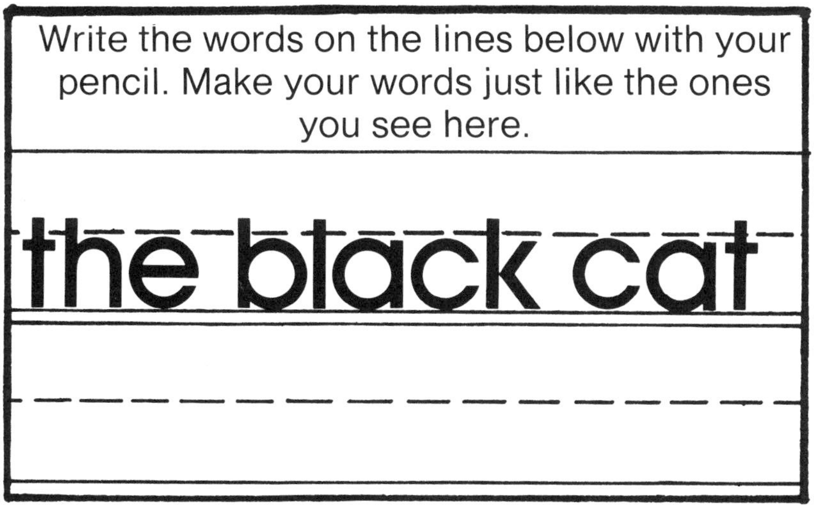

Write the words on the lines below with your pencil. Make your words just like the ones you see here.

the black cat

FIGURE 2.8
TASK H.

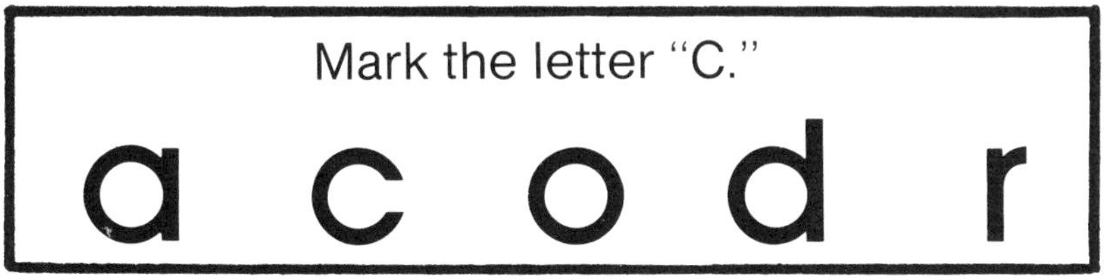

Mark the letter "C."

a   c   o   d   r

FIGURE 2.9
TASK I.

(Figure 2.9) requires that the student know the names of the letters. The task is to put a mark on the letter that the teacher names. Tests of letter name knowledge are also given individ-ually. The teacher shows letters to the student, and the student tells the name of the letter.

Other items test letter-sound relationships in words. In task J (Figure 2.10), the student is

FIGURE 2.10
TASK J.

FIGURE 2.11
TASK K.

asked to mark the picture whose name begins with the letter in the box; in task K (Figure 2.11), the student is asked to mark the picture that ends with the sound of the letter in the box.

Word Learning Tasks

A third kind of task is called a word learning task. The assumption underlying such a task is that in order to find out whether a child is ready to learn to read, one should try to teach the child to recognize words in print and discover whether or not he or she learns.

For example, children are taught words such as *walk, fly,* and *swim.* The children look at the words printed on the board and say the words as the teacher points to them. The words are presented on cards, and the children say them as the teacher presents each card and matches the word on the card to the word on the board. The words are used in several sentences by the teacher as the students look at the words: "Birds can fly. Airplanes can fly. You and I can't fly—except in an air-

Put a mark on the word
<u>swim</u>.

train   swim   build

FIGURE 2.12
TASK L.

Put a mark on the picture of
the baby.

FIGURE 2.13
TASK M.

plane." The teacher asks questions and holds up a card. The students must know the word on the card to answer: "Can fish do this (holding up *swim*)? Yes, fish can swim." Children are then tested on recognizing the words, as in task L (Figure 2.12). The test may be repeated an hour later.

Oral Language Comprehension

A fourth kind of task tests the students' understanding of oral language. The assump-

tion underlying these tasks appears to be that reading is a language comprehension skill, and if children understand oral language, they will probably become good readers.

In an example of an item testing vocabulary knowledge, the child might be shown a series of pictures, as in task M (Figure 2.13), and told to "put a mark on the picture of the baby." In an example of an item testing oral sentence comprehension, the child might be shown a series of pictures, as in task N (Figure 2.14), and told to "put a mark on the boy who is following after the girl."

FIGURE 2.14
TASK N.

Readiness Tasks Reflect Assumptions About Reading

The tasks presented above reflect a broad division among reading educators between those influenced by the empiricist tradition and those influenced by the rationalist tradition (see Chapter 1). The most obvious difference reflected in these tasks is whether those who created the tasks see learning to read as an atomistic enterprise or as a holistic enterprise.

READING AS AN ATOMISTIC ENTERPRISE

Tasks A through K, represented in Figures 2.1 through 2.11, reflect the empiricist view that learning to read is an atomistic enterprise. That is, a person learns to distinguish one shape from another and one sound from another; he or she then learns to distinguish letters and speech sounds from each other; he or she then learns to associate particular speech sound with particular letters; he or she then learns to match successive sounds with successive letters and thereby discovers the spoken counterpart of written words.

Teachers strongly under the influence of this tradition are likely to have a highly compartmentalized and hierarchical program of auditory and visual discrimination skills, letter naming, letter-sound association practice, and so on. When it is pointed out to such teachers that some of the students may already be reading whether they demonstrate mastery of these subskills or not, the teachers will often claim that they are *reinforcing* these skills, or that they are making explicit what some children seem to know implicitly. In any event, these teachers are not easily dissuaded from taking each child through each step in the program—and in a particular order.

READING AS A HOLISTIC ENTERPRISE

Although educators who view reading as a holistic enterprise are generally unsympathetic to the use of traditional readiness tests (because these tests reflect such a strong bias toward the atomisic view of reading), the rationale behind tasks like L, M, and N (Figures 2.12, 2.13, and 2.14) is more compatible with their view.

Task L, represented in Figure 2.12, reflects the rationalist view that learning to read is a holistic enterprise: What is important in learning to read is that the student somehow learns to associate spoken words in context with their printed representations. These tasks do not reveal whether the child is attending to the shape of the word, the first letter, the length, or any number of other possibilities. Some students may be doing one thing; some may be doing another; and a student's strategy may change from word to word. Tasks M and N, represented in Figures 2.13 and 2.14, reflect an even broader holistic concept of what it means to learn to read. Learning to read is seen as a skill that depends on facility with language and even more generally on knowledge of the world. A child who responds to these items correctly demonstrates that facility and knowledge and so is probably ready to learn to read.

Teachers strongly influenced by this tradition are likely to teach children to read whole words and sentences in context from the beginning. They may use such techniques as having the children make up captions for their own paintings or drawings and then trying to help the children read the captions. These teachers may even feel that learning to read should be as effortless as learning to speak seems to be, and they may be bewildered by children who do not learn to read "naturally."

Teachers influenced by this tradition may concede that readers obviously make distinctions between different letters and between different speech sounds, and that they rely on knowledge of letter-sound relationships at some point. However, these teachers tend to believe that one person may learn these things and employ them in reading in a different order from another person. Or one person may employ such knowledge at different times and with different emphasis from another person. These teachers may resist teaching such things as letter discrimination and letter-sound relationships, or they are likely to teach such things as they believe the need arises, rather than in a predetermined, orderly way (see, for example, Lee and Rubin, 1979).

• This may be a good place to stop and think about which of these traditions you are sympathetic toward. You might want to discuss the question with your classmates. Deciding where you stand on this matter is not a pointless intellectual exercise. Decisions regarding what to do, when to do it, and how to do it are ultimately based on the answers to such questions.

THE USEFULNESS OF PUBLISHED READINESS TESTS

Are the readiness concepts incorporated into traditional published tests useful? In reviewing the research, it becomes clear that the question can take three forms, and that the answer may vary depending on the form of the question. The three forms of the question are as follows:

— Are the concepts in published tests useful for predicting who will learn to read?
— Are the concepts useful for selecting who will be given instruction in reading and from whom instruction will be withheld?
— Are the concepts useful for diagnosing which skills a particular child needs to learn at the initial stages of reading instruction, and which teaching method will be most appropriate for a particular child?

Predicting Who Will Learn to Read

Most reading readiness research is done on a model that is very easy to understand. If one believes that a certain skill such as naming letters is a necessary prerequisite to learning to read, one can test children on letter names before instruction begins. If most of the children who know their letter names learn to read and most of the children who do not know their letter names do not learn to read, one would have strong evidence that learning letter names is an important prerequisite to learning to read. But studies are not usually that clearcut. What usually happens is that success in learning to read is far from infallibly predicted by scores on such tests as letter naming.

Using statistics, however, one can tell whether there is a relationship between children's scores on tests of such skills as letter naming, administered before instruction begins, and tests of reading administered after a year or so of instruction. If there is a relationship, one may infer that knowledge of letter names is an important prerequisite to learning to read. This inference may be called into question, as we shall see, but it is usually made in research of this kind. It is this inference to which educators refer when they speak of the *predictive validity* of reading readiness tests.

PUBLISHERS' CLAIMS

Publishers of readiness tests typically issue data to show that scores on their tests correlate with later success in learning to read, as measured by standardized tests of reading achievement. For example, the manual of directions for the Metropolitan Readiness Test (Hildreth et al., 1969) reports that scores on the following subtests correlate between .34 and .55 with scores on a paragraph meaning test administered after around six months of instruction:

— *Word Meaning,* similar to task M (Figure 2.13)

— *Listening,* similar to task N (Figure 2.14)
— *Matching,* similar to tasks A and D (Figures 2.1 and 2.4)
— *Alphabet,* similar to task I (Figure 2.9)
— *Copying,* similar to task E (Figure 2.5)

The manual of direction of the Murphy-Durrell Reading Readiness Analysis (Murphy and Durrell, 1965) reports that scores on the following subtests correlate between .48 and .59 with scores on a paragraph meaning test administered after around eight months of instruction:

— *Phonemes,* similar to task B (Figure 2.2)
— *Letter Names,* similar to task I (Figure 2.9)
— *Learning Rate,* similar to task L (Figure 2.12)

The manual for the Clymer-Barrett Pre-reading Battery (1969) reports that scores on the following subtests correlate between .42 and .66 with scores on a paragraph meaning test.

— *Visual Discrimination,* similar to tasks G and I (Figures 2.7 and 2.9)
— *Auditory Discrimination,* similar to tasks B and C (Figures 2.2 and 2.3)
— *Visual Motor Coordination,* similar to tasks E and H (Figures 2.5 and 2.8)

♦ This might be a good time to stop and think about the terms used to classify tests and the actual test items. Look at task I (Figure 2.9), for example. By what name is task I classified on the Metropolitan? On the Murphy-Durrell? On the Clymer-Barrett?

Look at task B (Figure 2.2). By what name is task B classified on the Murphy-Durrell? On the Clymer-Barrett? This inconsistency between terms used to classify tests and actual test items becomes particularly important when reading readiness tests are used to make decisions about what to teach and to whom.

RESEARCH FINDINGS

In addition to the claims of predictive validity supplied by publishers of tests, a great deal of research has been done by others to discover which skills predict reading success. A frequent and consistent finding is that letter name knowledge is among the best predictors of success in learning to read (deHirsh et al., 1966; Silvaroli, 1965; Bond and Dykstra, 1967; Chall, 1967; Durrell, 1958; Silverberg, 1968; Weiner and Feldman, 1963; Jansky and deHirsh, 1972). Visual discrimination has been found to correlate with later reading achievement (Wilson and Fleming, 1960; Bryan, 1964; Barrett, 1965; deHirsh et al., 1966; Chall, 1967). A child's ability to recognize words she or he has been taught to recognize has been found to predict later reading achievement (Gavel, 1958; deHirsh et al., 1966; Barr, 1971; Kibby, 1979). Tests of vocabulary knowledge have been found to predict reading achievement (Morgan, 1960; deHirsh et al., 1966; Loban, 1963; Robinson, 1963).

Research findings relating language development to success in learning to read are usually based on measures of children's oral language production. Measures of language development as a factor in reading readiness will be discussed below in a separate section.

WHY PREDICT SUCCESS?

The best way to discover whether a student will learn to read is to teach that student to read and see if he or she learns. Then why test readiness? There are two reasons generally put forward (when the question is asked—and it frequently is not asked). One is that by testing readiness, the teacher can decide which children he or she should begin to teach to read. That is, one tests readiness to *select* children for reading instruction. The sec-

ond is that by testing readiness, the teacher can determine what skills or knowledge individual children need before instruction begins. That is, one tests reading readiness to *diagnose* which skills a child will need to learn before that child can begin to learn to read.

Selecting Students for Reading Instruction

PREDICTING INDIVIDUAL SUCCESS ON THE BASIS OF CORRELATIONS

The practice of selecting students for beginning reading instruction on the basis of readiness tests is probably unjustified because it is based on several questionable assumptions. First of all, success or failure on individual tasks like A through N (Figures 2.1 through 2.14) or on tests made up of combinations of these tasks do not infallibly predict success in learning to read. Test manuals claim correlations of between .35 and .60 for individual tests and later reading scores. Similar correlations are consistently reported in the literature (see Spache, 1973; Weintraub, 1967).

Although these correlations are statistically significant, that simply means that low scorers on readiness tests *tend* to get low scores later on reading tests, and high scorers on readiness tests *tend* to get high scores later on reading tests. But in a large group some students can get high scores on one test and low scores on the other, and the correlations may still be significant. As a research tool, such tests and correlations are useful because they supply us with evidence about what skills are related to success in beginning reading. As predictors of which *individuals* will learn to read, they are not very useful.

A good analogy to keep in mind is that U.S. government studies have shown a significant correlation between cigarette smoking and incidence of lung cancer. But it is not possible to say with any certainty whether a particular cigarette smoker will contract lung cancer. In the same way, studies have shown a significant correlation between failure on certain reading readiness tasks and low reading achievement test scores after instruction. It is not possible to say with any certainty whether a particular student who failed these reading readiness tasks will fail on a reading achievement test after instruction. And, of course, we cannot be certain that an individual who does not smoke will not contract cancer; nor can we be sure that an individual who can perform reading readiness tasks will score high on a reading achievement test after instruction.

♦ You might reflect for a moment on the two charges given to the committee by the minister of education at the beginning of this chapter. The committee members want to make an additional 20 percent of the adult population literate in two years, and they have 95 percent of the population to choose from. Here is a case where tests with predictive validity might be useful. If they knew that people who do well on tasks like A through N (Figures 2.1 through 2.14) tend to learn to read better than people who fail on such tasks, they would be very wise to choose adults for the literacy program on the basis of such test scores. But to withhold instruction from children in the primary school (where universal literacy is the goal) on the basis of such tests presents a problem. They would almost certainly be withholding reading instruction from some children who would learn to read if they were taught.

EFFECTS OF WITHHOLDING INSTRUCTION

Advocates of selecting students for instruction on the basis of some concept of read-

iness appear to assume that there are no ill effects from beginning instruction with some children and withholding instruction from others. The assumption seems to be that those "not ready" will become ready (perhaps through readiness training) and will then begin to learn to read with no ill effects. People strongly influenced by the notion that learning is dependent on maturation may go so far as to say that beginning reading instruction of any kind with children who are not ready may be harmful (Furth and Wachs, 1974). However, these assumptions are questionable.

MacGinitie (1969) has argued that "nearly every six year old is ready to learn something about reading if this something is carefully selected in keeping with his abilities." Lee and Rubin (1979) have argued that "the decision in advance that certain children are high risk candidates for learning to read, and subsequent treatment of them as such, cannot help but provide negative feedback" (p. 271).

The practice of segregating children who are not ready—by whatever criteria—from children who are ready to learn to read is thoroughly out of keeping with both Vygotsky and Piaget. As noted in Chapter 1, Vygotsky (1962) believed that school learning should concentrate on areas of cognitive development that pupils cannot handle on their own, but that they can work on with others who are more advanced in the area. Piaget places great emphasis on learning through interaction with peers (Brainerd, 1978). Although Vygotsky finds much to argue with in Piaget's theories of development, both would agree that a good way to keep a concept from developing would be to keep children who do not have the concept segregated from children who do.

It has also been shown that when schools identify children who are likely to fail, the children usually do fail. It has been suggested that at least some of these failures are due to the phenomenon of the "self-fulfilling prophecy." Subtle changes in teachers' expectations and differential treatment of children increase the likelihood of failure (Rosenthal and Jacobson, 1968). Segregating children at the beginning stages of reading instruction may be particularly harmful and certainly ought not to be done on the basis of readiness tests for the reasons stated here. The practice of grouping children for instruction will be treated in Chapters 10, 11, and 12.

Diagnosis

The purpose of much of the research done in reading readiness is not to discover tasks that will enable teachers to select children for reading instruction, but to discover the skills necessary for learning to read or to discover the components of the reading task so that one knows what to teach. In his review of reading readiness research, MacGinitie (1969) states that there are two purposes for such research: " . . . [1] to understand better the nature of the process of learning to read, and [2] to learn how to make helpful predictions" (p. 399). "Helpful predictions," according to MacGinitie, are not predictions that lead to selecting students for instruction, but predictions regarding what *facet* of the reading process this particular child will be successful in learning at this point. Gates (1937) expressed similar views of the concept of readiness. Fry (1977) describes readiness as a "subskills theory" and says that it is "educational in nature" in that its followers believe a child who is not ready can be taught these skills and be made ready by proper education.

But viewing tests made up of items like tasks A through N as tests of skills that are essential to (or at least contribute to) successful reading is, again, based on questionable assumptions.

THE MEANING OF TEST NAMES

The first assumption is that if a teacher knows the *name* of a test on which a child performed poorly, the teacher knows precisely what tasks the child failed to perform. It has been pointed out that task I (Figure 2.9) is referred to as a test of visual discrimination on one standardized test and a test of letter names on another, and that task B (Figure 2.2) is referred to as a test of auditory discrimination on one test and a test of phonemes on another.

♦ What kind of lesson do you think would be in order if you were told that a child failed a test called Auditory Reception? Think about it for a minute.

The Auditory Reception test on the Illinois Test of Psycholinguistic Abilities (Kirk et al., 1968) consists of 50 questions of the following form: "Do wingless birds soar?" "Do children play?" Do you think the lessons you had in store for the child would have helped that child with whatever problem he or she experienced when he or she did poorly in answering these questions?

One must never assume from the name of a test that one knows what the test measures. If a teacher is going to base educational decisions on test results, he or she must look at the test items and decide for him or herself what the significance of success or failure on those items is.

THE MEANING OF INCORRECT RESPONSES

A second assumption is that if a child fails a test (or an item on a test), it is because that child does not possess the skill or knowledge the test (or item) was designed to measure. For example, if a child marks the present on task B (Figure 2.2), one assumes it is because she thinks *road* and *present* begin with the same sound—or, put another way, the child cannot hear a difference between /p/ and /r/.[1]

♦ Picture a normal, healthy 6-year-old (preferably one you know), and ask yourself: "If Suzie (or whoever) marked the present in task B, would the most plausible explanation be that she does not hear a difference between /p/ and /r/? What might some other explanations be?

• *Perhaps she does not understand the meaning of the phrase "begins with the same sound."*
• *Perhaps she does not understand that the words the teacher says for this task go with the pictures.*
• *Perhaps she was distracted and did not hear the choices and guessed at the answer.*

♦ There are many explanations for the incorrect response more plausible than the idea that the child cannot hear a difference between /p/ and /r/.

FINDING THE REASONS FOR INCORRECT RESPONSES

To discover the real reason why a child makes an incorrect response, one needs to sit down with the child and go over the items answered incorrectly. The child may give the correct response when given individual attention, or she may respond incorrectly and appear to be guessing. In that case, a lesson may be in order. For example:

TEACHER: All these words begin with the same sound: road, rip, Ron, roll. They all begin with /r/. Which of these words begins with /r/: run, ball?

All these words begin with the same sound: pot, Patsy, pull, punch. They all

[1]When letters appear between slashes as in /p/, read as follows: "The sound typically represented in English by the letter *p*."

begin with /p/. Which of these words begins with /p/: cat, pan?

Now let's look at the picture again. The pictures are rope, present, and train. Which begins with the same sound as road—rope, present, train—road?

In a short time one may discover what caused the child to make the wrong response, or it may take a long time. The point is that the problem may not be that the child does not discriminate between sounds. The problem may be something that is quite crucial to reading instruction. For example, the child may not know what the phrase "begins with the same sound" means in this context. This knowledge is quite necessary for success in some reading lessons. To find out that this is the problem and to go to work on correcting the problem is sound diagnostic teaching.

Or one may find that the child can do the task with a little coaching, but is unable to do it alone. The task is in the zone of proximal development (Vygotsky, 1962), and if the task is relevant to the instruction the child is receiving, practice with the teacher and other students who perform the task readily is in order. This too is sound diagnostic teaching. But to assume that because a child failed an item (or a series of items) like task B, the child does not distinguish between sounds, and to launch into a series of lessons where the child distinguishes between the sound of such things as a fire alarm and running water is a waste of time and energy, and that is bad teaching.

Never assume that because a child does not respond correctly to an item (or items) the child does not have the skill or knowledge the item (or test) is designed to measure. If a teacher is going to base educational decisions on test results, he or she should observe the child making responses to the test items and determine the reason for failure.

THE RELEVANCE OF INDIVIDUAL TASKS TO READING INSTRUCTION

A third assumption is that because some skill or knowledge is tested on a reading readiness battery, it is necessary to instill the skill or knowledge in a child before beginning to teach that child to read. Although some reading programs appear to be based on this assumption, it is rarely stated explicitly. The assumption is indefensible, and as soon as it is stated explicitly, its indefensibility becomes obvious.

If one's concept of beginning reading instruction is to teach the names of the letters, ought one to refrain from teaching the names of the letters until the child demonstrates mastery of every task demonstrated in Figures 2.1 through 2.14? If one's concept of beginning reading instruction is to have each child recognize one-word captions placed on appropriate objects, such as *desk, door,* and *clock,* ought one refrain from this teaching until the child has demonstrated mastery on every task demonstrated in Figures 2.1 through 2.14? Such an assumption is untenable.

Never assume that because a skill or knowledge is included on a battery of readiness tests, mastery of that skill is necessary before reading instruction begins. If a teacher is going to base educational decisions on test results, he or she should reflect on the connection between the skill or knowledge measured by the test and the content of the instruction he or she plans. If the connection is not clear, the student's performance on the test may be irrelevant.

Unexamined Assumptions and Unwarranted Practices

GROUPING CHILDREN WHO FAIL A TASK

Because these assumptions are not made explicit, they are not challenged. The practice in some first grades is to give readiness tests and to put all children who fail to respond correctly to items called Visual Discrimination into a group and put them through dozens of lessons (the materials for which are often purchased from the test publisher) designed to teach children to discriminate visually. Other groups are formed of children who failed the test called Auditory Discrimination, of children who failed the test called Alphabet Knowledge, and so on. Many of the lessons have little to do with the tasks the children failed on the tests, and many of the lessons have little to do with the tasks the children will be asked to perform in beginning reading lessons.

GROUPING CHILDREN WHO FAIL THE TEST

Because these assumptions are not made explicit and challenged, all children who get a low score on a whole battery of reading readiness tests are sometimes put into a general reading readiness program where they are given lessons on tasks that they *have* mastered, on tasks they were not tested on, and on tasks that have little apparent relevance (perhaps *no* relevance) to the reading activities in the particular program used in their classroom.

One survey (Carducci-Bolchazy, 1977) shows that of fifteen school districts surveyed, thirteen routinely use readiness tests. Of those thirteen districts, eight reported that readiness tests are used to establish cutoff points—children scoring below a particular point do not begin reading instruction. Nine of the districts reported that readiness tests are used to identify skill weaknesses.

It is not recommended that the traditional battery of reading readiness tests ever be used in their entirety for selecting students for beginning reading instruction or for diagnosis. The traditional uses of reading readiness tests have been fairly thoroughly discredited. On the other hand, the *concept* of reading readiness is still quite useful. Later in this chapter we will suggest that administering individual tasks (probing for actual causes of failure as described above) may be a useful option at certain times. Now we will look at how the concept of reading readiness is employed in an up-to-date classroom.

THE CONCEPT OF READINESS IN AN UP-TO-DATE CLASSROOM

To Test Readiness, Teach Reading

There are two very consistent findings in reading readiness research. First, tasks that are the best predictors of success in learning to read are the tasks that most resemble reading (MacGinitie, 1969). For example, success on tasks involving geometric figures, such as tasks D and E (Figures 2.4 and 2.5), would not be as reliable predictors of success in learning to read as tasks involving letters and words, such as tasks F and G (Figures 2.6 and 2.7). Second, training in skills that are quite clearly not reading but are supposedly reading readiness (or skills prerequisite to reading) does not improve performance on skills that are clearly reading, like discrimination of letters or word recognition. For example, training on a task involving geometric shapes, such as tasks D and E (Figures 2.4 and 2.5) will not enhance performance on tasks like letter matching, such as task F (Figure 2.6), or word learning, such as task L (Figure 2.12) (Pryzansky, 1972; Hammill et al., 1974; Harris, 1976; Paradis,

1974). These two facts lead to the following conclusion: The way to discover whether a child is ready to learn to read is to begin to teach that child and to observe that child's performance on skills actually used in the beginning lessons. This is the only way to find out whether *this child* is ready to learn to read in *this classroom*, with *these classmates*, from *this teacher*, using *these materials*—and if not, why not.

Two Widely Divergent Methods

THE LANGUAGE EXPERIENCE APPROACH

Supposing the beginning reading approach in a particular classroom is the language experience approach. Stauffer (1970) described a typical first lesson in this approach as one where the pupils gathered around the teacher, who had a white mouse in a cage (and out of the cage soon after). The children decided to call the mouse Snow White and the teacher printed "Snow White" on a large piece of lined paper on an easel where all the children could see. She then asked the children to tell about the mouse and said she would print what they said, just as she had printed "Snow White." Soon the paper contained the following "story":

SNOW WHITE

Dick said, "Snow White scratched around his cage."

Jane said, "Snow White has pink eyes."

Alice said, "He stood up on his hind legs and looked at us."

Jerry said, "His tail is two feet long."

Bill said, "Snow White ran around on the table."

Nancy said, "Snow White is soft and furry."

The teacher then read the story, pointing to each word as she said it; next she asked the children to read with her as she pointed to the words and said them. Finally, each child drew a picture of Snow White, and the teacher printed "Snow White" at the top of each child's paper as the children worked.

The next day the teacher reviewed the story with the children and had individuals say words they recognized. One child recognized "Snow White" and her own name. Another recognized "Snow White," her own name, and the names of the other children. Another child could read the whole story except for two words. By the end of the second day, the teacher knew that one child could read by any rough and ready standard and that some children recognized many words—indicating visual discrimination and visual memory.

As the program progressed, the teacher printed words each child recognized by sight on small cards. Each child kept his or her own cards in a "word bank." After a couple of weeks of learning words in this manner, the teacher began word recognition skills with one child who knew twenty-five words by sight and had these words on small cards. The teacher asked the child to find two of "her words" that began with the same sound as baker. When children had as many as thirty words committed to memory and written on small cards, the teacher supplied envelopes, each with an upper- and lower-case letter printed on them (Aa, Bb). The children put words into envelopes according to first letters.

In this manner, the teacher made observations about children's readiness skills when the skills were relevant to the method and materials, and "tests" were conducted under normal classroom conditions.

THE PHONIC-LINGUISTIC SYSTEM

In the first reading lesson of another, radically different approach known as the phonic-linguistic system (Walcutt and McCracken, 1981), each child opens his or her book to a page like Figure 2.15, and the teacher says something like this:

This is the letter a. A *stands for the first sound in* astronaut. A *stands for the first sound in* an, ant, accident, *and* animal.

A variety of activities is then introduced on the same day and on the following days to give the children experience with identifying the form of the letter *a*, with the sound /a/, and with associating the two. The following are some example activities.

The children are each presented with a small card with the letter *a* printed on it, and they play a game. The children hold up their cards while the teacher pronounces words such as *as, an, ant, be, afternoon*. The object of the game is for the children to put their cards down quickly when they hear a word that does not begin with /a/.

They are directed to use their fingers like a pencil and draw over the letters *a* and *A* as the teacher says words beginning with /a/.

They write upper- and lower-case As on the chalkboard.

They underline words on the chalkboard that do not begin with *a*, as in the following set:

Alma	act	do
am	it	Alice
boy	on	art

FIGURE 2.15
PAGE FROM PHONIC-LINGUISTIC SYSTEM READER.

Write <u>a</u> next to the pictures
whose name begins with the
first sound in <u>apple</u>.

FIGURE 2.16
TASK O.

They put circles around each *a,* as in the following set:

o   a   d   a   e
e   a   a   c   o

They print an *a* next to pictures whose names begin with /a/, as in Figure 2.16.

They put a circle around each *a* as in the following set:

A   B   C   A   O
a   c   a   o   g

They cross out the letter that does not belong in each row as in the following set:

A   A   A   L
a   c   a   a

The following lessons take up the letters *n, r, d, u,* and so on. After the letter *n* is introduced, the words *an, Ann,* and *Nan* are presented. The children are helped to become aware of the sounds in these words and the letters that spell the words. Thereafter, new words are taught as new letter-sound relationships are introduced (*ran, Dan, Dad,* and so on).

In this approach, as in the language experience approach, the teacher has many opportunities to observe pupil performance and to identify children who are not performing as expected. Traditional questions of reading readiness will arise.

- Is each child making the auditory and visual discriminations necessary *for the lessons taught?*
- Is the child's auditory and visual memory up to the tasks *these lessons introduce?*
- Does the child know the names and corresponding sounds of the letters *that have been introduced?*

Using this method, learning the names of letters and the sounds most frequently associated with letters is a crucial part of early word recognition. In the language experience approach, letter names and the sounds associated with letters have no part in initial word recognition.

In employing either of these two widely divergent methods, a teacher may observe that a child is not performing satisfactorily, and the teacher may find it useful to administer one of two specific subtests from a traditional reading readiness battery—remembering, of course, to test the assumptions one makes about using tests for diagnosis. The teacher may also find it useful to teach specific lessons on specific skills. But for many children, questions about particular reading readiness skills will never arise, although some of these same children would undoubtedly have failed some subtests if they had been given a complete formal battery before instruction began. Children will often display skills and knowledge in meaningful situations where motivation is high that they will not display in formal testing situations (Cazden et al., 1977; Adelman and Feshbach, 1971).

- You may have observed that the phonic-linguistic system grows out of the empiricist tradition (see Chapter 1). It is an atomistic approach made up of small steps that add up to reading. Such small steps are amenable to testing. On the other hand, the language experience approach is a holistic approach that grows out of the rationalist tradition (see Chapter 1). It is not nearly so compatible with testing of subskills—not at the early stages, at least. As a matter of fact, adherents to the language experience approach are the most vehement critics of the traditional use of reading readiness tests (see Lee and Rubin, 1979; Cramer, 1978).

You may also have observed that the two approaches sketched here are remarkably different and wondered which is "better." There is no simple answer to this question; how you answer it will be dictated by whether you are more influenced by the empiricist or the rationalist tradition. Practices that grow out of these two traditions will be discussed throughout this book.

THE CONCEPT OF READINESS AS A PREREADING CURRICULUM

Traditional Reading Readiness Skills

Tasks like task A (Figure 2.1) are often used in preschool and kindergarten as a vehicle for achieving many legitimate objectives, such as giving children experience in using pencils or in following directions. In such cases, teaching visual discrimination would be a secondary objective, or perhaps not an objective at all. But many skills and concepts are taught in preschool and kindergarten on the assumption that they are relevant to the reading process or to reading instruction.

Auditory discrimination and memory, visual discrimination and memory, and alphabet knowledge, as exemplified by tasks A through K (Figures 2.1 through 2.11), are often

Put a cross on the pictures of animals.

FIGURE 2.17
TASK P.

included in preschool and kindergarten programs. As a matter of fact, Durkin (1974) believes that one reason traditional reading readiness batteries are poor predictors of who will learn to read in first grade may be that some children have been taught the kinds of tasks one finds on the tests and others have not; therefore, success on the tests is often a result of training for the test rather than aptitude for reading.

Additional skills and concepts are taught in preschool and kindergarten explicitly because they are thought to be relevant to reading. They are often taught in combination with other objectives.

Concepts Related to Print and Reading

The following concepts are taught in many preschool and kindergarten programs:

1. Understanding that printing represents spoken language.
2. Proceeding from left to right on a page.
3. Proceeding from top to bottom on a page.
4. Proceeding from page to page.

Practice in proceeding from left to right and from top to bottom is worked into numerous activities. In reviewing the names of shapes, the teacher might hold up a triangle. When the children name it, the teacher puts it on the ledge of an easel and holds up a square. When the children name the square, the teacher puts it to the right of the triangle. Soon the shapes are lined up as in Figure 2.1, and the teacher reviews asking the children to name the shapes as he or she points to them, proceeding from left to right. On activity sheets, as in Figure 2.17, children are directed to put a cross on the pictures that have an animal in them, starting at the top on the left side of the sheet and working across to the right and then to the next row, and so on. This might be a lesson in following directions, but practice with left-to-right and top-to-bottom processing is incorporated into the lesson—as it is in other lessons having diverse objectives.

Teachers frequently read to children in preschool programs. The teacher may point to words as he or she reads, hold the book up, and proceed from page to page. Children's art work may be captioned and stapled into "books" that the children may go through, page by page, "reading" captions.

Many children come to first grade with a rich store of enjoyable experiences with books and print. They are quite used to proceeding from left to right, top to bottom, page to page. They are well aware that print represents spoken language. But some children have not had these experiences. It is not a good idea to view these skills and concepts as readiness skills in order to predict success or select children for beginning reading instruction, but it is wise to be aware that some children do not have these concepts and that for some children confusion about these concepts persists long after instruction begins (Clay, 1972).

Understanding the Vocabulary of Reading Instruction

Preschool and kindergarten programs include activities to teach children the meanings of terms that will be used early in nearly every reading program. A list of such terms is as follows:

above	last	beginning	in front of
after	letter	sound	looks like
alphabet	line	begins with	next to
before	next	different	rhymes with
below	number	from	same as
beside	page	ends with	sounds like
end	under	first letter	
first	word		

Preschool teachers take advantage of many opportunities to employ these terms in situations where the children will learn their meanings or get a wider understanding of their meanings. When the children are in line, the teacher may ask: "Who is first in line?" "Who is last?" "Who is standing next to Ann?" In more formal lessons, the teacher may ask the children to "find the one that's different from the others" in a row with three oranges and one banana.

However, all children have not had such preschool experiences or have not benefitted fully from such experiences. It has been observed by several authors (see Calfee and Venezsky, 1969; Cutts, 1975; Holden and MacGinitie, 1972) that some children may experience difficulty in reading lessons because they do not know the meaning of terms like those listed above. When children are not performing as expected, the teacher must be alert to the possibility that it is a lack of understanding or a misunderstanding of the terms used in the instructions.

♦ A formal procedure for discovering a child's knowledge of some of the concepts related to print and some of the vocabulary of reading instruction was developed by Clay (1972). Her "Concepts about Print Test" begins with the item "Show me the front of this book" and proceeds to test the child's knowledge of left to right progression, letters, words, punctuation marks, and so on.

Administering this test to several kindergartners and first-graders will probably heighten your awareness of the conventions and vocabulary connected with reading—conventions and vocabulary that accomplished readers respond to unconsciously, but that beginning readers must learn.

It would be a useful exercise to create a survey of your own to explore beginning readers' knowledge of the conventions of print and the vocabulary of reading instruction discussed in this section.

Concepts Related to Storybooks

The following skills are taught in many preschool and kindergarten programs:

1. Following the sequence of events in a story.
2. Recalling details to relate a story.
3. Interpreting pictures.
4. Making inferences.

Preschool and kindergarten curricula are replete with opportunities to learn, recite, recall, and listen to songs, poems, and stories. For example, teachers may teach songs like "There Was an Old Woman Who Swallowed a Fly" with the aid of cutout "creatures." With each new verse, the appropriate cutout is added to the flannel board or easel. Children are then encouraged to recall in what order the old woman swallowed the creatures after the cutouts are scrambled.

The same technique may be used with such poems as "The House That Jack Built" or stories such as *Jennie's Hat* (Keats, 1966). In this picture storybook, Jennie thinks her hat is too plain, so on each page she adds a new decoration, including flowers, birds' nests, and feathers. Some teachers bring in props to tell such stories and then leave them on a table where the children can come back to them and "play teacher" by telling the story to others using the props.

Children are also given experiences with interperting pictures of happy faces, sad faces, and angry faces. Pictures such as Figure 2.18 are used to give students opportunities to make up stories, to retell stories presented by others, and to make inferences (Why is the girl sad?).

Such activities in preschool and kindergarten are universally approved and are generally thought of as reading readiness activities, since following sequence, recalling details, interpreting pictures, and making inferences are all skills that are demanded in reading and reading instruction. Although such experiences are obviously beneficial to children, reading instruction can begin with pupils who have not had these experiences in preschool. And, of course, because reading instruction begins is no reason why these experiences should stop. Such experiences should continue through the primary grades, and the skills used should be employed in relation to reading as opportunities arise.

LANGUAGE DEVELOPMENT AND READING READINESS

Reading Skill and Language Development

There is general agreement that there is a relationship between language development and success in learning to read. Tiedt (1974) put it this way: "Reading is a language skill. All language skills reinforce each other, and no language [skill] can be taught in isolation." On the other hand, authors tend to become a little less definite when it comes to specifying how language development is related to learning to read. Rupley (1975) claims that "an understanding of how language develops, how this development is related to beginning reading instruction, and how language development and reading instruction can be taught concurrently *should* [italics added] enable teachers to become more effective teachers of beginning reading." Rupley says this *should* be true rather than that it is true.

Lapp and Flood (1978) state: "It is almost axiomatic to say that teachers who are preparing to instruct children in reading need to know a great deal about the language development of the child." To say that a fact is ax-

FIGURE 2.18
TELLING STORIES AND MAKING INFERENCES FROM PICTURES.

iomatic is to say that it is self-evident rather than that it has been demonstrated. And Cazden (1972) says: "Hopefully, their work [the work of teachers and educational researchers] will be improved with better understanding of the work of linguists, psycholinguists, and so-ciolinguists" (p. 1). The statement is qualified by the word *hopefully*.

The reason respected authors advise teachers to understand the language development of their pupils, but then qualify that advice by saying that such understanding *should* help, or will *hopefully* help, is that the precise nature of the connection is not known.

Numerous studies have shown that there is a relationship between measures of oral language performance and success in reading (Loban, 1963; deHirsh et al., 1966; Bougere, 1969; Brittain, 1970). From these studies it has been shown that children who score high on reading tests tend to say more words, say more different words, use words that are less frequent, use longer sentences, and use more complex relationships within and between clauses. Brittain (1970) showed that in second grade, good readers tended to form plurals and past tenses on invented words better than poor readers. But these sophisticated measures do not correlate with reading scores even as well as some traditional standardized reading readiness tests (Bougere, 1969).

But one does not need to justify teaching language development in terms of its effect on reading. Proficient oral language performance is itself an objective of the schools, and general language performance is basic to all school learning. Therefore, schools should provide rich and varied language experiences that will stimulate growth in language, an interest in language, and an understanding of the value of language. This topic will be treated repeatedly throughout this book. In the following section, we discuss attitudes toward language performance as a factor in reading readiness.

Assessing Language Development

As one might predict, how one approaches the question of language development as a factor in reading readiness is determined to a large extent by which sphere of influence one finds more compatible: empiricism or rationalism.

AN ATOMISTIC APPROACH

If one views language as a set of separate, observable, measurable skills, as the empiricist tradition has, one is likely to identify many language skills and concepts appropriate for first-grade students and to employ a checklist for the purpose of assessing language performance. The following items are typical of such a checklist:

1. Articulates clearly.
2. Speaks in a group with confidence.
3. Takes part in class discussion.
4. Expresses needs effectively.
5. Knows words used in primer.
6. Knows relationship words: up, down, top, bottom.
7. Knows comparison words: big, little, short, tall.
8. Listens to stories with apparent enjoyment.
9. Interprets experiences through dramatic play.
10. Knows words and concepts related to home and school: brother, teacher, room.
11. Knows nursery rhymes and traditional children's stories.
12. Describes places in the community.
13. Understands direction.
14. Can memorize short poems.
15. Listens attentively.
16. Describes actions and pictures.
17. Tells stories about pictures.
18. Knows words about time: before, after, when.
19. Knows abstract words: pretty, strong.
20. Knows words about space: behind, under, over, where.

Some language checklists attempt to put the elements of performance in an order—implying that one element will or should appear before those that follow. For example, one checklist that has been used to assess "certain aspects of readiness" (Lapp and Flood, 1978), proposes the following sequence in the appearance of "developmental tasks":

1. Give personal information.
2. Describe simple objects.
3. Relate words and pictures.
4. Define words.
5. Use correct grammar.

A HOLISTIC APPROACH

A contrasting attitude toward assessing and promoting language performance as a factor in reading readiness grows out of the rationalist tradition. It is exemplified by the activity described earlier in which children "wrote" a story about a white mouse they had named Snow White. Stauffer (1970) lists sixteen separate skills or tasks that the children gained experience with in performing this activity, including:

1. Telling about their reactions to the mouse
2. Sharing ideas in the dynamics of a classroom situation
3. Observing more carefully in response to teacher's questions
4. Listening to others to discover how they reacted to the same circumstances

In the same situation, the teacher had the opportunity to observe the children's:

1. Oral language usage
2. Choice of words

These lists are similar to the checklists presented in the last section. The difference is that here the subskills are seen as emerging as a result of focusing on a large, global language experience. In this approach, the assumption is that the parts will emerge if the whole is attended to. As this example demonstrates, the principle applies to assessment of skills as well as attempting to develop skills.

Selecting and Diagnosing on the Basis of Language Development

Whichever way one chooses to assess language development, the same practice sometimes emerges—that of withholding reading instruction from a child because that child's language performance is not up to some pre-established standard. Language skills checklists and lists of hierarchical developmental tasks can be interpreted as lists of skills that are prerequisite to reading instruction, and even the most holistic concepts of language development are sometimes employed as criteria for delaying formal reading instruction.

Monroe (1971) suggests that even before a language experience approach is used, the teacher must explore the language the children bring to school and assist those children who need help in developing vocabularies and syntax. And Robinson (1971) states:

There is a tremendous difference between what students meet on the printed page in most of the materials confronting them and what they are saying within their own peer and family environments. We must concentrate on language development first.

The same reasoning that was suggested in regard to selecting students for reading instruction on the basis of traditional tests of reading readiness applies to selecting students for reading instruction on the basis of language performance. Although correlations between various measures of language performance are statistically significant, they tend to be low; therefore, some students who score low on language performance measures may score high on reading tests if they are taught to read.

The practice of withholding instruction on the basis of the fact that a child's family and peers speak a language that is highly dissimilar to the language of the printed page is particularly dangerous, because it is almost certain to result in grouping children for instruction on the basis of social class membership.

Several authors (Midwinter, 1972; Cook-Gumperz, 1977; Finn, 1980) have argued that some difficulties in learning to read are related to social class habits of language use. However, none of these authors suggests delaying reading instruction because a child does not show much facility with certain uses of language. In fact, Levitas (1974) and McDermott (1977) have argued that to withhold instruction in reading because of differences between the language of the school and the language of the child is unnecessary and results in perpetuating social-class-related reading failure.

Development of oral language performance is in and of itself a goal of the school. Teachers must be concerned with language development. But using language development as a basis for delaying reading instruction is ill-advised. Furthermore, using assessment of language to gain diagnostic insights into reading problems must be used with the same questioning of assumptions as suggested in the use of traditional concepts of readiness.

SCHOOL READINESS AND READING READINESS

Readiness for Instruction

McDermott (1977) has observed that many children in schools spend their time in endless "relational battles" with the teacher rather than on learning tasks. DeHirsh, Jansky and Langford (1966) describe "failing readers" as hyperactive, distractible, impulsive, and disinhibited children who need many opportunities to move around the room and are resentful when required to sit still.

Mehan (1978) has described the classroom as a small society: He points out that there is a practical concern for order in a society, and in schools the rules are often implied rather than spelled out. For example, in taking turns for speaking (getting the floor, so to speak), the rule may be that the student raises his or her hand and is recognized, but on many occasions it is permissible for all the children to chorus an answer. Children must gain "social competence" in these matters to operate in the classroom and for the classroom to operate effectively.

Although these authors have slightly different perspectives and use different terminology, they are all making observations about the degree to which children are *school trained* (Sharp and Green, 1975). This is another factor that is "sometimes taken into account by teachers in judging whether or not a child is 'ready' to learn to read" (Fry, 1977).

There are several parallels in the way school readiness and language development are treated as factors in reading readiness. Both terms take in broad areas of behavior, and although experts agree that both characteristics are related to success in reading, the precise nature of the relationship is difficult to establish. Both are legitimate concerns of the school regardless of their connection with success in reading. Finally, two ways of approaching school readiness and language development are closely aligned with the empirical and rational traditions.

Assessing School Readiness

AN ATOMISTIC APPROACH

The empiricist approach is to enumerate the behaviors that seem appropriate to productive, socially competent first-graders and to use a checklist for evaluating these behaviors. The following items are typical of such a checklist:

1. Attends to tasks
2. Persists in attention to tasks
3. Works with a group
4. Takes share of responsibility
5. Takes turns in games
6. Takes turns in reciting
7. Occupies him or herself when finishing a task early
8. Accepts changes in routine
9. Takes pride in school work
10. Accepts opposition or defeat maturely
11. Appears happy and well adjusted

A HOLISTIC APPROACH

Once again, a contrasting attitude toward promoting school readiness as a factor in reading readiness is exemplified by Stauffer's (1970) comments on the Snow White lesson described earlier. Among the skills children may display in performing this activity are these:

1. Displaying curiosity
2. Displaying creativity
3. Sharing ideas in the dynamics of a classroom
4. Listening to others
5. Voting or expressing a preference (for the mouse's name)
6. Learning to accept the decision of the majority

And the teacher had the opportunity to observe the children's:

1. Willingness to move about the table and among one another

2. Attention span
3. Persistence
4. Cooperation

The social skills developed and evaluated in this approach grow out of the total experience in contrast to the checklist approach, where one attempts to make a comprehensive list of the social skills that apply to numerous contexts.

Selecting and Diagnosing on the Basis of School Readiness

It is not much in vogue to withhold instruction on the grounds that students are lacking in school readiness, but such practices are reported. For example, Fry (1977) states:

Some teachers would call children who are low in socialization "immature" and not ready to read. In extreme cases they force such children to repeat kindergarten . . . or put them into "junior first grade" in which reading instruction is delayed up to half a year or more. (p. 124)

Fry states that he does not approve of this practice, but Furth and Wachs (1974) report an incident where a boy who requested on several occasions to participate in formal reading instruction was dissuaded by his teacher, because in the teacher's opinion he was "not able to attend to a task or function in a group" (p. 63). These authors express approval of this decision.

Selecting students for reading instruction on the basis of school readiness rests on even shakier assumptions than selecting on the basis of traditional readiness tasks and language development. There is no reason to believe that the child whose enthusiasm leads him or her to answer continually out of turn, for example, would benefit from delaying instruction. Of course, children who are "disinhibited" will probably cause themselves and everyone else a certain amount of trouble if the beginning reading program demands a great deal of regimentation.

In this case, two courses of action seem to be in order. The teacher ought to try a beginning reading approach that does not demand as much regimentation and at the same time work with the child to help him or her gain the self-control necessary to function in the classroom. And both courses of action can proceed simultaneously.

School readiness can be a useful concept in seeking solutions to problems a child encounters while engaged in reading instruction. However, if a teacher bases decisions about reading instruction on a child's performance on school readiness tasks, he or she must question his or her assumptions in the same way as suggested for using traditional concepts of readiness for diagnosis.

SUMMARY

The meaning of the concept of reading readiness was developed in this chapter by posing the question of how a committee in a developing nation would select 20 percent of the adult population for literacy training and determine when to begin reading instruction in the primary school, where universal literacy is the goal.

Characteristics such as ability to make visual discriminations may be useful for predicting which adults would make good candidates for literacy and therefore may be useful in selecting adults for the program. But in the primary school, where universal literacy is the goal, the use of reading readiness tasks for predicting success and selecting pupils is inconsistent with the goal. In this situation, the concept of reading readiness may be more useful for deciding what to teach and how to teach individuals.

Tasks that typically appear on traditional published tests of reading readiness can be classified as those dealing with auditory and visual discrimination and memory, alphabet knowledge, word learning, and oral language comprehension. Tests of auditory and visual discrimination and memory reflect the view that reading is made up of individual observable subskills; these tests reflect the empiricist (atomistic) tradition. The rationalist (holistic) tradition is more likely to view word learning tasks and comprehension of oral language as reasonable indicators of readiness for learning to read, but the holistic view of reading is largely incompatible with the view reflected by published readiness tests.

Reading readiness tests have three traditional uses: predicting who will be successful in learning to read, selecting students for beginning reading instruction, and diagnosing (identifying causes of failure). Although success on traditional readiness tasks correlates with success in learning to read, one cannot be sure whether *an individual* will succeed in learning to read from his or her performance on traditional readiness tasks. Selecting students for reading instruction on the basis of performance on traditional reading readiness tasks is unjustified for the same reason. Furthermore, withholding instruction from some students while others are taught to read can be injurious.

Using traditional tests for diagnosis is often done without questioning the assumptions on which diagnosis is based. Test names are often deceiving, so one must examine the actual items on a test before deciding to take remedial action on the basis of poor performance. Poor performance is not necessarily the result of the student's not having the skill or knowledge the test is supposed to measure. One must observe an individual's performance on a test on an individual basis and discuss the reasons for the responses before taking remedial action. And many traditional reading readiness tasks may not be relevant to performance in early reading instruction.

Different approaches to beginning reading instruction make different demands on the learner. For example, different skills are necessary for the language experience approach and the phonic-linguistic system.

Skills and concepts are taught in preschool and kindergarten as preparation for reading intruction in first grade. These include the traditional tasks that appear on readiness tests, concepts related to print and reading, and the vocabulary of reading instruction. Lack of these skills and knowledge may cause difficulty in first-grade reading, but before taking remedial action teachers must question their assumption that any particular skill is lacking and that it is relevant to the instruction the child is receiving.

There is general agreement that language development and school readiness are necessary for success in learning to read, but the precise nature of these relationships is not known. School readiness and language development both take in broad areas of behavior that are legitimate concerns of the school in their own right as well as in terms of their relationship to reading.

Two approaches to assessing these areas of behavior grow out of the empiricist and rationalist traditions. Empiricists tend to enumerate the smallest categories of behavior that seem appropriate for children at a given age and develop checklists for assessment and for directing efforts toward developing these behaviors. Rationalists tend to create learning situations appropriate to a given age and to observe categories of language development and school readiness behaviors that grow out of the situation.

In viewing school readiness or language development as factors in diagnosing reading difficulties, one must question one's assumptions regarding whether the particular knowledge or behavior is truly lacking (or truly present, if it is undesirable) and whether it is relevant to the instruction the child is receiving.

FOR FURTHER READING AND DISCUSSION

Having read this chapter, the beginning teacher should understand the concept of reading readiness, be able to apply the concept in the classroom, and discuss the issue intelligently with parents and other educators. But there are topics related to reading readiness that have not been covered in this chapter because of space limitations.

In this section there are four brief statements of a topic followed by references. Some readers may want to pursue some of these topics on their own, or perhaps they can be pursued for further study by the class.

1. Education, like all human endeavors, has a history. The following are landmark publications in

the development of the concept of reading readiness.

Arthur, Grace. A quantitative study of the results of grouping first grade children according to mental age. *Journal of Educational Research*, 12 (1925): 173–85.

Holmes, Margaret C. Investigation of reading readiness of first grade entrants. *Childhood Education*, 3 (1927): 215–21.

Morphett, Mable V., and Carleton Washburne. When should children begin to read? *Elementary School Journal*, 31 (1931): 496–503.

Gates, Arthur I. The necessary mental age for beginning reading. *Elementary School Journal*, 37 (1937): 497–508.

Havighurst, Robert. *Human Development and Education.* New York: David McKay, 1953.

Bruner, Jerome. *The Process of Education.* Cambridge, MA: Harvard University Press, 1960.

MacGinitie, Walter H. Evaluating readiness for learning to read: A critical review and evaluation of research. *Reading Research Quarterly*, 4 (1969): 396–410.

2. Two ideas came together in the 1960s— first, that the years before age 5 are very important in intellectual development, and second, that many teachers believed economically deprived children were frequently not ready to learn to read when they entered first grade. The following publications record the theory and the educational-political activity that led to Head Start.

Educational Policies Commission. *Universal Opportunity for Early Childhood Education.* Washington, D.C.: National Education Association, 1966.

Hunt, J. McVicker. *Intelligence and Experience.* New York: Ronald Press, 1961.

Shaw, Frederick. The changing curriculum. *Review of Educational Research*, 36 (1966): 343–52.

3. Teachers are often asked by parents what they can do at home to improve their children's prospects of becoming successful readers. The following publications discuss this matter.

Almy, Millie. The importance of children's experience to success in beginning reading. In C. W. Hunnicutt and W. Iverson (eds.), *Research in the Three R's.* New York: Harper & Row, 1958.

Durkin, Dolores. *Teaching Them to Read.* Boston: Allyn and Bacon, 1974.

Hess, R. D., and V. C. Shipman. Early experience and the socialization of cognitive modes in children. *Child Development*, 36 (1965): 69–86.

Koppenhaver, Albert H. Reading and the home environment. In Malcolm P. Douglass (ed.), *Claremont Reading Conference 38th Yearbook.* Claremont, CA: Claremont Reading Conference, 1974, 122-29.

Milner, Esther. A study of the relationship between reading readiness in grade one school children and patterns of parent-child interaction. *Child Development*, 22 (1951): 95–112.

Swift, M. Training poverty mothers in communication skills. *Reading Teacher*, 23 (1970): 360–67.

4. For many years Delores Durkin has investigated children who learn to read before entering first grade. What kind of children learn to read before coming to first grade? How do they learn? Is such learning desirable? These questions are discussed in the following publications.

Clark, Margaret, M. *Young Fluent Readers: What Can They Teach Us?* London: Heinemann Educational Books, 1976.

Durkin, Dolores. *Children Who Read Early: Two Longitudinal Studies.* New York: Bureau of Publications, Teachers College Press, Columbia University, 1966.

————. When should children begin to read? *Innovation and Change in Reading Instruction: Sixty-Seventh Yearbook of the National Society for the Study of Education*, Part II. Chicago: University of Chicago Press, 1968, 30–71.

————. A language arts program for pre-first grade children: Two year achievement report. *Reading Research Quarterly*, 5 (1970): 534–65.

————. A six-year study of children who learned to read in school at the age of four. *Reading Research Quarterly*, 10 (1974): 9–61.

Ollila, Lloyd O. Pros and cons of teaching reading to four- and five-year-olds. In Robert Aukerman, (ed.), *Some Persistent Questions on Beginning Reading.* Newark, DE: International Reading Association, 1972, 53–61.

REFERENCES

Adelman, Howard, and Seymour Feshbach. Predicting reading failure: Beyond the readiness model. *Exceptional Children,* 37 (1971): 349–54.

Barr, Rebecca. *Development of a Word Learning Task to Predict Success and Identify Methods by which Kindergarten Children Learn to Read.* Final Report Project No. 9-E-125, Contract No. OE 6-5-70002(010) U.S. Department of Health, Education and Welfare, 1971.

Barrett, T. C. Visual discrimination tasks as predictors of first grade reading achievement. *Reading Teacher,* 18 (1965): 276–82.

Bond, G. L., and R. Dykstra. The cooperative research program in first grade reading instruction. *Reading Research Quarterly,* 2 (1967): 5–142.

Bougere, Marguerite B. Selected factors in oral language related to first grade reading achievement. *Reading Research Quarterly,* 4 (1969): 31–58.

Brainerd, C. J. *Piaget's Theory of Intelligence.* Englewood Cliffs, NJ: Prentice-Hall, 1978.

Brittain, Mary M. Inflectional performance and early reading achievement. *Reading Research Quarterly,* 5 (1970): 34–48.

Bryan, Q. Relative importance of intelligence and visual perception in predicting reading achievement. *California Journal of Educational Research,* 15 (1964): 44–48.

Calfee, R. C., and R. L. Venezky. Component skills in beginning reading. In K. S. Goodman and J. T. Fleming (eds.), *Psycholinguistics and the Teaching of Reading.* Newark, DE: International Reading Association, 1969.

Carducci-Bolchazy, M. A survey of use of reading readiness tests. *Reading Horizons,* 18 (1977): 209–12.

Cazden, Courtney B. *Child Language and Education.* New York: Holt, Rinehart and Winston, 1972.

Cazden, Courtney B., et al., Language assessment: Where, what and how. *Anthropology and Education Quarterly* (1977): 83–94.

Chall, Jeanne S. *Learning to Read: The Great Debate.* New York: McGraw-Hill, 1967.

Clay, M. M. *Reading: The Patterning of Complex Behavior.* London: Heinemann Educational Books, 1972.

Clymer, Theodore, and Thomas C. Barrett. *Clymer-Barrett Prereading Battery—Teacher's Manual.* Princeton, NJ: Personnel Press, 1969.

Cook-Gumperz, J. Situated instructions: Language socialization of school age children. In E. Ervin-Tripp and C. Mitchell-Kernan (eds.), *Child Discourse.* New York: Academic Press, 1977, 103–21.

Cramer, Ronald L. *Writing, Reading and Language Growth.* Columbus, OH: Charles Merrill, 1978.

Cutts, Warren G. Does the teacher really matter? *Reading Teacher,* 28 (1975): 449–52.

deHirsh, K., J. J. Jansky, and W. S. Langford. *Predicting Reading Failure.* New York: Harper & Row, 1966.

Durkin, Dolores. A six-year study of children who learned to read in school at the age of four. *Reading Research Quarterly,* 10 (1974): 9–61.

Durrell, D. D. First grade reading success story: A summary. *Journal of Education,* 140 (1958): 2–6.

Finn, P. J. *Failure in Learning to Read.* Edinburgh: Workers' Educational Association of South East Scotland, 1980.

Fry, Edward. *Elementary Reading Instruction.* New York: McGraw-Hill, 1977.

Furth, Hans G., and Harry Wachs. *Thinking Goes to School.* New York: Oxford University Press, 1974.

Gates, A. I. The necessary mental age for beginning reading. *Elementary School Journal,* 37 (1937): 497–508.

Gavel. S. R. June reading achievements of first-grade children. *Journal of Education,* 140 (1958): 37–43.

Hammill, D., L. Goodman, and J. L. Wiederbolt. Visual-motor processes: Can we train them? *Reading Teacher,* 27 (1974): 469–78.

Harris, Albert J. Practical applications of reading research. *Reading Teacher,* 29 (1976): 559–65.

Hildreth, Gertrude H., Nellie Griffiths, and May E. McGauvran. *Manual of Directions—Metropolitan Readiness Tests.* New York: Harcourt, Brace and World, 1969.

Holden, M. H., and W. H. MacGinitie. Children's conceptions of word boundaries in speech and print. *Journal of Educational Psychology,* 63 (1972): 551–57.

Jansky, J., and K. deHirsh. *Preventing Reading Failure.* New York: Harper & Row, 1972.

Keats, Ezra J. *Jennie's Hat.* New York: Harper & Row, 1966.

Kibby, Michael W. The effects of certain instructional conditions and response modes on initial word learning. *Reading Research Quarterly,* 15 (1979): 147–71.

Kirk, Samuel A., James McCarthy, and Winifred Kirk. *Illinois Test of Psycholinguistic Abilities,* rev. ed. Champaign: The Board of Trustees of the University of Illinois, 1968.

Lapp, Diane, and James Flood. *Teaching Reading to Every Child.* New York: Macmillan, 1978.

Lee, Dorris M., and Joseph B. Rubin. *Children and Language.* Belmont, CA: Wadsworth, 1979.

Levitas, M. *Marxist Perspectives in the Sociology of Education.* London: Routledge and Kegan Paul, 1974.

Loban, W. D. *The Language of Elementary School Children.* Champaign, IL: National Council of Teachers of English, 1963.

MacGinitie, W. N. Evaluating readiness for learning to read: A critical review and evaluation of research. *Reading Research Quarterly,* 4 (1969): 396–410.

McDermott, R. P. Social relations as contexts for learning in school. *Harvard Education Review,* 47 (1977): 198–213.

Mehan, Hugh. Structuring school structure. *Harvard Education Review,* 48 (1978).

Midwinter, E. *Priority Education.* Harmondsworth, Eng.: Penguin, 1972.

Monroe, Marion. The child and his language come to school. In C. Braun (ed.), *Language, Reading and the Communication Process.* Newark, DE: International Reading Association, 1971, 121–42.

Morgan, E. Efficacy of two tests in differentiating potentially low from average and high first grade readers. *Journal of Educational Research,* 53 (1960): 300–4.

Murphy, Helen A. and Donald D. Durrell. *Manual of Directions—Murphy-Durrell Reading Readiness Analysis.* New York: Harcourt, Brace and World, 1965.

Paradis, Edward E. The appropriateness of visual discrimination exercises in reading readiness materials. *Journal of Educational Research,* 67 (1974): 276–78.

Pryzwansky, W. B. Effects of perceptual motor training and manuscript writing on reading readiness skills in kindergarten. *Journal of Educational Psychology,* 63 (1972), 110–15.

Robinson, H. Alan. Communications and curriculum change. In C. Braun (ed.), *Language, Reading and the Communication Process.* Newark, DE: International Reading Association, 1971, 1–8.

Robinson, Helen M. Vocabulary: Speaking, listening, reading and writing. In H. A. Robinson (ed.), *Reading in the Language Arts.* Chicago: University of Chicago Press, 1963.

Rosenthal, Robert, and Lenore Jacobson. Teacher expectations for the disadvantaged. *Scientific American* (April 1968): 19–23.

Rupley, William. Language development and beginning reading instruction. *Elementary English* (1975): 403–8.

Sharp, Rachael, and Anthony Green. *Education and Social Control: A Study in Progressive Primary Education.* London: Routledge and Kegan Paul, 1975.

Silvaroli, N. J. Factors in predicting children's success in first grade reading. In J. A. Figurel (ed.), *Reading and Inquiry I.R.A. Conference Proceedings,* 10 (1965): 296–98.

Silverberg, N., et al. *The Effects of Kindergarten Instruction in Alphabet and Numbers on First Grade Reading. Final Report.* Minneapolis: Kenny Rehabilitation Institute, 1968.

Spache, G. D., and E. B. Spache. *Reading in the Elementary School.* Boston: Allyn and Bacon, 1973.

Stauffer, Russell G. *The Language Experience Approach to the Teaching of Reading.* New York: Harper & Row, 1970.

Tiedt, Iris. Input. *Elementary English,* 51 (1974): 757.

Vygotsky, L. S. *Thought and Language.* Cambridge, MA: MIT Press, 1962.

Walcutt, Charles, and Glenn McCracken. *Basic Reading, Book A* (teacher's edition). Philadelphia: Lippincott, 1981.

Weiner, M., and S. Feldman. Validation studies of a reading prognosis test for children of lower and middle socio-economic status. *Educational and Psychological Measurement,* 23 (1963): 807–14.

Weintraub, Sam. What research says to the reading teacher: Illustrations for beginning reading. *The Reading Teacher,* 20 (1967): 61–67.

Wilson, F. T., and C. W. Fleming. Grade trends in reading progress in kindergarten and primary grades. *Journal of Educational Psychology,* 31 (1960): 1–13.

3

TEACHING WORD RECOGNITION
WHOLE WORD METHOD

DEFINING WORD RECOGNITION

The Beginning Reader's "Concept of Word"
Learning Word Meaning Versus Learning Word
  Recognition

**APPROACHES USING THE WHOLE WORD
METHOD**

Paired-Associate Learning
Language Experience
Key Vocabulary
Whole Words in the Environment
Basal Readers

**SELECTING WORDS FOR THE WHOLE WORD
METHOD**

Criteria When Whole Word Is the Sole Method

INTEREST
FREQUENCY

Criteria after Other Methods Are Introduced

GENERALIZATIONS THAT WILL SOON BE
  TAUGHT
IRREGULAR SPELLING-SOUND
  RELATIONSHIPS

**SOME PRINCIPLES FOR TEACHING WHOLE
WORDS**

Presenting Words in Context
Pupils' Attention
Attention to Appropriate Stimulus
Use of Picture Clues
Practice

WHY USE THE WHOLE WORD APPROACH?

Purposeful Reading
Interest
Demonstrated Success
Directness

**A CONTRASTING VIEW: THE LINGUISTIC
APPROACH**

Consistent Spelling-Sound Relationships
Minimal Differences Between Words Taught

SUMMARY

FOR FURTHER READING AND DISCUSSION

REFERENCES

DEFINING WORD RECOGNITION

The Beginning Reader's "Concept of Word"

Beginning readers do not necessarily know that spoken words are represented in printed texts as groups of letters bound by spaces (Clay, 1972; Ehri, 1978). Morris (1981) and Morris and Henderson (1981) suggest a technique where children first memorize a nursery rhyme and then recite it with the teacher while the teacher points to the words of the rhyme printed on a card. After several trials, the child's "concept of word" is tested. For example, the child is asked to point at each word as he or she recites the poem and to say words as the teacher points to them.

Among students in a classroom where beginning reading instruction is being introduced, children vary in their success on such tasks. Some point accurately while reading and can identify words in the text and in isolation after a little practice; others cannot point accurately and cannot identify words in the text or in isolation after practice. This latter group may need to learn the concept of what a printed word is. Without this concept, no word recognition strategies can succeed. Morris and Henderson (1981) suggest the memorized nursery rhyme as a method of teaching the concept of word as well as testing it.

Learning Word Meaning Versus Learning Word Recognition

There is a difference between learning the meaning of a word and learning to recognize a word, and it is an important difference to keep in mind. The word *recognize* is made up of a Latin prefix and root, *re + cognize*, meaning "to know again; to identify something as a thing one has known or seen previously."

In teaching beginning reading, we are concerned with teaching children to recognize words in print that they already know in spoken form. Learning new words, which is an important part of language development and a legitimate concern of reading teachers, is a different matter from learning to recognize words in print that one already knows in speech. Learning new words will be treated in Chapter 9; Chapters 3 through 7 deal with word recognition.

Word recognition can be looked at in two ways:

1. How many words does a child recognize instantly in print?
2. What skills or techniques is a child able to use in order to recognize a word that he or she does not recognize instantly when he or she sees it in print?

It is important for a teacher to recognize that these are two different but interrelated questions. A child who instantly recognizes many words is likely to be skillful at recognizing words he or she does not instantly recognize; and a child who has well-developed techniques for recognizing words is likely to recognize many words instantly.

Because these two aspects of word recognition—*recognizing* words and knowing *how* to recognize words—are intimately connected, it is difficult to answer some very basic educational questions: Should you teach a child to recognize words, or should you teach a child *how* to recognize words? Should you teach both? Should you teach one before the other? Should you concentrate on one rather than the other in later stages of reading instruction? In answering such questions, one is led into questions concerning the nature of reading and language and the nature of learning.

Chapters 3 through 7 will present the time-honored practices in teaching word recognition and word recognition skills, introduce the reader to the vocabulary and concepts embodied in these practices, and present some issues or points of controversy surrounding these practices.

APPROACHES USING THE WHOLE WORD METHOD

The objective of the whole word method is that when a child sees a printed word, he or she identifies it immediately without thinking about it, puzzling over it, or analyzing it. But instant recognition is the *ultimate* objective of all recognition skills; there is something more separating the whole word method from other methods. The whole word method can also be classified by what the teacher does not do—the teacher does not refer to letters, to sounds of letters, to syllables, prefixes, suffixes, or roots.

Paired-Associate Learning

Because the immediate goal of the method is recognition without analysis, this approach is conducive to paired-associate, stimulus-response learning—the kinds of teaching and learning techniques associated with behaviorist psychology. One often observes teachers working with an individual—showing a word, saying it, asking the child to say it, and going on to the next word until several words are presented.

After this procedure is repeated several times, the teacher then shows a word. The child says the word and is rewarded ("That's right! Good!"); or the child does not say the word and is not rewarded—or is "punished" ("No! We'll put that back in the pile of words

you don't know."). Sometimes the rewards are more concrete—a token, piece of candy, or a penny; and sometimes the punishments are more concrete—a token, piece of candy, or a penny is withheld or taken away. Such procedures are used to introduce new words and to review words the child learned to recognize in previous lessons.

Language Experience

Many widely varying techniques are whole word techniques. The initial stages of the language experience approach described in Chapter 2 is a whole word approach. Children tell the teacher which words they recognize from the previous day's story, and the teacher copies them down for each child's own word bank. Over several weeks, if things go well, each child has his or her own bank of many words that he or she has learned as whole words.

Key Vocabulary

Sylvia Ashton-Warner is a New Zealand novelist and teacher who introduced an innovation in teaching beginning reading through a whole word approach that focuses on the interest of the individual child (Ashton-Warner, 1959, 1963, 1972). Her method is to elicit from each child words that are intimately connected with the child's life, words that have intense meaning.

She starts with words one presumes are connected with any child's inner world, such as *Mommy*, *kiss*, and *ghost*. Her aim is to elicit each child's individual words, whether they be *house*, *jet*, *tiger*, or *bomb*. For example, she recounts an incident in which some of her students were discussing what they were frightened of. A violent Maori (New Zealand na-

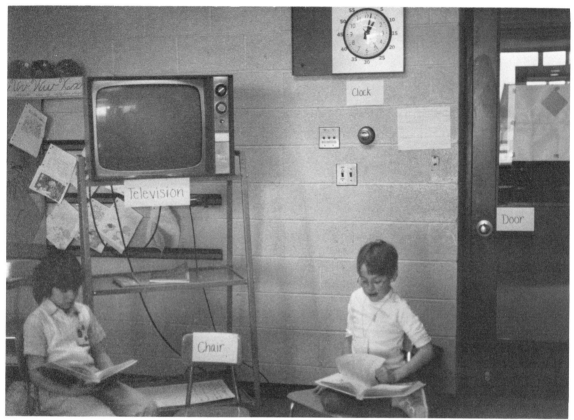

FIGURE 3.1
TEACHER-MADE LABELS FOR OBJECTS IN THE CLASSROOM.

tive) child shouted that he was frightened of nothing, that he would stick his knife into anything, even the tigers!

So I give him "tigers" [that is, she prints tigers on a card and gives it to him] and I never have to repeat this word to him, and in the morning the little card shows the dirt and disrepair of violent usage. (Ashton-Warner, 1963, p. 35)

Veatch and others (1979) recognize that the essence of Ashton-Warner's approach is that each child's key vocabulary is unique and largely unpredictable, and that if one elicits the right words from a child, the words are learned instantly (what Ashton-Warner calls "one-look words"). Veatch and others suggest that every few days the child go through his or her words and say them as fast as possible.

Those he cannot recognize instantly must be thrown away without criticism. "Oh, that just wasn't a good enough word to remember. You will think of a better one today or tomorrow." (Veatch et al., 1979, p. 16)

FIGURE 3.2
CALENDAR BOARD.

Whole Words in the Environment

Teachers often put nicely lettered labels on objects around the room, as in Figure 3.1. They call the students' attention to these words and encourage the students to remember them. Primary teachers often set aside an area for a "Calendar Board," as in Figure 3.2. They print the days of the week, months, and numerals on cards and encourage children to remember them by having the children choose the correct cards to put up the day's date each morning. Another permanent bulletin board may be set aside for "Today's Weather," as in Figure 3.3. Cards containing the words *sunny, rainy, cloudy, foggy, hot, cold, warm,* and so on are displayed. The words are discussed, and students are encouraged to learn to recognize them so they can add a weather dimension to the daily exercise of changing the date.

A science lesson can be the occasion for teaching new words through the whole word approach. The words *heat, cold, ice, melt,* and *water* might be part of a bulletin board display after they have been introduced during an ex-

FIGURE 3.3
WEATHER BOARD.

periment and added to a child's list of known words (see Figure 3.4).

The Problem of Function Words. Words like *a, and, is, of,* and *it* are called *function words* because their chief purpose is to show syntactic relationships in sentences. They do not have much meaning on their own, and because function words are unstressed in normal speech, some children may not recognize them in isolation (Huttenlocher, 1964; Ehri, 1975; Holden and MacGinitie, 1972).

It is clear that many children do not perceive the word *to* in "gonna go" nor the word *have* in "shoulda gone" nor the word *of* in "bag a' marbles." Written compositions show that even some college-age students fail to recognize function words as separate words in some contexts. Sloan (1979) finds that instances of such neologisms as *alot, noone, infact, nodoubt, intime,* and *fillup* are on the rise in college writing. But because function words appear frequently, it makes sense to teach children to recognize them early in their word learning careers.

FIGURE 3.4
SCIENCE BULLETIN BOARD.

Teachers incorporate function words into whole word recognition lessons by printing phrases or short sentences onto cards, as in Figure 3.5, rather than single words, as suggested on page 65. Flannel board activities can be created especially to encourage children to learn to recognize function words such as prepositions. An outline of a fishbowl and phrases printed on cards such as "in the bowl," "on the bowl," "under the bowl," "near the bowl" can become the center of a group activity and be put where individuals can work with them on their own or in small groups (see Figure 3.6).

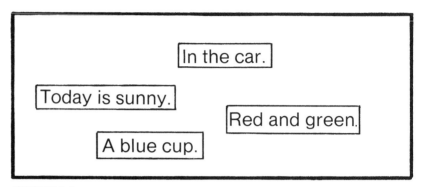

FIGURE 3.5
**INCORPORATING FUNCTION WORDS INTO WHOLE WORD
RECOGNITION MATERIALS.**

Basal Readers

Perhaps the most widespread use of the whole word approach is with basal readers. Many basal reading series begin with stories such as this:

Here is Father.
Father runs home.
Run, run, Father.
Run home.

Through many activities such as those discussed above, students are helped to learn these words as whole words. The words are then repeated in new stories, and words are gradually added until longer stories with more complex sentences appear.

♦ It is presumed that most readers of this book have themselves learned to read in American schools and will therefore know what basal readers are, since basal readers have been used in the overwhelming majority of American schoolrooms for many decades. However, some readers may not have used basals or were not aware that the books used to teach them were basals.

Basal readers are textbooks published in a series for use in the elementary grades, beginning with first grade. Each set of students' books is accompanied by a teacher's guide or teacher's manual with page by page suggestions and instructions for teaching reading using the materials in the books. Other materials such as workbooks and audiovisual teaching aids are published to accompany basal readers. The teacher's guide or manual gives suggestions and directions for using these materials as well.

An important aspect of basal readers is that each book (ideally, each lesson) is created as part of a grand design. Decisions of what to teach, when to teach, and how to teach are guided by the authors' and editors' beliefs about the nature of reading, how one learns to read, in what order skills ought to be presented, and so on. Questions of content, such as how minorities are portrayed, whether death will be portrayed, and so on are also answered in terms of a coherent policy. Schools often choose basal readers largely on the basis of the grand design or the policies that are reflected in the materials and teaching suggestions.

Basal readers are discussed or referred to throughout this book. It would be a good idea to visit a college or university materials center where several complete basal reading programs are available and "work through" one or two lessons at the primary, middle, and upper grades and examine the materials referred to in the lessons. Classroom pro-

FIGURE 3.6
FLANNEL BOARD ACTIVITY ENCOURAGING CHILDREN TO RECOGNIZE FUNCTION WORDS SUCH AS PREPOSITIONS.

cedures built around basal readers are described in some detail in Chapter 11.

SELECTING WORDS FOR THE WHOLE WORD METHOD

Criteria When Whole Word Is the Sole Method

Before instruction in other methods of word recognition is begun, two criteria deter-

mine the selection of words: interest of the children in the words and the frequency of the words.

INTEREST

From the start, particularly at the start, learning to read should be an exciting, stimulating, warm, human, useful, social, congenial, gregarious experience. Perhaps the aspect of the whole word approach that recommends it best is that children use reading from the first day. One does not wait till the child has learned some letter-sound relationships, or the names of letters, or how to print.

Key Vocabulary. The key vocabulary approach reflects the view that learning originates within the child as he or she develops. The child will learn his or her own words. It has been suggested that eliciting the child's key vocabulary is analogous to discovering the child's stage of development in a Piagetian sense (Duckworth, 1967; Hartman, 1977). One idea associated with this school of thought is that one cannot hasten the child's level of development. The teacher's job is to discover where the child is and give the child as many and as broad experiences on that level as possible. The main arena of learning is in the child's mind; we can only discover the stage of development of that mind and facilitate experiences appropriate to that level of development.

Experience Story and Words in the Environment. The experience story approach, and what has been called here "words in the environment," reflect the view that learning originates in society. In these examples, children are members of a learning community. They are engaged in a common enterprise. The teacher is talking and writing; the children are contributing. An interesting thing is happening. Some children know more than others. Some learn to recognize words faster than others.

But they are all in it together, and they have the opportunity to learn from the teacher and from one another. The main arena of learning is the social group, and as a member of that group the teacher can help children to extend their learning efforts into areas where

they may encounter a little difficulty—into Vygotsky's zone of proximal development.

Basal Reading Programs. Writers of basal reading programs take the interest of the children into account as well. Here, though, "interest" tends to be defined in terms of the "average" child. Primer stories are about mommies and daddies and puppies—things that 6-year-olds are presumably interested in. Words taught as sight words in these early stories are chosen because one can demonstrate that they are *frequent* words in most 6-year-olds' environments.

Authors of these series consult extensive word counts of young children's oral language (Murphy, 1957; Johnson, 1971; Moe et al., 1982) and counts of words in published schoolbooks (see next section).

The interest of the child is considered in all three methods, but different sources of interest are assumed in each (see Figure 3.7).

FREQUENCY

One problem with choosing words on the basis of interest only is that children often choose words to learn (or words arise in an activity) that may be interesting but not be very useful—that is, words that will probably not appear again very soon in the child's reading. An enthusiastic child may want to learn to recognize *Bunsen burner* after a science demonstration. The teacher knows that the child will probably not see these words in print again for years.

On the other hand, *the, of, then, so,* and *like* are among the most frequently used words in print. Frequent words tend to be function words, and as has been pointed out before, such words tend not to have much meaning in isolation. As a result, children are not likely to choose them out of interest. As a

FIGURE 3.7
HOW CHILD'S INTEREST IS TAKEN INTO ACCOUNT IN THREE WHOLE WORD TEACHING STRATEGIES.

KEY VOCABULARY

The child learns *tiger* because it's *his* or *her* word. This approach concentrates on the inner life of the child, appeals to the child's emotions, and stresses the child's individuality.

EXPERIENCE STORY

The child learns *mouse* because of a social event of which he or she was part. Some children will learn more, and some will learn less, but community and learning together and from each other are stressed.

TYPICAL BASAL READER

Children learn words that are presumed to be interesting to them. This presumption is based on frequency counts and the principle that usefulness, interest, and frequency are related. Emphasis is on what all children have in common rather than on interests generated from a common experience or interests that are unique to individual children.

matter of fact, it has been demonstrated that such words tend to be harder for children to learn to recognize than "content words"—nouns, verbs, adjectives, and adverbs (Ehri, 1976).

Word Frequency Counts and Basic Vocabulary Lists. Many studies have been done to discover the relative frequency of words. The first modern study in the field of education was done in 1921 by Thorndike (1921; Thorndike and Lorge, 1944), who counted word frequencies in a potpourri of English-language publications. His study included American and British literature, literature intended for children and adults, and literature that had been published recently as well as literature from the distant past.

Dolch (1936) counted word frequencies from school reading materials (preprimer to grade 6). Dolch developed the Dolch Basic Sight Vocabulary, consisting of 220 words (excluding nouns) and a list of 95 nouns that are common in primary reading materials (published as Dolch Picture-Word Cards [Garrard]).

Since the advent of computers, three important frequency counts have been done. Kucera and Francis (1967) counted a million running words of text published in the United States in 1961 in fifteen categories of writing representing types of journalism, scientific writing, and fiction and nonfiction trade books. This had an advantage over the Thorndike lists in that it was contemporary, American, published writing, and it was thought to give a better estimate of the probability of a word's being encountered by a contemporary American in daily reading.

Carroll, Davies, and Richman (1971) published a frequency count of over 5 million words published in texts and other materials used in American classrooms in 1969. This highly sophisticated study reports the frequency of words in the entire body of material, their frequency in each of seventeen subject categories (reading, math, library fiction, magazines, and so on), and their frequency in each of grades 3 through 9 and ungraded.

The study even reports the probability of one's encountering a word based on how often it was found plus *where* it was found. A word found fairly often in music books is not as likely to be encountered as a word found equally often in social studies books, because more time is spent in school reading social studies than music.

Harris and Jacobson (1972) counted words in six basal reading series and eight content area textbook series for grades 1 through 6.

Several word lists categorized by grade level are reported in this study, including "core" lists of 332 words categorized as preprimer, primer, and first reader words.

Fry (1972) reviewed frequency counts done by others and devised six lists of 100 words each which he believes are necessary for successful reading in grades 1 through 4. Fry calls words on these lists "instant words," referring to his belief that these words should be known instantly by students at the grade level identified for each list.

A glance at any of these lists will convince the reader that many words chosen for teaching on the basis of frequency would not be found on a list of words chosen on the basis of interest.

Uses of Basic Vocabulary Lists. Selecting frequent words. Basic vocabulary lists have come to be used for several purposes. One is to decide what words to teach at the early stages of reading. We can be sure that writers of basal readers consult such lists and that editors and teachers refer to them in arguing that the words in a particular book are too hard or too easy for the grade level. Such lists are also used by teachers who employ language experience, key vocabulary, and language in the environment approaches. With each new experience, one wants the children to gain more independence and to be better prepared for the next. Therefore, teachers want to call attention to words that will appear again and again.

Whatever approach one is using, words are sometimes introduced that will not probably be encountered again for some time. One wants to spend the time and effort of review on useful words and leave the others to each child's discretion. Although most teachers can trust their intuition on this question most of the time, frequency counts can help to decide on borderline cases.

Assessment of student progress. These lists are also often used for assessment of reading skills. Primary teachers often think of one aspect of a child's level of achievement in terms of how many of the Dolch Basic Sight Vocabulary Words or Dolch Picture Words a child knows, or whether the child has mastered the first hundred, second hundred, and so on of the Fry Instant Words, or the Preprimer, Primer, or First Reader List of the Harris-Jacobson Core Words.

Confusing the Two Uses. One must not, however, confuse the two traditional uses of these lists. To insist upon teaching the first twenty-five words on a particular list before the second, to decide not to teach *ice* and *water* because they are not on the primer list, to decide not to teach the word *vote* on election day because it is not on any list is to violate the first principle of word selection—*interest*.

Selection for whole word recognition is a matter of capitalizing on the interests of children at the moment and taking into consideration what their reading needs will be in the ongoing program. A teacher need not act on one criterion at the expense of the other; he or she can and should consider both.

Criteria after Other Methods Are Introduced

GENERALIZATIONS THAT WILL SOON BE TAUGHT

When even the most rudimentary principles of phonics or structural analysis are introduced, a third criterion for choosing words by the whole word method arises. It is to choose words on the basis of skills that will be introduced in the near future.

If, for instance, one has determined to teach the letter-sound correspondence of the initial *p* as in *pan* and *put,* one wants to be sure the child recognizes several words beginning with *p* as whole words. Much later, if some less obvious word analysis generalizations are going to be taught, such as where to divide two-syllable words ending in -*le,* one wants to be sure the child recognizes words like *able, title, sample,* and *wrinkle* as whole words.

IRREGULAR SPELLING-SOUND RELATIONSHIPS

As children progress, they learn to use phonics and structural analysis as aids to word recognition. At the same time, the words appearing in the materials they are asked to read become more diverse. When a new word appears at these later stages, the teacher must decide whether to use some combination of context, structure, and phonics or to use the whole word approach.

At this stage, the whole word approach may become something of a default option. If other methods will not work, use the whole word method. For example, *colonel* and *isthmus* represent very uncommon spelling-sound relationships. Words borrowed from other languages (such as *frijole, pinochle,* and *spiel*) often fall into this class. Ruddell (1974) gives many more such examples.

It is best to simply teach such words as whole words, perhaps with a comment on the unusual spelling. One should be aware of phonetic irregularity as a criterion for using the whole word approach at the very beginning stages of reading instruction as well. One of the most common words in English is *of;* it is the only word in English where /v/ is represented by *f.*

One can see from this discussion that the whole word method is not abandoned after the initial stages of reading instruction. It is perhaps the most commonly used method of teaching new words at all levels of reading instruction.

SOME PRINCIPLES FOR TEACHING WHOLE WORDS

The most commonly used, unadorned whole word method has been mentioned in several contexts in this chapter. That method is to say a word while the child is looking at its printed form and encourage the child to remember it so that he or she will recognize the printed form in the future. Several principles are involved in teaching words by this method and in follow-up techniques used to ensure future recognition.

Presenting Words in Context

One often stated rule of reading instruction is that one should always teach words in context. This is based on three observations: (1) Most words have more than one meaning. For example, *bear* can refer to the animal or mean "to carry." Out of context, a meaning may be ambiguous. (2) Many words have more than one pronunciation (for example, *read* in "I do read" and "I have read"). Such words do not have one correct pronunciation out of context. (3) Context helps to narrow down the possibilities of what an unrecognized word is and therefore helps the reader to recognize it. One does not confuse *bed* with *bad* in the sentence "He sleeps in bed."

This should not be taken to mean that every word must appear in a printed context. Smith (1976), in discussing children's earliest experiences with printed words, states that "words do not need to be in sentences to be meaningful, they just have to be in a meaningful context" (p. 229).

Suppose the teacher says "Let's learn the words *clock* and *door*. I'll print the word *clock* on this card and tape it next to the clock and I'll print the word *door* and tape it to the door. What else should I print cards for?" The teacher is using the words in the context of oral language and presenting the printed word in that context. He or she is also placing the printed word in a physical context. It *is* advisable to introduce function words in written phrases or short sentences, for the reasons discussed earlier.

Even Gray, who is often cited as an advocate of teaching words in context (see Hartley [1970], for example), does not suggest that words always appear in *written context:*

To make sure that every child will associate both sound and specific meaning with a sight word the first time he sees it, the teacher initiates an oral discussion in which the word is used informally with the same meaning as it has in the story that pupils are about to read. During the discussion, as she uses the word in a sentence, the teacher shows its printed form (usually on a word card at early levels). (Gray, 1960, p. 17)

Deciding how much written context to supply in presenting a new word depends on what part the teacher expects the written context to play in the child's recognition of the word. These factors will be discussed again in Chapter 6, when context is discussed as an aid to word recognition.

Pupils' Attention

The whole word method is often referred to as the look-and-say method, for obvious

reasons. Harris and Sipay (1975, p. 57) have pointed out that "look while you say" would be a better term because it would remind both the teacher and learner that the child's attention must be focused on the visual form and the spoken form of the word at the same time and that the connection between the two must be understood by the child.

Affixing a label to a door and a desk will not ensure that the child will learn these words, nor will the teacher's reading a story from a chart while pointing to each word accomplish much in the way of word recognition for a child who is gazing out the window.

Ensuring that children's attention is directed to the task at hand is a large part of the teacher's job. Although this seems an obvious point, it is one that teachers can lose sight of. Classroom observers have recorded extreme examples of teachers who appear to be oblivious to the need for attention or who seem inured to the lack of attention (McDermott, 1977). Rist (1973) reports the following example of what he calls a "phantom performance":

She asks the children to repeat the poem and no child makes a sound. She asks the children to repeat the poem line by line after her, first with words and then a second time through simply saying "lu, lu lu" in place of words. The children are completely baffled and say nothing. At the end of the second repetition she comments, "Okay, that was good. We will have to do that again next week." (p. 107)

One teacher commented to an observer:

It seems to me that some of the children at Table 2 and most all the children at Table 3 at times seem to have no idea of what is going on in the classroom and were off in another world all by themselves. It just appears that some can do

FIGURE 3.8
CALLING ATTENTION TO THE SHAPE OF WORDS.

it and some cannot. I don't think that it is the teaching that affects those that cannot do it, but some are just basically low achievers. (Rist, 1970, p. 425)

The observer clearly believed that the teacher made little effort to get the attention of the children at tables 2 and 3. The "bright" children in this kindergarten were seated at table 1.

Berliner (1981) defines academic learning time as time when students are engaged with materials and lessons and they produce a high rate of successful responses. He reports some middle-grade classrooms where as little as four minutes a day is spent in academic learning time in reading; he finds a direct relationship between academic learning time in reading and reading test scores. Less dramatic examples of the same problems are seen when flannel board displays, such as those suggested in Figure 3.6, are not used or attended to by children largely because the teacher has not made their purpose clear, or modeled for the children how they might be used.

Attention to Appropriate Stimulus

When employing a whole word approach to word recognition, it is difficult to say what aspect of a printed word enables an individual

child to recognize it. One child may respond to length, another to shape, another to first letter, and so on. One wants to be sure, however, that a child is not responding exclusively to some extraneous cue, such as that there is an inkblot on the card that has the word *man*, or that *Monday* is in the top slot of the calendar.

To ensure that children are responding to some aspects of the printed word itself, one wants to be sure that words appear in different contexts in connection with different activities and as different physical entities (that is, printed in chalk on the board, on a card in ink, in the child's book, and so on). Some authorities discourage writing *red* in red ink and *green* in green ink and other such gimmicks because they encourage children to rely on memory aids that are not intrinsic to the printed words.

Calling Attention to the Shape of Words. It is often recommended that the first words taught should look as dissimilar as possible. If a class is asked to remember *an*, *for*, and *elephant* on a particular day, *elephant* may be learned first by most children because it is the most different from the others. Teachers capitalize on this reliance on differences and on peculiarity of shape by drawing outlines around words, as in Figure 3.8.

Other memory aids are sometimes taught, such as that *bed* looks like a bed, *looks* has two "eyes", and *monkey* has a "tail," as in Figure 3.9. There is some objection to teaching aids

bed   looks   monkey

FIGURE 3.9
MEMORY AIDS FOR TEACHING SIGHT WORDS.

of this sort because *bad* also looks like a bed, *took* also has two eyes, and *money* also has a tail. One must bear in mind, however, that these suggestions are to aid memory only at the very earliest stages. Care is taken not to introduce both *bad* and *bed*, *took* and *look*, and *money* and *monkey* at this stage anyway, on the principle that the first words should be as dissimilar as possible.

Very early in the process, letter names are learned and letter-sound correspondences begin to be discussed; then differences between similar words can be discussed in terms that are relevant throughout the person's reading career. For example, one points out that *took* and *look* begin with different letters and correspondingly different sounds. But as soon as these clues are employed, one is no longer dealing with a purely whole word technique. Rudimentary phonics is involved.

Use of Picture Clues

Teachers frequently use pictures with words as clues to recognition. For example, the commercially available Dolch Basic Picture Words (Garrard) set may be used. Ninety-five frequently used nouns appear with a pic-

ture and the word on one side, and the word only on the other side.

Children can "learn" the pictures and words together and then turn the cards over to see how many words they can remember without the pictures. They can check their progress by turning the cards over again to see if they said the right word. They can work singly, in pairs, or in groups. The prudent teacher supervises such activities from time to time to make sure the child has not assigned the wrong word to the picture. Teachers can make cards (as in Figure 3.10) and use similar learning activities.

This same idea has been used with the weather board. The "picture and word" side of the cards is shown at first, and the "word only" side later, as in Figure 3.11. Children can choose the weather card for the day and check to see if they are right.

Teachers want to be careful that students progress to the stage where they identify words without the aid of pictures and that the students realize identification of the words without the aid of pictures is the ultimate goal. A commonly reported research finding is that *under experimental conditions*, children recognize words that have been presented alone (without accompanying pictures) better than words presented with pictures (Braun, 1969; Santostefano et al., 1965; and Samuels, 1967).

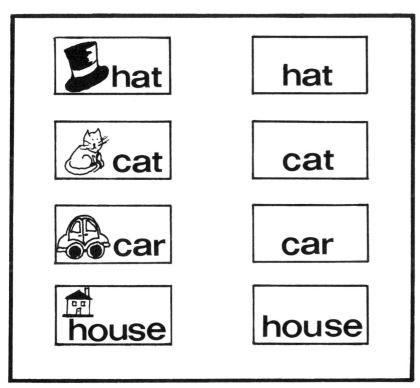

FIGURE 3.10
TEACHER-MADE NOUN CARDS.

Practice

Children need many exposures to some words before they recognize them, and they will forget many words if the words are not repeatedly seen and recognized. Both facts indicate a need for practice. Repeating words that have already been introduced in new stories, flannel board activities, flash cards, word banks, team games, and so on, is essential. Word recognition drill need not be ruled out but, like all activities, it should not be overused lest it become boring.

One way to ensure that drill does not become boring is to keep the sessions short by concentrating on words that have not been learned. Word cards like The Dolch Picture Words or The Dolch 220 (whether commercially prepared or teacher made) are particularly useful because soon each child's "hard words" will differ. An individual's hard words can then be identified and separated out and used for drill.

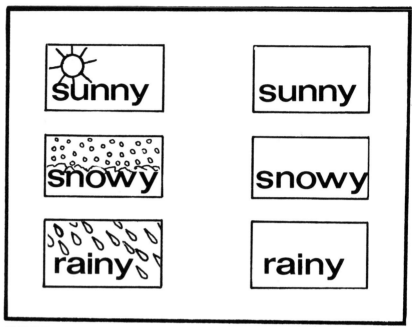

FIGURE 3.11
TEACHER-MADE WEATHER CARDS.

WHY USE THE WHOLE WORD APPROACH?

There are several sound reasons for using a whole word approach in the beginning of reading instruction.

Purposeful Reading. With the whole word approach, purposeful reading begins on the first day of instruction or soon after. Reading pages of the preprimer, writing and reading experience stories, doing calendar activities, weather activities, workbook pages, felt board activities, or team games can begin as soon as a child has learned to recognize a few words. One does not put off reading while children learn to recognize and name individual letters, or until they have learned the most frequent sounds associated with letters.

Interest. The whole word approach enables the teacher to capitalize on interest. Just as a teacher-introduced experience like taking a white mouse out of a cage and letting it run around a table may motivate children to write a story and learn some words from that story, events of the day outside school may generate interest in words like *snow, parade* or *vote*. From the start, written language is introduced as a thing that is relevant to the ordinary business of life.

Demonstrated Success. The whole word method is a time-honored approach to beginning reading. It was advocated by Horace Mann and began to be widely used in primers beginning around 1850 (Matthews, 1966). It has been advocated by the two most influential authorities on reading in this century: Edmund Huey (1908) and William S. Gray (1948), and it is still the most widely used method of teaching beginning reading.

Durkin (1966) has studied cases of children who have learned to read before they entered school and has discovered that many parents of such children claim that no one ever taught the children to read. Upon direct questioning, however, many parents reported that the children frequently asked "What's that word?" and were answered by attentive adults.

This is, of course, a whole word method. Parents do not recognize it as a teaching method either because it is initiated by the child, or because there is no letter-sound element involved. One might argue from this that the whole word approach is a "natural" approach if one defines *natural* as a method spontaneously initiated by many children who show an early interest in reading.

Directness. One great virtue of the whole word method is that it leads directly to the objective all methods are ultimately designed to achieve: instant, automatic word recognition. For this reason, the whole word approach is retained throughout reading instruction as one way to introduce new words.

A CONTRASTING VIEW: THE LINGUISTIC APPROACH

This chapter has presented the prevailing view of the function of sight words in beginning reading instruction. The information and advice given in this chapter is consistent with the teaching practices recommended by the most widely used basal reading series.

However, if one were to adopt the so-called linguistics approach to teaching reading, one would find much of the information and advice given in this chapter quite inconsistent with that approach. Fewer published reading programs use a linguistic approach, and they are not as widely used as the more traditional basal reading series. But this approach is used in a significant number of classrooms.

Consistent Spelling-Sound Relationships

The linguistic approach is derived from the belief that beginning readers would be harmed if forced to deal with the phonetic inconsistencies of English (Soffietti, 1955; Fries, 1962). It follows, then, that one would choose words for beginning reading instruction on the basis of the regularity of the letter-sound relationships the words represent.

That is, one would *not* teach *of* because *f* represents /v/ in this word—a highly irregular letter-sound correspondence. One would teach words like *can, man,* and *ran* because the words contain very regular spelling-sound relationships. If one taught *can,* one would not teach *cent* until much later in the program because the initial *c* represents two different sounds in the words *can* and *cent.*

Minimal Differences Between Words Taught

Bloomfield (1961) believed that from learning lists of highly similar words, students

FIGURE 3.12
A TYPICAL WORD LIST FROM A LINGUISTIC READER.

at	sat	fat
bat	mat	cat
hat	Pat	

FIGURE 3.13
A TYPICAL STORY FROM A LINGUISTIC READER.

The Hat on the Mat

Look at the hat.
The hat is on the mat.
Pat sat on the hat.

will discover that similar spellings represent similar sounds and that different spellings represent different sounds. Through learning words like *hen, pen,* and *men* as lists, students will learn to attend to the only clue in the word that can help—the difference in a single letter (see Figure 3.12). Therefore, through learning such lists students learn to attend to what Bloomfield believed is the only appropriate stimulus—letter-sound relationships, not the shapes of words or pictures on cards.

Although frequency and interest are taken into account, the overriding considerations for choosing words for the linguistic method are that the words employ letter-sound relationships that are regular, that words with inconsistent letter-sound relationships be avoided, and that words taught in the same lesson have minimal differences (single initial consonant letter contrasts, for example).

Certain function words such as *the* and *on* are introduced as sight words because they are needed to create sentences. Figure 3.13 shows a typical ''story'' from a linguistic reader.

SUMMARY

There is a difference between learning words and learning to recognize words. In teaching reading, *word recognition* refers to recognizing a word in print that one knows in spoken form. This chapter and the next several chapters are on word recognition. *Learning words* is taken up in Chapter 9.

The whole word method involves teaching children to recognize words without referring to letters, the sounds represented by letters, syllables, prefixes, suffixes, or roots.

The whole word method appears at some stage of many different approaches to reading instruction. Paired-associate learning, the language experience approach, the key vocabulary approach, whole words in the environment, many basal readers, and Bloomfield's linguistic method are based on different assumptions and employ different methods, but they all teach whole words.

Assumptions underlying the whole word method differ with the approach. Paired-associate learning rests on the assumption that when children are rewarded for the correct response to an external stimulus, they will make those responses in the future. The language experience and key vocabulary approaches rest on the assumption that children are *interested* and will learn things they want to learn. The language experience approach attempts to engender interest in words through group language activities; the key vocabulary approach attempts to discover words individuals are already interested in. Some basal readers attempt to capitalize on the interests of the ''average'' child and rely on paired-associate assumptions as well.

Selecting words for teaching by the whole word method depends on the approach as well. The interest of the child in the words is paramount in the key vocabulary and the language experience approaches. The frequency of words in the language is another consideration, however, because a child who does not learn to recognize *the, of,* and *and* will be severely handicapped in reading since these are very frequent words in written English.

Teachers and creators of materials for teaching reading use word frequency counts to guide their choices of words to include in recognition lessons. Some lists identify words by the grade level at which they are appropriately introduced.

These lists are sometimes used to get an estimate of a child's reading ability. Knowing that a child recognizes all the words in Fry's First 100 Instant Words (1972, p. 58) tells an experienced teacher something about a child's reading ability. Sometimes teachers do not use words in reading lessons because they do not appear on a list of words appropriate for the level they are teaching; this is an unfortunate use of these lists. These lists guide teachers in choosing words that ought to be taught because they are likely to be encountered frequently at a particular level. They are not intended to limit the words taught at a particular level.

In most programs, phonics, word structure, and use of context are introduced at some point as word recognition methods. Even then, words are sometimes taught as whole words because they represent phonic or structure generalizations that will soon be taught. Some words, such as *pinochle,* simply do not lend themselves to other methods. The whole word approach is a frequently used method of teaching word recognition at all levels of teaching reading.

Success in using the whole word approach depends on several principles. Words should be taught in context (written or oral language or physical context) so that the meaning of the word is not ambiguous, the correct pronunci-

ation is clear, and the learner can be helped to recognize the word through the context.

It is the teacher's responsibility to enlist the students' attention. The student should find it necessary to remember the word through appropriate visual clues (the first letter, the shape, the length). He or she should be kept from relying exclusively on irrelevant clues, such as the one place the word is always found in his or her experience.

Picture word cards are useful in that they permit a child to practice word recognition without the individual attention of the teacher. But research suggests that using pictures as aids to recognition may not be the most efficient way to learn to recognize words.

There are several sound reasons for using a whole word approach in the earliest stages of reading. Purposeful reading can begin soon after instruction begins. The approach capitalizes on student interest. The approach has a long history of success and has been advocated by many eminent scholars. Children who learn to read before coming to school and with no apparent instruction seem to learn to read through a whole word approach.

Bloomfield's linguistic approach begins by teaching whole words in a paired-associate fashion, but the paramount criterion for choosing words is neither interest nor frequency. Words are chosen because they represent regular letter-sound relationships; words that represent inconsistent letter-sound relationships are avoided, and groups of words having minimal differences are chosen. The assumption underlying this approach is that if words are carefully chosen, the student will discover for him or herself the regular letter-sound relationships of English.

All the approaches discussed in this chapter introduce letter-sound relationships and other methods of word recognition at some point following the whole word phase.

FOR FURTHER READING AND DISCUSSION

Words children use have been the focus of attention of scholars who wish to understand language and cognitive development. Writers of elementary school materials are interested in the words children use because they want to choose words for instructional material that will communicate with children. Teachers are interested in words children use because this knowledge helps them understand what they can expect children to know. Several lists of words children use are cited below.

Hopkins, C. J. The spontaneous oral vocabulary of children in grade one. *Elementary School Journal*, 79 (1979): 240–49.

Horn, E. Appropriate materials for instruction in reading. IN G. M. Whipple (ed.), *Report of the National Committee on Reading. Twenty-fourth Yearbook of the National Society for the Study of Education*. Bloomington, IL: Public School Publishing Company, 1925.

Johnson, D. D. A basic vocabulary for beginning reading. *Elementary School Journal*, 72 (1971): 29–34.

Moe, A. J., C. J. Hopkins, and R. T. Rush. The *Vocabulary of First-Grade Children*. Springfield, IL: Charles C. Thomas, 1982.

Murphy, H. The spontaneous speaking vocabulary of children in primary grades. *Journal of Education*, 140 (1957): 3–106.

Sherk, J. K. *A Word-Count of Spoken English of Culturally Disadvantaged Preschool and Elementary Pupils*. Kansas City: University of Missouri, 1973.

Obtain several of these lists and compare the methods by which the lists were compiled and the purpose the authors state for compiling the lists. How does the information contained in these lists differ from the word counts of published materials referred to in this chapter?

REFERENCES

Ashton-Warner, S. *Spinster*. New York: Simon and Schuster, 1959.

———— *Teacher*. New York: Simon and Schuster, 1963.

———— *Spearpoint: Teacher in America*. New York: Knopf, 1972.

Berliner, D. C. Academic learning time and reading achievement. In J. T. Guthrie (ed.), *Comprehension and Teaching: Research Reviews*. Newark, DE: International Reading Association, 1981.

Bloomfield, L. Teaching children to read. In L. Bloomfield and C. Barnhart, *Let's Read: A Linguistic Approach*. Detroit: Wayne State University Press, 1961.

Braun, C. Interest-loading and modality effects on textual response acquisition. *Reading Research Quarterly*, 5 (1969): 428–44.

Carroll, J. B., P. Davies, and B. Richman. *The American Heritage Word Frequency Book*. Boston: Houghton Mifflin, 1971.

Clay, M. M. *Reading: The Patterning of Complex Behavior*. London: Heinemann Educational Books, 1972.

Dolch, E. W. A basic sight vocabulary. *Elementary School Journal*, 36 (1936): 456–60; 37 (1936): 268–72.

Duckworth, E. Piaget rediscovered. In E. Victor and M. S. Lerner (eds.), *Readings in Science Education for the Elementary Schools*. New York: Macmillan, 1967, 317–19.

Durkin, D. *Children Who Read Early*. New York: Teachers College Press, Columbia University, 1966.

Ehri, L. C. Word consciousness in readers and prereaders. *Journal of Educational Psychology*, 67 (1975): 204–12.

————. Word learning in beginning readers: Effects of form class and defining contexts. *Journal of Educational Psychology*, 68 (December 1976): 832–42.

————.Beginning reading from a psycholinguistic perspective: Amalgamation of word identities. In F. Murray (ed.), *The Recognition of Words*. Newark, DE: Internatioanl Reading Association, 1978.

Fries, C. C. *Linguistics and Reading.* New York: Holt, Rinehart and Winston, 1962.

Fry, E. B. *Reading Instruction for Classroom and Clinic.* New York: McGraw-Hill, 1972.

Gray, W. S. *On Their Own in Reading.* Chicago: Scott, Foresman, 1948. Revised edition, 1960.

Harris, A. J., and M. D. Jacobson. *Basic Elementary Reading Vocabularies.* New York: Macmillan, 1972.

Harris, A. J., and E. S. Sipay. *How to Increase Reading Ability, 6th ed.* New York: David McKay, 1975.

Hartley, R. N. Effects of list types and cues on the learning of word lists. *Reading Research Quarterly,* 6 (1970): 97–121.

Hartman, T. The relationship among the ability to classify, retrieval time from semantic memory and reading ability of elementary school children. Ph.D dissertation, Memphis State University, 1977.

Holden, M. H., and W. H. MacGinitie. Children's conceptions of word boundaries in speech and print. *Journal of Educational Psychology,* 63 (1972): 551–57.

Huey, E. B. *The Psychology and Pedagogy of Reading.* New York: Macmillan, 1908. Reprinted, Cambridge, MA: MIT Press, 1968.

Huttenlocher, J. Children's language: Word-phrase relationship. *Science,* 143 (January 17, 1964): 264–65.

Johnson, D. D. A basic vocabulary for beginning reading. *Elementary School Journal,* 72 (1971): 29–34.

Kucera, H., and W. N. Francis. *Computational Analysis of Present-Day American English.* Providence, RI: Brown University Press, 1967.

Matthews, M. M. *Teaching to Read.* Chicago: University of Chicago Press, 1966.

McDermott, R. P. The ethnography of speaking and reading. IN R. W. Shuy (ed.), *Linguistic Theory: What Can It Say About Reading?* Newark, DE: International Reading Association, 1977.

Moe, A. J., C. J. Hopkins, and R. T. Rush. *The Vocabulary of First-Grade Children.* Springfield, IL: Charles C. Thomas, 1982.

Morris, D. Concept of word: A developmental phenomenon in the beginning reading and writing process. *Language Arts,* 58 (1981): 659–68.

————, and E. H. Henderson. Assessing the beginning reader's "concept of word." *Reading World* (May 1981):279-85.

Murphy, H. The spontaneous speaking vocabulary of children in primary grades. *Journal of Education,* 140 (1957): 3–106.

Rist, R. C. Student social class and teacher expectation. *Harvard Educational Review,* 40 (1970): 411–51.

————. *The Urban School: A Factory of Failure.* Cambridge, MA: MIT Press, 1973.

Ruddell, R. *Reading Language Instruction.* Englewood Cliffs, NJ: Prentice-Hall, 1974.

Samuels, S. J. Attentional processes in reading: The effect of pictures in the acquisition of reading responses. *Journal of Educational Psychology,* 58 (1967): 337–42.

Santostefano, S., L. Rutledge, and D. Randall. Cognitive styles and reading disability. *Psychology in the Schools,* 2 (1965): 57–62.

Sloan, G. The subversive effects of an oral culture on student writing. *College Composition and Communication,* 30 (May 1979): 156–60.

Smith, F. Learning to read by reading. *Language Arts,* 53 (1976): 297–99, 322.

Soffietti, J. P. Why children fail to read: A linguistic analysis. *Harvard Educational Review* (Spring 1955): 63–84.

Thorndike, E. L. *The Teacher's Word Book.* New York: Bureau of Publications; Teachers College, Columbia University, 1921.

————, and I. Lorge. *The Teacher's Word Book of 30,000 Words.* New York: Teachers College Press, Columbia University, 1944.

Veatch, J., F. Sawicki, G. Elliot, E. Flake, and J. Blakey. *Key Words to Reading.* Columbus, OH: Charles E. Merrill, 1979.

CHAPTER

4

PHONICS

DEFINITIONS

MORE PHONICS OR LESS PHONICS?

DECIDING WHAT TO TEACH

A Compromise Between Simplicity and Truth
Some Generalizations Are Interesting But Not
  Very Useful
Some Principles for Making Decisions

REGARDING CONTENT
REGARDING ATTITUDE

SOME COMMON GENERALIZATIONS

Definition of "Consonants" and "Vowels"

PHONOLOGICAL DEFINITIONS
PHONICS DEFINITIONS

Sounds Represented by Single Consonant
  Letters

ONE TO ONE CORRESPONDENCE
SINGLE CONSONANT LETTERS THAT
  REPRESENT MORE THAN ONE SOUND
A BRIEF REVIEW

Sounds Represented by Consonant Letters
  Together in a Syllable

CONSONANT DIGRAPHS
CONSONANT BLENDS
"SILENT" CONSONANT LETTERS

Spelling Clues to Vowel Sounds in One-Syllable
  Words

SINGLE VOWEL LETTERS
SINGLE VOWEL LETTERS IN WORDS ENDING
  IN *E*
TWO VOWEL LETTERS TOGETHER

Spelling Clues to Vowel Sounds in Two-
  Syllable Words

DEFINITION OF SYLLABLE
CLUES TO VOWEL SOUNDS IN TWO-
  SYLLABLE WORDS
DIVIDING UNRECOGNIZED WRITTEN
  WORDS INTO SYLLABLES
APPLYING CLUES TO VOWEL SOUNDS

Generalizations for Applying Stress (Accent)

KNOWING PHONICS AND KNOWING WHAT TO
TEACH

Examples of Generalizations of Questionable
  Utility

A CONSONANT LETTER-SOUND
  GENERALIZATION
A VOWEL SPELLING-SOUND
  GENERALIZATION
A CLUE TO SYLLABLE DIVISION

Examples of Fine Points

ARE SILENT LETTERS SILENT?
HOW MANY SYLLABLES IN *TABLE?*

SUMMARY

FOR FURTHER READING AND DISCUSSION

REFERENCES

DEFINITIONS

There are relationships between ordinary English spelling and the pronunciation of words. For example, there is a generalization that can be drawn between the initial sound and the initial letter in the words *dad, dog, den,* and *dime.* The generalization is that printed words which begin with the letter *d* usually begin with the sound /d/.

The study of the relationship between ordinary spelling and the pronunciation of words is called *phonics.* A collection of such generalizations into a body of knowledge is also called *phonics.* Teaching such generalizations to children as a method of word recognition is also called *phonics.*

Two other terms are sometimes confused with phonics. They are phonology and phonetics.

Phonology is the study of language sounds. A phonologist uses the same methods in studying the sounds of any language—for example, English, Russian, Greek, Arabic, or Chinese. The fact that these languages do not share a writing system is irrelevant, because the phonologist is studying the sounds of spoken language, not their writing systems.

Phonetics is a system of representing sounds in special symbols. For example, the International Phonetic Alphabet is a set of symbols that enables phonologists to represent the sounds of any language (see *The Random House Dictionary of the English Language,* 1968, under International Phonetic Alphabet). A phonetic representation of a language might not even resemble the symbols or ordinary spelling of the written form of the language.

Phonics, however, is concerned with the relationship between ordinary spelling and pronunciation.

MORE PHONICS OR LESS PHONICS?

The question of whether or not one should teach phonics is often raised in shrill tones. Critics of programs that do not emphasize phonics charge that children do not read as well today as they did in the past, and that this is true because phonics—which was the proved method of the past—has recently been abandoned for a whole word, look-and-say method where no phonic principles are ever taught. On the other hand, critics of phonics-based programs charge that the aim of such programs is to teach word calling rather than understanding and that in such programs children do not learn that language has meaning.

Attacks from both sides contain false assumptions. First of all, although historical trends toward more phonics and less phonics have been observed in America, the level of literacy among children who attend school in America has remained fairly constant (Matthews, 1966). Recent studies (Farr et al., 1978; Wray, 1978) show that reading test scores have not declined over recent decades, but have improved slightly. Copperman (1979), on the other hand, insists that there has been a decline in reading achievement in the upper grades of high school, but he does not attribute this decline to methods of teaching reading.

Second, although programs that teach phonics exclusively are available, they are intended to be used as supplements to regular reading programs. Among programs that are designed to be used as the major approach to reading instruction (for example, various basal reading programs, individual reading programs, and so on), one simply does not find programs that teach all phonics and no comprehension. Nor does one find programs that teach all comprehension and no phonics.

These programs differ in terms of when phonics generalizations are introduced, how many phonics generalizations are introduced, and the extent to which phonics generalizations are taught in isolation.

In this chapter, we present some phonic generalizations and some principles for deciding which generalizations to teach and when.

DECIDING WHAT TO TEACH

A Compromise Between Simplicity and Truth

Phonic generalizations seem easy if one knows them. They can seem hopelessly complicated if one does not know them or if one is trying to teach them to someone who does not know them. One reason phonic generalizations may appear to be so complicated is that they are not immutable laws.

A discussion of the sound represented by the consonant letter *b* will help to demonstrate the problem. The letter *b* usually represents the sound /b/, but it does not represent the sound /b/ in *climb* or *lamb*. So what does one teach?

No Rule. A person might decide not to teach any letter-sound correspondence for *b* since there is no hard and fast rule.

♦ This is clearly absurd, since anyone who can read knows that *b* nearly always represents /b/. In a computerized study of letter-sound relationships (Hanna et al., 1966), the letter *b* corresponds to the sound /b/ over 2,000 times, and it is "silent," as in *climb*, 27 times. Those 27 instances tend to occur in words beginning readers are not likely to encounter in print, such as *dumb, limb, plumb,* and *womb.*

A Complicated Rule That Is Always True. A person might decide that there is a generalization, but it is a bit more complicated: The letter *b* represents /b/ unless it is preceded by *m* at the end of a syllable.

♦ This may be too complicated for many students to understand. Imagine a child who has learned fifty words by sight. Does it seem wise to complicate a simple and widely applicable generalization by qualifying it so it will take into account a rare spelling?

A Simple Rule That Is Not Always True. A person might decide that there is a generalization and that it is so widely applicable and the exceptions so rare that he or she will teach it without qualifications, except to say "usually" instead of "always": The letter *b* usually represents the sound /b/. Later—perhaps years later—a qualification of the generalization can be dealt with explicitly: The letters *mb* at the end of a syllable usually represent the sound /m/.

♦ Teaching children that phonics generalizations are *usually* true is a major objective of phonics instruction. Children should learn that using phonics is something of a juggling act. When you encounter a word you do not recognize, you apply phonic generalizations on a trial and error basis. You are seeking a *probable* pronunciation that *approximates* or *suggests* a word you know and that makes sense in context. You realize that these generalizations may not apply in this particular case. If a set of generalizations does not suggest a word that you know and that makes sense, you are ready to try a different set of generalizations.

Some Generalizations Are Interesting But Not Very Useful

Does it ever make sense to teach the generalization that *mb* at the end of a syllable usually represents /m/ as a clue to word recognition? It is not a very useful rule because it applies to so few words.

Instead of teaching this generalization as

a clue to word recognition, it might be taught as an observation about a group of words one presumes students already recognize. One can imagine the word *tomb* occuring in a fifth-grade textbook. The teacher might take the opportunity to point out that this unusual spelling occurs in other words, such as *bomb, climb, comb, crumb, dumb, lamb, limb, numb,* and *thumb*.

Teaching this kind of generalization at this stage probably will not result in students' using the generalization to recognize as yet unencountered words. Instead, it is just one of dozens of facts about written English that people who love the study of language find interesting. Classrooms should be places where knowledge about language is esteemed and where discovery and discussion of such facts are a source of pleasure, regardless of their immediate utility.

One point to be taken from this discussion is that teachers of reading should know a lot about phonics, but they must not think they need to teach all they know all at once. Nor must they think that every phonics generalization they know will be useful to young readers for word recognition.

Some Principles for Making Decisions

REGARDING CONTENT

Some principles that will be developed in this chapter are these:

1. Teach generalizations that consistently apply to words children will encounter in beginning reading (such as that *b* usually represents /b/).
2. Avoid delving into qualifications until advanced stages of reading skill have been attained.

3. Realize that some qualifications of widely applied rules are legitimately taught as interesting facts about written language rather than as clues to word recognition.

REGARDING ATTITUDE

Children should be taught the uses and limitations of phonics from the start. Children should develop attitudes based on the following facts:

1. Phonics clues lead to approximate pronunciations; while part of the student's attention should be on spelling-sound possibilities, another part should be devoted to guessing at known words that conform to the suggested pronunciation and that make sense.
2. The spelling of some words is tricky, and therefore some words are best learned as whole words or recognized primarily through context rather than phonics.

SOME COMMON GENERALIZATIONS

Definition of "Consonants" and "Vowels"

PHONOLOGICAL DEFINITIONS

Phonologists talk about two kinds of speech sounds—consonant sounds and vowel sounds. The difference is a technical one having to do with the physiology of sound production. Speech sounds are made by the tongue, teeth, palate, and other organs. The one thing that all speech sounds in English have in common is that there is air moving out of the lungs during sound production.

If the movement of air is stopped (as in /t/ or /g/, for example), diverted (as in /m/ or /n/, for example), or obstructed (as in /f/ or /s/, for example), the sound is considered a consonant sound. If the movement of air is not stopped, diverted, or obstructed, the sound is considered a vowel sound.

PHONICS DEFINITIONS

But one need not know the technical physiological definition of consonant and vowel sounds in order to learn phonics generalizations. Most reading pupils (and many reading teachers) learn simply that the vowel letters are *a, e, i, o, u,* and that the vowel sounds are the sounds usually represented by these letters. Strictly speaking, *y* and *w* are sometimes involved in vowel spellings (as in *sky* and *how*). The consonant letters are all the rest. The consonant sounds are sounds usually represented by consonant letters.

Sounds Represented by Single Consonant Letters

The most consistent phonic generalizations are concerned with single consonant letters in one-syllable words. In phonics, "a single consonant letter" is one that does not appear next to another consonant letter in a syllable. In *dog* the *d* and *g* are single consonant letters. In *save* the *s* and *v* are single consonant letters. In *spark* there are no single consonant letters. Each consonant letter *s, p, r,* and *k* appears next to another consonant letter in the same syllable.

ONE TO ONE CORRESPONDENCE

There are fourteen consonant letters that usually represent only one sound each as long as they appear as single consonant letters. These letters are *b, d, f, h, j, k, l, m, n, p, r, t, v,* and *z.* Of course, these letters do not always conform to this rule. The single consonant letter *d* represents the sound /j/ in several

longer words (words of several syllables), such as *educate, gradual,* and *cordial.*

The question one must ask is whether this is an important qualification of the generalization or a confusing quibble. Are such words likely to appear in beginning reading? If a person is analyzing a word like *gradual* and presumes the *d* represents /d/, will that person not arrive at a pronunciation so close to the correct one that he or she will recognize the word? This is a case of the teacher deciding between what he or she knows to be true and what he or she believes it will be profitable to teach.

♦ If you were writing a reading program for first grade, how would you handle the fact that *d* sometimes represents /j/? How would you handle this fact in a fifth-grade program?

SINGLE CONSONANT LETTERS THAT REPRESENT MORE THAN ONE SOUND

Letters *w* and *y*.   When *w* and *y* appear as single consonant letters at the beginning of syllables, they each represent only one sound, as in *was* and *yet.*

When *w* and *y* do not appear as single consonant letters at the beginning of a syllable, they may represent other sounds. In *gym* and *cry, y* represents a vowel sound; in *how,* the *o* and *w* taken together represent a vowel sound.

The Letter *s*.   When *s* appears as a single consonant letter at the beginning of a syllable, it usually represents only one sound, /s/ as in *sing.* When it appears at the end of a syllable, it may represent /s/ as in *bus* or /z/ as in *has.*

The Letters *c* and *g*.   When *c* appears as a single consonant, it may represent the sound /k/ as in *cut,* or the sound /s/ as in *cent.* When *g* appears as a single consonant, it may represent the sound /g/ as in *gave,* or /j/ as in *gem.*

The fact is that there are very reliable spelling clues to the sounds of the letters *c* and *g.* If *c* is followed by *e, i,* or *y,* it usually represents the /s/ sound, as in *cent, city,* and *cycle.* If *c* is not followed by *e, i,* or *y,* it usually represents the /k/ sound, as in *cat, cot, cut, crab,* and *picnic.* If *g* is followed by *e, i,* or *y,* it usually represents the /j/ sound, as in *gem, gin* and *gym.* If *g* is not followed by *e, i,* or *y,* it usually represents the /g/ sound, as in *gave, got, gum, grow,* and *bug.*

A more generalized rule that covers the sounds represented by the letters *c* and *g* is that if these letters are followed by *e, i,* or *y,* they usually represent their "soft" (sibilant) sounds, /s/ or /j/. If they are not followed by *e, i,* or *y,* they represent their "hard" sounds, /k/ or /g/.

◆ The question is whether it is better to teach that *c* represents either /s/ or /k/. (If one sound does not suggest the pronunciation of a word the reader knows, he or she tries the other.) Or is it better to teach that the letter following *c* or *g* is a reliable clue to the correct option?

Based on what has been discussed before in this chapter, what criteria should you consider in deciding?

The Letter *q.* The consonant letter *q* is always followed by *u* and represents /kw/, as in *queen,* or /k/, as in *bouquet.*

◆ Although there are a half dozen moderately common words where *qu* represents /kw/ (*quarter, queen, question, square,* for example), there are no common words where *qu* represents /k/. Furthermore, many words where *qu* represents /k/ do not conform to English spelling-sound principles in other ways (*bouquet* and *marquise,* for example). As these facts are presented, the option of teaching that *qu* usually represents /kw/ and letting it go at that may seem more and more reasonable.

The Letter *x.* The consonant letter *x* represents the sound /ks/, as in *box,* or two consonant sounds /g/ plus /z/, as in *exist,* or /z/, as in *xylophone.*

◆ In the word frequency count of 5 million words in American schoolbooks (Carroll, Davies, and Richman, 1971), the most frequent word where *x* is pronounced /z/ is *xylophone;* according to this study, the statistical probability of encountering the word *xylophone* in an American schoolbook is less than one in every million words. The probability of encountering this word outside a music book is even less.

So if a class comes across *xylophone* in a story, does the teacher rush to teach that the *x* sometimes represents /z/? Of course not. You teach the word as a sight word, or a child may even "sound it out" using the usual sound of *x* and arrive at something like /ksi lō fōn/. If he or she knows the word, and it is in context, the child has probably arrived at a pronunciation close enough to the correct one to recognize it.

A BRIEF REVIEW

This section on sounds represented by single consonant letters touched upon some important facts about phonics in general and about teaching phonics. Before proceeding, it will be useful to reflect upon some of these facts and to make some facts explicit that have only been implied.

1. The position of a letter in a syllable may be relevant to the sound the letter represents. (Review the sections on the letters *w, y,* and *s.*)
2. Letters following a letter in a syllable may be relevant to the sound the letter represents. (Review the section on the letters *c* and *g.*)

Suggestions about the Content and Timing of Phonics Instruction. Single consonant letters sometimes represent more than one sound. In deciding whether to teach only the most frequent correspondence or to explicitly teach alternative correspondences, one wants to consider whether or not:

1. The alternative spelling-sound correspondences are likely to appear in many words the students will encounter at their level.

2. The alternative spelling-sound correspondences are similar enough to the most frequent ones that students will arrive at pronunciations which will enable them to recognize words in context.

3. The alternative spelling-sound correspondences are likely to be useful in word recognition or are simply interesting observations about written language and should be taught as such as students progress in reading.

♦ A good way to review the concepts presented in this section would be to decide what you would teach in beginning reading about the sounds represented by the single consonant letters *d, w, y, s, c, g, q,* and *x.* What would you teach about the sounds usually represented by these single consonant letters in third grade? In fifth grade? It might be instructive to discuss this with your classmates.

Sounds Represented by Consonant Letters Together in a Syllable

CONSONANT DIGRAPHS

Consonant digraphs are pairs of consonant letters that represent a single consonant sound that is different from the consonant sound either letter usually stands for. The letters *th* in *the* represents a sound different from /t/ or /h/. The most common digraphs are *ch* as in *church, sh* as in *ship, ph* as in *phone, ng* as in *ring,* and *th* as in *thaw* or *the.* Each of these represents a single sound except for *th,* which represents two subtly different sounds. The differences in the sounds represented by *th* is that one does not "voice" the initial sound of *thaw,* but one does voice the initial sound of *the.*

CONSONANT BLENDS

Consonant blends are consonant letters that appear together and represent the usual sound of each letter "blended" one into the other. Consonant blends that frequently appear at the beginning of syllables are *bl* as in *black* and *str* as in *stripe* (see Figure 4.1). Consonant blends that frequently appear at the ends of syllables are *ct* as in *act, nt* as in *rent,* and *st* as in *mist* (see Figure 4.2).

♦ In some dialects of American English, people pronounce and hear a difference between the words *witch* (pronounced /wich/) and *which* (pronounced /hwich/). In such dialects, most words spelled with the beginning letters *wh* are pronounced with the initial consonant blend /hw/. This is peculiar, because the order of the consonant letters is the reverse of the consonant sounds they represent in the word. In other equally standard dialects, *witch* and

FIGURE 4.1
COMMON CONSONANT BLENDS AT THE BEGINNING OF SYLLABLES.

bl *blue, blow, block*	**br** *brown, brave, brick*	**sp** *spell, space, spoon*
cl *clay, clock, clown*	**cr** *cross, crib, cry*	**st** *store, still, stop*
fl *flip, flag, flat*	**dr** *dress, drink, drum*	**sc** *scare, scream, school*
pl *plane, play, please*	**fr** *fright, frog, fry*	**sw** *swim, sweat, swan*
sl *sleep, slow, slip*	**tr** *tree, trick, tramp*	**tw** *twist, twelve, twig*

FIGURE 4.2
COMMON CONSONANT BLENDS AT THE END OF SYLLABLES.

ct	st	sk	sp	nt	lk	ld	nd
fa*ct*	mo*st*	a*sk*	cri*sp*	we*nt*	mi*lk*	mo*ld*	hi*nd*
ta*ct*	be*st*	de*sk*	gra*sp*	hu*nt*	su*lk*	fo*ld*	mi*nd*
a*ct*	che*st*	ma*sk*	ra*sp*	li*nt*	e*lk*	we*ld*	wi*nd*

FIGURE 4.3
SILENT CONSONANT LETTERS.

kn words	wr words	-ck ending	-mb ending	-lm ending
*k*nee	*w*rite	sa*ck*	co*mb*	a*lm*
*k*nob	*w*ring	blo*ck*	thu*mb*	ca*lm*
*k*nife	*w*rong	du*ck*	cli*mb*	pa*lm*

which are pronounced the same—/wich/—and in these dialects words spelled with the beginning letters *wh* are pronounced with the initial consonant /w/.

This might leave one in something of a quandary as to what to teach. A couple of suggestions may relieve your anxiety. (1) Teach that the letters *wh* at the beginning of a syllable represent the beginning sound of *what* and *when.* You need not explicitly state what that beginning sound is. (2) Teach the usual sound represented by *w* and the usual sound represented by *wh* on different days. Do not comment on the similarity or difference.

An interesting fact—not a clue to word recognition. In a sixth- or seventh-grade class, a teacher might comment on the pronunciation of the words *which* and *witch,* and the fact that some individuals pronounce *wh* in *which* as /hw/ and others pronounce it as /w/. But this is not a lesson in phonics as an aid to word recognition. It is a lesson in language study.

The objectives of the two lessons are very different and should not be confused. What might be hopelessly abstract and confusing to a 6-year-old trying to learn word recognition skills may be very interesting to a 12- or 15-year-old who recognizes all the words concerned but is learning something about phonology and the dialects of American English.

"SILENT" CONSONANT LETTERS

Sometimes two consonant letters appear together in a syllable, but they represent the usual sound of one letter. In *knee,* for example, the initial consonant sound is /n/; the *k* in the spelling is said to be silent. Other spellings that include silent letters are *ck, wr, lm,* and *mb,* as in Figure 4.3. "Double consonants" such as the two *l*s in *tall* and two *g*s in *egg* can be thought of as special cases of silent letters. One of the pair represents its usual sound, and the other is silent.

Spelling Clues to Vowel Sounds in One-Syllable Words

Relationships between vowel sounds and ordinary spellings are less consistent than relationships between consonant sounds and ordinary spelling. The inconsistency of the relationship between vowel sounds and spelling has led some authors to advise students to try to recognize unfamiliar words by sounding out the consonants only and uttering a neutral vowel sound like the *a* in *alone* for the vowels. The idea is that if a word is in context, thinking of the correct consonant sounds and the (possibly distorted) vowel sounds in sequence will result in a pronunciation so close to the real one that the word will be recognized.

This is not a bad idea, particularly for advanced readers dealing with multisyllabic words, but spelling-sound relationships for vowels in one- and two-syllable words are reasonably dependable. Once again, however, the teacher must be prepared to deal with the tension between the desire to teach generalizations that are easy and generalizations that are always true. In this section, generalizations will be presented that are easy to understand and that apply often enough to be worth learning.

FIGURE 4.4
SINGLE VOWEL LETTERS IN ONE-SYLLABLE WORDS FOLLOWED BY ONE OR MORE CONSONANTS.

bat	pep	bib	rod	hut
rap	den	fit	mom	bus
sand	bent	chimp	pond	just

SINGLE VOWEL LETTERS

In one-syllable words, a single vowel letter followed by one or more consonant letters usually represents the short sound of the vowel, as in *pan, get, bin, mop,* and *fun* (see Figure 4.4). In one-syllable words, single vowel letters at the end of the word (not followed by consonant letter[s]) usually represent the long sound of the vowel, as in *we, hi,* and *no* (see Figure 4.5).

FIGURE 4.5
SINGLE VOWEL LETTERS AT THE END OF ONE-SYLLABLE WORDS.

me	hi	go	gnu	by
he		so	flu	my

◆ The fact is that very few one-syllable words end with a single vowel letter. This generalization is useful, though, because it applies to syllables in longer words, as will be shown presently.

SINGLE VOWEL LETTERS IN WORDS ENDING IN *E*

In a one-syllable word, a single vowel letter followed by a single consonant letter and final *e* usually represents the long sound of the vowel. The *e* is silent, as in *take, bite, nose,* and *sure* (see Figure 4.6). In a one-syllable word, a single vowel letter followed by two consonant letters and a final *e* usually represents the short sound of the vowel and the final *e* is silent, as in *dance, else, since, bronze,* and *dunce* (see Figure 4.7).

FIGURE 4.6
LONG VOWELS REPRESENTED BY THE VOWEL-CONSONANT-SILENT *E* PATTERN.

cake	kite	rode	flute	Pete
plate	bride	pole	tube	gene
spade	quite	hose	June	eve

FIGURE 4.7
SHORT VOWELS REPRESENTED BY THE VOWEL-CONSONANT-CONSONANT-SILENT *E* PATTERN.

dance	else	since	bronze	dunce
prance	fence	bridge	lodge	judge
trance	twelve	ridge	dodge	fudge

FIGURE 4.8
TWO VOWELS TOGETHER REPRESENTING A LONG VOWEL SOUND.

ai	**ay**	**ea**	**ee**	**ie**	**oa**	**oe**
bail	bay	beach	beef	die	bloat	doe
drain	gray	cheat	cheese	lie	foam	hoe
frail	pay	east	freeze	tie	goat	toe

FIGURE 4.9
TWO VOWEL LETTERS TOGETHER REPRESENTING DIPHTHONGS.

oo	**oo**	**au**	**aw**	**ou**	**ow**	**oi**	**oy**
bloom	book	caught	awe	blouse	brow	broil	boy
boot	crook	fault	bawl	bounce	clown	choice	ploy
cool	good	cause	crawl	found	cow	foil	soy

TWO VOWEL LETTERS TOGETHER

In a one-syllable word, two vowel letters together may represent the long sound of the first vowel letter, as in *mail, pay, weak, beef, die, boat, snow,* and *sue* (see Figure 4.8). In a one-syllable word, two vowel letters together may represent one of the so-called glided vowel sounds or diphthongs, as in *tool, took, haul, law, out, down, oil,* and *boy* (see Figure 4.9).

Deciding whether two vowel letters together in a syllable represents a diphthong or the long sound of the first vowel letter is not as arbitrary as it may appear at first. Most of the common two vowel letter combinations usually represent one option or the other. Only the spellings *ow* (as in *how* contrasted with *row*) and *oo* (as in *tool* contrasted with *look*) frequently represent more than one sound.

Spelling Clues to Vowel Sounds in Two-Syllable Words

DEFINITION OF SYLLABLE

A *syllable* is part of a word with one vowel sound that may be preceded and/or followed by consonant sounds. A syllable can be a single vowel sound like the word *I* or the first syllable in *acorn* (pronounced /ā' korn/); or a consonant and vowel sound like the first syllable in *paper* (pronounced /pā' per/); or a vowel and consonant sound like the first syllable in *actor* (pronounced /ak' tor/); or a consonant, vowel, and consonant sound like the first syllable in *lantern* (pronounced /lan' tern/).

Once children begin to learn about vowel sounds, they can begin to identify spoken words with one, two, and three syllables by counting the number of separate vowel sounds they hear. This is a useful exercise for the purpose of learning the meaning of the word *syllable*. But for reading, students must learn to divide printed words they do not recognize into syllables for the purpose of applying phonic generalizations to the syllables.

Vowel letter spellings (single vowel letters or two vowel letters together) usually represent a single vowel sound and are clues to the presence of a syllable. Even if a student did not recognize the following words, he or she would be fairly confident that they were two-syllable words because there are two vowel spellings separated by one or more consonant letters: *final, afraid, detour, heinous, matter, poignant.*

As in one-syllable words, a final *e* after a consonant letter usually does not represent a separate vowel sound and is therefore not a clue to the presence of a syllable. Even if a student did not recognize the following words, he or she would be fairly confident they were two-syllable words because there are two vowel spellings separated by one or more consonant letters and a final *e* that does not represent an additional vowel sound: *pleasure, senate, commerce, orange, knowledge.*

However, a final *e* preceded by a consonant and an *l* usually is a clue to the presence of a syllable. Even if a student did not recognize the following words, he or she would be fairly confident that they were two-syllable words because there is a vowel spelling followed by a final syllable ending in *-le: cable, eagle, crumble, little, foible.*

The same generalizations apply to words having any number of syllables. One could determine that the following were three-syllable words because of the way they are spelled: *liberal, sufficient, tomorrow, camouflage, millionaire, orchestra, cuticle, boondoggle,* and *voluble.*

CLUES TO VOWEL SOUNDS IN TWO-SYLLABLE WORDS

The clues to vowel sounds in words of more than one syllable are the same as the clues to vowel sounds in one-syllable words, but there are two additional factors to consider:

1. One cannot apply some spelling-sound generalizations until one knows where syllables begin and end.

2. Syllables in English words having more than one syllable do not receive equal stress. Spelling-sound generalizations

apply regularly to stressed syllables, but vowels in unstressed syllables tend to sound like the vowel in the last syllable of *butter* or the first syllable in *alone,* regardless of how they are spelled.

DIVIDING UNRECOGNIZED WRITTEN WORDS INTO SYLLABLES

When we encounter a word we do not recognize, we do not know where one syllable ends and the next begins and we do not know which syllable is stressed. But, once again, there are fairly reliable generalizations for deciding where to divide words into syllables and for deciding which syllable to stress. Spelling clues to dividing written words into syllables are based on patterns of vowels and consonant letters.

Vowel-Consonant-Consonant-Vowel. When two consonant letters appear between two vowel letters, syllable division usually occurs between the two consonant letters, as in Figure 4.10.

FIGURE 4.10
SYLLABLE DIVISION FOR WORDS CONTAINING A VOWEL-CONSONANT-CONSONANT-VOWEL PATTERN.

af / ter	boun / ty	ac / count
sus / tain	al / ley	un / der
ar / gue	boul / der	bliz / zard

Vowel-Consonant-Vowel. When one consonant letter appears between two vowel letters, syllable division often occurs between the first vowel and the consonant, as in Figure 4.11.

♦ This generalization is not easy to justify on the grounds that it usually applies. When researchers

FIGURE 4.11
SYLLABLE DIVISION FOR WORDS CONTAINING A VOWEL-CONSONANT-VOWEL PATTERN.

di / ner	fi / nal	ti / tle
ba / by	lo / go	fo / cus
re / tain	i / con	li / lac

FIGURE 4.12
SYLLABLE DIVISION FOR WORDS CONTAINING -LE AT THE END.

ma / ple	strug / gle	i / dle
gam / ble	cy / cle	jin / gle
stee / ple	trem / ble	mum / ble

FIGURE 4.13
SYLLABLE DIVISION FOR WORDS CONTAINING CONSONANT DIGRAPHS.

e / ther	mar / shal
pa / thos	en / chant
tro / phy	or / phan

apply this generalization to lists of words in schoolbooks, it has been found to work about half the time or slightly less than half the time (Clymer, 1963; Bailey, 1967; Emans, 1967).

Sometimes the rule is stated as follows: When one consonant letter appears betweeen two vowel letters, syllable division occurs before the consonant letter (as in *ba/by*) or after the consonant letter (as in *ov/en*). This often leaves people scratching their heads. Which is it—before or after? Most authorities choose to state the generalization as it is stated above (that syllable division often occurs between the vowel and consonant (as in *ba/by*) so the student will have a consistent first approach.

But you want to keep in mind that the purpose of teaching syllabication generalizations is that they give the student a method for recognizing words that are unfamiliar at first sight. Visually breaking the word into syllables gives the student manageable, pronounceable units to which spelling-sound generalizations can be applied. If dividing the word one way does not suggest a word the student knows, he or she should try another way. This is what Wardaugh (1966) meant when he said that the concept of syllabication has no truth value, but it has pragmatic value.

Consonant -le at the End of a Word.   When a word ends in -le preceded by one or more consonants, syllable division usually occurs before the consonant closest to -le, as in Figure 4.12.

Consonant Digraphs.   When a consonant digraph appears in a word, the digraph is treated as a single consonant letter and the vowel-consonant-vowel rule or the vowel-consonant-consonant-vowel rule is followed, as in Figure 4.13.

APPLYING CLUES TO VOWEL SOUNDS

Look at the syllables resulting from applying the clues to syllable division in Figures 4.10 to 4.13. Apply the clues to vowel sounds in one-syllable words to these syllables. The procedure does not always result in exactly the same vowel sounds as one hears in the whole word, but it results in pronunciation close enough to the real one that it should lead to word recognition if the spoken word is familiar. This is particularly true if the word is in context.

This statement does not apply to the last syllable of words ending in a consonant plus -le, as in Figure 4.12. This spelling does not appear in one-syllable words.

• You do not want to confuse dividing unrecognized words into syllables for the purpose of applying phonics with the task of the typist, printer, or editor in dividing words at the end of a printed line. Conventions for dividing words at the end of a printed line reflect knowledge of how the word is pronounced (which is precisely what the reader does not know) and knowledge of scholarly conventions (which is something the reader does not need to know).

A child who divides the word *writer—wri/ ter*—and arrives at the correct pronunciation has accomplished his purpose. An editor who allows the word *writer* to be divided *wri/ter* at the end of a line is displaying ignorance of printing conventions. As a reading teacher, you are concerned with the performance of the child trying to identify an unfamiliar word. You are not concerned with the editor's knowledge of conventions for dividing words at the end of a line.

Generalizations for Applying Stress (Accent)

In two-syllable words, stress usually falls on the first syllable. In three-syllable words, stress usually falls on the first or second syllable. If a word contains a prefix or a suffix (as longer words often do), special considerations apply that will be taken up in Chapter 5.

In teaching about the application of stress in English words, it is most important to instill an attitude of flexibility and a willingness to experiment. There is some question as to whether the correct application of stress leads to recognition of words, or whether the recognition of words leads to the correct application of stress.

1. *Eisenhower was a cadet at West Point.*

For example, if a child does not immediately recognize the word *cadet* in sentence 1, his or her knowledge of dividing words into syllables and of phonics would lead to the pronunciation /kā det/ with equal stress on both syllables. If *cadet* is a familiar spoken word, the child may recognize it and correctly pro-

nounce it (/kə det'/) without further experimentation with stress.

2. *Put another potato into the soup.*

Likewise, if a child encounters *potato* in sentence 2 and does not immediately recognize it, he or she may arrive at the pronunciation /pō tā tō/ with equal stress on each syllable. If *potato* is a familiar spoken word, the child would no doubt recognize it without any further experimentation with stress and arrive at the correct pronunciation, /pə tā' tō/.

♦ In Figure 4.14 you will find a scrambled list of words that appear in Figures 4.10 through 4.13. It would be a good check on your understanding of this entire section to divide the words into syllables and apply the clues to vowel sounds to the resulting syllables. If this process does not result in a pronunciation that is very close to the actual pronunciation of the word, you have not followed the generalizations for dividing the words into syllables, or you have not followed the generalizations concerning vowel spelling and sound. Reread the section or check with your classmates to see where you went wrong.

FIGURE 4.14
WORDS FOR SYLLABICATION.

diner	logo	focus
after	alley	tremble
sustain	boulder	trophy
baby	account	lilac
orphan	struggle	idle
argue	maple	pathos
bounty	under	mumble
enchant	jingle	marshal
gamble	icon	steeple
retain	blizzard	final
cycle	ether	title

KNOWING PHONICS AND KNOWING WHAT TO TEACH

It will become apparent in Chapter 7 that in practice one teaches the generalizations presented here gradually and using words that appear in the reading program. As a result, learning and teaching phonics is not as abstract or as complicated as it may appear in this chapter, where generalizations are presented one after the other. However, the danger of phonics instruction becoming overly abstract and overly complex is always present.

Several phonics generalizations have been discussed here that are probably not very useful for word recognition, but one would expect a teacher of reading to know them. In this section, several more such generalizations will be discussed and two examples of extraordinarily fine points regarding phonics will be introduced as further examples of the kind of information one would expect a teacher of reading to have regarding phonics. But one would not expect to see them become part of the word recognition curriculum.

Examples of Generalizations of Questionable Utility

A CONSONANT LETTER-SOUND GENERALIZATION

The single consonant letter *t* usually represents the sound /t/, but there is a group of words where *t* represents /sh/. These are words ending in the spellings *-ation* and *-tion*, as in *action, adoption, installation,* and *accusation.* This spelling appears in a large number of English words, but they tend not to be high-frequency words in primary reading materials.

Second, the spellings *-ation* and *-tion* result from adding suffixes to root words such as

act, adopt, install, and *accuse.* For these two reasons, the generalization that *t* sometimes represents /sh/ is frequently taught as part of the structure clues to word recognition (see Chapter 5), rather than as part of the phonics program.

A VOWEL SPELLING-SOUND GENERALIZATION

Single vowel letters followed by *r* and the letter *a* followed by *l* in the same syllable usually represent a sound unlike the short sound of the vowel letter. For example, compare the vowel sound of *cab* and *car; bed* and *her; cob* and *for; sit* and *sir; hat* and *halt.*

♦ Will this additional set of vowel spelling sound relationships help or harm the learner in reaching the primary objective of teaching phonics—enabling him or her to recognize words he or she does not recognize instantly? In context, would trying the short sounds of the vowel lead to a pronunciation close enough to the word so that the learner would recognize the word?

We are back to the tension between wanting to teach a few generalizations that will be easy to apply and wanting to teach generalizations that will cover every case. Teaching an "*r*-controlled" vowels generalization will certainly complicate matters. Is it worth it?

A CLUE TO SYLLABLE DIVISION

In the discussion of spelling clues to vowel sound and in the discussion of determining the probable number of syllables in a word, it was stated that two vowel letters together in a word usually represent one vowel sound and therefore constitute one syllable (or part of one syllable). Burmeister (1968) found this to be true in frequent words. However, it is sometimes true that words divide into syllables between two vowel letters, as in:

cha/os	cre/ate	di/al
li/on	ne/on	bo/a

• Think of all the words you can where two adjacent vowel letters represent vowel sounds in separate syllables, such as in *neon.* Are these words children are likely to encounter in beginning reading? Does it seem worthwhile to qualify the generalization that two adjacent vowel letters in a word probably represent one vowel sound to accommodate these words?

Examples of Fine Points

ARE "SILENT" LETTERS SILENT?

Some reading specialists object to referring to the *e* in *safe* or the *i* in *mail* as "silent." They argue that referring to such letters as "silent" implies they are not related to the sound represented by the spelling of the word. But in fact these letters are part of the spelling code—they signal that the other vowel letter in the word represents its long sound.

There is some merit in this argument; however, most students are able to learn that the *e* signals the long sound of the other vowel letter in spellings of this kind and to understand what is meant when the *e*s are referred to as silent. Introducing this fine point into word recognition instruction does not seem advisable. With older children, a discussion of whether "silent letters" are silent may appeal to their interest in language, but it will probably not improve their word recognition skills.

HOW MANY SYLLABLES IN TABLE?

Phonologists have observed that it is possible to form a syllable by pronouncing /l/ after certain consonants (for example /b/) without inserting a vowel sound between them. Dictionaries record this fact by using what they refer to as a "syllabic *l.*" In the *Webster's New World Dictionary of the American Language* (1968), for example, the phonetic respelling of table is *tā b'l.* By the definition of

syllable used in this chapter, *table* would be considered a one-syllable word, since only one vowel sound is heard in pronouncing the word.

Shuy (1969) reports the case of a third-grade student who got into trouble with his reading teacher because he could hear only one vowel sound in *travel, weasel,* and *awful.* Shuy suggests that defining a syllable as "some kind of voiced continuant peak with borders which are, somehow, not like peaks" would account for syllabic consonants like the one in *table.*

The experience of most reading teachers would no doubt confirm that this is indeed a fine point. The untrained ear cannot distinguish between the last syllable in *bushel* (where phonologists agree that there is a vowel sound heard) and the last syllable in *cradle* (where phonologists hear a syllabic *l*). Attention to this difference would simply bewilder most readers.

Once again, this is a fact that may interest older students simply because they are interested in language; it would not contribute to word recognition skill.

• In this section several issues, some of them complex, have been introduced and discussed. In each case the conclusion was reached that it would not be useful to raise these issues in teaching word recognition skills to children. A fair and obvious question arises: Why bring these things up in this textbook?

The reason was discussed in Chapter 1. Reading teachers and the profession of teaching reading have never lacked for critics. Most linguists know more about phonology than most reading teachers. Many linguists know more about phonics than many reading teachers. It is not uncommon, therefore, for a linguist to discover that some aspect of the reading curriculum is not wholly compatible with the current state of knowledge in linguistics. When linguists point out the error of reading teachers' ways, it often results in a rout rather than a discussion because the reading teacher is overwhelmed by what seems like superior knowledge. It is very important that reading teachers respond to such suggestions from a position secure enough to enable them to ask questions and to evaluate these suggestions in the context of what they know—how to teach reading.

SUMMARY

Phonics is the study of the relationship between the ordinary spelling of words and the pronunciation of words. The set of generalizations derived from this study is called phonics. The method of teaching word recognition through reference to these generalizations is called phonics. Phonology is the study of spoken language sounds. It is something linguists study. Phonetics is a system of representing speech sounds with written symbols. Phonetics ignores conventional spelling.

Whether or not to teach phonics is often the topic of emotional debate. Extremists who defend phonics as the only way to teach reading often claim that today's students cannot read as well as students of former years because they are not taught phonics. In fact, reading ability among students who attend school in the United States has probably remained the same regardless of trends toward more or less phonics. In the past quarter century, reading performance may have improved slightly in the elementary school grades, where performance would seem to be most susceptible to methods of teaching word recognition. There is evidence that reading achievement has declined in the upper grades and high school, but there is no evidence that this decline is connected with methods of teaching word recognition.

Extremists who attack phonics claim that teaching phonics causes children to think that the purpose of reading is to decode words, and that students therefore never learn to comprehend printed language. However, most published programs introduce both phonics and comprehenison. Programs differ in terms of when phonics is introduced, how many generalizations are introduced, and whether phonics is taught separately.

Phonics generalizations can become very complicated if one tries to state them in a way that covers nearly all words. Children should be taught simple rules that apply widely to words they will encounter at the early stages of learning to read. Some phonics rules may be taught to children at later stages of reading development not to assist them in word recognition, but because they are interesting facts about written English, and learning to enjoy knowing about language is an important objective.

From the start children should be taught that phonics generalizations lead to *approximations* of the pronunciation of many words. They must learn to ask themselves whether the pronunciation they arrive at sounds similar to a word they know and if the word fits the context.

In producing English sounds, when air is stopped, diverted, or obstructed by the organs of speech, it is considered a consonant sound; when air is not stopped, diverted, or obstructed, it is considered a vowel sound. A less technical definition, and one that is preferable for teaching phonics, is that sounds usually represented by vowel letters (*a, e, i, o,* and *u*) are vowel sounds. Sounds usually represented by consonant letters (all letters except *a, e, i, o,* and *u*) are consonant sounds.

The most consistent phonic generalizations concern the sounds represented by single consonant letters. The single consonant letters *w, y, s, c, g, q,* and *x* represent two different sounds. The position in the syllable and letter following these letters often indicate which sound they represent.

Consonant digraphs are two consonant letters that appear together and represent a speech sound different from either letter (such as *ch* in *church*). When consonant letters appear adjacent to one another, they often represent their usual sounds blended together (such as *str* in *stripe*). These spellings are called consonant blends. Sometimes consonant letters appear adjacent to one another, but the usual sound of only one of the letters is represented (such as *lm* in *calm*). In such spellings, the consonant letter whose usual sound is not represented is often referred to as a "silent letter."

The relationships between vowel sounds and spellings are far less consistent than the relationships between consonant sounds and spelling. The letter or letters following vowel letters in a syllable often indicate what sounds the vowel letter represents. The sound a vowel letter represents may depend on the following spelling patterns:

- The vowel letter is the last letter in the syllable.
- It is followed by a consonant letter(s) in the syllable.
- It is followed by a consonant letter and the letter *e*.
- It is followed by two consonant letters and the letter *e*.
- It is followed by another vowel letter.

A syllable is part of a spoken word that has one vowel sound. Learning how to divide unfamiliar printed words into parts that probably represent syllables is useful for two reasons. It gives the reader manageable units to attempt to pronounce, and letter-sound correspondences are often signaled by the position of the letter in the syllable.

Patterns formed by spelling sequences of vowel and consonant letters suggest to the knowledgeable reader how many syllables an unrecognized word contains, and which letters begin and end syllables within the word.

The stress with which a syllable is pronounced often has an effect on vowel sound. Two-syllable words are usually stressed on the first syllable. In attempting to recognize a longer word, a reader who takes phonic generalizations into account and pronounces each syllable with equal stress will probably recognize a word if it is one he or she knows and if it is in context.

Although one would expect teachers of reading to know quite a lot about phonics, some generalizations are probably not very useful for aiding recognition of words—especially in the early stages of learning to read. Linguists sometimes get into extraordinarily fine points of phonology that are not very useful for a person struggling to recognize a word.

One must remember that the aim of phonics is to arrive at an approximate pronunciation. Teachers who do not know enough about phonics may be misled by suggestions from linguists who do not understand the teachers' purpose in teaching phonics. Therefore, reading teachers should know quite a lot about phonics so that they know what to teach—and what not to teach.

FOR FURTHER READING AND DISCUSSION

Criteria for Deciding What to Teach

The following three frequently cited studies were done to discover which phonics generalizations are useful at various grade levels. The findings of these studies seem to suggest that a different set of generalizations be taught than those suggested in this chapter.

Bailey, M. H. The utility of phonic generalizations in grades one through six. *The Reading Teacher*, 20 (1966–67): 413–18.

Clymer, T. The utility of phonic generalizations in the primary grades. *The Reading Teacher*, 16 (1962–63): 252–58.

Emans, R. The usefulness of phonic generalizations above the primary grades. *The Reading Teacher*, 20 (1966–67): 419–25.

You might read one or more of these studies and decide whether the phonics generalizations recommended for teaching in this chapter are the best ones after all. (If you are going to read only one study, read Clymer (1963) because the other two are based on Clymer's methods.) This exercise will enable you to reflect on a great many of the ideas presented in this chapter. The following questions may guide your thinking.

1. In the studies there are no generalizations regarding single consonant letters that have reliable sound correspondences (such as *b* usually represents /b/). How might this have happened? How might the conclusions have been different if this kind of generalization had been included?

2. The criteria for evaluating the usefulness of generalizations in these studies have to do with the number of words where the spelling in question occurs and the number of words where the *exact* sound predicted by the generalization is represented by the spelling. How do these criteria differ from the criteria stated in this chapter? Which set of criteria seems more desirable? Why?

Assumptions About How Students Use What Is Taught

Cunningham suggests in the following three articles that readers do not divide words into syllables and apply phonics generalizations to the syllables to identify words they do not immediately recognize. Instead, they break words into segments and pronounce them by comparing and contrasting the unrecognized word with known words. A child who does not recognize *employment* might compare and

contrast this word to known words *embarrass* and *empire* (yielding *em* = /em/), *boy* and *toy* (yielding *ploy* = /ploi/), and *bent* and *spent* (yielding *ment* = /ment/). Cunningham refers to this technique as a compare/contrast strategy of word identification.

Cunningham, P. M. Investigating a synthesized theory of mediated word identification. *Reading Research Quarterly*, 11 (1975): 127–43.

————. Decoding polysyllabic words: An alternative strategy. *Journal of Reading*, 21 (1978): 608–14.

————. A compare/contrast theory of mediated word identification. *The Reading Teacher*, 32 (1979): 774–78.

Read her description of this strategy and reflect on the following questions.

1. How much knowledge of phonics does one expect the student to have when this strategy is introduced?

2. What generalizations presented in this chapter would be discovered by a child who used this method?

This exercise will enable you to reflect on many of the ideas presented in this chapter. It may also set you to thinking about a question that will arise again in later chapters: Is it better (or is it necessary) to teach children certain generalizations about reading, or is it better to enable students to discover these generalizations on their own?

REFERENCES

Bailey, M. H. The utility of phonic generalizations in grades one through six. *The Reading Teacher*, 20 (1966–1967): 413–18.

Burmeister, L. E. Vowel pairs. *The Reading Teacher*, 21 (1967–68): 445–52.

Carroll, J. B., P. Davies, and B. Richman. *The American Heritage Word Frequency Book*. Boston: Houghton Mifflin, 1971.

Clymer, T. The utility of phonic generalizations in the primary grades. *The Reading Teacher*, 16 (1962–1963): 252–58.

Copperman, P. The achievement decline of the 1970s. *Phi Delta Kappan,* 60 (June 1979): 736–39.

Emans, R. The usefulness of phonic generalizations above the primary grades. *The Reading Teacher,* 20 (1966–1967): 419–25.

Farr, R., L. Fay, and H. Negley. *Then and Now: Reading Achievement in Indiana (1944–45 and 1976).* Bloomington: School of Education, Indiana University, 1978.

Hanna, R., Hanna, R, Hodges, and Rudolph. *Grapheme Phoneme Correspondence as Cues to Spelling Improvement.* Washington, D.C.: U.S. Government Printing Office, USOE, 1966.

Matthews, M. M. *Teaching to Read.* Chicago: University of Chicago Press, 1966.

Random House Dictionary of the English Language. New York: Random House, 1968.

Shuy, R. W. Some language and cultural differences in a theory of reading. In K. S. Goodman and J. T. Fleming (eds.), *Psycholinguistics and the Teaching of Reading.* Newark, DE: International Reading Association, 1969.

Wardaugh, R. Syl-lab-i-ca-tion. *Elementary English,* 43 (1966): 785–88.

Webster's New World Dictionary of the American Language. Cleveland: World, 1968.

Wray, M. A comparison study of the reading achievement of sixth grade students in 1917 and eighth grade students in 1919 with sixth and eighth grade students in 1978. Unpublished Master's thesis, Bowling Green, Ohio, Bowling Green State University, 1978.

ANALYSIS OF WORD STRUCTURE AS CLUES TO WORD RECOGNITION

DEFINITIONS

Morphemes

FREE MORPHEMES
BOUND MORPHEMES

Two Kinds of Suffixes

DERIVATIONAL SUFFIXES
INFLECTIONAL SUFFIXES
REGULAR AND IRREGULAR INFLECTIONAL
  SYSTEMS

TEACHING STRUCTURAL ANALYSIS

Purpose

AS A WORD RECOGNITION TECHNIQUE
AS CLUES TO THE MEANING OF UNKNOWN
  WORDS
AS AN AID TO WORD LEARNING
AS INTERESTING, CHALLENGING
  KNOWLEDGE ABOUT LANGUAGE

Timing

SOME LESSONS FOR BEGINNING READERS

Compound Words
Words with Inflectional Suffixes
Words with Derivational Suffixes
Words with Prefixes

WORDS WITH SUFFIXES: TWO ADDITIONAL
PROBLEMS

Spelling Changes
Changes in Pronunciation and Accent

EMPIRICISM AND RATIONALISM IN
CONSIDERING WORD STRUCTURE

SUMMARY

FOR FURTHER READING AND DISCUSSION

REFERENCES

Structural analysis, like syllabication, is a method that enables the reader to divide words that are not immediately familiar into smaller, manageable parts. Much of what is taught under the heading of structural analysis is derived from a branch of linguistics called morphology. *Morphology* is the study and description of word formation from meaningful parts called *morphemes.* In this section we present some facts regarding the structure of English words. In following sections some suggestions will be made for using these facts as the basis for word recognition.

DEFINITIONS

Morphemes

A morpheme is the smallest meaningful part of a word. There are two major categories of morphemes: free morphemes and bound morphemes.

FREE MORPHEMES

Free morphemes are English root words, such as *apple* and *walk*. They can usually appear with prefixes and suffixes, as in *coatless, recoat,* and *walked,* and they sometimes appear together as one word, as in *sometimes* or *carhop.* When a word is made up of two English root words, it is called a *compound* word.

English root words have approximately the same meaning when they appear alone or in combination with prefixes, suffixes, or other English root words; thus they are morphemes. They may appear by themselves as words; thus they are free morphemes.

BOUND MORPHEMES

Bound morphemes are meaningful word parts that appear in many words, but never appear alone as a word. The sound represented by s in *boys* and *trees* is a bound morpheme. The syllables *un-* in *unkind* and *unhappy* and *-er* in *worker* and *talker* are bound morphemes. They are word parts that have approximately the same meaning in many words where they appear (thus they are morphemes), but they never appear on their own as words (thus they are bound morphemes).

The bound morphemes in the example words are *affixes*—that is, they are added to base words to form new words. Affixes added to the beginning of base words are called *prefixes,* as in *unkind* and *resale.* Affixes added to the end of base words are called *suffixes,* as in *boys* and *worker.*

Another category of bound morphemes can be discovered by noticing the common element in such word lists as the following:

predict	inspection
diction	spectacular
valedictorian	spectator

The study of word history reveals that *dict* and *spect* are both derived from non-English words (Latin in these two instances), and they survive with approximately the same meanings in several English words. Thus they are classified as morphemes—meaningful word parts. They do not appear alone as English words; they appear with a prefix and/or a suffix, or they sometimes combine with other elements like themselves, as in *dictaphone* and *spectragraph.*

Because they do not appear alone, they are bound morphemes. But because suffixes and prefixes can be added to them and because they can combine with each other, they are considered *roots* or *root words.* A list of non-English roots appears in Figure 5.1.

♦ This would all be very simple if one had to deal only with English root words and affixes. English roots are free morphemes. Affixes are bound morphemes.

FIGURE 5.1
LIST OF NON-ENGLISH ROOT WORDS.

Latin Root	Examples
audire	audience, audition, auditorium
cedere	precede, succeed, exceed
dicere	predict, dictaphone, dictionary
phobia	claustrophobia, hydrophobia, agoraphobia
portare	import, report, transport
scribere	postscript, transcript, scribble

Greek Root	Examples
cyclo	cycle, cyclone, cyclist
graph	phonograph, autograph, mimeograph
logos	monologue, logic, geology
meter	thermometer, perimeter, metrical
phonos	phonics, phonograph, telephone
scope	telescope, periscope, microscope

What makes the discussion complicated is that non-English root words are like affixes in that they are bound morphemes, but they are like English root words because they combine together to make words and they combine with affixes to make words. It is easy to avoid this confusion by basing beginning lessons in word structure on words composed of familiar English root words and common affixes.

Two Kinds of Suffixes

DERIVATIONAL SUFFIXES

Suffixes serve two purposes in English. The difference between the two kinds of suffixes is determined by whether the suffix changes the function of the root word. For example, *predict* is usually used as a verb, as in sentence 1. By adding suffixes, new words

with different functions can be derived from *predict,* as in sentences 2, 3, and 4.

1. *I* predict *rain. (verb)*

2. *The* prediction *came true. (noun)*

3. *His* behavior *was* predictable. *(adjective)*

4. *Harry behaved* predictably. *(adverb)*

The suffixes added to *predict* to derive new parts of speech in sentences 2, 3, and 4 are called *derivational* suffixes. A list of derivational suffixes that appear frequently are listed in Figure 5.2.

INFLECTIONAL SUFFIXES

Other suffixes do not create new words with different functions. Instead, they "modulate" (Brown, 1973) the meaning of the root word without changing its basic function. Nouns may take plural and possessive inflection, as in sentences 5 and 6.

5. *One* boy *chased two* boys.

6. *One* man *took another* man's *hat.*

Verbs are inflected to show differences in tense. Examples of three English tenses appear in sentences 7, 8, and 9.

7. *I* walk *to school. (Indicative—often called "present" tense)*

8. *I* walked *to school. (past tense)*

9. *I am* walking *to school. (present progressive tense)*

Verbs are also inflected to agree with the subject in certain cases, as in sentence 10.

10. *I* go *to school and she* goes *to work.*

♦ It is often asserted that when you want to change a singular noun to plural, you add *-s;* and if you want to change an uninflected verb to past tense, you add

-ed. That assertion is usually true when you are re-ferring to written language, but if you stop to think about it, that assertion is not true in a large number of cases when you are referring to spoken language.

In spoken language, if you want to make *hat* or *cup* plural, you add /s/; but if you want to make *boy* or *pad* plural, you add /z/. Likewise, if you want to make *braid* or *defeat* past tense, you add /əd/; but if you want to make *play* or *hum* past tense, you add /d/ and if you want to make *laugh* or *pass* past tense, you add /t/.

FIGURE 5.2
LIST OF DERIVATIONAL SUFFIXES.

Suffix	Derivative
-y	rainy shiny
-ful	careful cheerful graceful
-ous	mountainous riotous
-er	farmer builder
-or	actor director
-ist	organist soloist
-tion	invention protection
-ness	sweetness greatness
-able	lovable movable
-ity	popularity polarity
-ive	excessive expressive

These differences in the pronunciation of inflec-tional suffixes depend on the final sounds of the word to which they are added. Since the inflectional system is such an integral part of English, we learn to utter the proper inflection for nouns and verbs without being conscious of the "rules" we are fol-lowing. That is why we can say that we add *-s* to nouns and *-ed* to verbs— even when we are refer-ring to spoken language and people know what we mean. More accurately, most people are not aware that what we have said is not always true.

Adjectives are inflected to show degrees of comparison, as in sentences 11, 12, and 13.

11. *Ann is tall.*

12. *Sue is* taller *than Ann. (comparative degree)*

13. *Mary is the* tallest *of the three girls. (super-lative degree)*

REGULAR AND IRREGULAR INFLECTIONAL SYSTEMS

Although the inflectional systems in English consist almost entirely of regular in-flectional suffixes, there are small sets of words that conform to irregular systems. The plural of *mouse* is not *mouses* but *mice*; the past tense of *take* is not *taked* but *took*. Other nouns and verbs that conform to irregular inflec-tional systems are listed in Figures 5.3 and 5.4. Notice that most of the irregular inflected forms of nouns and verbs in Figures 5.3 and 5.4 do not contain suffixes at all; they result from a change in the pronunciation of the root word.

TEACHING STRUCTURAL ANALYSIS

The brief look in the last section into the study of English morphology revealed many facts about the structure of English words, but it also led into some fairly complex concepts,

FIGURE 5.3
NOUNS THAT CONFORM TO IRREGULAR INFLECTIONAL SYSTEMS.

mouse	mice	woman	women
goose	geese	child	children
ox	oxen		

FIGURE 5.4
VERBS THAT CONFORM TO IRREGULAR INFLECTIONAL SYSTEMS.

bring	brought	tell	told
kneel	knelt	win	won
mean	meant		

such as the concepts of bound and free morphemes, of root words and affixes, of English and non-English root words, of prefixes and suffixes, of derivational and inflectional suffixes. Dealing with these concepts led into the consideration of word functions (parts of speech), regularly and irregularly formed noun plurals, and regularly and irregularly formed verb tenses.

In the course of a child's schooling, many of these facts and issues may become relevant to learning standard English usage in speaking and writing, to learning spelling, and to developing vocabulary. But many of the issues raised here are not directly useful in learning to recognize words. What aspects of word structure are useful as aids to word recognition? What other purposes are served by teaching structural analysis in the reading curriculum?

Purpose

AS A WORD RECOGNITION TECHNIQUE

For the purpose of word recognition, the study of word structure has much in common with the whole word technique. The point is to help students recognize word parts—prefixes, suffixes, and roots—on sight and to know how they are usually pronounced. A child who sees *nonreturnable* may not recognize it immediately; if he or she recognizes *non-* and *-able* as affixes, he or she is left with *return*. The child may recognize *re-* as another affix and *turn* as an English root. If through this process he or she recognizes a word he or she knows and that makes sense in the context, the child has used structural analysis for word recognition.

Notice nothing has been mentioned here about the meaning of *non-*, *re-*, and *-able*. It is presumed that the reader knows the meaning of the word *nonreturnable*, but does not recognize the word. In fact, consideration of the meanings of *re-* and *turn* would only cause confusion in this case, but recognizing *re-* and *turn* as familiar word parts, or morphemes, would be using word structure as a word recognition technique.

AS CLUES TO THE MEANING OF UNKNOWN WORDS

Structural analysis may be useful in figuring out the meanings of words that are unknown words for the reader—that are not in the reader's speaking or listening vocabulary. For example, knowledge of word structure may aid a reader in figuring out what *unquenchable* means in sentence 14..

14. *The first sign of his illness was his unquenchable thirst.*

The reader may recognize *un-* and *-able* as probable affixes and know how these affixes usually relate to the meanings of words. He or she may guess from this that *unquenchable* means that something could not be done to or changed about thirst. Whether *quench* is a familiar word or not, the reader may guess the actual meaning of the word from this sentence or from the larger context; but if he or she did not know the word *unquenchable* before this encounter, this process would not lead to recognition. One must know a word before one can be said to recognize it. The use of structural analysis for clues to the meaning of unknown words will not be discussed further in this chapter, but will be taken up again in Chapter 9.

AS AN AID TO WORD LEARNING

Many techniques for vocabulary development involve structural analysis. The biology teacher may refer to non-English roots in teaching the meanings of *hydrotropic* and *geotropic*. The reading teacher who is introducing the word *harmonious* before assigning a reading selection may discuss the fact that it is derived from *harmony* and related to the words *philharmonic, harmonic,* and *harmonize.*

In this case, word structure is used as an aid to learning the meanings of several presumably new words and is not taught primarily as a word recognition technique. This use of knowledge of word structure will be taken up in Chapter 9.

AS INTERESTING, CHALLENGING KNOWLEDGE ABOUT LANGUAGE

The study of morphology in English reveals many interesting facts that are of no apparent value as aids to word recognition, as clues to meanings of unknown words, or as aids to learning new words. For example, the reason *about* and *because* are stressed on the second syllable rather than the first (two-syllable words in English are usually stressed on the first syllable) is that the first syllables of these words were originally prefixes, and stress rarely falls on affixes in English words.

A second example of an interesting idea related to word structure is that the suffix *-less* appears to have the same meaning in *hatless* and *helpless,* but the meaning is not exactly the same. A hatless person is a person without a hat, but a helpless person is not a person without help. A helpless person is a person who cannot help himself.

If one loves the study of language, this kind of information is interesting and may increase one's love for the study of language. And learning such facts may inspire the love of the study of language in a person who is not particularly interested to begin with.

♦ If you do not see that these are four *different* ways structural analysis may be useful, or if you confuse the four ways, you may make some unwise teaching decisions. For example, you may want students to recognize the prefixes *re-* and *dis-* in such words as *retreat* and *disfigure* as a strategy for recognizing words students do not immediately recognize. But if you begin to discuss the meaning of *re-* and *dis-* in words such as *retreat* and *disfigure,* you are going to be in trouble.

It is interesting to talk about the stress pattern of *about* in terms of word structure. To introduce the possibility that unrecognized words beginning with *a* may be stressed on the second syllable because the *a* may have at one time been a prefix is madness. It could only confuse students struggling with word recognition.

Timing

As a student progresses from beginning reading through elementary school and beyond, the nature of words he or she encounters changes in terms of structure. In beginning material words are overwhelmingly one- or two-syllable English root words without prefixes or derivational suffixes. All the basic vocabulary lists confirm this statement. Inflectional suffixes (plural nouns and past tense verbs, for example) appear from the beginning, and therefore the first lessons in word structure usually treat inflectional suffixes.

Durkin (1980) suggests teaching both derivational and inflectional suffixes before prefixes on the grounds that English root words are more obvious when suffixes are added at the end than when prefixes are put at the beginning. That is, *play* is more apparent in *plays* and *player* than in *replay* (p. 402).

A reasonable principle to guide the introduction of later lessons on structural analysis for the purpose of word recognition is to teach suffixes, prefixes, and root words as they become frequent in reading materials and as the level of reading skill increases. Some examples of lessons in structural analysis for the purpose of word recognition follow.

SOME LESSONS FOR BEGINNING READERS

Compound Words

The concept a student must learn in order to use word structure for word recognition is that words can sometimes be divided into parts based on the meanings of the parts (in contrast to dividing words into syllables based on pronunciation). This concept can be demonstrated by using compound words composed of English root words that students already recognize. Exercises for teaching recognition of compound words through structural analysis are presented in Figures 5.5 through 5.9.

FIGURE 5.5
FLANNEL BOARD ACTIVITY.

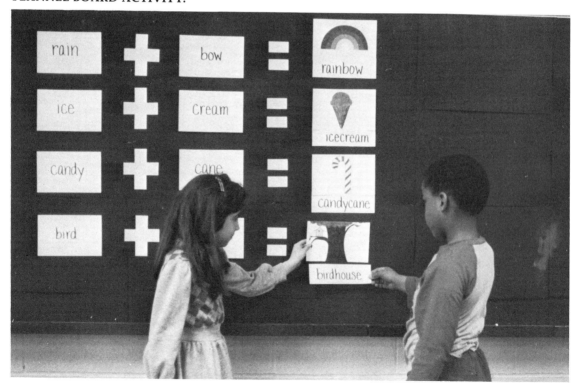

FIGURE 5.6
COMPOUND MATCH.
Directions: The words in columns A and B can be placed together to form one new word. Write the two words together under column C. Say the new compound word you have formed.

A	B	C
some	day	someday
school	house	
any	one	
air	port	
drive	way	

FIGURE 5.7
COMPOUND MATCH.
Directions: Each word under column A can be added to a word in column B to form a new compound word. Find the two words that go together and write the new compound word in column C.

A	B	C
grand	port	grandmother
school	mother	
tooth	house	
air	ache	
drive	way	

FIGURE 5.8
FIND THE COMPOUND.
Directions: Read each sentence. Underline the compound words you see. Draw a line between the two words in the compound word. The first one is done for you.

A. Grand/mother made us some cup/cakes.
B. The sailboat halfway overturned in the storm.
C. The schoolhouse was closed due to the snowstorm.
D. The basketball game that afternoon was exciting.

FIGURE 5.9
GAME ACTIVITY—JIGSAW PUZZLE PIECES.

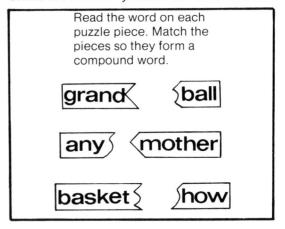

Words with Inflectional Suffixes

Hearing Inflectional Suffixes. An early objective of lessons in word structure is to make the learner aware of the auditory distinction between the inflected and uninflected forms of words and how these forms relate to meaning. This may be accomplished through exercises such as those presented in Figures 5.10 through 5.12.

Recognizing Inflectional Suffixes in Printed Words. Next, using previously taught words that are easily recognized, lessons can be devised to call attention to spelling differences between inflected and uninflected words by using exercises such as those presented in Figures 5.13 through 5.15.

♦ The presence or absence of inflectional suffixes is one of the most striking differences between dialects spoken in America. Labov (1970) observed

FIGURE 5.10
EXERCISE FOR HEARING INFLECTIONAL SUFFIXES.

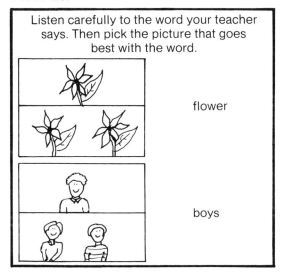

Listen carefully to the word your teacher says. Then pick the picture that goes best with the word.

flower

boys

FIGURE 5.11
EXERCISE FOR HEARING INFLECTIONAL SUFFIXES.

Listen carefully to the sentence as your teacher says it. Mark the picture that best goes with the sentence.

"Mark the biggest airplane."

FIGURE 5.12
EXERCISE FOR HEARING INFLECTIONAL SUFFIXES.

Listen carefully to the sentence as your teacher says it. Mark the picture that best goes with the sentence.

"The milk spills."

FIGURE 5.13
EXERCISES CALLING ATTENTION TO SPELLING DIFFERENCES BETWEEN INFLECTED AND UNINFLECTED WORDS.

Mark the sentence that goes with the picture in the gray box.

"I see the smallest pig."
"I see the biggest pig."

that the black youngsters he studied tended to pronounce the verbs in the following three sentences identically. That is, the inflectional suffixes on the verb *jump* in sentences 2 and 3 tended not to appear in the speech of these youngsters.

1. *They jump back quickly.*
2. *He jumps back quickly.*
3. *He jumped back quickly.*

In fact, the past tense morpheme would tend not to appear in the speech of most Americans in sentence 3. Whether inflectional suffixes appear in speech or not depends in part on the speech sounds before and after the suffixes—and that is true in all dialects, including standard English.

From a reading teacher's point of view, the important thing is that the student understands there is a difference in the *meanings* of sentences 2 and 3. Whether or not the student *pronounces* the inflection is not a reading problem—if it is a problem at all. The question of dialects and whether or not they interfere with learning to read is taken up again in greater detail in Chapter 10.

FIGURE 5.14
MULTIPLE-CHOICE QUESTIONS REQUIRING THE PUPIL TO PUT PROPER ENDINGS ON WORDS.
Directions: Read the following sentences. Circle the word that has the correct ending for the sentence.

1. The girl was (look, looks, looking) out the door.

2. That is (funny, funnier, funniest) than the last joke you told.

3. The boys came (late, later, latest) than their scoutmaster.

FIGURE 5.15
WORD WHEEL—EXERCISE CALLING ATTENTION TO SPELLING DIFFERENCES BETWEEN INFLECTED AND UNINFLECTED WORDS.

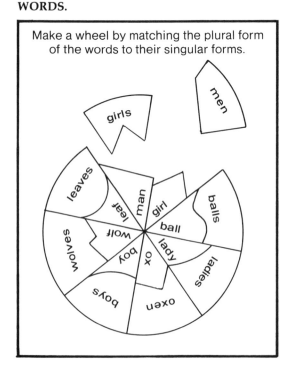

Make a wheel by matching the plural form of the words to their singular forms.

Words with Derivational Suffixes

As the need arises, students can be taught to recognize derivational suffixes by using exercises such as those presented in Figures 5.16 through 5.19.

FIGURE 5.16
SUFFIX STRIPS.

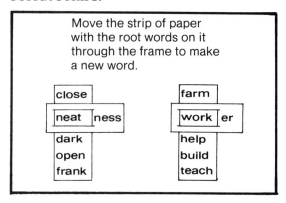

Move the strip of paper with the root words on it through the frame to make a new word.

FIGURE 5.17
A BULLETIN BOARD FOR WORKING WITH DERIVATIONAL SUFFIXES.
Directions: See how many sentences you can complete by using root words in the first slot and a root word with a suffix in the second slot.

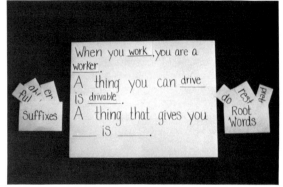

FIGURE 5.18
SENTENCE PRACTICE.
Directions: Write three sentences using the three different forms of the root word *joy*.

joyful   joyfully   joyous

Sample sentences:

1. Henry was a joyful child.

2. Mary laughed joyfully.

3. Christmas is a joyous occasion.

Similar exercises could be constructed using additional root words and adding suffixes to them.

Words with Prefixes

Recognition of prefixes can be taught by using exercises such as those presented in Figures 5.20 through 5.23.

FIGURE 5.19
BASKETBALL MATCH.
Directions: Match as many basketballs (suffixes) to basketball hoops (root words) as you can to form new words.

FIGURE 5.20
EXERCISE FOR TEACHING RECOGNITION OF PREFIXES.

FIGURE 5.21
WORD MATCH.
Directions: Match the root word in column A with a word containing that root in column B.

A	B
happy	dislike
use	disappear
like	unhappy
appear	repack
pack	disuse

FIGURE 5.22
BUILDING NEW WORDS.
Directions: The prefix *un* means "not." Place the prefix *un* at th beginning of the following words and give their new meanings.

_____ known   _____ healthy

_____ able   _____ interesting

_____ important

FIGURE 5.23
SENTENCE SENSE.
Directions: Read the following sentences. Cross out the word that does not belong.

1. Ann (tied, untied) the string to see what was inside the box.
2. It is (safe, unsafe) to play with matches.
3. The poor boy had not eaten in weeks and was very (healthy, unhealthy).

WORDS WITH SUFFIXES: TWO ADDITIONAL PROBLEMS

Spelling Changes

When suffixes are added to English root words, the resulting word is often spelled root plus suffix, as in *cloudy*, *walks*, and *warmer*. But when root words have certain spellings, there are slight spelling changes. The plural of *match* is *matches* (the plural morpheme is spelled *-es* rather than *-s*) and the plural of *half* is *halves*. In some words ending in *y*, the *y* is cahnged to *i* before adding a suffix, as in *happier*, *puppies*, and *married*. In root words ending in silent *e*, the *e* is usually dropped before adding a suffix, as in *taking*, *baker*, and *operation*. In some words ending in a single consonant letter, the final consonant is doubled before adding a suffix, as in *winner*, *digging*, and *skipped*.

These spelling changes are not haphazard; the conditions under which they occur are presented in Figures 5.24 through 5.28. Although it is useful to learn when these spelling changes occur in order to become a good speller, the task of the reader is to recognize roots and suffixes in words where these spelling changes appear. In other words, the job of readers is to realize that when they do not recognize a word like *digging*, they should sus-

FIGURE 5.24
CONDITIONS FOR ADDING SUFFIXES AND SUBSEQUENT SPELLING CHANGES.
If a word ends in *x*, *ss*, *sh*, or *ch* or *z*, we usually add *es* to make the plural form of the word.

church	churches	dish	dishes
glass	glasses	fizz	fizzes

FIGURE 5.25
CONDITIONS FOR ADDING SUFFIXES AND SUBSEQUENT SPELLING CHANGES.
When a word ends in silent *e*, we drop the *e* before adding a suffix that begins with a vowel.

like	liked	love	loved
write	writer	skate	skater
trace	tracing	make	maker

FIGURE 5.26
CONDITIONS FOR ADDING SUFFIXES AND SUBSEQUENT SPELLING CHANGES.
When a word ends in a single consonant preceded by a short vowel sound, we usually double the consonant before adding a suffix that begins with a vowel.

tag	tagged	hop	hopped
fat	fatter	swim	swimming
bat	batter	chop	chopping
rip	ripped	sip	sipped

FIGURE 5.27
CONDITIONS FOR ADDING SUFFIXES AND SUBSEQUENT SPELLING CHANGES.
When a word ends in *y* after a consonant, change the *y* to *i* before adding the ending.

puppy	puppies	cherry	cherries
marry	marries	penny	pennies

FIGURE 5.28
CONDITIONS FOR ADDING SUFFIXES AND SUBSEQUENT SPELLING CHANGES.
When a word ends in *f*, we sometimes change the *f* to *ve* and add *s*.

calf	calves	ourself	ourselves
hoof	hooves	thief	thieves
loaf	loaves		

FIGURE 5.29
SHIFTS IN STRESS PATTERNS RESULTING FROM ADDING SUFFIXES.

symbol	symbolic	trivial	triviality
patriot	patriotic	conscience	conscientious
popular	popularity	pretense	pretentious

pect that *-ing* is a suffix and that the root is not *digg* but *dig*. When they do not recognize a word like *crazier*, they should suspect that *-er* is a suffix and that the root word is not *crazi* but *crazy*.

Changes in Pronunciation and Accent

When words are created by adding suffixes to root words, the root word is often pronounced the same in both its original and its derived form, as in *delerious* and *deleriousness*. Frequently, however, the accent pattern and even the pronunciation of the root word changes in a derived form, as in *courage* and *courageous*.

Some examples of shifts in accent and resulting changes in pronunciation are presented in Figure 5.29. Once again, it is well to remember that the principal task of the reader is to recognize known words. Suppose a reader does not recognize a word like *symbolic*, but suspects that *-ic* is a suffix and then recognizes *symbol*. If the reader knows the word *symbolic*, he or she will undoubtedly recognize it and know how to pronounce it. For this reason, explicit lessons in shifts in stress patterns resulting from adding certain affixes are taught late in the reading program, and taught as interesting facts about language, rather than as a word recognition skill.

EMPIRICISM AND RATIONALISM IN CONSIDERING WORD STRUCTURE

Osburn (1954) suggests that if one teaches the fifteen most common first and last syllables, children will recognize the first and last syllables of numerous common words. Advocates of teaching word structure point out that if one teaches the most common prefixes and suffixes and roots, children will recognize parts of numerous common words. These approaches emphasize teaching frequently encountered parts and presume that recognition of wholes will result from recognition of parts. The emphasis on frequency and part-to-whole learning places these approaches under the empiricist sphere of influence.

Cunningham (1975, 1978, and 1979) suggests that when children learn a store of words, they will begin to recognize common syllables, affixes, and roots and will learn to recognize momentarily unrecognized words by comparing and contrasting word parts in known words and the unrecognized word. Therefore, Cunningham emphasizes teaching wholes and presumes that recognition of parts will result from knowledge of wholes. The emphasis on whole-to-part learning and on the learner's aggressive discovering patterns in words place this approach under the rationalist sphere of influence.

Once again, in considering word structure one discovers contrasting views that are identified with empiricist and rationalist schools of learning theory.

SUMMARY

The branch of linguistics that studies word parts is called morphology. Morphology is the study of how words are formed from meaningful parts. A morpheme is the smallest meaningful word part. Free morphemes are English root words such as *window* and *walk.*

Bound morphemes are meaningful word parts that appear in many words, but do not appear alone as words. One category of bound morphemes is made up of affixes; affixes are added to root words to form new words. *Un-* in *unkind* and *-er* in *worker* are affixes. Affixes that appear before root words are called prefixes. Affixes that are added after root words are called suffixes.

Non-English root words such as *dict* in *diction* and *predict* comprise another category of bound morphemes. Non-English root words combine with affixes (as in *diction*) or with each other (as in *phonograph*) to form words.

Derivational suffixes change the function of a word. For example, the noun *boy* is changed to an adjective through adding the derivational suffix *-ish* to form *boyish.* Inflectional suffixes "modulate" the meaning of words without changing their function. For example, inflectional suffixes signal plural and possessive on nouns, tense on verbs, and degrees of comparison on adjectives.

The inflectional system in English is made up almost entirely of regular inflectional suffixes, but there are some irregular inflected forms. For example, the regular plural suffix is *-s*, but the plural of *mouse* is *mice* and the plural of *man* is *men.*

Four purposes are served by teaching students about word structure. (1) Recognizing parts of words often enables a reader to recognize a word he or she did not recognize immediately. (2) Recognizing parts of a word and knowing what those parts frequently mean sometimes enables a reader to guess at the correct meaning of a word he or she does not recognize. (3) Teaching the meanings of word parts is often used as a technique for teaching new words to students. (4) Finally, there is a great deal that is interesting about language that comes under the heading of word structure. Helping children to develop an interest in the study of language is a goal of reading teachers.

Teaching word structure usually begins with teaching about compound words made of English root words the children recognize. Inflectional suffixes are taught next for two reasons. (1) It is believed that familiar root words are more recognizable when suffixes are added to them than when prefixes are placed before them. (2) Inflectional suffixes appear in the very earliest reading material.

Students are usually taught to recognize inflectional suffixes on spoken words and then to recognize them in print. Children are taught to recognize derivational suffixes and prefixes as they begin to appear in reading materials frequently enough to merit attention.

One complication that arises in teaching children to recognize suffixes is that the spelling of English root words sometimes changes when a suffix is added. A second problem is that the stress pattern and pronunciation of root words sometimes changes when a suffix is added. These spelling, stress, and pronunciation changes are not haphazard. The spelling pattern may be taught as part of the spelling curriculum. Students should be made aware that when they recognize a root plus a suffix, it may be a word they know but one that is not pronounced exactly like the root word.

Some advocates of teaching word structure argue that teaching children to recognize the most common affixes will help them to recognize the thousands of words that contain these common affixes. This is a bottom-up, part-to-whole approach characteristic of the empirical sphere of influence. Other advocates of teaching word structure believe that through learning to recognize many common words, students will discover frequently appearing word parts and apply their discovered knowledge in future recognition strategies. This is a top-down, whole-to-part approach characteristic of the rationalist sphere of influence.

FOR FURTHER READING AND DISCUSSION

When Is a Prefix Not a Prefix?

In the discussions cited below, Durkin and Stotsky discuss prefixes in terms that are not used in this chapter.

Durkin, D. *Strategies for Identifying Words*. Boston: Allyn and Bacon, 1976.
Stotsky, S. L. Teaching prefixes: Facts and fallacies. *Language Arts*, 54 (1977), 887–90.

Durkin refers to "active prefixes" and "absorbed prefixes." She defines absorbed prefixes as syllables that originally functioned as prefixes but no longer do. Her examples are the *a-* in *above* and the *be-* in *between*. She does not define active prefixes, but some of her examples are the *un-* in *unhappy* and the *non-* in *nonstop*.

Stotsky makes a distinction between prefixes and "historical or etymological elements." Prefixes are dependent meaning-bearing elements attached to independent words. Etymological elements may appear to be prefixes, but they are not attached to independent words. The *in-* in *incorrect* is a prefix. The *in* in *inspect* is an etymological element. Read Stotsky and Durkin, pages 27–31.

1. Discuss Durkin's distinction between active prefixes and absorbed prefixes in terms of bound morphemes, free morphemes, non-English root words, and English root words.

2. Discuss Stotsky's definition of prefix and etymological elements in terms of bound morphemes, free morphemes, non-English root words, and English root words.

3. Which term do you think is best to describe word parts like the *in-* in *inspect* and the *be-* in *between*: historical element, etymological element, or absorbed prefix? What concept do all three terms refer to?

4. Durkin suggests that bright children might "profit from a careful study of absorbed prefixes" (p. 28). Regarding other children, she writes: "What *is* necessary for each child is, first, the ability to identify words like *above* and *between* and, second, an understanding of their meanings. Going beyond these essentials can lead to problems, especially with children who are not overly bright" (p. 27). Discuss this advice in terms of the material in this chapter under "Teaching Structural Analysis."

5. Stotsky comments that older elementary students should have little trouble discovering when a word contains a prefix and when it contains an etymological element. *Dis-* in *disturb* is an etymological element because *-turb* is not an English root word. *De-* in *delight* is an etymological element because *-light* is not an English word *in the sense required*. That is, the *-light* in

delight is not the English word *light* because its meaning is different. *Pre-* in *preheat* is a prefix because *heat* is an English word. Relate this discussion to the section in this chapter entitled "Teaching Structural Analysis."

More about Suffixes

The following classic study examines 90 derivational suffixes.

Thorndike, E. L. *The Teaching of English Suffixes.* New York: Bureau of Publications, Teachers College, Columbia University, 1941. Reprinted, New York: AMS Press, 1972.

Four kinds of data are reported for each suffix: (1) The frequency of the words containing the suffixes. (2) An analysis score, which is an estimate of how recognizable the suffix is when it appears in a word. For example, *-ness* in *carefulness* is rated 100 percent; *-ic* in *boric* is rated near zero. (3). An inference score, which is an estimate of the likelihood that a student will guess the meaning of a word if he or she recognizes the suffix and knows the root word. For example, *structureless* is rated 100 percent; *unction* is rated near zero. (4) The number of different meanings the suffix represents in the sample.

1. Relate the four kinds of data (frequently, analysis score, inference score, and number of different meanings) concerning suffixes to the four reasons for teaching structural analysis stated in this chapter in the section "Purposes."
2. What data in the Thorndike study would be relevant to the question of when to introduce particular suffixes into the curriculum—that is, the question addressed in this chapter in the section entitled "Timing?"
3. Look at this study and try to decide what suffixes you would want to teach for the purpose of word recognition. For example, *-most* as in *topmost* is given an analysis score of 99, but it appears in only 23 words and most of these words are very rare. Thorndike's advice: "The less said about *-most* the better" (p. 54). In another example, *-al* as in *cultural* is given an analysis score

of only 35, but it appears in 506 words, 21 of which are among the more common words in English.

4. Look up the derivational suffixes appearing in Figures 5.18 through 5.21 in the Thorndike study. Based on the analysis score and the frequency of the words containing the suffixes, decide which suffixes should be taught as part of the word recognition curriculum.

Differences Between Affixes and Syllables

Osburn's syllable count raises some questions about what one is doing when one teaches word structure.

Osburn, W. J. Teaching spelling by teaching syllables and root words. *The Elementary School Journal,* 55 (1954), 32–41.

Osburn identified initial, medial, and final syllables in the 14,571 words of the Rinsland (1945) list. He points out that recognition of the fifteen most common first syllables would enable a child to recognize the first syllable of 1,660 polysyllabic words on the Rinsland list, and that recognition of the fifteen most common final syllables would enable a child to recognize the final syllable in 3,038 polysyllabic words on the Rinsland list. (Although the title of this article mentions teaching spelling and does not mention reading, Osburn addresses the usefulness of his syllable count in reading as well.)

Of the fifteen most common first syllables identified in this study, eight often appear as prefixes combined with English root words. They are *re-, in-, de-, ex-, un-, dis-, en-,* and *pro-.* The remaining seven may appear as prefixes combined with Non-English root words.

Of the fifteen most common final syllables, six often function as inflectional suffixes. They are *-ing, -ed, -er, -es, -est,* and *-en.* Six may function as derivational suffixes. They are *-ly, -tion, -y, -ty, -al,* and *-ment.*

1. As far as word recognition is concerned, is there any advantage to teaching that prefixes and suffixes are anything other then frequently occur-

ring first and last syllables? Consider the affixes *super-* and *inter-* and *-ation* and *-able.*

2. Relate Osburn's suggestion to Cunningham's (1975, 1978, 1979) suggestions for the compare/contrast method of word recognition. (The Cunningham articles were suggested for further reading and discussion at the end of Chapter 4. You may want to refer to the brief description of Cunningham's proposal on page 104.)

REFERENCES

Brown, R. *A First Language: The Early Stages.* Cambridge, MA: Harvard University Press, 1973.

Cunningham, P.M. Investigating a synthesized theory of mediated word identification. *Reading Research Quarterly,* 11 (1975): 127–43.

————. Decoding polysyllabic words: An alternative strategy. *Journal of Reading,* 21 (1978), 608–14.

————. A compare/contrast theory of mediated word identification. *The Reading Teacher,* 32 (1979), 774–78.

Durkin, D. *Teaching Young Children to Read.* Boston: Allyn and Bacon, 1980.

Labov, W. The reading of the -ed suffix. In H. Levin and J. P. Williams, *Basic Studies in Reading.* New York: Basic Books, 1970, 222–45.

Osburn, W. J. Teaching spelling by teaching syllables and root words. *The Elementary School Journal,* 55 (1954): 32–41.

Rinsland, H. D. *A Basic Vocabulary of Elementary School Children.* New York: Macmillan, 1945.

CONTEXT

THE NECESSARY UNIFYING MEDIUM FOR ALL WORD RECOGNITION SKILLS

DEFINING THE USE OF CONTEXT

USE OF CONTEXT CLUES BY EXPERIENCED READERS

TEACHING THE USE OF CONTEXT CLUES

   Physical Context
   Picture Context
   Linguistic Context
   Teaching the Use of Context When the Need
     Arises

THE ULTIMATE GOAL: INTEGRATING CLUES TO WORD RECOGNITION

SUMMARY

FOR FURTHER READING AND DISCUSSION

DEFINING THE USE OF CONTEXT

A precise definition of what is meant by "the use of context" in a discussion of word recognition is not easy to come by. As Supreme Court Justice Potter Stewart said of pornography, "I can't define it, but I know it when I see it." In order to arrive at an understanding of what is meant by the use of context for word recognition, it will be useful to think about how one is able to guess what words are missing from the following sentences.

How would one explain the fact that most Americans would complete sentence 1 with the word *red?*

1. *Three cheers for the* _____, *white, and blue.*

How would one explain the fact that most people would complete sentence 2 with the word *little, small,* or perhaps *tiny?*

2. *A daddy is big; a baby is* _____.

Why would one expect most people to choose *wore* to fill the blank in sentence 3 instead of *reviled?*

3. *Alexandra always* _____ *a red dress.*
   a. *wore*
   b. *reviled*

Why would one expect most people to choose *slowly* rather than *walnut* to fill the blank in sentence 4?

4. *The ship sailed* _____ *into the sunset.*
   a. *walnut*
   b. *slowly*

Why would it be more startling for a person to choose *walnut* for sentence 4 than for a person to choose *reviled* for sentence 3? One might arrive at the following answers to these questions:

- The phrase "red, white, and blue" embodies a concept in our culture. When we are given part of the phrase, we recognize the concept and supply the missing part.
- Sentence 2 is an analogy. We realize that the missing word relates to *baby* in the same way as *big* relates to *daddy.*
- In sentence 3 we realize the missing word is a verb that states a relationship between a girl and a dress. *To wear* states a more typical relationship than *to revile.*
- And finally, in sentence 4 we realize that *walnut* cannot be the right word, because *walnut* is a noun and an adverb is needed.

These suggestions reflect the facts that we can guess missing words from context because (1) we have knowledge of the world, of our culture, and of our language; and (2) when dealing with a missing part, we recognize wholes and guess what is missing.

USE OF CONTEXT CLUES BY EXPERIENCED READERS

In sentences 1 through 4, a word has been replaced with a blank. When one uses context to recognize words in a normal reading task, however, the word is present. Examples of how experienced readers use context to recognize words follow:

The reader encounters the word *victuals* in sentence 5.

5. *The hungry cowboys crowded around the fire, tin plates in hand, as the smell of hearty victuals filled the crisp night air.*

He momentarily presumes (through phonics clues) that the word is pronounced /vik' tū els/; but that pronunciation does not suggest a word he knows. He guesses from context that it means "food," and he remembers a term for food that he particularly associates with cowboys. That word is pronounced /vit' els/. The spelling of *victuals* is close enough for him to conclude he has identified the word.

The reader encounters the word *apropos* in sentence 6.

6. *The jury could not help but notice that the witness's costume was not apropos to an appearance in court.*

Through phonics she arrives at the pronunciation /ap' rō pos/; but that does not suggest a familiar word. From context she guesses that the phrase *not apropos* means "not proper" or "not fitting," and realizes that the word is one she knows; it is pronounced /ap rə pō'/.

These examples were chosen because *victuals* and *apropos* are words not frequently seen in print, and therefore they may be "new" to many readers. Second, the correspondence between their spelling and pronunciation is irregular, and therefore they may not be recognized immediately by many readers.

On the other hand, the use of context clues for word recognition is not necessarily secondary to the use of phonics or structure clues. Context may induce such high expectations of what a word will be that the reader attends to the word only to check to see if the expectations are correct. An avid reader of Westerns, for example, might recognize *victuals* in sentence 5 without an instant's hesitation because through context he might be certain of what the word is before he comes to it.

The use of context in correctly identifying words so permeates the reading process that it is usually taught explicitly from the beginning of reading instruction, and all methods of word recognition are taught in combination with the use of context.

TEACHING THE USE OF CONTEXT CLUES

Physical Context

From their first encounter with print, children should be reminded as often as possible and in as many ways as possible that reading makes sense—that it fits in with what we know of the world and what we recognize as sensible language.

When looking at yesterday's experience story, the children are reminded that the words centered at the top of the sheet are the title of yesterday's story.

"What are the words?"
"Snow White."
"Yes. Let's see who can find those words later on in the story."

The words on the attendance board are children's names.

"Who can find his or her own name?"
"Who can find Jim's name and put it in the 'absent' column?"

The words on the calendar board are names of days and months. There are numbers here too.

"Today starts a new week. What day is it?"
"Who can find Monday *on the Calendar board and put it in 'Today's Date'?"*

These are all examples of using physical context to aid in word recognition. Further examples are calling attention to words labeling the clock, door, and desk and identifying words on the science table that were printed during a recent lesson. The point is that we expect certain words in certain places because of the meaning we have learned to attach to those places.

Picture Context

Children learn that sometimes words go with pictures. Teachers label children's drawings. Children learn sight words from picture word cards. Children write sentences to go with pictures. Children draw pictures to go with stories they have written. Many books have a fixed relationship between words and pictures, as in Figures 6.1 and 6.2.

Reminding children that the words they are trying to read "go with" pictures in some way gives them practice in using context for word recognition. The larger context (pictures) narrows the possibilities of what the words are and suggests what the words may be.

Linguistic Context

As children progress in reading, there are more and more occasions where physical context and pictures are not very useful, and they need to rely on the language of the text to help identify words they do not immediately recognize. But the principle remains the same. The unrecognized word cannot be just any word because not just any word would make

many people

many doors

FIGURE 6.1
BOOK PAGES SHOWING A FIXED RELATIONSHIP BETWEEN WORDS AND PICTURES.
(From James Steel Smith's *City Song*. New York: Holt, Rinehart and Winston, 1970.)

FIGURE 6.2
BOOK PAGES SHOWING A FIXED RELATIONSHIP BETWEEN WORDS AND PICTURES.
(From *Brown Bear, Brown Bear, What Do You See?* by Bill Martin, Jr. New York: Holt, Rinehart and Winston, 1970.)

sense: and context may suggest only a few words that would make sense in this place.

Examples of the use of context for word recognition were presented above with the words *apropos* and *victuals*. Teaching the use of this technique presents certain problems, because one cannot be certain which word a reader will not recognize, and it is very difficult to tell precisely what aspect of the linguistic context restricts word possibilities or suggests probable words. Therefore, lessons are constructed where blanks are substituted for words and where the clues to the identity of the missing words appear to be obvious.

For example, nouns are deleted before appositives, as in Figure 6.3; or words are deleted from similes, as in Figure 6.4; or words are deleted from a series of words with the same features, as in Figure 6.5.

In using context to identify a word one does not immediately recognize, however, one must take the spelling into account in arriving at the word. One might have guessed *grub* in sentence 5, but the spelling of the word rules it out. In this example, the word was recognized partly by guessing the meaning through context and partly by arriving at a pronunciation through phonics.

To make lessons in using context for word recognition more like the task of the reader who does not immediately recognize a word, lessons sometimes supply part of a word (a letter, syllable, or affix) so that the student has two systems to benefit from—and two systems that must be taken into account in arriving at the word. Examples appear in Figure 6.6.

Teaching the Use of Context When the Need Arises

Teachers should always be alert for opportunities to suggest the use of context for

FIGURE 6.3
NOUNS DELETED BEFORE APPOSITIVES.

_____, or men who travel in outer space, wear air-tight space suits.

The _____, a lizard that can change colors, makes an interesting pet.

The shoppers rode the _____, which is a moving staircase, to reach the second floor.

FIGURE 6.4
WORDS DELETED FROM SIMILES.

Mary had a little lamb whose fleece was white as _____.

The beautiful maiden's lips were as red as a _____.

She was as busy as a _____.

FIGURE 6.5
WORDS DELETED FROM A SERIES OF WORDS WITH THE SAME FEATURE.

1. The flowers were red, blue, and _____.

2. They ran, jumped, and _____ in the park.

3. They ate apples, oranges, and _____.

clues to word recognition. When a child does not know a word when reading orally or when a child asks the teacher what a word is when reading silently, the teacher can often help the child through questioning or by modeling. If,

FIGURE 6.6
LESSONS SUPPLYING PART OF A WORD (LETTER, SYLLABLE, AFFIX).

Our basketball t_____ won the game.

We had br_____d and butter.

He is the cap_____ of the ship.

She won a gold med_____ at the Olympics.

The baby drank from his bot_____.

They had to re_____ the house after the fire.

When she returned she began to un_____ her suitcase.

---

for example, the child does not recognize the word *vehicles* in Figure 6.7, the following scenario may take place:

TEACHER: Read the whole sentence and just say "mmm" for the word you don't know.

CHILD: He had no showroom so he parked both "mmms" in front of his store.

TEACHER: What did the father have that he parked in front of the store? What do you *park* on a street?

CHILD: Cars.

TEACHER: The word must mean . . . ?

CHILD: Cars.

TEACHER: Divide the word into syllables. What do you think the first syllable is?

CHILD: Vee Hi Kuls. Oh! It's *vehicles!*

Or the teacher might model the process:

TEACHER: Let's see. He parked both "mmm" in front of his store. The father has two cars

FIGURE 6.7
A PASSAGE WHERE CONTEXT MAY HELP WITH WORD RECOGNITION.

Automobiles played a large part in our family life. My father owned a drugstore in 1912, but he decided to become an Oldsmobile dealer on the side to make some easy money. To get the dealership he had to buy two cars, a blue sedan and a somewhat sportier red one. He had no showroom so he parked both vehicles in front of his store.

---

in this story, so it probably says he parked both cars. Let's see. I would divide that word—*v-e* (long *e*), *h-i* (long *i*), *c-l-e-s* (probably a word ending in *le* and the *s* is plural). *C-l-e* at the end of a word is probably "kel." That's "vee-hi-kel-s." Oh! Of course! It's *vehicles!*

THE ULTIMATE GOAL: INTEGRATING CLUES TO WORD RECOGNITION

In discussing word recognition, it is difficult for one to know whether to start or to finish with context, because context interacts with other word recognition skills from the very beginning. That is true for the most inexperienced beginner (as discussed above in connection with physical context clues and picture clues) and the most sophisticated reader dealing with the most difficult text. The fundamental questions regarding reading—what one teaches; how one learns; how one defines comprehension; how one describes the process of reading—all lead to the consideration of how successful readers utilize context.

Although teaching sight words, phonics, structure, and context can be thought of as separate activities, the goal of teaching reading is for the student to be able to recognize most words he or she encounters automatically and to use all the clues present (phonics, structure and context) when he or she encounters a word he or she does not recognize immediately.

According to Biemiller (1970), beginning readers' errors in oral reading demonstrate a heavy reliance on context and little reliance on graphic information (the spelling of the word) at first. However, successful readers soon begin to take graphic information into account and rely on both context and graphic information. Poor readers seem to continue to rely on context alone for a longer period of time. It follows that teachers should give attention to integrating the use of word recognition clues.

In the example above, it was shown how a teacher might help a child who is reading to recognize *vehicles* in Figure 6.7. Similar scenarios might be constructed based on the recognition of the words *apropos* and *victuals* in the contexts described earlier. In such examples, the teacher would lead the student through the process of employing all the clues available through questioning or modeling.

However, for such lessons to take place spontaneously takes a great deal of luck and considerable skill on the part of the teacher. The lessons can be planned, however, by the teacher who reads a passage, judges which words may not be recognized by the pupil, and plans which clues to emphasize in leading the pupil to recognize them.

For example, if one were going to assign a fifth-grade class to read the passage in Figure 6.7, one might expect the majority of the words to be recognized as sight words, but that some students would not immediately recognize some of the following words: *automobiles, drugstore, Oldsmobile, dealer, dealership, sedan, sportier,* and *vehicles.* In questioning students or in modeling the process, one might stress clues for each word in order of usefulness, as listed below:

— *automobiles*—structure, phonics, context (Note that strong context clues come much later in the passage. One must read ahead to get to them.)
— *drugstore*—structure, phonics, context
— *Oldsmobile*—structure, context, phonics
— *dealer*—structure, phonics, context
— *dealership*—structure, phonics, context
— *sedan*—phonics, context
— *sportier*—structure, phonics, context (very weak)
— *vehicles*—context, phonics, structure

♦ It would be good exercise to stop and think out the scenario that might take place if you were the teacher and if a fifth-grader in your class "got stuck" on one of the words in this passage. You might try this exercise for several of the words suggested and discuss the exercise with classmates who have also tried it.

A teacher who creates such lessons must keep in mind that they are based on predictions of which words will cause trouble and which clues will be most salient for the students reading the passage. A particular child may recognize *vehicles* immediately and get stopped by *somewhat.* Another child may arrive at the correct pronunciation of *sportier* through phonics and recognize the word without ever reflecting on the fact that this word is related to the words *sport* and *sporty.*

The purpose of lessons in integrating clues to word recognition is to teach the child to use everything that is handy, rather than to dictate that structure will be referred to here and context will be referred to there.

SUMMARY

In general we think of using context for word recognition in terms of what experienced readers do when they encounter a word they do not recognize. Experienced readers rely on their knowledge of the world, of culture, and of language to arrive at an idea of what the word means and how it functions in the sentence. From their understanding of the whole, they make inferences about the missing part (the unrecognized word).

They are aided in their inference making by the presence of the word. Through applying structural analysis, syllabication, and phonics, they are also able to make inferences about how the word is pronounced. All these sources interact to enable the experienced reader to recognize words.

Teaching the use of context may proceed from the use of physical context (the child knows the words in a certain place are names of days of the week, for example) to the use of picture clues, and finally to the use of linguistic context alone. At every stage the children are reminded that when they think they recognize a word, they should ask themselves whether the word makes sense in that context and whether the pronunciation of the word is suggested by the printed word in question.

Because one cannot predict which words any child will not immediately recognize, blanks are sometimes used to replace words, and children are taught how to arrive at the identity of the word that belongs in the blank through using context. Sometimes parts of the deleted words are supplied so that the students learn to use both spelling and context

clues and so that they learn that the word they seek must be compatible with both the linguistic context and the spelling.

Teachers should always be alert to teach the use of context for word recognition as the need arises. Asking leading questions or modeling the process are suggested as ways of teaching the use of context for word recognition. However, incidental teaching of this kind cannot be relied upon exclusively. Many teachers preread passages and try to identify words students will not immediately identify. Through questioning or modeling, students are led to identify these words, and what the teacher believes to be the most useful source of word recognition is emphasized for each word.

Although the use of context for word recognition is formally presented in this book after the use of the whole word approach, phonics, and structural analysis, the use of context has been referred to repeatedly in earlier chapters. The use of context pervades all word recognition activity. Able readers use whole word recognition, phonics, structure, and context simultaneously; they are able to emphasize one source of information after another until they are satisfied that they have recognized the word—or that they are dealing with a word that is not familiar to them. This facility is the ultimate goal of all teaching of word recognition skills.

FOR FURTHER READING AND DISCUSSION

Classifying Context Clues

Categories arrived at experimentally. At the beginning of this chapter it was stated that it is easy to tell when someone is using context for word recognition, but it is not easy to analyze the process.

The following article will help you understand the difficulty of trying to define or describe the use of context for word recognition.

Ames, W. S. The development of a classification scheme of contextual aids. *Reading Research Quarterly*, 2 (1966): 57–82.

Ames inserted nonsense words in place of selected words in passages that had appeared in popular magazines and asked adults to read the passages and tell him what the nonsense words meant and how they decided what they meant. In analyzing 334 instances where readers arrived at the correct meaning of the word, he arrived at fourteen categories of contextual aid. The categories range from "clues derived from language experience or familiar expressions" as in guessing *faces* for the nonsense word in the expression "it was written all over their *herats*" to "preposition clues" in guessing *freeway* or *highway* for the nonsense word in the sentence "He sped northward along a California *cliotol*."

1. Read the Ames article and discuss the difficulty one has in stating precisely what a person does when he or she uses context to determine the meaning of an unrecognized word.

2. For each of his fourteen categories, Ames supplies three examples of text and readers' explanations of how they arrived at the meaning. It might be interesting to copy this article and cut the examples with their explanations out and paste each one on an individual card without any identification of which of Ames' categories they demonstrate. Mix the examples up and sort them into the fourteen category titles supplied in the article. Discuss the difficulties you encounter with your classmates.

3. Take these forty-two examples of text with their explanation and ask some students who are not familiar with Ames' categories to decide which

ones go together and how they would describe or name the categories they formed. Discuss the proposition that a precise definition of what is meant by "the use of context" is not easy to come by.

Commonsense categories. Several schemes for classifying context clues have been suggested as a logical first step in an instructional program. Several examples are cited below.

Artley, A. S. Teaching word meaning through context. *Elementary English Review,* 20 (1943): 68–74.

Deighton, L. C. *Vocabulary Development in the Classroom.* New York: Teacher's College, Bureau of Publications, 1959.

McCullough, C. M. Learning to use context clues. *Elementary English Review,* 20 (1943): 140–43.

Seibert, L. C. A study on the practice of guessing word meanings from context. *Modern Language Journal,* 29 (1945): 296–322.

Examine some of these classification schemes and discuss their usefulness in preparing materials to teach the use of context in early grades; middle grades; upper grades.

Discuss the merits of prepared lessons in using context, as suggested by these authors (and in this chapter), and teaching the use of context on a more incidental basis, as suggested in the section entitled "Teaching the Use of Context When the Need Arises."

CHAPTER

7

TEACHING WORD RECOGNITION SKILLS
PRACTICES, ISSUES, AND SUGGESTIONS

HOW IS WORD RECOGNITION TAUGHT?

Typical Lesson: First-Grade Phonics-Emphasis Basal Reader
Typical Lesson: First-Grade Eclectic Basal Reader
Differences Between the Lessons

DIFFERENCES OBSERVABLE IN THE LESSONS
SIMILARITIES IN THE LESSONS
DIFFERENCES IN THE PROGRAMS AND UNDERLYING ASSUMPTIONS

HOW ARE WORD RECOGNITION SKILLS LEARNED AND USED?

If Taught Phonics, Must Children Use It?
If Taught Context, Must Children Use It?

WHICH IS THE BEST APPROACH?

Straw Man Arguments

ATTACKS ON THE PHONICS APPROACH
ATTACKS ON THE ECLECTIC APPROACH

What Is Happening in Real Classrooms?
Research Findings
The Role of the Teacher

TEACHING AND LEARNING BY DEDUCTIVE AND INDUCTIVE METHODS

Differences and Similarities
Tradition Associated with the Methods

THE DEDUCTIVE METHOD AND THE EMPIRICIST TRADITION
THE INDUCTIVE METHOD AND THE RATIONALIST TRADITION

Which Is Better: Inductive or Deductive Teaching?

SUPPORT FOR THE INDUCTIVE METHOD
SUPPORT FOR THE DEDUCTIVE METHOD

ADVICE TO THE BEGINNING TEACHER

SUMMARY

FOR FURTHER READING AND DISCUSSION

REFERENCES

In this chapter and in Chapter 9 the actual practice of teaching reading as it is done in the vast majority of American classrooms will be examined and discussed. Although there are a great variety of published materials designed for use with teaching reading, surveys consistently find that the basal reading series are the predominant or exclusive tools of reading instruction. (Austin and Morrison, 1963; Spache, 1972). Therefore, this chapter will focus on issues inherent in teaching word recognition from basal readers. At the end of the chapter, the reader will be invited to examine some of the other widely used reading materials and to evaluate them in terms of the questions raised about basal readers.

There are over a dozen widely used basal reading series on the market, but they can be grouped into two categories: phonics emphasis and eclectic. The word *eclectic* means "selecting; choosing from various sources." We will discuss the differences between the two kinds of basal readers in this chapter.

HOW IS WORD RECOGNITION TAUGHT?

Here are two word recognition lessons from first-grade basal readers. The first is typical of lessons from widely used phonics-emphasis readers. The second is a typical lesson from a widely used eclectic reader.

Typical Lesson: First-Grade Phonics-Emphasis Basal Reader

The purpose of this lesson is (1) to present the spellings *ou* and *ow* and two sounds these letter pairs represent, and (2) to provide practice in analyzing words containing the spellings and sounds. In preparation for the lesson,

the teacher writes the sentence in Figure 7.1 on the board and prepares cards lettered *ou* and *ow*, as in Figure 7.2. The lesson proceeds as in Figure 7.3.

FIGURE 7.1
SENTENCES WRITTEN ON THE BOARD IN PREPARATION FOR THE LESSON PRESENTED IN FIGURE 7.3.

Do not growl, Spot.

I will pour the food into this bowl.

Spot found the food.

FIGURE 7.2
LETTER CARDS MADE IN PREPARATION FOR THE LESSON PRESENTED IN FIGURE 7.3.

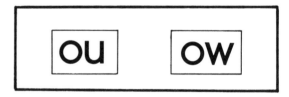

Typical Lesson: First-Grade Eclectic Basal Reader

The purpose of this lesson is (1) to teach the children to recognize the words *cat*, *get*, *stop*, and *help*; and (2) to teach the children to recognize unfamiliar words by relying on spelling and context clues. In preparation for the lesson, the teacher writes the sentences in Figure 7.4 on the board. The lesson proceeds as in Figure 7.5.

♦ A person who is not an experienced reading teacher might have difficulty seeing any differences

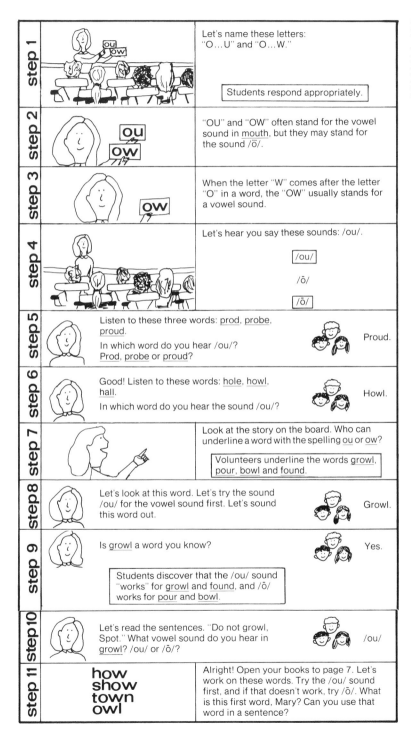

FIGURE 7.3
**TYPICAL WORD
RECOGNITION LESSON
FROM A FIRST-GRADE
PHONICS-EMPHASIS
BASAL READER.**

step 1

Let's name these letters:
"O...U" and "O...W."

Students respond appropriately.

step 2

"OU" and "OW" often stand for the vowel
sound in mouth, but they may stand for
the sound /ō/.

step 3

When the letter "W" comes after the letter
"O" in a word, the "OW" usually stands for
a vowel sound.

step 4

Let's hear you say these sounds: /ou/.

/ou/

/ō/

/ō/

step 5

Listen to these three words: prod, probe,
proud.
In which word do you hear /ou/?
Prod, probe or proud?

Proud.

step 6

Good! Listen to these words: hole, howl,
hall.
In which word do you hear the sound /ou/?

Howl.

step 7

Look at the story on the board. Who can
underline a word with the spelling ou or ow?

Volunteers underline the words growl,
pour, bowl and found.

step 8

Let's look at this word. Let's try the sound
/ou/ for the vowel sound first. Let's sound
this word out.

Growl.

step 9

Is growl a word you know?

Yes.

Students discover that the /ou/ sound
"works" for growl and found, and /ō/
works for pour and bowl.

step 10

Let's read the sentences. "Do not growl,
Spot." What vowel sound do you hear in
growl? /ou/ or /ō/?

/ou/

step 11

how
show
town
owl

Alright! Open your books to page 7. Let's
work on these words. Try the /ou/ sound
first, and if that doesn't work, try /ō/. What
is this first word, Mary? Can you use that
word in a sentence?

in these two approaches—but very important differences do exist.

Perhaps you would like to think about and discuss the differences between the two lessons before reading on.

Differences Between the Lessons

DIFFERENCES OBSERVABLE IN THE LESSONS

In the lesson from the phonics-emphasis reader (Figure 7.3):

1. The teacher presents letters in isolation (not as spellings of words). (step 1)
2. The teacher presents a letter-sound rule to the children before any written words are introduced. (steps 2, 3)
3. The children pronounce sounds in isolation. (step 4)
4. The children listen for sounds in words and identify words that contain target sounds in an auditory discrimination task. (steps 5, 6)
5. The children find words in the story on the board that contain the target spellings—a visual discrimination task. (step 7)
6. The children look at *growl* and try the /ou/ sound and are satisfied, because they recognize /groul/ as an English word. (steps 8, 9)
7. The children finally read the word *growl* in context and are asked again to reflect on the vowel sound of the word. (step 10)
8. More words having the vowel spelling *ou* or *ow* are presented in isolation for the children to recognize and use in sentences. (step 11)

In the lesson from the eclectic basal reader (Figure 7.5):

1. Words are presented, discussed, and recognized as parts of sentences, not in isolation. (steps 1, 3, 4, 5)

FIGURE 7.4
SENTENCES WRITTEN ON THE BOARD IN PREPARATION FOR THE LESSON PRESENTED IN FIGURE 7.5.

It is a lion.
It is not a cat.
He will go.
He will get the cat.
He will go.
He will not stop.
Dan will go.
He will get help.

2. Letters are discussed, named, and so on, as parts of words, not in isolation. (steps 2, 5)
3. Children are encouraged to rely on what the word must mean in the given context. (step 4)
4. Children are encouraged to rely on spelling clues to recognize the word. (steps 2, 5)

SIMILARITIES IN THE LESSONS

On the other hand, there are similarities in the two lessons that should not be overlooked.

1. Both lessons teach the children to rely on the relationship between English spelling and the sounds that spellings generally represent. That is, sooner or later they both teach phonics.
2. Both lessons present words in written context, sooner or later.
3. Both lessons assume the children have acquired a sight-word vocabulary.

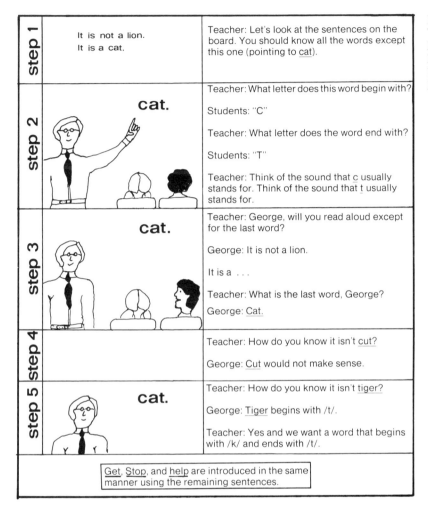

FIGURE 7.5
TYPICAL WORD RECOGNITION LESSON FROM A FIRST-GRADE ECLECTIC BASAL READER.

DIFFERENCES IN THE PROGRAMS AND UNDERLYING ASSUMPTIONS

Some differences that may not be obvious to people who are not experienced reading teachers are as follows.

Number of Words Introduced and Criteria for Choosing Words. In the phonics-emphasis lesson, many new words are introduced because they demonstrate and give students practice with the rule that is being taught. In the eclectic lesson, many fewer words are introduced. They are chosen because they are very frequent words and are therefore considered necessary sight words for even the "easiest" reading. They do not demonstrate a particular phonics rule.

Complexity of Phonics Rules Introduced Early in the Program. More difficult and more detailed phonic generalizations are taught at an earlier stage in phonics-emphasis readers than in eclectic readers.

Empiricist Versus Rationalist Traditions. The phonics approach builds from parts to wholes. It concentrates on the outer aspect of the reading process (letter-sound relationships) and proceeds to the inner aspect of the reading process (meaning). The assumption is evident throughout this lesson that each step of the process must be taught to the child.

There is an implication that the child is passive and does not actively search out stimuli and organize them in a meaningful way; instead, the lesson implies that the child performs each step as it is presented and waits for the next step to be presented.

The eclectic approach focuses first on wholes (sentences and meaning) and proceeds to analyze the parts (meaning of the "new word" and finally the letter-sound relationships in the new word). Therefore it focuses first on the inner aspect of reading (meaning) and proceeds to the outer aspects (letters and sounds and their relationships).

This lesson allows for the fact that the reader may make cognitive leaps. After the "new word" is recognized, "wrong words" are suggested so the child will be forced to reflect on the role of phonics and context in recognizing the word. This happens because there is an assumption that the child may have recognized the word without conscious reference to phonics or context.

Synthetic Versus Analytic Methods. The phonics approach is sometimes called a *synthetic* approach because it focuses on parts (letters and sounds) and puts the parts together (or synthesizes them) to recognize words and understand sentences. The eclectic approach is sometimes called an *analytic* approach because it focuses on wholes (sentence meaning, words) and later looks at parts (analyzes words into parts—letters and sounds) to

discover generalizations about how the parts are related.

HOW ARE WORD RECOGNITION SKILLS LEARNED AND USED?

Everyone agrees that the ultimate goal of teaching word recognition is the instant recognition of words in context. Advocates of the two approaches differ in the way they teach because of different assumptions about the way children learn. One assumption that teachers often make, and an assumption that ought to be reflected upon (but often is not), is that children learn what teachers teach. A discussion of the two lessons presented earlier in this chapter should show that this assumption is not necessarily accurate.

If Taught Phonics, Must Children Use It?

In the phonics emphasis lesson, the teacher writes the sentence "Do not growl, Spot" on the board in preparation for the lesson. It has been pointed out that the children are expected to recognize *do, not,* and *Spot*. It is also obvious from the lesson that the children are expected to know the usual sound represented by the initial consonant blend *gr* and the final consonant *l*.

The teacher begins the lesson by presenting the letters *ou* and *ow* and proceeds to identify the two sounds these spellings usually represent. She gives the students practice in recognizing these sounds in spoken words, in discriminating these sounds in spoken words, in finding words with these spellings. Finally, she calls attention to the word *growl* in the sentence on the board. Presumably, all the steps in the lesson lead up to recognition of the word *growl*.

How does the teacher know that certain children in the class did not recognize the word *growl* because of the initial sound and the context, or because they learned the word *owl* as a whole word from a picture book and made the connection between *owl* and *growl*? The fact is that the teacher does not know whether some children are relying on context or whether some have discovered a spelling-sound relationship on their own.

If Taught Context, Must Children Use It?

In the eclectic approach, the teacher writes the sentence "It is a cat" on the board and calls attention to the "new word" *cat*. She or he calls attention to the beginning and ending consonant letters and the sounds they usually represent. The teacher then asks a pupil to read the sentence and asks what the word is. Presumably, the teacher has enabled the children to recognize the word by causing them to consider the constraints of context and spelling. How does the teacher know that certain children in the class recognized the word *cat* because they know *at* and *rat* and made the connection between *cat*, *at*, and *rat*?

When the teacher says, "How do you know it isn't *cut*?" the proper response is "*Cut* wouldn't make sense." But some children may distinguish between *cut* and *cat* because they know them both as sight words or because they know the usual sound represented by *a* and *u* in words like *bat*, *mat*, *but*, and *nut*. Once again, the teacher does not know whether the child who gives the correct answer has arrived at that answer by the process implied by the lesson.

Realizing this fact does not help a teacher to know which method to stress or which basal series to use; but it should help a teacher to avoid wasting valuable energy insisting he or she has found the one correct system. It should also enable the teacher to recognize children who are arriving at the correct answers through alternative processes and to reflect on whether a particular child's process will carry him or her through to adequate reading skill. If they will, the lesson's goal is accomplished. If not, of course, in future lessons the teacher should take particular care that the child is attending to the process she or he is attempting to teach, rather than focusing on correct answers as criteria for success.

WHICH IS THE BEST APPROACH?

Straw Man Arguments

In discussing the relative merits of the phonics-emphasis approach and the eclectic approach, it is necessary to establish boundaries of what one is talking about. It is not difficult to find examples of any position that are so extreme as to be indefensible and to attempt to discredit the entire position by discrediting the extreme example.

In this chapter, the two approaches to teaching word recognition are defined as the approaches found in the widely used phonics-emphasis and eclectic basal series listed below. The reader is urged to examine one or two of these sets of materials from each of the two categories and to refer to what is in these materials when evaluating charges made about them and claims made for them.

The following series are frequently identified as phonics-emphasis basal readers:

— Economy
— Lippincott
— Open Court

The following series are frequently identified as eclectic basal readers:

— Ginn
— Harcourt Brace Jovanovich
— Holt, Rinehart and Winston
— Houghton Mifflin
— Laidlaw
— Macmillan
— Scott, Foresman

ATTACKS ON THE PHONICS APPROACH

Downing (1975) charges that:

Many children today are being confused by ill-conceived phonic methods and materials. These often overemphasize the coding method to the neglect of the communicative purpose of writing. This type of instruction misleads the beginner into believing that reading is decoding one set of meaningless visual symbols (letters) into another set of meaningless auditory symbols (phonemes). (p. 144)

Whether *many* children are exposed to the kind of materials described here is questionable. But it is certainly not true that the widely used phonics-emphasis basal readers are guilty of this charge.

ATTACKS ON THE ECLECTIC APPROACH

On the other hand, for many critics, the chief difference between phonics-emphasis and eclectic readers is that phonics-emphasis readers teach word recognition through phonics and eclectic readers teach word recognition through whole word look-and-say methods.

Rudolph Flesch (1979) has recently charged that if the authors of one of the most widely used eclectic readers were honest and plain-speaking, they would say to seventh- and eighth-grade teachers:

You probably don't know that the students in your class have been taught by the look-and-say method and don't know how to read. Many of them have never caught on to the fact that the letters stand for sounds. Please do the exercises in the back of the manual with them to help them learn to read. (pp. 2–3)

The reader is urged to examine one or two of the eclectic basal reading series listed earlier. To call these "look-and-say readers" is a misrepresentation. To imply that after six years of learning from these materials students would not know that letters stand for sounds is preposterous.

What Is Happening in Real Classrooms?

One should always respond to charges about outrageous practices by asking first what evidence there is that these practices actually exist anywhere. Over the years, several scholars have attempted to discover how prominent a role phonics has played in reading lessons in actual classrooms.

Russell (1955) examined the views of 220 primary teachers, intermediate teachers, and supervisors from 33 states on the topic of phonics teaching. The results clearly show that phonics is taught in a vast majority of classrooms, but exclusive attention to phonics occurs in practically none. Eighty-three percent of the respondents expressed the view that the word attack technique children find most useful is a combination of phonics, structural analysis, context, and sight recognition.

Austin and Morrison (1963) report that in 90 percent of the school systems visited, "Basal reading series which emphasize phonics as *one* of several techniques to be used in word identification" were in use (p. 29).

Research Findings

Numerous research projects have been conducted to discover whether the phonics-emphasis or the eclectic approach is the best method. The results of small-scale studies often favor one method or the other; but because the findings of such studies are inconsistent, they are of little help in answering the question.

Two major research efforts in the 1960s attempted to overcome the shortcomings of the small-scale studies. Chall (1967) attempted to reach a conclusion through a comprehensive review of the literature. Her conclusion was that "code emphasis" appeared to produce better results than the eclectic approaches current in the 1950s and 1960s. However, Chall's review of the literature has been criticized for not being exclusive enough—that is, she did not attempt to exclude poorly designed research from her survey.

The second research effort was a large-scale experimental effort funded by the federal government in 1964–65. It is usually referred to as the First Grade Studies (Stauffer, 1967). This research involved not only the phonics-emphasis and eclectic methods discussed here, but more extreme methods of teaching reading. These studies were followed up in second grade (Dykstra, 1968) and third grade (Fry, 1967; Hayes and Wuest, 1967; Harris et

al., 1968; Ruddell, 1968; Schneyer and Cowen, 1968; Sheldon et al., 1967; Stauffer and Hammond, 1969; Vilscek and Cleland, 1968).

A review of this extensive research reveals that:

1. There are no consistent advantages for any method when followed through third grade.
2. Combinations of programs such as basal readers, supplemental phonics programs, and individual reading programs (see Chapter 11) are often superior to single programs.
3. Other factors, such as characteristics of the neighborhood, school environment, quality of teaching, and student ability, are more important factors in determining success in reading than the method of instruction.
4. The number of children who fail to learn to read is about the same from method to method.

All methods result in a certain number of reading failures. The conventional wisdom is that if a child fails to learn to read using one method, a different method should be used. This is a further reason why it is desirable for reading teachers to remain open-minded about methods. When a child fails to learn by one's favorite method, it is sheer folly to refuse to try other methods that have been demonstrated to be effective with some children because of a dogmatic commitment to one method or a prejudice against another method.

The Role of the Teacher

A repeated finding in research that attempts to compare learning in classrooms is that the most important variable, and one that often overshadows methods, is the teacher.

This was one of the major conclusions of the First Grade Studies and related studies. Weikart (1973) compared a Piagetian preschool program to two other kinds of programs and found that when teachers were motivated, conscientious, and hard-working, the curriculum did not make a difference. Brainerd (1978), in reviewing preschool programs, concludes:

> There is a suggestion that the teacher, not the curriculum being administered, is what makes the big difference. To me, this suggests that we might do well to spend less time arguing educational doctrines and more time developing highly motivated teachers. (p. 295)

And Chomsky, who is the foremost figure in the resurgence of rationalist assumptions in the study of language and language learning (see Chapter 1), only once turned his attention to teaching reading when he wrote a chapter on how the study of phonology might contribute to research on problems of literacy. His remarks on teaching are as follows:

> [T]here is little reason to doubt that the dominant factor in successful teaching is and will always remain the teacher's skill in nourishing, and sometimes even arousing, the child's curiosity and interest and in providing a rich and challenging intellectual environment in which the child can find his own unique way toward understanding, knowledge, and skill. It is difficult to imagine that psychology or linguistics or any other academic discipline will make much of a contribution to this end; correspondingly, it may be that their contribution to education will be quite restricted. The final judgment on this matter must be that of the teacher in the classroom. More generally, it is quite clear that the professional psychologist, linguist, mathematician, and so on has no particular competence, as a professional, to determine the educational goals that provide the framework for the choice of a curriculum or the manner of its implementation. (Chomsky, 1970, pp. 3–4)

TEACHING AND LEARNING BY DEDUCTIVE AND INDUCTIVE METHODS

Figures 7.6 and 7.7 show two lessons in word structure that might be taught in fourth grade. In the first lesson (Figure 7.6), the deductive method is employed. In the second lesson (Figure 7.7), the inductive method is employed.

Differences and Similarities

Of course, the salient difference between these two lessons is that in the deductive method, the teacher presents the rule to the children and the rule is then applied to words. In the inductive method, words are presented that demonstrate the rule and children are led to discover the rule from the example words. The rule is then applied to new words.

♦ The phrases "rule—egg" and "egg—rule" may help you remember this distinction. "Egg" stands for "example" ("egg" being a play on the pronunciation of the first syllable of *example*.) In deductive teaching, one goes from the rule to examples; in inductive teaching, one goes from examples to the rule. Inductive teaching is often referred to as "the discovery method" because students are led to discover the generalization that one wants them to learn.

In both lessons, the teacher is quite clear on the rule to be taught. This is important to remember because the discovery (inductive) method is sometimes unjustly associated with haphazard goals and lesson planning. In both lessons, the students are expected to apply the rule to words not used in the lesson when the lesson is over.

step 1	When a singl a single vowel, adding		Teacher: Today we're going to work on some words whose spelling changes when a suffix is added. The rule is "When a one syllable word ends with a single consonant letter preceded by a single vowel, the consonant letter is doubled before adding a suffix beginning with a vowel."
step 2	fun funny hop hopped	get getting fat fatter	Teacher: Here are some examples: Fun; funny. Get; getting. Hop; hopped. Fat; fatter.
step 3		tub bag sun	Teacher: How would I spell these words if I add the suffix -y to them? Students: t-u-b-b-y Students: b-a-g-g-y Students: s-u-n-n-y
step 4	dot plan tip		Teacher: How would I spell these words if I add the suffix-ed to them? Students: d-o-t-t-e-d Students: p-l-a-n-n-e-d Students: t-i-p-p-e-d
step 5	hit let pin		Teacher: How would I spell these words if I add the suffix -ing to them? Students: h-i-t-t-i-n-g Students: l-e-t-t-i-n-g Students: p-i-n-n-i-n-g
step 6	mad red big		Teacher: How would I spell these words if I add -er to them? Students: m-a-d-d-e-r Students: r-e-d-d-e-r Students: b-i-g-g-e-r

FIGURE 7.6
A LESSON IN WORD STRUCTURE TAUGHT BY THE DEDUCTIVE METHOD.

Traditions Associated with the Methods

THE DEDUCTIVE METHOD AND THE EMPIRICIST TRADITION

The deductive method is the usual method in reading programs based largely on empiricist assumptions, including phonics-emphasis programs. There are several reasons for this.

This method is compatible with the view of the learner as a receiver of stimuli to which an appropriate response is expected. Reading skills are analyzed, isolated, sequenced, and

FIGURE 7.7
A LESSON IN WORD STRUCTURE TAUGHT BY THE INDUCTIVE METHOD.

step 1	I like fun. Pam is funny. Here is a bag. His shirt is baggy.	Teacher: Let's read these sentences and look at the underlined words. How is the word fun like funny and the word bag like baggy.
step 2	(fun)ny (bag)gy	Students: Fun is the root word fun plus the suffix y. Teacher: Let's circle the root words and suffixes. What is left over in each word? Where did the extra letter come from?
step 3		Students: You double the last letter when you add y. Teacher: Yes. Sometimes, when we add the suffix y to some words, we double the last letter. But not always. Let's look at these word pairs. Let's see what the difference is.
step 4	fun funny bag baggy sun sunny fruit fruity tear teary rain rainy	Teacher: Fun, bag and sun are one syllable words. Fruit, tear and rain are one syllable words. Fun, bag and sun end in single consonant letters. Fruit, tear and rain end in single consonant letters. What is the difference? Students: Fun, bag and sun are spelled with a single vowel letter but fruit, tear and rain are spelled with two vowel letters.
step 5	fun funny bag baggy sun sunny sand sandy string stringy mess messy	Teacher: Good! Let's look at the next list and see what the rule is. Students are led to discover that the root word must end in a single consonant letter.

In like manner the rule is derived for the suffixes -ed, -ing, and -er and finally the generalization is drawn that the rule works for suffixes beginning with a vowel letter.

presented when they are needed for the next stage. When the learner is ready, he or she is trained to attend to the appropriate stimuli and to make the appropriate response. The learner is then given practice in making appropriate responses.

The method begins with parts. In Figure 7.6, the student is directed to consider roots and suffixes, consonant letters, vowel letters, and so on, and is given a rule for putting suffixes and roots together. The method focuses first on parts that are brought together (synthesized) into wholes.

Empiricists view the learner as comparatively passive, waiting to be presented with stimuli and rules for organizing the stimuli and rules for making the proper responses. Empiricists focus on the outer aspects of language; they see learning as proceeding always from part to whole. It follows that empiricists teach rules before teaching words where such rules apply.

THE INDUCTIVE METHOD AND THE RATIONALIST TRADITION

The inductive method is the usual method in reading programs based on rationalist assumptions, including eclectic basal reading series. There are several reasons for this.

This method is compatible with the view that the learner is an active seeker and organizer of stimuli and an active discoverer of useful relationships. The method introduces new words in context (calls attention to meaning) and encourages the learner to rely on context and phonics simultaneously. The method focuses first on wholes (words) and proceeds to analysis of the wholes to discover parts (roots and suffixes) and to discover how the parts are related (the spelling rule).

Rationalists view the learner as active and aggressive, not merely responsive. Rationalists focus on the inner aspects of language (meaning); they see learning as proceeding from wholes to parts. It follows that rationalists teach whole words in context before they focus on the spelling rules that apply to those words.

♦ The fact that phonics-emphasis basal readers are based on empiricist assumptions and that eclectic basal readers are based on rationalist assumptions explains their differences much more fully and satisfactorily than the difference in emphasis in phonics teaching. The differences in emphasis in phonics teaching follows from the basic assumptions on which the programs are built.

The fact that phonics readers typically use deductive methods and eclectic readers typically use inductive methods follows from the same source: One is compatible with empiricist assumptions, and the other with rationalist assumptions.

The fact that phonics readers teach rules and then introduce words where the rule is used, whereas eclectic readers teach rules after a number of words where the rule is applied have been introduced follows from the same source: The former method is compatible with empiricist assumptions,

and the latter is compatible with rationalist assumptions. Figure 7.8 shows the relationship graphically.

Which Is Better: Inductive or Deductive Teaching?

SUPPORT FOR THE INDUCTIVE METHOD

There is considerable consensus among experts in the mainstream of educational thought favoring the inductive method of teaching, particularly for reading and language arts. For example, Farr and Roser (1979), commenting on a sample lesson, state:

The concept was presented so that learning was inductive. That is, the children were given a number of examples, and discovered for themselves the idea that objects and words began alike. Having children discover such relationships, as opposed to telling them, encourages them to seek other such relationships on their own. (p. 215)

And Durkin (1976) states:

Inductive phonics instruction is often recommended for children with the hope that it will foster a better understanding of generalizations, and further, that it will enable children to make their own systematic observations about written words. It is viewed then as a way of helping them learn how to learn. (p. 78)

However, it is important to notice that these two statements are undocumented; that is, there is no reference to research findings. In fact, there is no published research that clearly supports or refutes these assertions. One reason the inductive method is in favor today is because, as was pointed out in Chapter 1, the

FIGURE 7.8
HOW THE PHONICS-EMPHASIS APPROACH AND THE DEDUCTIVE METHOD GROW OUT OF EMPIRICISM, AND HOW THE ECLECTIC APPROACH AND THE INDUCTIVE METHOD GROW OUT OF RATIONALISM.

Empiricism	Rationalism
Focuses on outer aspects of language	Focuses on inner aspects of language
Focuses on how separate parts contribute to whole	Focuses on whole and how parts relate within wholes
Views language as perceived in parts that are added up to wholes (bottom-up)	Views language as perceived in wholes that are analyzed into parts (top-down)
Views the mind as a comparatively passive receiver of stimuli that attends to the most frequent or most intense stimuli	Views the mind as an active seeker and organizer of stimuli that will attend to stimuli because they are meaningful or fit into a perceived organization
In reading, focuses on perception of letters and words, relationship of print to sound, frequency of words as indicators of ease of learning, brings the atomistic and mechanical aspects of reading together finally to consider meaning	In reading, focuses on meanings and on wholes, analyzes wholes to consider perception of words and letters and the relationship of print to sound finally to consider mechanical relationships of parts
From Which Follows ↓	*From Which Follows* ↓
The phonics-emphasis approach to teaching word recognition	The eclectic approach to teaching word recognition
↓	↓
The deductive method	The inductive method

mainstream of thought in philosophy, psychology, and education is presently influenced by the rationalist tradition.

SUPPORT FOR THE DEDUCTIVE METHOD

There are, as a matter of fact, three reasons that recommend the deductive method.

Results. The first reason is that it does undeniably work. People do learn things that one tells them. The reader will remember that Piaget's theories (Chapter 1) of how young

children learn concepts rely heavily on maturation and self-discovery. But it has been demonstrated that even when dealing with the kinds of concepts Piaget studied, teaching rules does indeed result in learning (Beilin, 1964). Under certain conditions, rule instruction is superior to discovery for learning certain of these concepts (Botvin and Murray, 1975).

Efficiency. The inductive method is very time-consuming and can become laborious and boring. Notice that in the sample deductive lesson (Figure 7.6), all the necessary conditions of the generalization were presented at once: (1) one-syllable words; (2) ending in a single consonant letter; (3) preceded by a single vowel letter; and (4) suffix beginning with a vowel letter. In the inductive lesson, more time and energy was needed to present the first three conditions, and only the suffix *y* had been considered. The idea that this generalization applies to all suffixes beginning with a vowel had not yet been introduced.

♦ You might question whether presenting more in a shorter span of time means that students learn more in a shorter span of time. It is because this kind of question arises that the debate over which method is better has not been decisively answered.

Timing. The third reason is that, because the inductive method is time-consuming and relies on the students' being able to recognize several words where the rule applies before the rule is taught, rules are introduced late. This can result in introducing rules that are not very useful for word recognition.

For example, the spelling *oo* is pronounced /o͞o/ as in *book* in very few words. One would be hard pressed to think of a word outside the twelve listed in Figure 7.9 (other than words derived from a word in Figure 7.9, such as *woodwork*). Since several of these are frequent words and since the spelling-sound relationship is fairly reliable, this rule is taught early by the deductive method in phonics-emphasis readers. But one wonders if it is worth the effort to teach a rule about the vowel spelling-sound relationship represented by words in Figure 7.9 after four or five of the words have been learned by sight. There would not be many more than five other words where the rule applies.

Durkin (1976) observes that inductive phonics instruction may be viewed as a method of teaching children how to learn, but she further observes that if one evaluates

FIGURE 7.9
TWELVE COMMON WORDS IN WHICH THE LETTERS *OO* REPRESENT THE SOUND /o͞o/ AS IN *LOOK*.

book	foot	hook	took
brook	good	look	stood
cook	hood	shook	wood

phonics instruction strictly in terms of how useful it is when applied directly to decoding words, "Some combination of inductive and deductive teaching will be elected" (p. 78).

♦ This leads to a topic that has been discussed earlier in this book; that is, keeping your objectives clear.

Suppose students recognize *book, cook, good, look, took,* and *wood* as sight words. Would you teach that *oo* is usually pronounced /o͞o/ as in *look*:

1. As a phonics rule that will be useful in recognizing a large number of "new words"? That would be a poor use of time.
2. As a lesson in discovering spelling-sound relationships—or more broadly as a lesson in inductive thinking? That is a legitimate reason; but it should be kept clearly separate from the usual objective of phonics lessons—to facilitate recognition of "new words."

ADVICE TO THE BEGINNING TEACHER

As a beginning teacher of reading, one is sometimes not consulted about what materials will be available. Most beginning teachers will find two or more basal reading series available in the school system from which to choose. Of the mainstream basals discussed in this chapter, there is no clear evidence that one works better than the others. It makes sense to choose the basal that falls into the category (empiricist–deductive-phonics-emphasis, or rationalist–inductive-eclectic) that one finds most compatible with one's personality and intellectual commitment.

The evidence is clear that most teachers use a basal series as the center of their reading programs and supplement it with other materials and methods. Since some children's failure may be attributed to the fact that their learning style is not compatible with the learning assumptions of the program, it makes sense to choose at least some supplemental materials and methods from "another camp."

Both the deductive and inductive methods of teaching have been demonstrated to be effective. One's choice of a basal reader will influence the method most often suggested, but a teacher who is conscious of the differences between these methods can convert an inductive lesson into a deductive one, and viceversa. Which approach is used will depend on the teacher's objectives.

Finally, research has repeatedly shown that the quality of teaching is a far more important variable than materials or method. Arousing and nourishing a child's curiosity and "providing a rich intellectual environment in which the child can find his own unique way toward understanding, knowledge and skill" (Chomsky, 1970, p. 3) is not accomplished by a slavish acting-out of prescribed lessons or by a mindless enthusiasm for a given method. It is accomplished by understanding the many moving variables in the process of learning to read and by hard work and enthusiasm born of interest in the process and in the success of each child.

SUMMARY

Two lessons for teaching word recognition were discussed in this chapter. One lesson is typical of those found in phonics-emphasis basal reading series and the other is typical of those found in eclectic basal reading series.

The two differ in that in the phonics-emphasis approach, letters are presented in isolation; letter-sound correspondences are taught before words demonstrating the correspondences are learned; letters are presented as a visual discrimination task, and speech sounds are presented in words as an auditory discrimination task; the letter-sound correspondence taught is used to recognize new words; the students are reminded that the word they "sound out" must be a word they recognize—if it is not, the generalization probably does not apply to the word.

In the eclectic reader lesson, words are presented, discussed, and recognized as parts of sentences, not in isolation; letters and the sounds they probably represent are presented and discussed as parts of words in sentences, not in isolation; and children are encouraged to rely on phonics generalizations and context simultaneously to recognize words.

The lessons are similar in that both refer to phonics generalizations, sooner or later; both present words in context, sooner or later; and both presume the children have acquired a sight word vocabulary.

The lesson that is typical of the phonics-emphasis basal reader reflects the empiricist tradition in that it proceeds from parts to wholes in a stepwise progression. It concentrates on the outer aspects of reading and proceeds toward dealing with the inner aspects. The lesson that is typical of the eclectic reader reflects the rationalist tradition in that it focuses on wholes first and then proceeds to parts. The lesson allows for the possibility that the student will make cognitive leaps rather than incremental steps leading to word recognition.

The phonics approach demonstrated in this lesson is sometimes called the synthetic method because it focuses on parts and synthesizes them into wholes. The eclectic approach is sometimes called an analytic approach because it focuses on wholes and analyzes the wholes into parts to discover generalizations about how the parts relate to the whole.

Teachers tend to adopt a phonics-emphasis, synthetic approach or an eclectic, analytic approach because of their beliefs about the reading process and learning. However, one cannot be sure that a child who recognizes a word has arrived at that point through the process *as it was taught.* This fact should help teachers avoid being doctrinaire about what works and what does not work. It should also help teachers evaluate the effectiveness of their lessons; correct answers do not ensure that students are learning the process the teacher believes he or she is teaching.

Although there is no shortage of dogmatic pronouncements in favor of one approach and attacking the other, years of research have failed to show that the phonics-emphasis or the eclectic approach is consistently superior. A review of this research suggests that some children fail to learn to read, regardless of the approach, and that other variables such as the teacher's skill and commitment are more important than method. Therefore, it makes sense to spend less time and energy arguing which method is best and to spend more becoming committed teachers who have the knowledge and skill to teach reading through several approaches.

Two lessons (Figures 7.6 and 7.7) were presented showing how the deductive and inductive methods are used to teach a lesson related to structural analysis. In the deductive method, children are taught rules and then taught to apply the rules to words. In the inductive method, the children are presented a list of words and led to discover the rule that applies to the words on the list. In both lessons, however, the teacher is quite clear on what rule is being taught and in both lessons the students are expected to apply the rule to words that are likely to be "new"—that is, not sight words.

The deductive method tends to appear regularly in phonics-emphasis programs because both the phonics-emphasis program and the deductive method rely on empiricist assumptions. Empiricism tends to view the learner as relatively passive and focuses on parts first. This is compatible with teaching small steps to the learner in a predetermined order.

The inductive method appears regularly in eclectic programs because both eclectic programs and the inductive method rely on rationalist assumptions. Rationalism tends to view the learner as aggressive and focuses on wholes first. This is compatible with presenting whole words and helping the learner to discover generalizations that apply to parts of the words.

There is considerable sentiment in favor of the inductive method of teaching reading because it is believed that this method not only teaches the lesson at hand, but helps children to learn a technique for approaching problems. However, the deductive method has some characteristics that recommend it as well. It works, people do learn from being told. Second, it is usually more direct, and therefore less time-consuming. Finally, in regard to teaching word recognition, children can learn a rule before they recognize any word to which the rule applies. Therefore, the deductive method permits one to introduce rules earlier, perhaps when they are useful as tools for word recognition. Since each method offers its own advantages, it is advisable to use both.

Most reading teaching is done using basal readers. If one is going to use a basal series, one ought to be aware of which series are phonics-emphasis and which series are eclectic and choose the series compatible with one's beliefs and intellectual commitment. However, teachers often supplment the basal reading program with other materials. Since some children will undoubtedly experience difficulties with whatever approach is adopted, supplementary materials that represent the point of view not taken in the basal program are a good idea.

Basal programs tend to emphasize deductive or inductive teaching methods. There are advantages to both methods. Teachers who understand the two methods can convert an inductive lesson to a deductive lesson, and vice-versa.

The teacher's knowledge, skill, commitment, and hard work are the most important ingredients in successful teaching. In this chapter, the assumptions on which several programs and teaching methods rest have been examined. The programs and methods have been discussed. This kind of knowledge is one prerequisite to good teaching. Skill is acquired through experience and keeping an open mind. Sensitivity to the great responsibility teachers bear toward their students and the pleasure teachers find in helping children learn to read are sources of motivation for commitment and hard work.

FOR FURTHER READING AND DISCUSSION

Other reading programs have been suggested to replace the basal programs discussed in this chapter. Read the following materials (or examine them) and answer the following questions: Is the recommended approach based on the empiricist or the rationalist assumption? Is the approach largely deductive or inductive? What is the role of the teacher as leader, planner, and model?

Language Experience Approach

Allen, R. V., and C. Allen. *Language Experiences in Reading: Teachers' Source Book.* Chicago: Encyclopaedia Britannica Press, 1966.

Stauffer, R. G. *The Language Experience Approach to the Teaching of Reading.* New York: Harper & Row, 1970.

Veatch, J., F. Sawicki, G. Elliot, E. Flake, and J. Blakey. *Key Words to Reading: The Language Experience Approach Begins.* Columbus, OH: Charles E. Merrill, 1979.

Individualized Reading Program

Veatch, J. *Reading in the Elementary School,* 2nd ed. New York: John Wiley & Sons, 1978.

Augmented Alphabet

Mazurkiewicz, A. J. The initial teaching alphabet (augmented Roman) for teaching reading. In A. J. Mazurkiewicz, *New Perspectives in Reading Instruction.* New York: Pitman, 1964.

Computer-Assisted Instruction

Atkinson, R. C., and D. M. Hensen. Computer-assisted instruction in initial reading. *Reading Research Quarterly,* 7 (1966): 5–25.

Programmed Learning

Sullivan Readers
Distar

Linguistic Readers

Merrill
Miami
Palo Alto

REFERENCES

Austin, M. C., and C. Morrison. *The First R: The Harvard Report on Reading in Elementary Schools.* New York: Macmillan, 1963.

Beilin, H. Perceptual-cognitive conflict in the development of an invariant area concept. *Journal of Experimental Child Psychology*, 1 (1964): 208–26.

Botvin, G. J., and F. B. Murray. The efficacy of peer modeling and social conflict in acquisition of conservation. *Child Development*, 46 (1975): 796–99.

Brainerd, C. J. *Piaget's Theory of Intelligence.* Englewood Cliffs, NJ: Prentice-Hall, 1978.

Chall, J. S. *Learning to Read: The Great Debate.* New York: McGraw-Hill, 1967.

Chomsky, N. Phonology and reading. In H. Levin and J. P. Williams, *Basic Studies in Reading.* New York: Basic Books, 1970.

Downing, J. What is decoding? *The Reading Teacher*, 29 (1975): 142–44.

Durkin, D. *Strategies for Identifying Words: A Workbook for Teachers and Those Preparing to Teach.* Boston: Allyn and Bacon, 1976.

Dykstra, R. Summary of the second-grade phase of the cooperative research program in primary reading instruction. *Reading Research Quarterly*, 4 (1968): 49–70.

Farr, R., and N. Roser. *Teaching a Child to Read.* New York: Harcourt Brace Jovanovich, 1979.

Flesch, R. Why Johnny still can't read. *Family Circle Magazine* (November 1979).

Fry, E. *Comparison of Three Methods of Reading Instruction (ITA, DMS, TO): Results at the End of Third Grade.* Final report, Project No. 3050. New Brunswick, NJ: Rutgers, The State University, 1967.

Harris, A. J., C. Morrison, B. L. Serwer, and L. Gold. *A Continuation of the CRAFT Project: Comparing Reading Approaches with Disadvantaged Urban Negro Children in Primary Grades.* Final Report, U.S.O.E. Project No. 5-0570-12-1. New York: Selected Academic Readings, 1968.

Hayes, R. B., and R. C. Wuest. *Factors Affecting Learning to Read.* Final Report, Project No. 6-1752. Harrisburg, PA: State Education Department, 1967.

Ruddell, R. B. *A Longitudinal Study of Four Programs of Reading Instruction Varying in Emphasis on Grapheme-Phoneme Correspondences and Language Structure on Reading Achievement in Grades Two and Three.* Final Report, Project Nos. 3099 and 78085. Berkeley: University of California, 1968.

————. Teachers' views on phonics. *Elementary English* (1955): 371–75.

Sheldon, W. D., et al. *Comparison of Three Methods of Teaching Reading in the Second Grade.* OEC 6-10-076. CRP-3231. Ed 023-524, 1967.

Schneyer, J. W., and S. Cowen. *Comparison of a Basal Reader Approach and a Linguistic Approach in a Second and Third Grade Reading Instruction.* Final Report, Project No. 5-0601. Philadelphia: University of Pennsylvania, 1968.

Spache, G. D. *The Teaching of Reading.* Bloomingdale, IN: Phi Delta Kappa, 1972.

Stauffer, R. G. *The First Grade Reading Studies: Findings of Individual Investigations.* Newark, DE: International Reading Association, 1967.

————, and W. D. Hammond. The effectiveness of language arts and basic reader approaches to first grade reading instruction—extended into third grade. *Reading Research Quarterly*, 4 (1969): 468–99.

Vilscek, E. C., and D. L. Cleland. *Two Approaches to Reading Instruction.* Final Report, Project No. 9195: Pittsburgh, PA: University of Pittsburgh, 1968.

Weikart, D. P. *Development of effective preschool programs: A report on the results of the High/Scope Ypsilanti preschool projects.* A paper presented at the High/Scope Educational Research Foundation Conference, Ann Arbor, Michigan, 1973.

CHAPTER 8

READING COMPREHENSION
WHAT IS IT?

WHAT DOES READING COMPREHENSION MEAN?

CONCEPTS DERIVED FROM PSYCHOLOGICAL AND LINGUISTIC EXPERIMENTATION

Comprehension Depends on Knowledge of Language

EMPHASIS ON SYNTAX
EMPHASIS ON HOLISTIC SEMANTIC EVENTS

Comprehension Depends on Knowledge of the World

KNOWLEDGE SHARED BY ALL SPEAKERS OF A LANGUAGE
KNOWLEDGE OF A PARTICULAR CONTEXT

Comprehension Depends on the Reader's "Schema"

"SCHEMA" IN ITS BROADEST SENSE
"SCHEMA" IN A NARROWER SENSE—"STORY GRAMMAR"

Comprehension Is Demonstrated by Evidence of Psycholinguistic Processes

MISCUES
RETELLING

Definitions of Reading Comprehension

CONCEPTS DERIVED FROM THEORIES OF EDUCATIONAL MEASUREMENT

Theory of Independent Subskills

FACTOR ANALYSIS

Theory of Hierarchically Related Subskills

HIERARCHIES BASED ON RESEARCH
LOGICAL HIERARCHIES

The Usefulness of a Subskills Approach

THE SPECIAL PLACE OF VOCABULARY KNOWLEDGE

The Aptitude Interpretation
The Instrumental Interpretation
Knowledge of the World Interpretation

IS READING COMPREHENSION DIFFERENT FROM
GENERAL LANGUAGE COMPREHENSION?

Is Reading Comprehension Unrelated to
Listening Comprehension?
Is Reading Comprehension Decoding plus Oral
Language Comprehension?

EMPHASIS ON DECODING
EMPHASIS ON ORAL LANGUAGE SKILLS
EMPHASIS ON TRANSFER OF ORAL
LANGUAGE SKILLS

Are Reading Comprehension Skills Different
from Oral Language Comprehension Skills?

FORMAL DIFFERENCES IN BEGINNING
MATERIALS
DIFFERENCES BETWEEN SPEECH AND
"INSTITUTIONAL WRITING"

Teaching Comprehension Skills

SUMMARY

FOR FURTHER READING AND DISCUSSION

REFERENCES

WHAT DOES READING COMPREHENSION MEAN?

The last chapter began with the notion that it is easier to recognize the use of context as an aid to word recognition than it is to define it. The idea was developed that using context to recognize words depends on the reader's knowledge of the world, culture, language, and ability to understand the whole phrase, clause, and thought of which the unrecognized word is a part. Understanding wholes enables the reader to supply missing parts.

Of course, one might have stated that the use of context for word recognition depends on *comprehension* of the surrounding text, because comprehension of written language, as we shall see, involves knowledge of the world, of one's culture and language, and the ability to understand whole phrases, clauses, and thoughts and their relationships in written text.

CONCEPTS DERIVED FROM PSYCHOLOGICAL AND LINGUISTIC EXPERIMENTATION

Comprehension is an event that takes place in the mind; it cannot be observed. Definitions of comprehension are therefore derived from observable behaviors that one looks for to determine whether comprehension has taken place or to measure the extent to which it has taken place. A brief review of the literature will demonstrate that a wide range of behaviors are observed as indicators of comprehension and that these behaviors imply a wide variety of concepts of just what comprehension includes.

Comprehension Depends on Knowledge of Language

EMPHASIS ON SYNTAX

Bormuth (1969, 1970) proposed that reading achievement test items could be generated from any written text by transforming sentences in the text into questions using transformational grammar. A sentence such as sentence 1 could be transformed by rules into several types of questions, such as 1a, 1b, and 1c.

1. *The boy rode the horse.*

   a. *Who rode the horse?*

   b. *By whom was the horse ridden?*

   c. *By whom was the steed mounted?*

One may presume that question 1a (a "wh-" item) could be answered easily because the answer could be derived by simply observing what words in the original sentence *(the boy)* were replaced by the *wh-* word *(who)*. Question 1b (a transform item) would be more difficult because it would require the reader to recognize that the question is derived from sentence 1 after it had been transformed into the passive voice, as in sentence 2.

2. *The horse was ridden by the boy.*

Answering 1b would demonstrate that the reader understood that sentences 1 and 2 are synonymous. In the vocabulary of transformational grammar, sentences with the same meaning are said to have the same "deep structure," and therefore one might say that answering question 1b would demonstrate that the reader understood the deep structure of sentence 1.

Question 1c (a semantic substitute item) would be more difficult than 1a or 1b because it would require the reader to recognize that not only had sentence 1 been transformed in the passive voice as in sentence 2, but that synonyms had been substituted for some words in sentence 2 before question 1c was derived.

It has been demonstrated that questions like 1a, 1b, and 1c are progressively more difficult (Bormuth, Manning, Carr, and Pearson, 1970). Anderson (1972), in summarizing the work of Bormuth and others on test items to measure comprehension, concludes: "Whether a test item measures comprehension depends upon the relationship of the wording of the test item to the wording of the instruction" (p. 167).

The relationship between comprehension and ability to recognize synonymous sentences (sentences derived from the same deep structure) was demonstrated by Simons (1972) as well. He devised a 25-item test and asked fifth-graders to choose the one sentence out of three that is not a paraphrase of the other two, as in 3 and 4.

3a. *The boy gave the book to the girl.*

3b. *The book was given the girl by the boy.*

3c. *The book was given the boy by the girl.*

4a. *He painted the red house.*

4b. *He painted the house red.*

4c. *He painted the house that was red.*

He showed that success on this test is highly related to reading comprehension.

It is important to notice the dates of the research reported in this section. Since the research was published during the heyday of interest in transformational grammar and syntax, it is not surprising that success on tasks derived from transformations of sentences was seen as an important aspect of reading comprehension.

♦ One of the important things you should learn from this chapter is that it is not easy to define reading comprehension. At the end of this section, you will find several definitions that have been proposed. It might be useful for you to stop and try to formulate a definition of reading comprehension that is implied by the several research ventures reported in this section. It would be helpful for you to discuss these definitions with your classmates.

EMPHASIS ON HOLISTIC SEMANTIC EVENTS

Bransford and Franks (1971) tested the question of whether subjects remember individual sentences or "holistic, semantic ideas." They constructed Idea Sets composed of seven sentences. Four sentences (as in sentences 5 to 8) each contained one idea. The fifth contained two of the ideas contained in the first four sentences (as sentence 9). The sixth and seventh sentences contained three and four of the ideas each (as in sentences 10 and 11).

One-idea sentences:
5. *The ants were in the kitchen.*
6. *The jelly was on the table.*
7. *The jelly was sweet.*
8. *The ants ate the jelly.*

Two-idea sentence:
9. *The sweet jelly was on the table.*

Three-idea sentence:
10. *The ants in the kitchen ate the sweet jelly.*

Four-idea sentence:
11. *The ants in the kitchen ate the sweet jelly which was on the table.*

Some of these sentences were presented orally to subjects and others were not during the *acquisition phase* of the experiment. During the *recognition phase*, some of these sentences were presented and subjects were asked whether the sentence had appeared in the earlier phase or not. Subjects were also asked to express how confident they were that they had (or had not) heard the sentence.

Subjects tended to report that they had *not* heard sentences that contained only one idea (like sentences 5 to 8) even when they had, and reported that they had heard sentences that contained more than one idea (like sentences 9 to 11) even when they had not. The authors concluded: "Individual sentences lost their unique status in memory in favor of more holistic representation of semantic events" (p. 348).

♦ Can you formulate a definition of reading comprehension that follows from the research reported in this section?

Comprehension Depends on Knowledge of the World

KNOWLEDGE SHARED BY ALL SPEAKERS OF A LANGUAGE

In an ingenious set of experiments, Bransford and Johnson (1973) set out to show that comprehension involves relating new information to old. They report an experiment similar to the Bransford and Franks study cited above, in which subjects were asked whether sentences presented to them during the recognition phase were the same as sentences presented to them during the acquisition phase.

Subjects presented with sentence 12a during the acquisition phase were very confident that 12b was the sentence that had been presented to them, but subjects who were presented with 13a during the acquisition phase were doubtful that 13b was the sentence that had been presented to them.

12a. *Three turtles rested on a floating log and a fish swam beneath them.*

12b. *Three turtles rested on a floating log and a fish swam beneath it.*

13a. *Three turtles rested beside a floating log and a fish swam beneath them.*

13b. *Three turtles rested beside a floating log and a fish swam beneath it.*

If comprehension is merely understanding input sentences, subjects who were presented with 12b and 13b should be equally likely to detect the pronoun change in the recognition item. However, the pronoun change in 12b is consistent with general knowledge of spatial relationships—if the turtles were on the log and the fish swam under them (the turtles), the fish must also have swum under it (the log). But the pronoun change in 13b may not be consistent with general knowledge of spatial relationships—if the turtles were beside the log and the fish swam under them, the fish may or may not have swum under it.

This experiment demonstrated that comprehension is more than understanding sentences or ideas as they appear in the text. Comprehension involves integrating what one learns from the text with what one already knows. Slight differences in sentences may therefore be understood as significant differences in meaning if they evoke significantly different knowledge of the world.

KNOWLEDGE OF A PARTICULAR CONTEXT

In order to demonstrate that a person can comprehend each sentence in a passage and still fail to comprehend the whole passage, Bransford and Johnson (1973) read the passage in Figure 8.1 to subjects under two conditions: In the no context condition, the passage was read to the subject with no preparation. In the context condition, the subjects looked at the picture in Figure 8.2 for thirty seconds before the passage was read.

Subjects were asked to rate the passage on a comprehension scale from 1 (very hard) to 7

FIGURE 8.1
THE BALLOON PASSAGE, DEMONSTRATING HOW CONTEXT CAN DETERMINE WHETHER OR NOT A READER CAN COMPREHEND. (From Bransford and Johnson, 1973, pp. 392–93.)

If the balloons popped the sound wouldn't be able to carry since everything would be too far away from the correct floor. A closed window would also prevent the sound from carrying, since most buildings tend to be well insulated. Since the whole operation depends on a steady flow of electricity, a break in the middle of the wire would also cause problems. Of course, the fellow could shout, but the human voice is not loud enough to carry that far. An additional problem is that a string could break on the instrument. Then there could be no accompaniment to the message. It is clear that the best situation would involve less distance. Then there would be fewer potential problems. With face to face contact, the least number of things could go wrong.

(very easy). They were also asked to write down as many ideas from the passage as they could. Subjects in the no context condition rated the passage as very difficult to comprehend and did not recall many ideas; subjects in the context condition rated the passage as easy to comprehend and recalled twice as many ideas as subjects in the no context condition.

The researchers reached the following conclusions:

1. *Context has a marked effect but people can "learn" things they don't understand. [That is, subjects who did not see Figure 8.2 could not have understood the passage, but they could recall ideas from it.]*

2. *Subjects forget things they do comprehend.*

3. *More research is needed to get at relationships between comprehension, retrieval and mem-*

ory but absence of context can seriously effect acquisition. (Bransford and Johnson, 1973, p. 397)

Bransford and Johnson (1973) relate their findings to the field theory of the German-Austrian psychologist Karl Buhler (1879–1963). Field theory states that for communication to take place, speaker and hearer must share the same field (knowledge, context, and language) to a certain degree.

♦ Can you formulate a definition of reading comprehension that follows from the research reported in this section?

Comprehension Depends on the Reader's "Schema"

"SCHEMA" IN ITS BROADEST SENSE

Anderson and others (1977) asked two groups of college students to read the passage in Figure 8.3. One group of students was made up of music majors, and the other group of physical education majors. There are two ways this passage could be interpreted: as a card game, or as a rehearsal of a woodwind ensemble. The results of the experiment showed that physical education majors tended to interpret this as a passage describing a card game (as do most adult readers), but the music majors tend to interpret it as a rehearsal. Three further results emerged from this experiment.

First, when asked to recall the story, subjects from both groups stated ideas that were not in the story or that were only implied in the story. These "added ideas" revealed whether the subjects interpreted the story as a card game or music rehearsal. Second, these authors considered such "recall" of information not in the story as evidence of compre-

FIGURE 8.2
APPROPRIATE CONTEXT FOR THE BALLOON PASSAGE, FIGURE 8.1. (From Bransford and Johnson, 1973, p. 394).

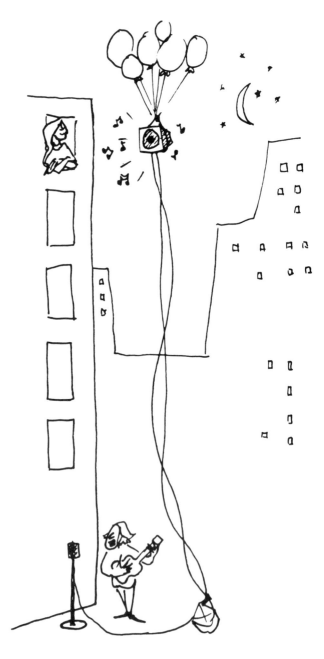

FIGURE 8.3
THE CARD/MUSIC PASSAGE. A PASSAGE WHICH COULD BE GIVEN TWO DISTINCT INTERPRETATIONS. (From Anderson et al., 1977, p. 372.)

Every Saturday night, four good friends get together. When Jerry, Mike, and Pat arrived, Karen was sitting in her living room writing some notes. She quickly gathered the cards and stood up to greet her friends at the door. They followed her into the living room but as usual they couldn't agree on exactly what to play. Jerry eventually took a stand and set things up. Finally, they began to play. Karen's recorder filled the room with soft and pleasant music. Early in the evening, Mike noticed Pat's hand and the many diamonds. As the night progressed the tempo of play increased. Finally, a lull in the activities occurred. Taking advantage of this, Jerry pondered the arrangement in front of him. Mike interrupted Jerry's reverie and said, "Let's hear the score." They listened carefully and commented on their performance. When the comments were all heard, exhausted but happy, Karen's friends went home.

hension. Third, when questioned after the experiment, more than 80 percent of the subjects reported that while reading the story, only one interpretation ever occurred to them. That is, subjects adopted an overview or a "big picture" of what the passage described, and their understanding of words, phrases, clauses, and ideas was governed by this overview.

Anderson and his colleagues propose these results show that the "knowledge structures the reader brings to the text" are more important than the "structures which are in some sense 'in' the text" (p. 369). They refer to these knowledge structures the reader brings to the text as "high-level schemata" (p. 367).

It is important to notice that these authors are not referring to bringing particular knowledge to a text, such as knowledge that the subjects who saw the picture in Figure 8.2

brought to the text in Figure 8.1. If a person has the "card game schema," for example, he or she knows how to participate in a card game, knows what to expect from others in a card game, and knows how to organize information he or she is told or reads about a card game. A thousand details can change from card game to card game, but the general outline remains the same.

The concept and the term *schema* (or its plural form *schemata*) is traced to Kant, the eighteenth-century rationalist philosopher mentioned in Chapter 1. Kant introduced the term in his discussion of human thinking (Kant, 1963; originally published in German in 1781). Bartlett (1932) is credited with directing the attention of modern scientists who are interested in the study of memory of spoken and written discourse to schema theory.

"SCHEMA" IN A NARROWER SENSE—"STORY GRAMMAR"

In recent years, scientists interested in language have turned their attention to a particular application of the concept of schema that has come to be known as *story schema* or *story grammar*.

Certain story outlines are well known. For example, a man and woman appear in a story; they meet; they fall in love; they have a misunderstanding; they separate; they reconcile; they marry. Or a promising athlete appears in a story; he sets his heart on winning a competition; he suffers setbacks; he perseveres; he wins. An outline or set of expectations even more general than the two described above is as follows: Characters are introduced; they set a goal for themselves; they attempt to reach the goal; they encounter setbacks; they make further attempts; they reach the goal.

Although all three outlines are abstract, the third is considerably more abstract than the first two. A conceptual outline of stories at this high level of abstraction has come to be called a *story grammar.*

Story grammars have been proposed by Rumelhart (1978), Mandler and Johnson (1977), Stein and Glen (1979) and Thorndyke (1977). A simplified version of the Mandler and Johnson (1977) story grammar might be stated as follows: A story is a *setting* followed by one or more *episodes.* An *episode* is made up of a *beginning, reaction, attempt, outcome,* and *ending.* An example of a two-episode story that conforms to this grammar is presented in Figure 8.4.

A considerable amount of research has been devoted to the question of whether story grammar plays a part in comprehending and remembering spoken and written texts. The following proposals have been examined in this research: (1) There is an underlying structure that can be detected and described for all or most stories. This underlying structure is described by story grammars. (2) The human mind is an avid organizer of past experience. After hearing and reading a number of stories, people formulate general outlines or sets of expectations or schemata for stories. These schemata are described by story grammars. (3) Once these schemata are internalized, people rely on them to organize the content of stories as they read or listen to them—that is, in the process of comprehension. (4) Once these schemata are internalized, people rely on them for recalling or remembering stories.

Several studies (Applebee, 1978; Stein and Glen, 1977; Whaley, 1981) have shown that children expect stories to conform to story grammars such as the one proposed by Mandler and Johnson (1977). In the Whaley study, for example, children were presented with stories similar to the one in Figure 8.4, but one grammar category (setting, beginning, and so on) was deleted and replaced by blank lines. The children were asked to read the story and supply the missing part. The results confirmed

FIGURE 8.4
A TWO-EPISODE STORY CONFORMING TO THE MANDLER AND JOHNSON (1977) STORY GRAMMAR. (From Mandler, 1978.)

Setting	Once there were twins, Tom and Jennifer, who had so much trouble their parents called them the unlucky twins.
Beginning 1	One day, Jennifer's parents gave her a dollar bill to buy the turtle she wanted, but on the way to the store she lost it.
Reaction 1	Jennifer was worried that her parents would be angry with her so she decided to search every bit of the sidewalk she had walked.
Attempt 1	She looked in all the cracks and in the grass along the way.
Outcome 1	She finally found the dollar bill in the grass.
Ending 1	But when Jennifer got to the store, the petstore man told her that someone else had just bought the last turtle, and he didn't have any more.
Beginning 2	The same day, Tom fell off a swing and broke his leg.
Reaction 2	He wanted to run and play with the other kids.
Attempt 2	So he got the kids to pull him around in his wagon.
Outcome 2	While they were playing, Tom fell out of the wagon and broke his arm.
Ending 2	Tom's parents said he was even unluckier than Jennifer and made him stay in bed until he got well.

the proposition that children expect the categories specified by the grammar in the order specified by the grammar.

Other studies have shown that stories which conform to story grammars are better understood and remembered than stories which do not conform to story grammars (Bower et al., 1979; Feldman, 1983; Mandler, 1978; Poulsen and others, 1979; Rumelhart, 1978; Stein and Nezworski, 1978). These studies provide ample support for the proposal that there is an underlying structure common to most stories and that readers internalize this structure or schema and rely on it for organizing the content of stories as they read and for recalling or remembering stories.

♦ Can you formulate a definition of reading comprehension that follows from the research reported in this section?

Comprehension Is Demonstrated by Evidence of Psycholinguistic Processes

In an article that reiterates and to some extent summarizes a decade of their own work (K. Goodman, 1967, 1969; Y. Goodman, 1976; Y. Goodman and Burke, 1972), Kenneth and Yetta Goodman (1977) propose that under certain conditions, observing a child's oral reading performance and his retelling of what he has read yields valuable insights into the process of comprehending, as well as an idea of what is retained from the comprehension process.

MISCUES

For example, Figure 8.5 shows the first three sentences in a story and a transcript of a 9-year-old girl's oral reading of these sentences. The Goodmans point out that the things the child says which are not in the text (what might be called "oral reading errors," but what the Goodmans prefer to call "miscues") can be explained, but they cannot be explained in terms of any single process.

For example, in sentence 1 the child says "he threw" for the printed words *he thought.* She is probably paying some attention to letter-sound correspondences (what the Goodmans refer to as "processing graphic information") since *threw* and *thought* begin with the same letters, but she is obviously not trying slavishly to "sound out" the words. She is undoubtedly relying on some knowledge of language (however unconsciously), since she produces a subject and verb where a subject and verb are called for. She is undoubtedly paying attention to the meaning of the language. She apparently cannot make sense of the next words when they follow *he threw,* and so she goes back, probably pays closer attention to the graphic information, and corrects herself.

A similar process seems to ensue in the second sentence, when the child renders *What do you do all day* as "I want you do all day," and then she corrects herself. But interestingly, in the same sentence the child reads *while I am away cutting wood* as "when I am always cutting wood." Neither the child's knowledge of letter-sound relationships, nor her knowledge of syntax, nor her knowledge of the world are violated by this rendering; therefore she does not check the clause again, although she has substituted *when* for *while* and *always* for *away.*

The Goodmans propose that this process, miscue analysis, reveals what readers do in the process of comprehending. Readers appear to draw on graphic information and their knowledge of letter-sound correspondences, syntax, semantics, and sentence transformations—as well as on their knowledge of the world.

RETELLING

A second phase of miscue analysis calls for the child to retell what was in the text

FIGURE 8.5
**THE FIRST THREE SENTENCES OF A WRITTEN TEXT AND THE TRANSCRIPT OF A CHILD'S
ORAL READING OF THE TEXT.** (From Goodman and Goodman, 1977, p. 318.)

TEXT	TRANSCRIPT
(1.) Once upon a time there was a woodman who thought that no one worked as hard as he did.	(1.) *Once upon a time there was a woodman. He threw . . . who thought that no one worked as hard as he did.*
(2.) One evening when he came home from work, he said to his wife, "What do you do all day while I am away cutting wood?"	(2.) *One evening when he . . . when he came home from work, he said to his wife, "I want you do all day . . . what do you do all day when I am always cutting wood?"*
(3.) "I keep house," replied the wife, "and keeping house is hard work."	(3.) *"I keep . . . I keep house," replied the wife, "and keeping . . . and keeping . . . and keeping house is and work."*

without prompting or leading questions. In analyzing the child's retelling, the observer is interested in how the child organizes (or reorganizes) what he or she learned from the text, and whether the child uses his or her own language or the author's language. Retelling also reveals a child's conceptions and misconceptions about the text.

For example, this child's retelling of the story (Figure 8.6) reveals that she knows *woods* and *forest* are synonyms, but she also seems to know that the author used *forest*, since she first says *woods* and corrects herself to say *forest*. For a further example, her retelling appears to confirm what her miscues suggest—that she is not familiar with the terms *keep house* and *keeping house*, although she apparently recognized the words *keep, keeping,* and *house*.

The Goodmans see the process of comprehending as one of constructing meaning, a process in which readers integrate their knowledge of reading, language, and the world to construct meaning while interacting with the printed page. They assert that the idea that every written text contains a precise meaning which readers passively receive is a

misconception. This view of the reading process is known as the *psycholinguistic model of reading.*

♦ You may want to look back at Chapter 1, where the meaning of the word *psycholinguistics* is discussed as a term applied to an empirical science in the 1950s and to a rationalist science by the end of the 1960s. The term as it is used by the Goodmans refers to the *rationalist* science, as you can see from its top-down approach and its strong emphasis on the reader's aggressive use of knowledge of language and the world in constructing meaning. Besides Kenneth Goodman, the person most widely known for promoting acceptance of this model is Frank Smith (1971, 1977).

♦ It would be useful to compare and contrast the definition of comprehension implied by each of these ingenious pieces of research.

If asked to recall the card game-rehearsal passage, might a person fail to report that the event took place every Saturday night but still answer the *Wh-* rote question "When do four good friends get together?" if it is asked explicitly? Might the child described by the Goodmans answer the question "Who would keep house?" correctly—despite the fact that her miscues and retelling indicate that she was unfamiliar with the term *keep house?*

In the Anderson experiment, adding information that was missing or only implied in the original

FIGURE 8.6
THE FIRST SEGMENT OF A CHILD'S RETELLING OF A STORY AFTER ORAL READING. (From Goodman and Goodman, 1977, p. 321.)

um . . . it was about this woodman and um . . . when he . . . he thought that he um . . . he had harder work to do than his wife. So he went home and he told his wife, ''What have you been doing all day.'' And then his wife told him. And then, um . . . and then, he thought that it was easy work. And so . . . so . . . so his wife, so his wife, so she um . . . so the wife said, ''well so you have to keep,'' no . . . the husband says that you have to go to the woods and cut . . . and have to go out in the forest and cut wood and I'll stay home. And the next day they did that.

passage was seen as evidence of comprehension. In the Goodmans' observations, correcting some oral reading miscues and *not* correcting others was seen as evidence of comprehension.

The point is that comprehension and passing tests of comprehension appear to be two separate things. This distinction becomes important when one considers *teaching* comprehension as distinct from *testing* comprehension.

Definitions of Reading Comprehension

Perhaps, after having considered the various definitions of comprehension that are implied by the selected studies reported above, the reader will appreciate why explicit definitions tend to be very abstract. The following are two classic defiitions of reading comprehension.

The first is from Edward L. Thorndike (1917), who proposed:

Understanding a paragraph is like solving a problem in mathematics. It consists of selecting the right elements of the situation and putting them together in the right relations, and also with the right amount of weight or influence or force for each. The mind is assailed as it were by every word in the paragraph. It must repress, reflect, soften, emphasize, correlate and organize, all under the influence of the right mental set or purpose or demand. (As reprinted in the Reading Research Quarterly, 6 *[1971]: 431)*

Arthur I. Gates (1949), in referring to the ''nature of the reading process,'' states:

[Reading] is essentially a thoughtful process. However, to say that reading is a ''thought-getting'' process is to give it too restricted a description. It should be developed as a complex organization of patterns of higher mental processes. It can and should embrace all types of thinking, evaluating, judging, imagining, reasoning, and problem-solving. . . .

In wholehearted reading activity the child does more than understand and contemplate; his emotions are stirred; his attitudes and purposes are modified; indeed, his innermost being is involved. (pp. 3–4)

Examples of more recent definitions of comprehension come from Bormuth (1969):

[C]omprehension ability is thought to be a set of generalized knowledge-acquisition skills which permit people to acquire and exhibit information gained as a consequence of reading printed language. (p. 50)

and Athey (1977):

Reading is an activity in which the highest human abilities—perceptual, intellectual, and linguistic—interact and support one another in pursuit of a single goal, the processing and assimilation of written information. (p. 94)

and Pearson and Johnson (1978):

Comprehension is building bridges between the new and the known. (p. 24)

Such definitions should remind a person that concentrating on the performance of a particular task leads one to consider comprehension too narrowly. On the other hand, such definitions may leave one overwhelmed by the complexity of the subject. Ideally, a teacher will adopt concepts of comprehension that permit him or her to devise achievable aims, lessons, and evaluation procedures, but at the same time remain aware that comprehension is a complex, many-faceted operation.

CONCEPTS DERIVED FROM THEORIES OF EDUCATIONAL MEASUREMENT

Theory of Independent Subskills

Definitions of comprehension refer to several apparently related mental abilities rather than to a single mental skill. Important questions arise from a teacher's point of view if the process of comprehension does in fact involve several skills and abilities.

1. Can a person possess several of these skills and be missing just one or two, causing that person to fail to comprehend?
2. Can we identify skills a person possesses and skills a person is missing so that we can spend time and energy efficiently by teaching only those skills that are lacking?
3. Can we isolate skills and teach them one at a time?
4. Are these skills only *logically* separable; are they in fact always found together so that it is not possible to demonstrate that a person possesses some and is missing others? Are they in fact so intimately connected that it is impossible to isolate single skills and teach them in isolation?

The reader undoubtedly recognizes a by now familiar division. Is reading comprehension a global affair (a view rationalists are apt to embrace) or is it atomistic—a set of subskills that can be considered, tested, and taught separately (a view empiricists are apt to embrace)? This question led to a body of literature in the field of measurement that has had a profound effect on the teaching of reading in the schools.

FACTOR ANALYSIS

Some very complicated statistical procedures have been used to explore the question of whether or not it is useful to think of comprehension as a global skill or as a set of related subskills. One technique is called factor analysis. *Factor analysis* is used to analyze right and wrong answers to individual test items to see if the items are measuring the same or discrete kinds of knowledge or skill.

The Rationale Behind Factor Analysis.   The rationale behind factor analysis is as follows. Suppose one gave the nine-item test in Figure 8.7 to one hundred 15-year-old students. One would not be baffled by a student who answered the first three right and the remainder wrong, or who answered 4, 5, and 6 right and the remainder wrong, or who answered 7, 8, and 9 right and the remainder wrong. Conversely, one would not be baffled by a student who answered all right except 1, 2, and 3; or all right except 4, 5, and 6; or all right except 7, 8, and 9.

The reason these patterns would not be surprising is that there are clearly three kinds of questions on this test—grammar, history, and science. Students who have one kind of knowledge may not have the other two kinds. Logically, the three kinds of knowledge are discrete and independent.

FIGURE 8.7
AN ACHIEVEMENT TEST THAT PRESUMABLY MEASURES THREE SEPARATE KINDS OF KNOWLEDGE.

GRAMMAR

1. What is the subject of the following sentence?
   Three boys were playing ball.

2. Which noun in the following sentence is plural?
   The women ran a race.

3. Which noun is possessive in the following sentence? *You've got Mary's hat.*

HISTORY

4. Who discovered America?
   a. Drake   b. Balboa   c. Marco Polo
   d. Columbus

5. Who was the first president of the United States?
   a. Franklin   b. Washington   c. Jefferson
   d. Adams

6. When was the Declaration of Independence signed?
   a. 1492   b. 1609   c. 1776   d. 1789

SCIENCE

7. At what temperature does water freeze?
   a. 32°F   b. 0°F   c. 100°C   d. 32°C

8. What elements are in H_2O?
   a. Hydrogen and nitrogen
   b. Helium and oxygen
   c. Water and air
   d. Hydrogen and oxygen

9. Which statement is true?
   a. An ounce of sugar is heavier than an ounce of water.
   b. An ounce of sugar is heavier than a gram of water.
   c. An ounce of sugar weighs the same as a gram of water.
   d. You can't tell if an ounce of sugar is heavier than a gram of water.

Of course, if you actually gave this test to one hundred 15-year-olds, you would get very confusing results. Some children would answer all the questions right, and some would answer all wrong. The performance of these children would not lend support to assertions that three discrete kinds of knowledge were being tested by these nine items. Students also make mistakes. They give wrong answers when they know the correct answers. Students are also lucky at times and answer questions correctly when indeed they do not know the answer. And knowledge is not acquired in air-tight categories. For example, many people who have never studied history know that Columbus discovered America.

But if these are discrete and independent categories of knowledge, the tendency to be right or wrong on all questions *within a group of questions* would be stronger than the tendency to get all right, all wrong, or to answer randomly right and wrong across all questions. Factor analysis is a statistical procedure that reveals separate factors—that is, groups of questions which seem to be measuring the same kind of knowledge, and knowledge different from knowledge measured by other questions or groups of questions on a test.

As a matter of fact, certain demands of the factor analysis procedure would make it necessary to write many more than three items for each category before using this procedure on test results. A forty-five-item test with fifteen items in each category would be much more likely if this procedure were actually performed. Presumably, then, if one were to administer a longer version of the test in Figure 8.7 and perform a factor analysis on the results, one would discover that there are three factors being tested by these items: one factor being addressed by items like 1, 2, and 3; a second factor being addressed by items like 4, 5, and 6; and a third factor being addressed by items like 7, 8, and 9.

Several presumptions that are quite consistent with one's intuition follow from this discovery.

1. That grammar, history, and science are separate kinds of knowledge, ability, or skill.

2. That students can possess one kind of knowledge, ability, or skill and not the other two; or two and not the other one.

3. That one can teach these areas separately and independently.

Factor Analysis and Reading Comprehension Testing. Using the same kind of reasoning and the statistical procedure called factor analysis, Davis (1944) published a paper claiming to show that a particular test on reading comprehension measured nine separate factors, as follows:

1. Knowledge of word meanings

2. Ability to select the appropriate meaning for a word or phrase in the light of its particular contextual setting

3. Ability to follow the organization of a passage and to identify antecedents and references in it

4. Ability to select the main thought of a passage

5. Ability to answer questions that are specifically answered in a passage

6. Ability to answer questions that are answered in a passage but not in words in which the question is asked

7. Ability to draw inferences from a passage about its contents

8. Ability to recognize the literary devices used in a passage and to determine its tone and mood

9. Ability to determine a writer's purpose, intent, and point of view—to draw inferences about a writer

A short time later, Thurston (1946) published a paper claiming to show that the test in question measured only one factor—reading ability. Davis (1946) reacted to the Thurston paper by claiming that

Comprehension in reading involves at least five independent mental abilities, which appear to be:

1. Word knowledge,

2. Ability to reason in reading,

3. Ability to follow the organization of a passage and to identify antecedents and references in it,

4. Ability to recognize the literary devices used in a passage and to determine its tone and mood,

5. Tendency to focus attention on a writer's explicit statements to the exclusion of their implications. (p. 254)

A long, interesting, and controversial literature has emerged regarding the contention that one can identify "independent mental abilities" which contribute to reading comprehension. See Davis (1944, 1946, 1968, and 1972), R. L. Thorndike (1973), Thurston (1946), Spearritt (1972), and Lennon (1962).

♦ This controversy is another example of how the reading teacher is confronted with philosophical questions and asked to make practical decisions based on how those questions are answered.

Is reading comprehension an atomistic affair? Is it true that one learns to comprehend literal meanings at one time and to predict outcomes at another time, and that at some point a critical mass of these separate skills comes together and one "comprehends reading"?

Or is reading comprehension a global affair? Are such components as "identifying the main idea" so bound up with every other component (such as knowing vocabulary, understanding details, or sensing the author's intent) that to think of these components as things that exist separately is to live in a dream world?

Questions like these were raised in earlier chapters in relation to readiness and word recognition. The questions are so fundamental to the life of the mind it is not surprising that they appear and reappear in a discussion of teaching reading, since reading has been described as the highest psychological function known to humans (Huey, 1908).

Several lists of "factors" or "components" of reading comprehension have been proposed. For example, Lennon (1962) proposed four components of reading ability. Lennon's four factors and the skills, knowledge, outcomes, and abilities he believes are inherent in the factors are as follows:

1. A general verbal factor
   a. Breadth of vocabulary
   b. Depth of vocabulary
   c. Scope of vocabulary
   d. Extensive word mastery
   e. Fluency in handling words
2. Comprehension of explicitly stated material
   a. Locating specifically stated information
   b. Comprehension of literal meaning of what is written
   c. Ability to follow specific directions in what is read
3. Comprehension of implicit meanings
   a. Draw inferences from what is read
   b. Predict outcomes
   c. Derive the meaning of words from context
   d. Perceive the structure of what is read
      (1) To perceive the main idea or central thought
      (2) To perceive the hierarchical arrangement of ideas
   e. Interpret what is read
      (1) Applying information to solution of a problem
      (2) Deriving some generalization or principles
   f. All those abilities that demand active, productive, intellectual response and activity on the part of the reader
4. An element that might be termed "appreciation"
   a. Sensing the intent or purpose of the author
   b. Judging the mood or tone of the selection
   c. Perceiving literary devices

Although Lennon proposes this list, he hedges on the separateness of the factors. He concedes that the existence of items listed under category 4 has not been established to be *separate* from those listed under 1, 2, and 3. He also concedes that factors 2 and 3 (comprehension of explicitly and implicitly stated material) cannot be differentiated. He observes that one would expect comprehension of explicitly and implicitly stated material to go together "because the ability to get at the implicit meaning of what is read presupposes the ability to understand the explicit or literal meaning" (p. 334).

Theory of Hierarchically Related Subskills

The factor-analytic and subskills approach implies that there are two possibilities: There are independent subskills, or reading comprehension is a single-factor, global affair. Lennon's explanation of why factors 2 and 3 cannot be differentiated (that one ability presupposes the other) offers a third possibility: There are separate subskills, but they are not independent; one presupposes the other. In other words, there are separate subskills, but they are hierarchically related.

HIERARCHIES BASED ON RESEARCH

Researchers have explored the possibility that reading comprehension can be usefully thought of as a group of subskills, but that the subskills are related in a hierarchical fashion.

For example, one would presume that any subject who could answer the second question in the following pairs could answer the first, but not all subjects who could answer the first question could answer the second.

14a. *Which number is larger, 3 or 7?*

14b. *What is 3 plus 2?*

15a. *How many points does a football team get for a field goal?*

15b. *If team A had 6 points and team B had 12 points and team A made a field goal, which team would be winning?*

Again, because of various sources of error, actual results of tests to determine hierarchies of knowledge or skills produce confusing results—even when the hierarchical relationship is as logically clear as it is in the sentences above. Confusion is much more pronounced when the logical relationship is less clear-cut, as it is among subskills presumed to exist in comprehension. As a result, various experimental techniques and statistical procedures have been used to test hierarchical theories. For example, Chapman (1971) used a statistical procedure known as the Rausch model to demonstrate that comprehension is made up of skills that are separate but related because more complex skills depend on and include more basic skills.

"Who" Questions and "Why" Questions. Trabasso (1981) reported a "provocative" study by Wimmer (1979). The study used a story consisting of 36 action statements in which an elaborate chain of events is first proposed and later occurs (see Figure 8.8). Wimmer read this story to groups of 4- and 8-year-olds. After each statement was read, a question was asked about the statement. Some children were asked *who/whom* questions (such as 16) after each statement; other children were asked *why* questions (such as 17) after each statement.

16. *Who went to the cow?*

17. *Why did the farmer go to his cow?*

At the end of this procedure, each child was asked to retell the story. The results were that children who answered all the *who/whom* questions correctly did not do as well on recalling the story as children who answered all the *why* questions correctly. Wimmer's conclusion was that one can understand individual sentences (answer *who/whom* questions) before one understands connections between sentences (answer *why* questions) and that recalling and retelling a story is dependent on understanding connections between sentences.

Perhaps Trabasso calls this a provocative study not only because of its very interesting results, but also because of the question it raises and leaves unanswered: Does asking *why* questions after each statement promote understanding of connections between statements? This question is simply not addressed. The study is reported here because it presents evidence that understanding individual statements in a story may precede understanding relations between statements and that recall depends on the latter. In other words, there is evidence here of a hierarchy of comprehension skills.

Sentences and Paragraphs. Chapman (1971) showed that training in sentence comprehension improves paragraph comprehension, but training in paragraph comprehension does not improve sentence comprehension. The implication is, of course, that understanding sentences and understanding paragraphs are hierarchically related.

FIGURE 8.8
THE FARMER AND THE DONKEY STORY USED TO DEMONSTRATE THAT SENTENCE COMPREHENSION MAY OCCUR PRIOR TO COMPREHENSION OF CONNECTIONS BETWEEN SENTENCES. (From Trabasso, 1981, p. 67.)

1 There was once an old farmer

2. who owned a very stubborn donkey.

3. One evening the farmer was trying to put his donkey into its shed.

4. First, the farmer pulled the donkey,

5. but the donkey wouldn't move.

6. Then the farmer pushed the donkey,

7. but still the donkey wouldn't move.

8. Finally, the farmer asked his dog

9. to bark loudly at the donkey

10. and thereby frighten him into the shed.

11. But the dog refused.

12. So then, the farmer asked his cat

13. to scratch the dog

14. so the dog would bark loudly

15. and thereby frighten the donkey into the shed.

16. But the cat replied,

17. "I would gladly scratch the dog

18. if only you would get me some milk."

19. So the farmer went to his cow

20. and asked for some milk

21. to give to the cat.

22. But the cow replied,

23. "I would gladly give you some milk

24. if only you would give me some hay."

25. Thus, the farmer went to the haystack

26. and got some hay.

27. As soon as he gave the hay to the cow,

28. the cow gave the farmer some milk.

29. Then the farmer went to the cat

30. and gave the milk to the cat.

31. As soon as the cat got the milk,

32. it began to scratch the dog.

33. As soon as the cat scratched the dog,

34. the dog began to bark loudly.

35. The barking so frightened the donkey

36. that it jumped immediately into its shed.

Word Recognition and Syntax. Cromer (1968) devised a method of grouping words in passages into phrases to help poor readers. The presumption was that this aid to perceiving syntactical relationships would aid in comprehension. Poor readers who were good at word recognition benefitted from the scheme, but poor readers who were not good at word recognition did not benefit. The implication is that word recognition and perceiving syntactic relationships are hierarchically related.

♦ The studies reported here imply a hierarchical relationship of word, to phrase, to sentence, to intersentence, to paragraph meaning, to passage comprehension.

These studies clearly characterize reading comprehension as a bottom-up affair. You don't want to forget that this scheme of comprehension does not go unchallenged. The studies reported earlier in this chapter demonstrate that the reader's knowledge of the world and the reader's schemata affect comprehension at all lower levels, including comprehension of meanings of words and sentences.

Whether one views comprehension as a bottom-up or top-down affair will certainly affect one's teaching decisions.

LOGICAL HIERARCHIES

In 1948 a group of college examiners met informally at the American Psychological Association convention. It was proposed that there would be better communication among people engaged in test construction if they could agree on the goals of education and classify these goals into educational objectives. A series of annual meetings led to the publication of a little book with a long title: *Taxonomy of Educational Objectives—The Classification of Educational Goals—Handbook I: The Cognitive Domain* (Bloom et al., 1956). It is usually referred to as "Bloom's taxonomy." This book has had an important influence on the way comprehension is conceptualized by people who determine the reading curriculum.

Bloom's Taxonomy.   Bloom's taxonomy classifies the intellectual objectives of education into two categories: (1) knowledge; and (2) intellectual abilities and skills.

Knowledge is further divided into:

1. Knowledge of specifics
2. Knowledge of ways and means of dealing with specifics
3. Knowledge of universals and abstractions

Intellectual abilities and skills are further divided into:

1. Comprehension (the lowest level of understanding)
2. Application (use of abstraction in concrete situations)
3. Analysis (breakdown of communication into parts)
4. Synthesis (putting together elements to form a whole)
5. Evaluation (judgments about the value of material)

Each of these categories is further divided. In the condensed version of the taxonomy (pp. 201–7) there are twenty more categories arranged under knowledge or intellectual abilities and skills.

Hierarchical Taxonomies of Reading Comprehension.   Several scholars have developed classification schemes for reading comprehension skills and abilities. Barrett (in Clymer, 1968) refers to his taxonomy as one of "cognitive and affective dimensions of reading comprehension." His major headings are:

1. Literal comprehension
2. Reorganization
3. Inferential comprehension
4. Evaluation
5. Appreciaton

Each of these categories is further divided so that in the entire taxonomy there are thirty-five categories arranged under these five major headings.

The Usefulness of a Subskills Approach

Although the research on the question of identifying separate factors in reading comprehension has been fraught with dissension, the terms and concepts discussed in this literature have entered the materials used for teaching reading in the schools. Lists of kinds of knowledge, skills, outcomes, and abilities such as those presented above are frequently presented as objectives in reading programs.

Even if these skills cannot be shown to be separate, it is useful for teachers to think of them as separate so that teaching comprehension becomes conceivable and manageable. The question then becomes one of whether reading comprehension skills and abilities should be considered to be independent of one another or hierarchically related.

If one presumes there is a hierarchy involved in reading comprehension skills and abilities, one would teach them in a particular order in relation to a written passage. If one presumes comprehension skills and abilities are separate and fairly independent of one another, one would not teach them in any particular order or address them in any particular order in relation to a written passage. In Chapter 9 some techniques for teaching reading comprehension will be presented, and suggestions for deciding which skills and abilities to teach and the order in which to teach them will be discussed.

THE SPECIAL PLACE OF VOCABULARY KNOWLEDGE

There is one undisputed fact in the literature concerning subskills and comprehension. If vocabulary knowledge is treated at all in the study, it emerges as the major contributor to comprehension as a whole. Differences of opinion emerge as to whether there are as many as eight *other* separate factors (Davis, 1944) or as few as only one *other* separate factor (Thorndike, 1973). But there is no dispute as to whether word knowledge is a major factor in comprehension.

There is some question about what this undisputed fact means, however. To understand how this question arises, it is necessary to know how the fact has been established. The fact was established by showing that subjects who score high on tests of word knowledge tend to score high on tests of reading comprehension.

Most widely used standardized reading tests have two parts—a test of word knowledge and a test of reading comprehension. If you look at a copy of a standardized reading test, you will discover that the words and topics treated on the word knowledge subtest are distinct from the words and topics treated on the reading comprehension subtest.

This relationship was *not* established by giving subjects a test of vocabulary that appears in a particular passage and then giving them a test on comprehension on the same passage. The statement that vocabulary knowledge is a major factor in reading comprehension means that one's knowledge of vocabulary *in general* is highly related to ability to comprehend written English *in general.* In other words, people with good vocabularies tend to be good at reading comprehension, and people with poor vocabularies tend to be poor at reading comprehension.

Anderson and Freebody (1981) have proposed that this fact has been interpreted in three different ways: as (1) an aptitude interpretation, (2) an instrumental interpretation, and (3) a knowledge of the world interpretation.

The Aptitude Interpretation

The aptitude interpretation is the oldest and perhaps the most widely held. It is based on the well-known fact that word knowledge is an excellent indication of how well one will score on an intelligence test (Terman, 1918). The aptitude interpretation simply states that intelligent people know a lot of words and intelligent people are good at reading comprehension. Both large vocabulary and good reading comprehension spring from the same source—high intelligence.

The Instrumental Interpretation

This view is something of a commonsense interpretation of the relationship. The instrumental interpretation is that people with large vocabularies are likely to know more words in any given passage than people with small vocabularies; therefore it is knowledge of word meanings that is the source of success on both measures—the vocabulary test and the comprehension test. This interpretation implies that if one knows all the words in a passage, one will automatically comprehend the passage; conversely, unknown words in a passage will cause failure to comprehend the passage.

The common sense of this interpretation is quite compelling, and it is appealing to teachers because it suggests something for them to do: To increase comprehension of a particular passage, teach the meanings of the words in the passage; to increase comprehension in general, teach the meanings of a lot of words in general.

But experiments designed to explore this interpretation do not always support it. For example, Tuinman and Brady (1974) reported that when they taught difficult vocabulary in a passage to fourth-, fifth-, and sixth-graders, the subjects' scores on vocabulary tests of the words taught improved, but the scores on comprehension tests of the passages did not improve. Furthermore, it was demonstrated by Bransford and Johnson (1973) that knowledge of individual words does not ensure comprehension of a text.

Knowledge of the World Interpretation

This interpretation is based on the assumption that people who have wide exposure to culture learn two things: First, they learn a lot of words, because the concepts, categories, procedures, attributes, and relationships that are important to a culture are encoded in the vocabulary of the culture. Second, they learn a lot of knowledge structures or schemata—that is, they acquire over-

views, "big pictures," of what to expect in a card game or a woodwind quartet rehearsal or wedding or a ball game or an arithmetic lesson or a mystery story or a travelog or a chapter in a physics book. The fact that the reader's possession of such schemata or such knowledge of the world plays an important part in text comprehension was discussed earlier in this chapter.

This interpretation of the relationship between word knowledge and comprehension states that people who have wide exposure to culture acquire a large number of words (and are therefore good at vocabulary tests) and a large number of schemata (and are therefore good at comprehension tests).

♦ These three interpretations of the relationship between word knowledge and comprehension are not air-tight categories. Like empiricism and rationalism, they are spheres of influence that teachers would profit from reflecting on when they make decisions concerning curriculum and method. Some similarities and contrasts among these three interpretations are shown in Figure 8.9.

The aptitude interpretation is no help to teachers. It seems to say if you want better reading comprehension, produce more intelligent people. The instrumental interpretation indicates that if your students learn more word meanings, they will become better comprehenders. The knowledge of the world interpretation indicates that if your students are exposed to the concepts, procedures, attributes, and relationships that are important in their culture, particularly the literate culture they have access to, they will not only learn the vocabulary, but will also acquire the schemata that will facilitate comprehension of written texts.

IS READING COMPREHENSION DIFFERENT FROM GENERAL LANGUAGE COMPREHENSION?

There are three possible views regarding the relationship between language processing abilities used in listening comprehension and

FIGURE 8.9
CONTRASTS AND SIMILARITIES IN THREE INTERPRETATIONS OF THE RELATIONSHIP BETWEEN VOCABULARY AND COMPREHENSION.

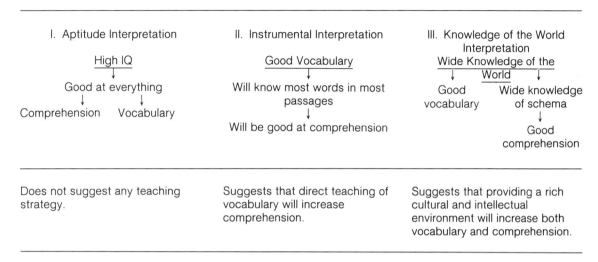

I and III suggest that vocabulary and comprehension are independent, but are caused by a common antecedent.

II suggests that good vocabulary is a direct cause of good comprehension.

II and III suggest teaching strategies; I does not suggest any teaching strategy.

II suggests direct teaching of vocabulary; III suggests indirect teaching of both vocabulary and comprehension.

But note well: The first causes in the models—IQ in I, good vocabulary in II, and wide knowledge of the world in III—may be very highly related. For this reason, people tend to slip from one model to another without being aware of it.

language processing abilities used in reading. They are:

1. That they are separate. That children who understand oral language must learn to understand written language as an unrelated, independent skill.
2. That they are essentially the same thing— reading comprehension is nothing more than decoding plus oral language comprehension.

3. That there is a great deal of overlap between language processes employed in understanding spoken and written language, but there are some language processing abilities uniquely relevant to understanding written language (see Figure 8.10).

The validity and implications of these three positions will be discussed in this section.

Is Reading Comprehension Unrelated to Listening Comprehension?

This position is patently untenable, and it receives no positive support from the literature. If it receives any support, it is in the form of what is implied by some teaching procedures. Sometimes teachers present written sentences like 18 to normal second-graders and ask questions like 19 and 20.

18. *The red ball hit the old barn.*

19. *What color is the ball?*

20. *What word tells you what color the ball is?*

If the teacher views this as a lesson to teach the child to comprehend the sentence, there is a clear implication that the teacher thinks comprehension of written language is separate from comprehension of spoken language, since a normal second-grader would be expected to comprehend sentence 18 in its spoken form. However, when teachers engage in such lessons, most of them do not presume to be teaching comprehension directly; they are attempting to teach students to reflect on the way language works, or they are attempting to demonstrate to the students that those language processing abilities used in the comprehension of oral language apply to written languages as well.

Is Reading Comprehension Decoding plus Oral Language Comprehension?

Several implications follow when one presumes that reading comprehension is nothing more than decoding plus those language skills developed in understanding oral language.

FIGURE 8.10
POSSIBLE RELATIONSHIPS BETWEEN LANGUAGE-PROCESSING ABILITIES NECESSARY TO COMPREHEND SPOKEN LANGUAGE AND TO COMPREHEND WRITTEN LANGUAGE.

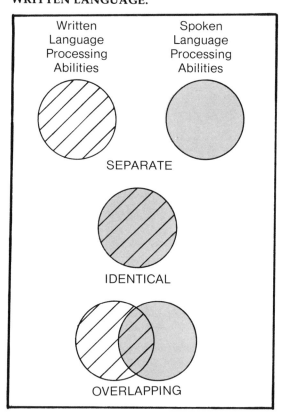

EMPHASIS ON DECODING

Perhaps the most straightforward statement of this position was written by Barnhart (1961): "The child [beginning reader] has had five or six years' experience in acquiring meanings, and he uses them readily in many kinds of syntactical patterns. He knows how to speak the English language, but he does not know how to read the forms of words" (pp. 9–10). The logical conclusion is that teaching reading is teaching the "forms of words"—the word recognition skills.

Some experts argue that inability to recognize words or slow, laborious word recognition processes so impede the entire process that the language comprehension component cannot function. They therefore emphasize rapid word recognition as a prerequisite for teaching reading comprehension. See, for example, LaBerge and Samuels (1974), Perfetti (1977), and Perfetti and Lesgold (1979).

This position implies a one-way relationship between decoding and written language comprehension—that is, decoding facilitates comprehension. However, it has been demonstrated by numerous writers (many of them cited earlier in this book) that *comprehension also facilitates decoding.*

EMPHASIS ON ORAL LANGUAGE SKILLS

Berger (1975) has demonstrated that in early grades, children who are superior in listening comprehension are also superior in reading comprehension. This relationship leads some experts to the conclusion that there is a ceiling imposed on reading comprehension by oral language comprehension, and that if oral language comprehension can be improved, reading comprehension will naturally follow.

EMPHASIS ON TRANSFER OF ORAL LANGUAGE SKILLS

There is a great deal of evidence, however, that children do not automatically use what they know about oral language comprehension when they are attempting to comprehend written language. Kennedy and Weener (1973), for example, have shown that comprehension training with written material leads to greater improvement in reading comprehension tasks than comprehension training with oral language.

Griffin (1977) identified a group of what she calls "middle range readers" as those who can "read," but who receive minimal information or enjoyment from reading. One problem she identifies in this group is what she calls "the gap." These readers do not realize that there are similarities between how one uses language in reading and how one uses language in speech. One powerful argument in favor of the language experience approach to beginning reading is that the relationship between oral language and written language is apparent. The teacher writes what the children say, and the written text becomes reading material.

Are Reading Comprehension Skills Different from Oral Language Comprehension Skills?

Although a child who does not use what he or she knows about understanding spoken language to understand written language is mostly decidedly in trouble, it is a mistake to think that written language is simply "talk written down."

FORMAL DIFFERENCES IN BEGINNING MATERIALS

The language of the texts children are asked to read even at the very earliest stages is different from oral language. In an effort to create a text using a limited number of words, sequences of sentences that would almost never appear in speech appear in beginning reading material.

— *We will go to the zoo.*

— *We will go on a bus.*

— *Will you come?*

— *Will you come to the zoo?*

— *Will you come on the bus?*

Also at the very earliest stages, the formality of written language intrudes, and children are asked to read sentences that are worded differently from what one would expect in a child's usual experience with oral language. One sees *He will go* or *He'll go*, rather than *He's gonna go*, as one would expect in speech.

Children in the first half of first grade are not expected to recognize very many words, and it is very difficult to write stories using only the words the children are expected to recognize. This leads to two peculiarities. Beck and her associates (1979) refer to these two problems as alternative wording and omitted information.

Alternative Wording. Among the stories presented very early in the Ginn series (Clymer, 1976a) is an account of the fable of the tortoise and the hare. The story is entitled "Rabbit and Turtle." This is a story of a race, and one of the important events is that the overconfident rabbit stops to rest and falls to sleep. But because of the children's limited word recognition facility, the word *race* is not used in the text.

The authors overcome this problem by a combination of "roundabout language" in the children's text and suggestions to the teacher in the teacher's manual. In the text, Turtle says: "See the park. You and I will run. We'll run to the park." In the teacher's manual (Clymer, 1976a), the following suggestion is made to the teacher:

Ask what Turtle meant by saying "We'll run to the park." If the idea of a race is not men-

tioned, suggest it. Help the children realize that Turtle was challenging Rabbit to a race. (p. 117)

Omitted Information. At times, elements of stories are omitted in beginning reading stories. For example, in a story entitled "Who Said 'Hello'?" the children's text runs as follows:

— *"Come with me, Ben.*

— *I want to see the zoo," said Bill.*

— *Ben said, "Stop, Bill.*

— *Who said 'Hello'?*

— *Who said 'Hello' to me?" (Clymer, 1976b, p. 7)*

This text has a serious omission: There is no mention that anyone said "hello" to Ben. Beck et al. note that this is a serious omission and suggest that it could be remedied by supplying the missing information as part of the reading lesson. The teacher might say, "When Ben and Bill got to the zoo, Ben heard someone say something to him. Read this page and find out what someone said to Ben."

These are typical examples of attempts to "teach" comprehension in the initial stages of reading instruction. Notice it is not presumed that the children can simply apply what they know about understanding spoken language to the stories. On the contrary, the very legitimate concern for the comprehension of these stories has to do with the fact that the written texts are unlike spoken language.

DIFFERENCES BETWEEN SPEECH AND "INSTITUTIONAL WRITING"

A frequently made observation is that when a child's reading skills have progressed to where he or she can read materials written at around the fourth-grade level, the child begins to devote less energy to learning to read and more to reading to learn. At about the fourth-grade level, children begin to encounter materials that are designed more to convey information, rather than to teach children to read. Reading materials begin to display those characteristics that are typical of written language in general, or what Stubbs (1980) refers to as "institutional writing."

Stubbs defines *institutional writing* as "all normal published books and, therefore, the vast bulk of written material" (p. 108). He distinguishes this writing from personal correspondence such as a postcard from grandmother. The language skills necessary for reading personal correspondence closely correspond to the language skills used in listening and speaking. The language skills necessary for reading institutional writing include some skills not usually needed in understanding oral language.

Differences Arising from Institutional Writing.

In a chapter entitled "The Function of Written Language," Stubbs (1980) points out important ways in which writing is used that separate written from spoken language.

Writing enables us to record language in a way that is accurate, permanent, and transportable. Therefore, writing communicates over time and space and provides an "external social memory." Historically, writing was first put to use in recordkeeping for government and commerce. Such records have little in common with spoken language. They are often lists or tables and are not read in sequence, but are arranged so the reader can find that portion of the list or table that interests him or her without "reading" what comes before or after it.

Many intellectual advances that followed the invention of writing appear to have been impossible without writing. Science and history, as we know them, could not have developed without writing. First, the limitations of human memory would not permit it, and second, writing makes it convenient to state beliefs and theories publicly, explicitly, and accurately. Public, accurate, and explicit statements can be challenged. Without this process, science and history could not progress. Goody and Watt (1968) argue that with the advent of widespread literacy in Greece, many inconsistencies in the oral tradition were noticed, and this process led to challenges to accepted world views.

Unique Characteristics of Institutional Writing.

Each of the following traits characterizes institutional writing. They are important to this discussion because they specify important differences between institutional writing on one hand, and spoken language and personal written communication on the other.

— *Institutional writing is public rather than private.* The personal identity of the author is not important, and the writing is not addressed to any individual. The focus is on the content of the writing.

— *Institutional writing is accurate.* Because of the formality of the channel and the writer's ability to stop and check facts and reformulate statements, the inaccuracy and generality of spoken discourse is replaced by accurate, researched facts and precisely stated details.

— *Institutional writing is explicit.* Because of the distance and lack of familiarity between writer and reader, the author cannot assume the reader holds any particular opinion or knows any particular fact. Because the reader cannot stop the writer to ask for clarification, descriptions and explanations must be complete and arguments spelled out exactly.

— *Institutional writing is edited.* Institutional writing is often rewritten several times and by both an author and an editor. Stubbs (1980) has pointed out that this should make written language easier to understand than spoken language, since it is better organized and can be reread. But editing results in denser, less redundant language that is more difficult to understand.

Because these characteristics are unique to institutional written language and distinct from spoken language and personal written communication, they may tap comprehension skills untapped by spoken language that will, according to Stubbs (1980), "require a great deal of explanation and practice."

Teaching Comprehension Skills

In the next chapter we present methods of teaching reading comprehension. The methods concentrate on comprehension strategies that apply to both listening and reading. Some of these strategies deal with oral language, and attempts are made to show how they apply to reading as a second step.

Other methods will be presented in the next chapter that concentrate on the comprehension strategies demanded by the particular characteristics of writing, particularly institutional writing. Some of these strategies appear early in reading programs because from the start, written language has characteristics one does not find in oral language. Lessons of this type continue throughout the reading program because, as the student progresses into the middle and upper grades, the characteristics of institutional written language become more pronounced in the texts children are expected to read. Lessons in study skills and reading in content areas pay particular attention to comprehension of information con-

veyed through written texts and other print media, such as graphs, maps, and charts.

SUMMARY

Some concepts of reading comprehension have been derived from psycholinguistic research. Early psycholinguistic research concentrated on sentence comprehension, particularly as it related to sensing relationships between sentences based on transformational grammar. Additional research showed, however, that people may understand individual sentences, but they remember semantic events—not individual sentences.

Later research has concentrated on the relationship between the knowledge readers bring to the printed page and comprehension. Whether or not language is ambiguous sometimes depends on the reader's previous knowledge. Language sometimes depends on the context to which it refers to a degree that it is incomprehensible without knowledge of the context.

Much recent research in comprehension has dealt with schema theory. Experience teaches more than simple isolated facts. The human mind perceives relationships between facts and imposes order on information. Soon one uses structures based on previously determined relationships in perceiving and making sense of new experiences. These structures are called schemata. Comprehension depends to a certain extent on the schemata the reader possesses.

Forms of literature (stories, essays, editorials) follow general outlines. Stories, for example, often have the same structure—setting, beginning, reaction, attempt, outcome, and ending. This kind of outline is called a story grammar, and it describes a story schema. Research has shown that readers rely on story schema in their comprehension and recall of stories.

Observing the oral reading miscues of children reveals that comprehension is a complex process involving word recognition, knowledge of syntax and semantics, and previous knowledge of the world. The psycholinguistic model of reading is based on observations of this type. Proponents of this model stress the importance of the reader's knowledge of language and knowledge of the world; they deemphasize the "outer" aspects of reading, such as word recognition skills.

Because of the great complexity of comprehension and the many factors involved, definitions tend to be abstract. Several definitions from recognized authorities were presented in this chapter.

Practices of teaching comprehension have been greatly influenced by theories of testing comprehension. Tests have been developed that attempt to measure the subskills thought to make up the comprehension process—such as perceiving the main idea, recalling details, and sensing the author's purpose. Attempts to demonstrate through factor analysis that these subskills are separate have not been successful.

One explanation for the failure of factor analysis to demonstrate the separateness of subskills is that the subskills may be related hierarchically. It has been suggested, for example, that one can understand sentences and fail to understand relationships between sentences, but one could not understand relationships between sentences without understanding the sentences. It would follow that there is a hierarchical relationship between sentence comprehension and paragraph comprehension—paragraph comprehension being the "higher" skill.

Hierarchical taxonomies based on logic rather than experimentation have had an enormous effect on the way reading comprehension is conceptualized and taught. The most influential of these taxonomies was developed by Bloom and his colleagues (1956) for testing educational objectives in general. This taxonomy has been tailored to apply specifically to reading comprehension by several authors such as Barrett (in Clymer, 1968).

One undisputed fact emerges from all experimental evidence: Vocabulary or word knowledge is intimately related to comprehension. This fact has been interpreted in several ways.

It is proposed that people with a great capacity for learning acquire large vocabularies and are good at comprehension—thus comprehension and vocabulary are related because they both spring from intelligence. This is the *aptitude interpretation.*

It has been proposed that people who have good vocabularies are less likely to encounter words they do not know the meaning of than people who have poor vocabularies—thus comprehension and vocabulary are related because comprehension depends on vocabulary. This is known as the *instrumental interpretation.*

It has been proposed that people who experience a rich cultural and intellectual environment acquire both good vocabularies and schemata that are relevant to the literature of the culture—thus comprehension and vocabulary are related, because both depend on rich cultural and intellectual experiences. This is known as *the knowledge of the world interpretation.*

An important question for people who propose to improve reading comprehension is how reading comprehension is related to listening comprehension. The proposition that they are not related is patently false. The position that comprehension of written and spoken language are essentially the same thing has many adherents. On one side, this assumption leads to an emphasis on rapid, effortless decoding, since reading comprehension is viewed as listening comprehension (which students presumably can already do) plus decoding. However, this same position leads others to conclude that teachers should emphasize spoken language comprehension skill or transfer of spoken language skills to reading.

The final position is that written language comprehension draws heavily on the same skills as oral language comprehension, but because of the use to which written language is put, some characteristics of written language are not present in oral language. This position leads to the conclusion that those characteristics unique to institutional written language need to be explained to students, and students need to be given practice in dealing with them. Strategies for teaching study skills and reading in content areas tend to concentrate on these characteristics of institutional written language.

FOR FURTHER READING AND DISCUSSION

One of the longest-standing controversies in the field of reading scholarship is the question of whether a subskills theory of comprehension can be demonstrated by statistical procedures. Read the following works, which are landmarks in this debate. What does the evidence seem to suggest?

Davis, F. B. Fundamental factors of comprehension in reading. *Psychometrika*, 9 (1944): 185–197.

Thurston, L. L. Note on a reanalysis of Davis' Reading Tests. *Psychometrika*, 11 (1946): 185–88.

Davis, F. B. A brief comment on Thurston's note on a reanalysis of Davis' Reading Tests. *Psychometrika*, 11 (1946): 249–55.

Lennon, R. T. What can be measured? *The Reading Teacher* (1962): 326–37.

Spearritt, D. Identification of subskills of reading comprehension by maximum likelihood factor analysis. *Reading Research Quarterly*, 8 (1972): 92–111.

There is a great deal involved in the study and teaching of reading comprehension. Authors sometimes contradict one another. On the other hand, when one author stresses a particular aspect of the process and another author stresses a different aspect of the process, they may only *appear* to contradict one another.

1. The following two articles stress the role of decoding (word recognition skills).

Perfetti, C. A., and A. M. Lesgold. Coding and comprehension in skilled reading and implications for instruction. In L. B. Resnick and P. A. Weaver, *Theory and Practice of Early Reading*. Hillsdale, NJ: Lawrence Erlbaum Associates, 1979, 57–84.

LaBerge, D., and S. J. Samuels. Toward a theory of automatic information processing in reading. *Cognitive Psychology*, 6 (1974): 293–323.

2. The following two articles deemphasize decoding and stress the similarity and continuity between oral language processing and written language processing.

Goodman, K. S., and Y. M. Goodman. Learning about psycholinguistic processes by analyzing oral reading. *Harvard Educational Review*, 47 (1977): 317–33.

Smith, F. Making sense of reading and reading instruction. *Harvard Educational Review*, 47 (1977): 386–95.

3. The following book chapter stresses the dissimilarity between oral language and the written language encountered in textbooks.

Stubbs, M. The functions of written language. In *Language and Literacy.* London: Routledge & Kegan Paul, 1980, 97–115.

4. The following article stresses the importance of the child's possessing a story schema for comprehension.

Whaley, J. F. Readers' expectations for story structure. *Reading Research Quarterly,* 17 (1981): 90–114.

Read the articles cited under 1 and 2 above. Do these authors contradict one another, or do they simply focus on different aspects of the comprehension process? If they contradict one another, which do you agree with? If you think they differ only in emphasis, which emphasis do you think is more useful for teachers of reading?

Read the articles cited under 2 and 3 above. Do these two authors contradict one another, or do they simply focus on different aspects of the process? If they contradict one another, which do you agree with? If you think they differ only in emphasis, which emphasis do you think is more useful for teachers of reading?

Read the articles cited under 2 and 4 above. Both articles deemphasize the role of word recognition skills and focus on the knowledge the reader brings to the reading process. Are they talking about the same or different kinds of knowledge? Do you think one is a more useful discussion than the other?

REFERENCES

Anderson, R. C. How to assess achievement tests to assess comprehension. *Review of Educational Research,* 42 (1972): 145–70.

————, and P. Freebody. Vocabulary knowledge. In J. T. Guthrie, *Comprehension and Teaching: Research Reviews.* Newark, DE: International Reading Association, 1981, 77–117.

Anderson, R. C., R. E. Reynolds, D. L. Schallert, and E. T. Goetz. Frameworks for comprehending discourse. *American Educational Research Journal,* 14 (1977): 367–81.

Applebee, A. N. *Child's Concept of Story: Ages 2–17.* Chicago: University of Chicago Press, 1978.

Athey, I. Syntax, semantics and reading. In J. T. Guthrie, *Cognition, Curriculum and Comprehension.* Newark, DE: International Reading Association, 1977, 71–98.

Barnhart, C. L. The story of the Bloomfield system. In L. Bloomfield and C. L. Barnhart, *Let's Read. A Linguistic Approach.* Detroit: Wayne State University Press, 1961, 9–18.

Bartlett, F. C. *Remembering.* Cambridge, Eng.: Cambridge University Press, 1932.

Beck, I. L., M. G. McKeown, E. S. McCaslin, and A. M. Burkes. *Instructional Dimensions That May Affect Reading Comprehension: Examples from Two Commercial Reading Programs.* Pittsburgh: Learning Research and Development Center, University of Pittsburgh, 1979. ERIC Document 197322.

Berger, N. An investigation of linguistic competence and organizational processes in good and poor readers. Unpublished Ph.D. dissertation, University of Pittsburgh, 1975.

Bloom, B. S., M. D. Engelhart, E. J. Furst, W. H. Hill, and D. R. Krathwohl. *Taxonomy of Educational Objectives. The Classification of Educational Goals. Handbook I: Cognitive Domain.* New York: David McKay, 1956.

Bormuth, J. R. An operational definition of comprehension instruction. IN K. S. Goodman and J. T. Fleming (eds.), *Psycholinguistics and the Teaching of Reading.* Newark, DE: International Reading Association, 1969, 48–60.

————. *On the Theory of Achievement Test Items.* Chicago: University of Chicago Press, 1970.

————, J. Manning, J. Carr, and D. Pearson. Children's comprehension of between- and within-sentence syntactic structures. *Journal of Educational Psychology,* 61 (1970): 349–57.

Bower, G. H., J. B. Black, and T. J. Turner. Scripts in memory for text. *Cognitive Psychology,* 11 (1979): 177–220.

Bransford, J. D., and J. J. Franks. The abstraction of linguistic ideas. *Cognitive Psychology,* 2 (1971): 331–50.

Bransford, J. D., and M. K. Johnson. Considerations of some problems of comprehension. In W. G. Chase (ed.), *Visual Information Processing.* New York: Academic Press, 1973, 383–438.

Chapman, C. A. A test of a hierarchical theory of reading comprehension. Unpublished Ph.D. dissertation, University of Chicago, 1971.

Clymer, T. (senior author). *Teacher's Guide for Reading 720, Level 3.* Lexington, MA: Ginn, 1976a.

———— (senior author). *Teacher's Guide for Reading 720, Level 4.* Lexington, MA: Ginn, 1976b.

————. What is 'reading'? Some current concepts. In H. M. Robinson (ed.), *Innovation and Change in Reading Instruction. Sixty-seventh Yearbook of the National Society for the Study of Education, Part II.* Chicago: University of Chicago Press, 1968, 7–29.

Cromer, W. The effects of "pre-organizing" reading material on two levels of poor readers. Unpublished Ph.D. dissertation, Clark University, 1968.

Davis, F. B. Fundamental factors of comprehension in reading. *Psychometrika,* 9 (1944): 185–97.

————. A brief comment on Thurston's note on a reanalysis of Davis' Reading Tests. *Psychometrika,* 11 (1946): 249–55.

————. Research in comprehension in reading. *Reading Research Quarterly,* 3 (1968): 499–545.

————. Psychometric research on comprehension in reading. *Reading Research Quarterly,* 7 (1972): 628–78.

Feldman, M. J., Evaluating pre-primer basal readers using story grammar. Unpublished Ph.D. dissertation, State University of New York at Buffalo, 1983.

Gates, A. I. Character and purposes of the yearbook. In N. B. Henry (ed.), *The Forty-Eighth Yearbook of the National Society for the Study of Education—Part II. Reading in the Elementary School.* Chicago: University of Chicago Press, 1949, 1–10.

Goodman, K. S. Reading: A psycholinguistic guessing game. *Journal of the Reading Specialist,* 6 (1967): 126–35.

————. Analysis of reading miscues: Applied psycholinguistics. *Reading Research Quarterly,* 5 (1969): 9–30.

————, and Y. M. Goodman. Learning about psycholinguistic processes by analyzing oral reading. *Harvard Educational Review,* 47 (1977): 317–33.

Goodman, Y. M. Miscues, errors and reading comprehension. In J. E. Merritt (ed.), *New Horizons in Reading.* Newark, DE: International Reading Association, 1976, 86–93.

————, and C. L. Burke, *Reading Miscue Inventory.* New York: Macmillan, 1972.

Goody, J., and I. Watt. The consequences of literacy. In J. Goody (ed.), *Literacy in Traditional Societies.* London: Cambridge University Press, 1968, 27–68.

Griffin, P. Reading and pragmatics. In R. W. Shuy, *Linguistic Theory: What Can It Say about Reading.* Newark, DE: International Reading Association, 1977, 123–42.

Huey, E. B. *The Psychology and Pedagogy of Reading.* New York: Macmillan, 1908. Reprinted, Cambridge, MA: MIT Press, 1968.

Kant, I. *Critique of Pure Reason* (N. Kemp Smith, translator). London: Macmillan, 1963. Originally published 1781.

Kennedy, D. K., and P. Weener. Visual and auditory training with the cloze procedure to improve reading and listening comprehension. *Reading Research Quarterly,* 8 (1973): 524–41.

LaBerge, D., and S. J. Samuels. Toward a theory of automatic information processing in reading. *Cognitive Psychology,* 6 (1974): 293–323.

Lennon, R. T. What can be measured? *The Reading Teacher* (1962): 326–37.

Mandler, J. M. A code in the node: The use of a story schema in retrieval. *Discourse Processes,* 1 (1978): 14–35.

————, and N. S. Johnson. Remembrance of things parsed: Story structure and recall. *Cognitive Psychology,* 9 (1977): 111–51.

Pearson, P. D., and D. D. Johnson. *Teaching Reading Comprehension.* New York: Holt, Rinehart and Winston, 1978.

Perfetti, C. A. Language comprehension and fast decoding: Some psycholinguistic prerequisites for skilled reading comprehension. In J. T. Guthrie, *Cognition, Curriculum and Comprehension.* Newark, DE: International Reading Association, 1977, 20–41.

————, and A. M. Lesgold. Coding and comprehension in skilled reading and implications for instruction. In L. B. Resnick and P. A. Weaver, *Theory and Practice of Early Reading.* Hillsdale, NJ: Lawrence Erlbaum Associates, 1979, 57–84.

Poulsen, D., E. Kintsch, W. Kintsch, and D. Premack. Children's comprehension and memory for stories. *Journal of Experimental Child Psychology*, 28 (1979): 379–403.

Rumelhart, D. E. Understanding and summarizing brief stories. In D. LaBerge and J. Samuels (eds.), *Basic Processes in Reading: Perception and Comprehension*. Hillsdale, NJ: Lawrence Erlbaum Associates, 1978.

Simons, H. D. Reading comprehension: The need for a new perspective. *Reading Research Quarterly*, 6 (1971): 338–63.

————. Linguistic skills and reading comprehension. In H. A. Klein (ed.), *The Quest for Competency in Teaching Reading*. Newark, DE: International Reading Asociation, 1972, 165–70.

Smith, F. *Understanding Reading: A Psycholinguistic Analysis of Reading and Learning to Read*. New York: Holt, Rinehart and Winston, 1971.

————. Making sense of reading and reading instruction. *Harvard Educational Review*, 47 (1977): 386–95.

Spearritt, D. Identification of subskills of reading comprehension by maximum likelihood factor analysis. *Reading Research Quarterly*, 8 (1972): 92–111.

Stein, N. L., and C. G. Glenn. The role of structural variation in children's recall of simple stories. Paper presented at the Society for Research in Child Development, New Orleans, 1977.

————. An analysis of story comprehension in elementary school children. In R. O. Freedle (ed.), *Discourse Processing: Multidisciplinary Perspectives*. Hillsdale, NJ: Ablex, Inc., 1979.

Stein, N. L., and T. Nezworski. The effects of organization and instructional set on story memory. *Discourse Processes*, 1 (1978): 177–93.

Stubbs, M. *Language and Literacy*. London: Routledge and Kegan Paul, 1980.

Terman, L. M. Vocabulary test as a measure of intelligence. *Journal of Educational Psychology*, 9 (1918): 452–66.

Thorndike, E. L. Reading as reasoning: A study of mistakes in paragraph meaning. *Journal of Educational Psychology*, 8 (1917): 323–32. Reprinted in *Reading Research Quarterly*, 6 (1971): 425–34.

Thorndike, R. L. *Reading Comprehension Education in Fifteen Countries*. New York: Wiley, 1973.

Thorndyke, P. Cognitive structures in comprehension and memory of narrative discourse. *Cognitive Psychology*, 9 (1977): 77–110.

Thurston, L. L. Note on a reanalysis of Davis' Reading Tests. *Psychometrika*, 11 (1946): 185–88.

Trabasso, T. On the making of inferences during reading and their assessment. In J. T. Guthrie, *Comprehension and Teaching: Research Reviews*. Newark, DE: International Reading Association, 1981, 56–76.

Tuinman, J. J., and M. E. Brady. How does vocabulary account for variance on reading comprehension tests? A preliminary instructional analysis. In P. Nacke (ed.), *Interaction: Research and Practice for College-Adult Reading*. Clemson, SC: National Reading Conference, 1974, 176–84.

Whaley, J. F. Readers' expectations for story structure. *Reading Research Quarterly*, 17 (1981): 90–114.

Wimmer, H. Children's comprehension and recall of hierarchically structured stories. Paper presented at the meeting of the Society for Research in Child Development, San Francisco, March 1979.

CHAPTER
9

TEACHING READING COMPREHENSION
ISSUES, PRACTICES, AND SUGGESTIONS

DEFINITIONS: COMPREHENSION INSTRUCTION

ASSUMPTIONS ABOUT TEACHING AND
LEARNING COMPREHENSION

Comprehension Can Be Taught Directly
Comprehension Can Be Taught Indirectly

EXPOSURE TO RICH AND VARIED
LANGUAGE EXPERIENCES
METALINGUISTIC AWARENESS
AWARENESS OF LANGUAGE IN A GENERAL
SENSE
AWARENESS OF PARTICULAR LANGUAGE
STRUCTURES

THE DIRECTED READING LESSON

The Preparation Stage

SUPPLYING BACKGROUND KNOWLEDGE
VOCABULARY
PURPOSE SETTING

The Question/Discussion Stage

QUESTIONING AS A TEACHING METHOD
FRAMEWORKS FOR GENERATING
QUESTIONS
A WORD IN DEFENSE OF LITERAL, FACTUAL
QUESTIONS
COMPREHENSION QUESTIONS AND
METACOGNITION

The Skills Development Stage

SENTENCE COMPREHENSION SKILLS
PARAGRAPH AND PASSAGE
COMPREHENSION SKILLS

TEACHING NEW VOCABULARY

The Complexities of Word Meaning
What Does It Mean to Know a Word?

OPPORTUNITIES ARISING FROM THE
COMPLEXITY OF WORD MEANING
LESSONS SUGGESTED BY WORDS IN
READING SELECTIONS

Teaching Words Related Through the
"Semantic Network"

SEMANTIC FEATURE ANALYSIS

Teaching Words Having the Same Morphemes

COMPREHENSION, FLUENCY, RATE OF READING,
AND FLEXIBILITY

Fluency
Rate of Reading

MEASURING RATE
HOW SLOW IS TOO SLOW?
MECHANICAL READING PACERS

Flexibility

  SPEEDING UP AND SLOWING DOWN A
    SINGLE PROCESS
  SWITCHING FROM ONE PROCESS TO
    ANOTHER
  ADVANTAGES AND DISADVANTAGES OF
    CHANGING RATE

Increasing Rate and Flexibility: Two Different
Goals

TEACHING COMPREHENSION AS "READING TO
LEARN"

Teaching Reading in the Content Areas
  VOCABULARY
  INFORMATION IN GRAPHIC,
    DIAGRAMMATIC, AND PICTORIAL FORM

Teaching Study Skills

  LOCATING INFORMATION
  INTERPRETING INFORMATION
  RECORDING INFORMATION
  RECALLING INFORMATION
  A FORMULA FOR EFFECTIVE STUDY: SQ3R

The Reading Teacher's Responsibility

SUMMARY

FOR FURTHER READING AND DISCUSSION

REFERENCES

DEFINITIONS: COMPREHENSION INSTRUCTION

When Durkin (1979) set out to observe classroom instruction to discover what was being done to teach comprehension, her first task was to define *comprehension instruction* so she would recognize it when she saw it. To her surprise, she found she could not find a definition in the literature. In formulating her own definition, she was faced with two choices. One choice was to define comprehension instruction as everything that helps children to read. That would include, of course, word recognition, phonics, word meaning, and so on. In short, teaching comprehension would be equivalent to teaching reading. A second choice was to exclude from comprehension instruction all instruction concerned with single isolated words and to include only efforts "(a) to teach children the meaning of a

unit that is larger than a word, or (b) to teach them how to work out the meanings of such units" (p. 487).

Reading was observed in twenty-four fourth-grade classrooms for 4,469 minutes. Using Durkin's definition, comprehension instruction was observed during only twenty-eight minutes, less than 1 percent of the time! Durkin comments:

Practically no comprehension instruction was seen. Comprehension assessment, carried on for the most part through interrogation, was common. Whether children's answers were right or wrong was the big concern. (p. 520)

Hodges (1980) used the same observational data as Durkin but adopted a broader definition of reading comprehension instruction. Hodges found that comprehension instruction was observed 23 percent of the time. The difference is accounted for by the fact that

Hodges defined many more activities as teaching comprehension. She accepted, for example, teaching new vocabulary in context, setting a purpose for reading, discussing the story background, asking questions after the child had read, and presenting feedback on written comprehension assignments. By far, most of the comprehension instruction observed using the Hodges definition was questioning after reading and feedback on written assignments.

In another study, Wilder (1977) asked teachers in five schools that were identified as having outstanding reading programs what they did when they taught comprehension. They mentioned comprehension exercises in publishers' materials used in their classrooms, use of questions, group discussions, listening exercises, vocabulary development, and broadening children's experiential base. They did not present a definable, concentrated set of principles or procedures related to instruction for comprehension.

Wilder's conclusion is that comprehension instruction is not thought of in isolation by reading teachers, but is part of "exposure to language in all forms" (p. 277).

ASSUMPTIONS ABOUT TEACHING AND LEARNING COMPREHENSION

Four positions will be examined here. The first is that comprehension can be taught directly. The remaining three maintain that comprehension cannot be taught directly, but can be improved, facilitated, and enhanced (1) through exposure to rich and varied language experiences; (2) through experiences that encourage students to reflect upon and make explicit the connection between *their general use of language,* their experience, and their knowl-

edge of the world; and (3) through exercises and experiences that encourage students to reflect upon and make explicit the connection between *their use of particular aspects of language* (those known to cause difficulty), their experience, and their knowledge of the world.

In order to explore, contrast, and compare these four positions, imagine a normal third-grade child who recognizes each word in Figure 9.1, but who reads sentence 1 and reports that it says George went to the movies or Bob did the dishes.

1. *George will go to the movies if Bob will do the dishes.*

One can presume that word recognition is not the cause of difficulty, but that comprehension or comprehension skills are to blame. What action would be indicated by each of the positions stated above?

Comprehension Can Be Taught Directly

This position would indicate that the child could be taught the meaning of this sentence directly through teaching the meanings of words such as *will* (indicating future) and *if* (indicating condition), or through teaching the child to recognize main clauses and subordinate clauses, and the relationship between the clauses in sentences like sentence 1.

This is an extreme position, and it does not receive much support. Durkin (1979) adopted this position in defining comprehension for her classroom observation study. She found comprehension teaching by this definition to occur less than 1 percent of the time spent in reading instruction. One interpretation of this finding is that practically no teachers share Durkin's presumption about how comprehension is learned or how it should be taught.

FIGURE 9.1
ALPHABETICAL LIST OF WORDS IN SENTENCE 1.

Bob	do	go	the
dishes	George	if	to
		movies	will

Bormuth (1969) seemed to have adopted the position that comprehension can be taught directly when he wrote:

[T]he content of comprehension instruction might be said to be the rules describing how the language system works to transmit information, and the tasks of research in reading comprehension instruction are: (1) to enumerate these rules; (2) to develop teaching tasks for shaping children's behaviors in the manners described by these rules; and (3) to organize them into a systematic sequence for instruction by determining their relative complexities. (p.50)

But in the next paragraph Bormuth insists he is not advocating the teaching of formal grammar or rhetoric and asserts that children can respond to the signaling systems of language without conscious knowledge of grammar or rhetoric (p. 51). This leads to a more often stated position that teaching comprehension is teaching how language works, but that children learn this indirectly rather than directly.

Comprehension Can Be Taught Indirectly

EXPOSURE TO RICH AND VARIED LANGUAGE EXPERIENCES

There are many adherents of the point of view that children do not "learn" language from being taught directly but acquire language through maturation and experience. If a child is involved in a great many activities involving language, he or she will undoubtedly be exposed to many sentences having the structure *A will happen if B happens* (such as in sentences 2 and 3) in contexts where the child understands the relationship between A and B.

2. *I will give you a cookie if Mommy brings some home.*

3. *Bill will see Ernie and Bert if he watches "Sesame Street."*

Given enough cognitive development and enough such experience, the child will learn to understand sentences like 1. Adherents of this point of view tend to consider providing any and all language experiences as teaching comprehension. It is this view that Wilder (1977) expresses when she concludes: "An effective reading program includes . . . exposure to language in all its forms (written, spoken, poetry, prose, etc.) and . . . comprehension is directly related to the amount, intensity and affect connected with the exposure" (p. 277).

Adherents of this point of view tend to put their faith in the "amount, intensity and affect" of language experience rather than in lessons focused on particular language structures. One would not expect such teachers to create lessons specifically concerned with sentences containing *if* clauses or with any other particular language structure.

Indirect teaching that tends toward general language development rather than focused language development is not without its critics, however. Singer and Balow (1981), in reviewing large-scale programs for increasing learning among disadvantaged preschoolers and primary grade students, conclude: "If you want pupils to learn a particular skill or knowledge it is more efficient to teach it directly than to expect it to transfer from other learnings'' (p. 309).

METALINGUISTIC AWARENESS

Another point of view is that one does not learn to comprehend through learning definitions and rules, and one does not learn to comprehend through indiscriminate language experiences. Rather, one learns to comprehend through reflecting upon and making explicit one's knowledge of how language works. Conscious, explicit knowledge of how language works is referrred to as *metalinguistic awareness*.

AWARENESS OF LANGUAGE IN A GENERAL SENSE

Two methods for encouraging children to reflect on what they know about language have received considerable attention in recent years. One is the cloze technique, and the other is sentence combining.

The Cloze Technique.   When using the *cloze technique*, one deletes words from a printed passage and replaces the words with blank lines, as in Figure 9.2. Students using the cloze technique write the words into the blank lines that they think must have been the words deleted. There are many ways to vary this technique. One can delete every fifth word, every tenth word, or whatever other numbered interval one wishes. One can delete only nouns, or nouns and verbs, or any words except function words. Another variation is to supply mulitple-choice responses for the student to choose from in filling the blanks, as in Figure 9.3.

The cloze technique was first suggested as a measurement technique. It is used to discover how difficult a written text is to compre-

FIGURE 9.2
EXAMPLE OF A PASSAGE FROM A BASAL READER MADE INTO A CLOZE EXERCISE WITH EVERY FIFTH WORD DELETED.
(From ''The Sea Turtle'' by Keith G. Hay in W. K. Durr, V. O. Windley, and J. E. Kittell, *Kaleidoscope.* Boston: Houghton Mifflin, 1971, p. 157.)

Directions: The following passage was taken from a book and some of the words were replaced by blanks. Write the word in each blank that you think was in the original passage.

Roaming the oceans are the largest turtles in

the world. These giant reptiles are _____ sea

turtles.

If _____ and your whole family _____

get on the bathroom _____ at one time,

your _____ weight would not equal _____

of the leatherback.

hend. In this capacity, it is considered a technique for measuring readability. It is also used to discover how well particular subjects understand a given text. In this capacity, it is considered a technique for measuring reading comprehension.

Kingston and Weaver (1970) (cited in Jongsma, 1971) used a clozelike procedure of deleting lexical items from first-graders's experience stories, having children suggest words that made sense, and discussing how the words were related to context. Martin (1968) (cited in Jongsma, 1971) used a clozelike technique with college freshmen. She replaced lexical words with two choices. After students completed the task individually, the teacher lead a discussion of why certain responses were correct and why others were

FIGURE 9.3
EXAMPLE OF A PASSAGE FROM A BASAL READER MADE INTO MULTIPLE-CHOICE CLOZE EXERCISE.
(From "The Sea Turtle" by Keith G. Hay in W. K Durr, V. O. Windley, and J. E. Kittell, *Kaleidoscope.* Boston: Houghton Mifflin, 1971, p. 157.)

Directions: Circle the word under each blank that you think fits best into the blank so the passage will make sense.

Roaming the oceans are the largest turtles in

the world. These giant reptiles are

_____ sea turtles.
(misnamed,   called,   quickly)

If _____ and your
     (you,   nobody,   orange)

whole family _____ get on
              (snake,   shall,   could)

the bathroom _____ at one
              (table,   scale,   about)

time, your _____ weight would not
          (combined,   separate,   already)

equal _____ of the leatherback.
     (friendly,   these,   that)

---

not. This procedure was followed by cloze tasks having blanks only (no word choices supplied) and a discussion of the choices made by students.

The results of both techniques were promising. In contrast to these studies, there have been several attempts to show that simply having students complete cloze exercises would increase reading ability. These have proved to be disappointing (Jongsma, 1971). It appears that the cloze technique can be valuable when it is used as a vehicle to promote discussion of language—to reflect upon and

make explicit what students know about how language works. But simply performing cloze tasks without the additional discussion and reflection on what one is doing has no benefit. The same conclusion was reached by Bortnick and Lopardo (1973).

Sentence Combining. In the *sentence combining* technique, one presents at least two sentences and a relation between them, and the student writes (or orally recites) the sentence that results from combining the sentences. The sample lesson in Figure 9.4 demonstrates the basic idea of sentence combining. Examples of more complex combining lessons appear in Figures 9.5 and 9.6.

Sentence combining was first suggested as a technique for improving written composition (Hunt, 1965; Mellon, 1969; O'Hare, 1973). Reading researchers have suspected it might have a positive effect on reading comprehension for two reasons: The first is the notion that the language arts are related and that what influences one will influence another. If sentence combining improves written composition, it is likely to improve reading comprehension (Pearson and Camperell, 1981). The second reason is that comprehending complex sentences may be the reverse of creating complex sentences, so increasing skill in creating complex sentences (sentence combining) will facilitate ability to do the reverse—to see the separate sentences and the relations between them when reading (Froese and Kurushima, 1979).

Froese and Kurushima (1979) and Straw (1978) found that sentence combining lessons designed to promote participation by students in discussion improved some measures of comprehension among third- and fourth-grade students. Sentence combining activities are another way that teachers can encourage students to reflect upon and make explicit

FIGURE 9.4
A LESSON IN SENTENCE COMBINING (1).
(Abridged from Lesson 1, Greenberg, McAndrew, and Melerski, 1975, pp. 2–3).

Lesson 1

This is the first type of problem in the workbook. It is also the simplest type. Once you understand how to do these, they will all be easy for you.

Every sentence combining problem has a *matrix sentence* and one or more *insert sentences.* The way to solve the problem is to combine all the insert sentences with the matrix sentence.

The insert sentence will be indented underneath the matrix sentence, like this:

The zebra ate the grass.
    The zebra is *striped*.

The answer to this sample problem would be:

The striped zebra ate the grass.

There might be more than one insert sentence, like this:

The zebra ate the grass.
    The zebra is *striped*
    The grass is *green*.

The answer would be:

The striped zebra ate the green grass.

All you do is take the word *striped* from the first insert sentence and the word *green* from the second insert sentence. You put these words into the matrix sentence where they best fit. You don't have to change any of the words in the matrix sentence; all you do is add words to the *matrix sentence from the insert sentences.*

FIGURE 9.5
A LESSON IN SENTENCE COMBINING (2).
(Abridged from Lesson 5, Greenberg, McAndrew, and Melerski, 1975, pp. 9–12).

Look at this sample:

The dog ran down the street.
    The dog *had lost his master.* (*who*)

Here is the answer:

The dog who had lost his master ran down the street.

Notice the word *who* in parentheses next to the insert sentence. This is a clue word that must also be added to the matrix sentence. From now on, whenever you see a word in parentheses next to an insert sentence, *you must use it in the answer.* The words *who had lost his master* form a clause that can be added to the matrix sentence.

Let's look at another example:

My father can still hit the basket from half court.
    My father *played varsity basketball in high school.* (who)

Here is the answer to this:

My father who played varsity basketball in high school can still hit the basket from half court.

what they know about language and how it relates to their experience and knowledge of the world.

AWARENESS OF PARTICULAR LANGUAGE STRUCTURES

Research and observation have determined that particular language structures may cause comprehension difficulties. For example, Bormuth and others (1970) showed that fourth-graders were considerably more successful in answering questions about sentences like 4 than they were in answering questions about sentences like 5. Likewise, sentences like 6 were easier than sentences like 7.

4. *Finding him was easy.*

5. *For us to find him was easy.*

6. *Joe runs faster than Bill.*

7. *Joe runs as fast as Bill.*

Carol Chomsky (1969) showed that some primary-grade children interpret the question

FIGURE 9.6
A LESSON IN SENTENCE COMBINING (3).
(Abridged from Lesson 12, Greenberg, McAndrew, and Melerski, 1975, pp. 29–32.)

Now let's combine all the different kinds of problems that you know how to do. Look at this one:

(a) The king wanted SOMETHING.
(b)   The king was lonely.
(c)   The king had never had a wife. (*who*)
(d)   He married the Princess Guinevere. (*to marry*)
(e)   Guinevere was beautiful.

The answer you should get is:

The lonely king who never had a wife wanted to marry the beautiful Princess Guinevere.

We've lettered the lines to help discuss this one. By now you should be able to tell that line (a) is the matrix sentence. Line (b) is a simple word embedding problem. You simply have to add the word *lonely* to the matrix sentence. Line (c) requires that you add the clause *who never had a wife* to the matrix sentence. Line (d) you just learned how to do. You remove the word *something* from the matrix sentence and replace it with the words *to marry the Princess Guinevere*. Line (e) is an insert sentence. It requires you to put the word *beautiful* into the insert sentence above it, so that you end up with *to marry the beautiful Princess Guinevere* as the phrase that replaced the word *something*.

FIGURE 9.7
CLASS ACTIVITY TO PROMOTE COMPREHENSION OF SENTENCE TYPES KNOWN TO CAUSE COMPREHENSION PROBLEMS.

Choose a Partner. Choose a Card on which one of the following sentences is printed. Act out the Sentence on the card. Does the class agree that you have acted out the sentence correctly?

Bob put on his hat after Sue rang the bell.

Willie sat down before Bill turned on the water.

As Mary looked out the window, Jane clapped her hands.

Before Wanda stood up, Jane closed the door.

Make it so it is hard for the doll to see.

Make it so it is hard to see the doll.

Dwayne asked Susan what to give to Sandra.

Gus told Rita what to give the teacher.

"Is the doll easy to see?" to mean "Is it easy for the doll to see?" Athey (1977) suggested that teachers attuned to these kinds of research findings can be alert to clarify, introduce new examples, or otherwise exploit the "teachable moment" (p. 90) when students' comprehension goes awry and knowledge of how language works may be the problem (see Figures 9.7 and 9.8 for suggestions on how one might do this).

If a student did not seem to fully understand a sentence like sentence 1, teachers who adopt this point of view would not attempt to teach the definition of the word *if* or *will*; nor would they rely on general language stimulation to accomplish their purpose. Instead, they would deal specifically with those aspects of

FIGURE 9.8
CLASS ACTIVITY TO PROMOTE COMPREHENSION OF COMPARISONS STATED IN ELLIPTICAL SENTENCES.

language that appear to be the source of the problem in some of the following ways.

They may present sentences like 1 and ask questions like 8, 9, and 10.

8. *Does the sentence say George went to the movies?*

9. *Does the sentence say that Bob will do the dishes if George goes to the movies?*

10. *Do you think George will be glad if Bob does the dishes? Why?*

Or the teacher may create sentences like 11 and 12 and ask questions modeled on 8, 9, and 10 about them.

11. *The children will stay inside if it is raining.*

12. *Mary will write if her pencil is sharp.*

Or the teacher may ask why sentences like 13 and 14 are silly, and how they can be changed so they make sense.

13. *It will be sunny if we play outside.*

14. *We will be hungry if we eat.*

Or the teacher may ask students to match the sentence parts that "go together" in an exercise such as the one in Figure 9.9 or to make up clauses to fit into sentences, as in Figure 9.10.

Here the teacher does not presume to teach the meaning of the word *if* or to teach how to recognize and interpret conditional clauses. Lessons like these are usually based on the observation that children behave as if they understand sentences like sentence 1 when they appear in a context that supports their meanings, but children do not reflect on their knowledge of how language works in such situations or pay particular attention to it. The presumption is that if children were to reflect on their knowledge of language and pay attention to it through exercises like those suggested here, their reading comprehension would improve.

♦ It is not suggested here that sutdents be given duplicated sheets of exercises or workbook pages on nominalizations (sentences 4 and 5) or comparatives (sentences 6 and 7) or conditional clauses (sentences 1–3, and 11–14). What are suggested are activities designed to make children reflect on what they already appear to know. Exercises like those presented in Figures 9.9 and 9.10 may be assigned to individuals as preparation for disucssion or for assessment. Such exercises done by individuals working alone have little or no instructional value.

THE DIRECTED READING LESSON

Reading lessons in eclectic basals and in many other materials used in teaching reading involve four steps:

FIGURE 9.9
EXERCISE TO PROMOTE METALINGUISTIC AWARENESS OF CAUSAL RELATIONSHIPS IN SENTENCES.

Match the cards so the sentences make sense. Work in pairs or groups of three.

Bill will be warm	if Mary is not in school.
The teacher will send a note home	if Father builds a good fire.
The birds will fly south	if the weather turns cold.

FIGURE 9.10
EXERCISE TO PROMOTE METALINGUISTIC AWARENESS OF CAUSAL RELATIONSHIPS IN SENTENCES.

Directions: Write a sentence that fits in the blank. Discuss your work with your classmates when you are finished. Do your sentences make good sense?

Bill will stop at Zeke's house if _____.

Jane will buy ice cream if _____.

We will not have school on Monday if _____.

1. Preparation
2. Reading
3. Questions/discussion
4. Skills development

This four-part lesson scheme is known as a *directed reading lesson.* In this section, we present selected practices for teaching comprehension in the framework of a directed reading lesson.

The Preparation Stage

During the preparation stage, three kinds of activities are designed to facilitate comprehension. They are supplying knowledge that the author of the text presumes the reader to have, presenting vocabulary, and setting a purpose for reading. The examples cited here are taken from Beck and others (1979).

SUPPLYING BACKGROUND KNOWLEDGE

A story in a third-grade reader (Durr, 1976a) is about a village in China in 1913. The action of the story revolves around the fact that an airplane lands near the village, and the people are very surprised. To mark this amazing event, the village holds a kite-making contest. The story opens with the line: ''In the Year of the Water Ox, a long time ago. . . .''

The program writers foresaw two possible impediments to a third-grader's comprehension of the story. One is the reference to the Year of the Water Ox, and the second is that a 9-year-old might not understand that an airplane would be unfamiliar in China in 1913. The teacher's guide simply suggests that the teacher tell the children that each year in the old Chinese calender is named for an animal and that 1913 was the year of the Water Ox, and that airplanes and automobiles were not commonly seen in China in 1913.

An innovative teacher might do more with these ideas; he or she might find out what the present year is in the old Chinese calendar or find pictures of 1913 airplanes, cars, or American street scenes to help the children understand how different the world was then. But the important point in terms of a directed reading lesson is that reading selections are previewed to determine whether comprehension may be impeded because the students are unfamiliar with concepts necessary for understanding the story.

This is an example of an application of a very old idea: Comprehension is relating information contained in a text to information already in the reader's possession. Some authorities believe that when students reach the point where they can read intermediate-level (grades 4–6) materials, the major cause of comprehension failure is limited knowledge on the part of the readers; that is, when students fail to comprehend texts, it is because they do not have the necessary background information to which to relate the text information. (Carver, 1981, Stitch et al., 1974.)

VOCABULARY

In the primary grades, care is taken to introduce only those words that are already in the students' speaking-listening vocabularies. The objective is not to teach students new words in reading, but to teach them to *recognize* printed words whose meanings are familiar. In intermediate grades, words whose meanings may not be known begin to appear in texts.

Teacher's guides for basal readers supply lists of words whose meanings may be unknown to the students. Teachers are urged to write the words on the chalkboard and use them in a strong oral context. Some teacher's guides supply sentences such as sentence 15 for ''target words.''

15. *After days of climbing the party reached the* summit, *the highest point on the mountain.*

Some basal readers identify words as either general vocabulary or specialized vocabulary. In a story about a weaver, for example, the words *woof* and *warp* and *shuttle* might be identified as specialized words. *Hardship* and *toil* and *efficient* might be identified as general words. Attention to specialized vocabulary is more likely to be left up to individual teachers. The presumption seems to be that knowledge of specialized words is necessary for comprehension of the particular story, so they must be given some attention, but they are not likely to appear again soon in a child's reading, so they should not be given too much attention.

The practice of presenting words from a selection as an unrelated list of words whose meanings are to be learned before reading is based on the instrumental interpretation of the relationship between word knowledge and comprehension (see Chapter 8)—that if one knows the words in a text, one will probably understand the text. Another, slightly more complicated rationale for these kinds of lessons is proposed by Beck et al. (1979): If a person does not recognize the meaning of a word in a text automatically, some of the energy that should be devoted to comprehension is diverted toward trying to assign a meaning to the word. Comprehension suffers. When this happens frequently, comprehension may break down completely.

At times the line between filling in background knowledge and teaching vocabulary becomes indistinct. For example, in a story about the black heroine Harriet Tubman, the following words might be identified for attention before reading: *Quaker, Underground Railroad, free states, slave states, overseer, traders, bloodhounds, runaways,* and *patrol.* A discussion of the list of words would supply a great deal of necessary background information for this story, and vice-versa.

When word lists like this appear, teaching them before reading is based on the knowledge of the world interpretation of the relationship between vocabulary knowledge and reading comprehension (see Chapter 8). As one gains knowledge of the history and culture of one's people, one learns concepts and words simultaneously. The understanding of the concepts is so bound up with the knowledge of the vocabulary involved that it does not make sense to say simply that vocabulary knowledge causes comprehension. The fact is that comprehension facilitates vocabulary knowledge as much as vocabulary knowledge facilitates comprehension. This is what Vygotsky (1962) meant when he wrote:

The relation of thought to word is not a thing but a process, a continued movement back and forth from thought to word and from word to thought. In that process the relation of thought to word undergoes changes. . . . Thought is not merely expressed in words; it comes into existence through them. (p. 125)

Vocabulary is also taught during the skills development phase of some directed reading lessons and also as a separate or supplemental program. Therefore, the topic of vocabulary development and comprehension will appear again later in this chapter.

PURPOSE SETTING

Purpose setting usually consists of remarks by the teacher intended to: (1) get the students thinking along the lines of the story they are about to read, and (2) identify particular information the students should be alert to or a question the students should keep in mind as they read the selection.

In beginning reading, when a major objective of instruction is to teach children that printed sentences have meaning, the story is often divided into short segments, and the preparation, reading, questioning cycle is repeated several times during the course of a story. At this stage, one is apt to find purpose-setting questions to be very concrete and designed to focus on one item of information that is explicitly stated in the text.

But beginning in the intermediate grades, purpose-setting questions that focus on one or two items of explicitly stated information are considered to be undesirable. Anderson and Biddle (1977) and Frase (1977) have pointed out that directing the reader's attention to small portions of the text may enhance recollection of that portion of the text but result in failure to recall the overall selection.

Beyond primary grades, good purpose-setting activities "should prepare children to construct the meaning of a text by evoking a network of relevant associations. . . . direction setting activities should provide a framework for the organization of events and concepts in the text so that many aspects of the text become interrelated and thus memorable" (Beck et al., 1979, p. 87). Another way of stating this definition is to say that good purpose-setting activities supply readers with a schema (see Chapter 8) or framework into which they may fit the content of the selection they are about to read.

The following example of a good purpose-setting activity is found in the teacher's manual at the second-grade level of a basal reading program (Durr, 1976b). The story is about a girl who attempts to convince a boy that she can pursue any profession she wishes regardless of her sex. In the teacher's manual it is suggested that the teachers say:

How many of you think that you know just what jobs you want to have someday? . . . Let's hear about some of these jobs. . . . Following these responses, go around the group asking pupils the questions, "How would you like to be a _____ *? Why or why not?" Ask the girls about occupations that have often been associated with boys—pilot, firefighter, police officer, football coach, engineer, dentist, farmer, etc. Ask the boys about occupations that have often been associated with girls—nurse, kindergarten teacher, nursery school teacher, baby sitter, secretary, dietitian, etc. Through questioning and discussion, guide them to arrive at the conclu-*

sion—or to begin thinking in the direction—that there are really no valid reasons why a boy can't be a nurse or a girl can't be a pilot, provided that each is trained or prepared or educated for the job.

In today's story, you're going to read about a boy and a girl who have some disagreements. You'll find out what those disagreements are and how they are settled. (Durr, 1976b, p. 127)

What recommends this purpose-setting activity is that it does not focus on some particular facts in the story the children are about to read; instead, it prompts the students to think along the lines of the story they are about to read, to identify the social issue of this story, and to recall what they know about this issue and the attitudes they have heard expressed about it. This activity gives the readers an orientation or ideational framework (or schema) that will enable them to recognize important elements in the story and to relate those elements to some larger design.

The Question/Discussion Stage

The most common classroom practice that is identified as teaching comprehension is asking questions. This is a curious fact, since one would think that the reason a teacher asks questions would be to *test* comprehension rather than teach it. Durkin (1979) observed that she saw practically no teaching of comprehension, but she did see a great deal of question asking, or assessment of comprehension.

There is, however, good reason to believe that questioning, *if done properly*, does teach comprehension. Suggestions as to how questioning can be used as a legitimate and effective method of teaching comprehension can be found in many sources; several are reviewed on the following pages.

QUESTIONING AS A TEACHING METHOD

Dewey. Dewey (1933) described the "art of questioning" as the art of showing pupils how to "direct their own inquiries and so to form in them the independent habit of inquiry" (p. 266). Dewey offered five suggestions to accomplish this goal.

1. Questions should require students to use information rather than to produce it literally and directly.

2. Emphasis should be on developing the subject and not on getting the one correct answer.

3. Questions should keep subject matter developing; each question should add to a continuous discussion. Questions should not be asked as if each one were complete in itself so that when the question is answered, the matter is disposed of, and another topic can be taken up.

4. There should be periodic reviews of what has gone before in order to extract the net meaning and focus on what is significant in prior discussion and to put old material into the new perspective that later material has supplied.

5. At the end of a question/discussion session there should be a sense of accomplishment and an expectation and desire that more is to come.

Vygotsky. Two of Vygotsky's notions of cognitive development support the belief that one can teach comprehension through questioning. The first is Vygotsky's belief that speech arises in society, in a child's interactions with others, and that only after habits of solving problems are developed through speech interaction does a child use egocentric speech to solve similar problems on his or her own. Eventually egocentric speech becomes inner speech. Thus, thought evolves from speech interactions with others (Vygotsky, 1962).

The second notion that supports the idea of using questions to teach comprehension is Vygotsky's belief that cognitive growth takes place in the "zone of proximal development"—that is, the concepts children are ready to learn are the concepts that are beyond their grasp as individuals but that they can cope with in collaboration with others who have the concepts (Vygotsky, 1978).

From these two notions it follows that a child acting alone may be able to read a story about Andrew Jackson and see it as a collection of facts about an American patriot. Collaborating with a knowledgeable adult, the child may realize that the story also tells how democratic ideas were especially useful for life on the frontier. A skillful teacher can bring such understanding out through questioning. If done frequently enough, the student will begin to ask him or herself the kinds of questions the teacher asked and reach higher levels of comprehension when acting on his or her own. In this manner, comprehension is improved by collaborating with a skilled adult in dealing with concepts in the student's zone of proximal development. Social speech (questions and answers) becomes egocentric speech and finally inner speech or thought.

FRAMEWORKS FOR GENERATING QUESTIONS

The Story Map Framework. Beck and her associates (1979) propose two reasons for asking questions after reading. The first is to test comprehension. This function of questioning is not pertinent to the present discussion. The second is to aid in comprehension of the text. In this capacity

. . . questions for a story should be generated with the aim of promoting the development of a unified conception of the story which we will call a

map *of the story. Any coherent story map must interweave the explicit and implicit story concepts. . . . To promote the development of a story map, the information elicited by each question should build on what has preceded. There are two notions here. First, questions should proceed in a sequence that matches the progression of ideas or of events in the story. Second, questions should be framed to highlight the interrelationship of story ideas.*

After a story map has been established through questioning and discussion, additional questions can then appropriately extend discussion to broader perspectives. (pp. 105–6)

For example, in a story in a second-grade reader (Clymer, 1976) a family is harassed by a mischievous ghost to the point where they decide to move to another house. As the truck with the family and its belongings pulls away from the haunted house, the ghost perched on top of the load says ''We're off! Away we go!'' Well-constructed questions would establish the problem (a troublesome ghost), the solution (the decision to move), the outcome (the ghost moves with them), and the ensuing problem (a troublesome ghost) in that order.

Final questions might lead the children to talk about what the family might do next, or whether this is a typical ghost story, or to relate this story to other stories in which the antagonist outwits the protagonist. These kinds of questions will enhance comprehension only if the story map has been well developed through earlier questions.

Practices That Violate the Story Map Framework. Some common questioning strategies violate the principle of constructing questions from a story map. For example, a series of factual questions such as those in 16, 17, and 18 does not relate to the main ideas of the story and does not promote a unified concept of the story.

16. *How many children were in the family?*
17. *How long did the family live in the house?*
18. *What was the father's name?*

Sometimes teachers begin with questions such as 19 and 20 that ask for speculations or emotional responses.

19. *How would you feel if a mischievous ghost lived in your house?*
20. *When do you think this family will discover their problem has not been solved?*

Such questions do not contribute to re-creating the progression of ideas or events in the story. In fact, such questions divert the students' attention away from the text; therefore they should not be asked until the story map has been established.

Fact and inference questions are sometimes separated in story questions. This leads to taking the children through the story to recount the facts and then starting over to discuss the inferences. Even if the teacher does an excellent job of selecting the facts and inferences relevant to the story map, the opportunity to create a unified concept of the story is lost.

Implications of the Story Map. The story map concept of relating questioning to teaching comprehension echoes in some ways Dewey's (1933) suggestions for showing pupils how to use questions ''to direct their own inquiries and so to form in them the independent habit of inquiry'' (p. 266). Dewey's first point suggests that facts always be recalled in relation to a unified concept of the story: points 2, 3, and 4 suggest that questions should show a progression of interrelated ideas; and point 5 suggests that the final step should be to extend the discussion to broader perspectives.

This belief is wholly compatible with Vygotsky's ideas (1) that much thought begins as social speech and travels inward to become egocentric speech and finally inner speech, and (2) that learning takes place in the zone of proximal development. Through collaboration with a knowledgeable adult, a student can reach a level of comprehension that is beyond his or her grasp when working alone, and through such collaboration, the student will eventually attain that level of comprehension on his or her own.

Although Beck and her associates never say so explicitly, they clearly believe that when children repeatedly go through the process of answering questions derived from the story map, they internalize this procedure and begin to create maps of texts they read on their own. Through this process, therefore, children learn to comprehend written materials. This clearly reflects the notion of story schema and the belief that story schema is used by proficient readers both in understanding and in recalling stories.

The Skills by Level of Comprehension Framework. Although the idea of using questioning as a device for teaching comprehension is widely recommended, the distressing fact classroom observations repeatedly reveal is that by and large teachers' questions require factual information stated explicitly in the text (Durkin, 1979; Hodges, 1980; Ruddell and Williams, 1972; Guzak, 1967). Such procedures are a far cry from those recommended as long ago as 1933 (by Dewey) and as recently as 1979 (by Beck and others). Guzak (1967) claims that such questions "lead the student away from basic literal understanding of story plots, events, and sequences."

The traditional response to such criticism is to encourage teachers and writers of reading programs to consider a "wider range of questions." Advocates of the idea that reading

comprehension is composed of separate factors, skills, or abilities suggest that lists of abilities, such as those proposed by Lennon (1962) (Chapter 8) be consulted and that questions tapping each ability (as far as possible) be derived from each passage in a directed reading lesson. Advocates of the notion that reading comprehension is composed of hierarchical subskills or taxonomies (see Chapter 8) suggest that questions tapping more elementary skills be asked first and "higher" skills be tapped with questions asked later.

Ruddell (1978) incorporated the notion that comprehension is composed of separate components in the "factor analytic" sense (Davis, 1944) and in the "taxonomy of objectives" sense (Bloom et al., 1956). He proposed a "skills by level of comprehension framework," as shown in Figure 9.11. The questions that appear in Figure 9.13 are derived from the passage in Figure 9.12 and are classified in terms of the comprehension framework in Figure 9.11. Ruddell suggests that teachers refer to the comprehension framework to be certain that their questions cover the seven skill competencies listed at the three comprehension levels.

The Skills by Level of Comprehension versus the Story Map Framework. Question-generating schemes derived from separate comprehension skills or levels of comprehension stress Dewey's first point—that questions should tap more than factual information stated explicitly in the passage. These schemes also encourage compliance with Dewey's fifth suggestion; they encourage questions that lead away from recalling facts and details and toward activities like "valuing" (Ruddell's term) and applying knowledge gained in reading the passage. Through this process one would expect students to be left with an "expectation and desire that more is to come."

FIGURE 9.11
SKILLS BY LEVEL OF COMPREHENSION FRAMEWORK BASED ON SEPARATE SKILLS AND LEVELS OF COMPREHENSION. (From Ruddell, 1978, p. 112.)

Questions may be generated from a passage to fit each cell in the framework where an X appears.

Skill Competencies	Comprehension Levels		
	Factual	Interpretive	Applicative
1. Details			
a. Identifying	X	X	
b. Comparing	X	X	X
c. Classifying		X	X
2. Sequence	X	X	X
3. Cause and Effect	X	X	X
4. Main Idea	X	X	X
5. Predicting Outcome		X	X
6. Valuing			
a. Personal judgment	X	X	X
b. Character trait identification	X	X	X
c. Author's motive identification		X	X
7. Problem solving			X

However, schemes like these do not ensure that questions will stress a sense of wholeness, development, and continuity in comprehending a passage, as Dewey's second, third, and fourth suggestions emphasize. One gets the sense in examining the three sample questions in Figure 9.13 that each question could be considered complete in itself—so that, in Dewey's words, "when that question is answered that particular matter is disposed of and another topic can be taken up" (p. 267).

Dewey's suggestions and the story map strategy both urge the teacher to induce in the student through questioning a holistic, organic notion of comprehension. This is a top-down strategy in which parts are always seen in re-

FIGURE 9.12
PASSAGE FROM E. B. WHITE'S *CHARLOTTE'S WEB* **(1952).**

On foggy mornings, Charlotte's web was truly a thing of beauty. This morning each thin strand was decorated with dozens of tiny beads of water. The web glistened in the light and made a pattern of loveliness and mystery, like a delicate veil. Even Lurvy, who wasn't particularly interested in beauty, noted the web when he came with the pig's breakfast. He noted how clearly it showed up and he noted how big and carefully built it was. And then he took another look and he saw something that made him set his pail down. There, in the corner of the web, neatly woven in block letters, was a message. It said:
                    SOME PIG!
    Lurvy felt weak. He brushed his hand across his eyes and stared harder at Charlotte's web.

FIGURE 9.13
QUESTIONS DERIVED FROM A PASSAGE IN *CHARLOTTE'S WEB* **(FIGURE 9.12) AND CLASSIFIED BY THE SKILLS BY LEVEL OF COMPREHENSION FRAMEWORK (FIGURE 9.11).** (From Ruddell, 1978, p. 113.)

1. What was written in Charlotte's web?
   Answer: SOME PIG!
   Comprehension level/skill competency: Factual—identifying details.

2. Why did Lurvy feel weak?
   Answer: Interpretation suggests that Lurvy believed it a rather unusual phenomenon to find the words SOME PIG! woven into a spider's web, and his actions express astonishment and surprise.
   Comprehension level/skill competency: Interpretive—cause and effect.

3. If you had been the first person to see Charlotte's web that morning, how would you have reacted?
   Answer: Responses will vary.
   Comprehension level/skill competency: Applicative—predicting outcomes.

lation to and derived from the whole. Questioning strategies based on separate skills and taxonomies start by stressing parts and pull the parts together at the end through questions that evaluate the passage and apply information gained in reading to other situations. This is a bottom-up strategy. One sees here the classic division of empiricism and rationalism.

The idea that comprehension is *taught* through questioning is based on the assumption that children will eventually internalize the questioning process to which they are repeatedly and systematically exposed. Different questioning strategies would follow from the three notions of comprehension introduced in the last chapter and again in this chapter: If comprehension is thought of as a global, holistic affair, one would adopt a story map strategy of relating all questions to a unified conception of text. If comprehension is thought of as a hierarchy of objectives and levels, one would adopt something like a comprehension framework strategy, as proposed by Ruddell. If comprehension is thought of as separate and independent subskills, one would focus on asking a variety of questions rather than on some organizing principle from which questions were derived.

Which strategy one chooses will depend on which strategy one believes is more conducive to learning, or which strategy more closely approximates useful thinking patterns.

A WORD IN DEFENSE OF LITERAL, FACTUAL QUESTIONS

Treating Literal, Factual Questions as Taboo. It is an often documented fact that teachers ask many literal, factual questions. This has disturbed reading experts and others who are concerned with the intellectual at-

mosphere of the classroom. As a result, literal-factual questions have almost become taboo in some circles.

It has been suggested that this abhorrence of literal, factual questions and esteem for questions that call for inference, analysis, speculation, and critical reaction may in fact lead not to improving comprehension, but to teaching children to have little regard for what is on the printed page. One may unwittingly teach students that it is not important to read for precise understanding of a passage. The second danger is that one may unwittingly teach students they do not have to read the passage *at all* to participate in a reading lesson or exercise.

Foster (1978) (borrowing from Adler's [1940] *How to Read a Book*) suggests that in reading one must understand, interpret, and evaluate. Foster claims that most of us evaluate without understanding or interpreting: "We give a critical analysis of a book before we understand what it says. We judge a book to be right or wrong before we interpret its meaning" (pp. 58–59). Mary McCarthy (1979) has complained that many of her readers, even book reviewers, do not get the simple facts of her novels straight before going on to analyze and criticize them. McCarthy has come to the conclusion that the reading public, who once could read, no longer can. Finn (1980) suggests:

Perhaps it would be more accurate to say that they do not read the text because they have not been taught that it is important to read the text. The result is that McCarthy's fears are realized. People who once could read as she understands the term no longer do. (p. 12)

Beck (1977) reports a conversation with a teacher who was using a reading program in which group lessons with follow-up questions were taught only about every two weeks. The teacher observed that when she asked her beginning second-graders to read two pages (six to ten sentences) to themselves, many of the children could not answer factual questions that could be answered by sentences in the text until after she told them to reread the pages. After rereading most children could answer the questions, and by the end of the story (several such rounds of reading and questioning), the children could answer the question without rereading (p. 117). Beck (1977) speculates that this happened because the children were simply not reading the text the first time; they were distracted because they were not used to being asked questions they could not answer without having read the text.

Fact Questions to Assess Silent Reading Performance. Classroom observers sometimes criticize what teachers do because they impute the wrong motives to the teacher. For example, if a teacher asks several factual questions that are explicitly answered in the text and only a few interpretive questions, an observer may assume the teacher thinks he or she is teaching comprehension by having students recount facts explicitly stated. That assumption may be unfounded.

A teacher may ask a few factual questions for the very mundane purpose of keeping everyone honest (checking to see if all have read what they are supposed to have read) and then go on to the most inspired interpretive and applicative questions. But an observer who is merely categorizing and counting questions might truthfully report that the teacher is asking a majority of factual questions.

Many teachers believe that habitually asking a few such questions encourages students to read the text, whereas habitually asking purely speculative questions causes the children to think they do not need to read the text to participate successfully in the reading lesson.

COMPREHENSION QUESTIONS AND METACOGNITION

As stated several times earlier in this book, Vygotsky believed some thinking processes originate as social speech that becomes egocentric speech and finally inner speech and thought. Meichenbaum (1977) has adopted this belief and suggested the process can be enhanced by actually teaching students to "talk to themselves" by teaching them what to say to themselves when confronted with a problem. In order to do this, Meichenbaum believes that

[F]rom the onset one needs the pupil to be a collaborator in the generation of the cognitive strategies. It is important to insure that the purpose and rationale for the training is explained to the pupil as fully as possible. (1980, p. 17)

Teaching about the Story Map Strategy. Translated to the use of questions for teaching comprehension, this advice would seem to suggest that teachers who generate questions from a story map should make the connection between the questions and the story map as explicit as possible.

For example, in a story (Brand, 1969) in an upper-grade reading anthology, a villain's water canteen is filled with wine instead of water by his suspicious host. When the villain does great injury to the host and makes his escape across the desert, he is doomed to die because the wine will not satisfy his bodily need for water. Question 21 would be a factual question derived from a story map of this story; question 22 would make it clear to the students that this fact is crucial to understanding the climax of the story, thus making the connection between the fact and the story map explicit.

21. *What was kept in the jars by the door? (Water in one jar and wine in the other.)*

22. *Why is that fact important later in the story?*

In the middle and upper grades, lessons might also be devised in which the class works out a story map and derives questions from it. Students might evaluate suggested questions in terms of how the questions promote the development of a unified conception of the story. A question like 21 would be judged to be good by this criterion. A question like 23 would be judged to be poor because, although the information is in the story and it is interesting, it is an incidental fact rather than one that is necessary to the development of the story.

23. *Why were the jars made of porous stone? (The liquid evaporating through the pores kept the contents of the jars cool.)*

This kind of lesson would enable the students to share in the intellectual exercise engaged in only by the teacher or writer under normal circumstances, despite the fact that it is this very process that one hopes the student will learn to accomplish through asking comprehension questions. Lessons like this one would provide explicit instruction in the questioning strategy, rather than relying on the students' abstracting and internalizing the strategy from repeated systematic experience with it.

Teaching about the Skills by Level of Comprehension Strategy. In explaining the rationale for training as fully as possible in a comprehension framework strategy, one would not expect teachers simply to generate questions in different cells (using Ruddell's scheme, Figure 9.11, for example), but to explain the rationale for the questions as they are asked. For example, a teacher might say: "Let's answer a few questions to see if every-one read the whole story." "Let's answer a few questions to see if we all understood the order in which things happened in the story." "Let's answer a few questions that will help us think about how we feel about the story." Such explicit statements of the rationale for the training will, according to Meichenbaun, ensure that the process will become internalized and lead to habits of thinking.

Such statements would clear up the misunderstanding of teachers' motives by classroom observers. More important, this practice may clear up the misunderstanding of teachers' motives by students. Students who are learning (mistakenly) that the object of reading is to give the one right answer to factual questions will be set straight by a teacher who discusses the rationale for the questions as a routine part of the question discussion segment of directed reading lessons.

The Skills Development Stage

The actual content of a particular reading selection suggests and restricts the kinds of comprehension skills that can be taught in the preparation and question discussion stages. Comprehension lessons that are not easily worked into these stages of a directed reading lesson are often treated in the skills development stage. The reading selection is often used as a springboard for the skills development lesson. For example, a lesson in Greek and Latin roots may start with several words from the reading selection that contain Greek and Latin roots and go on to consider the meanings of many other words that contain Greek and Latin roots but do not appear in the selection.

Comprehension skills that appear in the skills development stage are also often taught in lessons separate from directed reading lessons. Suggestions for teaching such skills appear in the following sections.

SENTENCE COMPREHENSION SKILLS

Comprehension difficulties that may arise at the level of single sentences were discussed earlier in this chapter. Typical exercises and activities designed to address these comprehension difficulties are found in that section. Sentence combining exercises are another obvious way of addressing the problem of sentence comprehension and of encouraging students to reflect on how relationships of ideas are expressed through combining sentences.

Although cloze exercises are constructed over passages containing several sentences and often several paragraphs, there is evidence that students engaged in cloze exercises rely on their knowledge of syntax and their understanding of the meanings of individual sentences in completing most blanks (Kibby, 1980). Completing and reflecting upon cloze exercises encourages students to reflect on the syntax and meaning of individual sentences to a large extent, and therefore may be thought of as a technique for teaching comprehension at the sentence level as well as at the paragraph or whole passage level.

PARAGRAPH AND PASSAGE COMPREHENSION SKILLS

The influence of Davis's assertion that comprehension could be usefully conceived of as separate, independent factors can be seen in current reading programs. Many comprehension lessons deal directly with the comprehension skills Davis (1944) identified. For example, Figures 9.14 and 9.15 show lessons in identifying the main idea in paragraphs.

TEACHING NEW VOCABULARY

The Complexities of Word Meaning

The question of why vocabulary knowledge is so closely related to reading comprehension was raised in the last chapter. Three possible answers were suggested, but no one answer has been agreed upon. The relationship between word knowledge and thought is an age-old topic of study. Psychologists have shown that word knowledge is a good measure of intelligence. Vygotsky (1962) has noted that the relationship between thought and word is an "immense and complex problem" (p. 153). He concludes by saying:

Words play a central part not only in the development of thought but in the historical growth of consciousness as a whole. A word is a microcosm of human consciousness. (p. 153)

It is no wonder, then, that there is no clear, easy definition of what it means to *know* a word.

What Does It Mean to Know a Word?

Ways of Defining Words. Johnson and Pearson (1978) list seven ways of defining words (p. 45):

1. Using words in a sentence.
2. Giving a synonym.
3. Giving an antonym.

FIGURE 9.14
AN EXERCISE IN IDENTIFYING PARAGRAPH MEANING. (From *The Laidlaw Program Skills Book to Accompany Voyages,* Laidlaw Bros., Publishers, 1982, p. 110.)

"The Hunt for the Mastodon," 338–347   Literal Comprehension: Finding the main idea
Teacher's Edition, 278   Study Skills: Making an outline

1. Scientists believe that the first horses were small animals between 10 and 20 inches high. They had high, arched backs and looked something like thin racing dogs. The size and shape of horses today is far different from that of the earliest horses.

2. No one knows for sure when horses were first tamed. However, it is known that cave people hunted horses and ate the meat from horses. For thousands of years people have tamed horses and have used them for riding and for pulling carts. Stone tablets 3,500 years old show pictures of horses pulling chariots.

3. Scientists have evidence that the earliest horses were native to North America, although they later disappeared. When explorers came from Europe, they brought their own horses. Some of these horses escaped and became the forerunners of the wild horses of the American West. Long before colonial families came to America, the native Americans were using horses for hunting. The colonial families themselves used horses for riding and for such work as pulling plows and wagons.

4. With the development of farm tractors, steam engines, trucks, and automobiles, horses became less and less important in America. The use of horses for work and for riding decreased. The number of horses in villages, in cities, and on farms declined greatly. In 1910 American farmers owned about 20 million horses; by 1970 there were fewer than 8 million horses in the United States.

Write the number of the paragraph beside the phrase that best states what the paragraph is about.

_2_ How people of early days used horses   _4_ Why the number of horses declined

_1_ What the first horses looked like   _3_ How horses were used in North America

110   Provide help with the words *chariots* and *declined*. Then ask the pupils to read the paragraphs and to follow the directions on pages 110 and 111.

FIGURE 9.15
AN EXERCISE IN IDENTIFYING THE MAIN IDEA IN PARAGRAPHS. (From *Reaching Out: Reading Skills Workbook,* Teacher's Edition, HBJ Bookmark Reading Program, by Margaret Early et al. Harcourt, Brace and Jovanovich, Inc., 1979, p. 64.)

Finding the Topic and Main Idea of a Paragraph

The **topic** of a paragraph is what all or most of the sentences are about. It can be stated in just a word or phrase. The **main idea** is the most important thing the paragraph says about the topic. A main idea must be stated in a sentence. The main idea is often the first sentence of a paragraph. But it can also appear at the end or in the middle.

Find the topic and the main idea in the following paragraph.

There are many kinds of muffins. You may have eaten corn muffins or bran muffins, to name two. Some muffins, like blueberry muffins, have berries in them. You may have also tasted muffins with raisins.

The topic of the paragraph is *muffins.* The main idea is "There are many kinds of muffins."

Read each paragraph. Write the topic and the main idea after each paragraph. Use the Answer Key to check your answers.

1. Some waterfalls are unusually long. The series of lower, middle, and upper falls at Yosemite in California drops 728 meters. Tugela Falls in South Africa plunges 604 meters in five jumps. Venezuela's Angel Falls is the world's highest falls (964 meters) with the longest uninterrupted drop.

Topic _____ waterfalls _____

Main idea _____ Some waterfalls are _____

_____ unusually long. _____

4. Classifying (A *woman* is an adult female human being.)

5. giving an example (Lassie is an example of a *canine.*)

6. Giving a comparison (An *ocean* is like a lake, but larger.)

7. Describing a physical relationship (An *arm* is connected to the shoulder and to the hand.)

Denotative and Connotative Meanings. It is a commonplace observation that words have both denotative and connotative meanings; that is, to say that a man is *rugged* and to say that he is *uncouth* may refer to the same characteristics of the man (*rugged* and *uncouth* have similar denotations). But *rugged* implies that the speaker approves of the characteristics, and *uncouth* implies the speaker does not approve (*rugged* and *uncouth* have different connotations.) It is impossible to say whether the denotative or connotative meanings of words are more important without a thorough knowledge of the context in which they appear.

Nuances. Words can take on nuances that are too subtle and too specific for any dictionary to record. When a Quaker says in a Quaker meeting that he is "concerned," he means what the average American means— but he means something more because of the long tradition connected with the word *concern* among Quakers.

Insider's Meaning. Slang is deliberately invented so that "outsiders" will not know what is being said among members of groups such as musicians, teenagers, and other subcultures. To "be cool" has nothing to do with one's temperature or the temperature of the room. A built-in problem with dictionaries of slang is they are outdated almost as soon as they are published. When the meaning of slang terms becomes widely known, they are abandoned by "insiders" and new terms are invented.

Historical Change. Meanings of words change over time. A glance at a glossed edition of any Shakespeare play will reveal dozens of examples. For example, in *Julius Casear* the word *emulation* means *jealousy,* and the word *napkins* means *handkerchiefs.*

Sarcasm, Irony, and Humor. Sarcasm, irony, and humor prompt people to use words to mean the opposite of what they usually mean. A person may ask why someone is "all dressed up" when the person is actually in particularly sloppy attire; or a person may comment on another's stinginess by asking why he is so generous.

"Narrowing" Meaning. People use words in particular contexts to denote only part of the usual meaning of the word. A married man whose wife is away for a weekend may refer to himself as a bachelor. A person may remark on a man's general attractiveness by saying "He's no Robert Redford."

OPPORTUNITIES ARISING FROM THE COMPLEXITY OF WORD MEANING

Given the profound implications of the relationship between word knowledge, reading comprehension, and thought, and given the rich variation in connotation, denotation, historical change, local variation, and creative use of language, it is no wonder that there is no pat curriculum for teaching vocabulary. On the other hand, it is no wonder that so many interesting things can be done with vocabulary in connection with nearly every reading selection or as separate exercises. Herr (1977), for example, lists 155 different activities for vocabulary development in grades 1 through 6.

LESSONS SUGGESTED BY WORDS IN READING SELECTIONS

Figure 9.16 presents a lesson that follows selections in an upper-grade literature anthology (Dunning et al., 1969) under the heading, "Words in Action." It is an example of a way in which reading selection can be used as an entrée into word study. Similar examples can be found in other anthologies, basals, and materials designed for teaching reading.

Teaching Words Related Through the "Semantic Network"

Johnson and Pearson (1978) have used the scheme referred to as a *semantic network* (Collins and Quillian, 1969) as a basis for creating vocabulary lessons. A semantic network portrays relationships between words in terms of class, example, and property.

A few examples will demonstrate the meaning of the terms class, example, and property. The word *animal* represents a class; fish, birds, and mammals are examples of this class; the examples have common properties: They are living; they do not manufacture food. The examples have particular properties: Fish have scales, fins, gills, and live in water; birds have feathers and wings; mammals have hair, mammary glands, and give birth to living offspring.

Vehicles are a class of things; bicycles, rowboats, and cars are examples of this class; the examples share some properties and not others. They are all used to transport people and goods. Bicycles have wheels and are powered by the rider's energy; a rowboat has no wheels, moves on water, and is powered by the rider's energy; a car has wheels and is powered by an engine.

FIGURE 9.16
EXAMPLE OF A VOCABULARY ACTIVITY FOLLOWING A STORY IN A READING ANTHOLOGY. (From Dunning et al., 1969, p. 187.)

After a selection about a famous performer's childhood career in vaudeville.

Words in Action

Words often have a special meaning among people in a particular trade or profession. What do the following expressions mean to people in the occupations named?

1. **line:** dancer, telephone operator, printer, salesman, railroad engineer

2. **mugger:** actor, policeman

3. **wings:** actor, airplane pilot, house builder, politician

4. **get booked:** actor, policeman

SEMANTIC FEATURE ANALYSIS

Johnson and Pearson (1978) suggest exercises that will help children to see the class, example, and property relationships among words. One such exercise is called semantic feature analysis. In this scheme, properties of a word such as "living," "feathered," "flies" are called *semantic features.*

In one exercise, the teacher suggests a class such as "vehicles." Examples of the class are listed down the left side of the board, and students are asked to name properties (or features) that at least one of the examples possesses. These properties are listed across the top of the board. Then students are asked whether each example has the property named in the column, and a plus or minus sign is put beside each example under each property, as shown in Figure 9.17.

Once this technique is learned, students are encouraged to add new words belonging to the class, to add new semantic features, and

to continue to expand the chart with plus and minus signs. Students are encouraged to discover and discuss the similarities and differences between words in terms of features that are shared and not shared. The technique can be used with new classes of words, beginning with familiar, concrete classes such as games, tools, and pets and proceeding to less familiar, more abstract categories such as moods, shapes, and entertainments.

The advantage of this kind of exercise is that it enables children:

1. To learn new words within a class.
2. To learn new properties, or properties they had not thought of.
3. To view the meanings of words in a more complete and precise way.
4. To see that word meanings are related but that no two words' meanings are identical.

Teaching Words Having the Same Morphemes

Identifying prefixes, suffixes, and roots was discussed in Chapter 5 as a method of word recognition. A student who was familiar with the word *graceful* in spoken form might not recognize it in print, but if he or she realized that *-ful* is a common suffix, the student might analyze the word as *grace/ful* and recognize *grace* as a sight word or through phonics.

Vocabulary lessons are frequently based on words having the same prefix, suffix, or root. These lessons differ from word recognition lessons in that the point is not to teach recognition of familiar words through structural analysis; the point is to teach the students the meaning of words that may not be familiar to them and to recognize those words in print.

FIGURE 9.17
EARLY STAGES OF A SEMANTIC FEATURE ANALYSIS FOR THE CLASS "VEHICLES." (From Johnson and Pearson, 1978, p. 39.)

	Two Wheel	Four Wheel	Motor	Passengers	Enclosed	Handlebars	Rubber Tires
Bicycle	+	−	−	+	−	+	+
Motorcycle	+	−	+	+	−	+	+
Car	−	+	+	+	+	−	+
Skateboard	−	+	−	−	−	−	−

Lists of non-English root words (Figure 5.1) and derivational suffixes (Figure 5.2) are found in Chapter 5. A list of the most commonly used prefixes appears in Figure 9.18. Three examples of lessons that concentrate on word structure as a vehicle for teaching new vocabulary appear in Figures 9.19, 9.20, and 9.21.

COMPREHENSION, FLUENCY, RATE OF READING, AND FLEXIBILITY

Fluency

It has been noted several times that the demands on the reader change as he or she masters the skills of beginning reading and proceeds to read more difficult materials and to use reading as a tool for learning. In the early stages, the energy of a child engaged in reading is devoted almost entirely to *learning to read.* For the accomplished reader, reading becomes a tool that he or she uses with little conscious effort; nearly all energy while reading is devoted to *reading to learn.* At this last stage, the reader is said to be *fluent.*

Before students become fluent in reading, the rate at which they read is determined largely by the degree to which the text chal-lenges their skills. Attention to increasing rate at this point is inappropriate. The question of speed of reading shoud not arise until the reader is fluent.

FIGURE 9.18
COMMONLY USED PREFIXES.

Prefix	Meaning
anti	against
auto	self
de	from, down
dis	not, away
in, im	into, not
inter	between
il, ir	not
mis	wrong
multi	many
non	not
out	over, surpass
para	beside
post	after
pre	before
re	back
semi	half
sub	under
super	above
trans	across
ultra	above
un	not

FIGURE 9.19
WORKBOOK EXERCISE: USING PREFIXES TO BUILD WORD MEANING.
(From *Catch the Wind:* Skills Practice Book, Series *r*, Macmillan Publishing Co.,
1980, p. 48.)

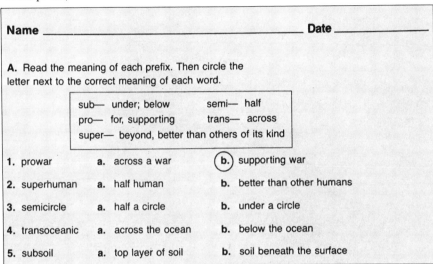

Name _____ Date _____

A. Read the meaning of each prefix. Then circle the
letter next to the correct meaning of each word.

> sub— under; below   semi— half
> pro— for, supporting   trans— across
> super— beyond, better than others of its kind

1. prowar   **a.** across a war   **b.** supporting war

2. superhuman   **a.** half human   **b.** better than other humans

3. semicircle   **a.** half a circle   **b.** under a circle

4. transoceanic   **a.** across the ocean   **b.** below the ocean

5. subsoil   **a.** top layer of soil   **b.** soil beneath the surface

Fluency is usually achieved through practice. If students are encouraged to read material which is interesting, which has very few words that present recognition problems, and which can be read with a high level of comprehension, both fluency and a reasonable rate of reading will usually develop. However, when a student attains fluency but his or her rate lags seriously behind that of classmates, steps should be taken to help that student increase his or her rate of reading.

Rate of Reading

MEASURING RATE

Reading rate is usually reported in words per minute. A simple procedure to measure rate is to give the students a passage of several hundred words and tell the students to copy the last number on the board onto their papers as soon as they have finished reading. After about one minute, the teacher begins to write the time lapses in ten-second intervals: 1:00, 1:10 . . . , 2:00, 2:10, 2:20, ... Each student's rate is calculated by dividing the number of words in the passage by the time expressed in minutes and fractions of minutes. (One minute and fifteen seconds is *not* 1.15 minutes; it is one and one-fourth minute, or 1.25 minutes).

An alternative method is to tell everyone to stop reading at precisely the same time (at the end of three minutes, for example) and to circle the word they are reading at the moment they are told to stop. Each student's rate is calculated by dividing the number of words read by the number of minutes elapsed before time was called.

HOW SLOW IS TOO SLOW?

Norms for standardized tests of rate of silent reading vary widely. Harris and Sipay

FIGURE 9.20
WORKBOOK EXERCISE: USING SUFFIXES TO BUILD WORD MEANING. (From *Catch the Wind:* Skills Practice Book, Series *r,* Macmillan Publishing Co., 1980, p. 30.)

Name _____ **Date** _____

When the suffix -*ic* is added to a word, the new word is
an adjective (*angel: angelic*). When the suffix -*ure*
is added to a word, the new word is a noun (*create:
creature*).

A. Add the suffix -*ic* to the underlined word to
complete each sentence.

1. A person who is a hero is a heroic person.

2. Sounds with the quality of rhythm are _____ sounds.

3. One with the quality of an acrobat is called _____.

4. A word that describes one who is an artist is _____.

5. A person who is a democrat is a _____ person.

B. Drop the final -*e* or -*y* from the underlined word.
Then add the suffix -*ic* to the word to complete each
sentence.

1. An event for an athlete is an athletic event.

2. A thing with the shape of a cube is called _____.

3. Maps showing the geography of an area are _____ maps.

4. A song with a nice melody is a _____ song.

C. Add the suffix -*ure* to the underlined word to complete
each sentence. If the underlined word ends in e, drop the
e before adding -*ure*.

1. If a thing happens to fail, it is called a failure .

2. When you press against something, you apply _____.

3. If things please you, they give you _____.

4. When you sculpt clay, you make a _____.

Macmillan Publishing Co., Inc

"The Lost Shepherd Girl," pages 141-151 (Softcover: pages 37-47)
Objective: Identify the meaning of words with the suffixes -*ure,* -*ic* (*Decoding Skills*)

FIGURE 9.21

WORKBOOK EXERCISE: USING GREEK ROOT WORDS TO BUILD WORD MEANING. (From *The Laidlaw Program Skills Book to Accompany Voyages*, Laidlaw Bros., Publishers, 1982, p. 74.)

You Press the Button, We Do the Rest." 246–251   Word Meaning Identifying the meaning of words containing
Teacher's Edition, 195   Greek roots

Greek Root	Meaning		Greek Root	Meaning
auto	self		phono	sound
graph	write		photo	light
meter	measure		scope	see
micro	small		tele	distant
phobia	fear		thermo	heat

Read each pair of sentences. Circle the letter of the
words that complete the last sentence of each pair. Use
the Greek roots and the meanings in the box to help you.

1. A telescope is used to see distant objects. A microscope is used ___.

   (A) to see small objects
   B. to measure far distances
   C. to test flexible substances

2. Something that is automatic works by
itself. Something that is autographed
has been ___.

   D. exposed to rough materials
   (E.) signed personally
   F. clamped together

3. Someone who is photosensitive has a
sensitivity to light. Someone with a
photophobia has ___.

   G. a lanky body
   H. a camera
   (I.) a fear of light

4. A thermometer is used to measure
heat. A photometer is used ___.

   J. to cut thatch
   (K) to measure light
   L. to forecast weather

5. A photograph reproduces light images.
A phonograph reproduces ___.

   (M) sound
   N. freight
   O. exposures

6. A micrograph is used to produce small
writing. A micrometer is used ___.

   P. to decorate small objects
   Q. to focus on small objects
   (R) to measure small objects

Use a pencil to color each box that contains a letter
you circled above. There is a message for you.

G A O K O R D I J M O E B

74 Ask the pupils to follow the directions on the page.
● For Can-Doers Tell the pupils to use the Greek roots
in the box to form other words that exist in the English
language. The words are to be written on a sheet of paper

and checked in a dictionary. Classmates are to read the
words and to write a short definition for each, using the
meanings in the box as clues.

(1980) report that the average speed of reading on several standardized tests varies from 171 to 230 words per minute at grade 6, and from 216 to 295 words per minute at grade 12 (p. 556).

The question of how slow is too slow cannot be answered in terms of numbers alone. If a student reads slowly because of lack of fluency, efforts to increase the student's rate are inappropriate. One study (Shores and Husband, 1950) showed that among bright students, faster readers appear to comprehend better, while among less bright students slower readers comprehend better.

The one category of student where rate of reading should unquestionably be addressed is composed of students who are fluent readers of average or better intelligence who read very slowly from habit. Timing these students on easy materials and giving them comprehension tests may convince them that they *can* read faster without loss of comprehension, and this may be all they need. Encouraging them to read widely in easy and interesting materials and to remind themselves to read as fast as they can may also help.

MECHANICAL READING PACERS

There are about ten mechanical devices on the market that expose reading material to a student at a controlled rate, either by a shutter that descends over a page of print from top to bottom or by projecting words, phrases, or lines of print onto a screen. The Controlled Reader (Educational Development Laboratories, New York) and the Reading Accelerator (Science Research Associates, Chicago) are two such devices.

Enthusiasts claim these devices engender a great deal of interest and motivate students to improve their reading rate (Fry, 1972, p. 409). Those who are less enthusiastic point out that these devices present reading material in a highly artificial format, that there may be little carryover to normal reading situations, and that students can be motivated through less expensive and less cumbersome means.

Flexibility

SPEEDING UP AND SLOWING DOWN A SINGLE PROCESS

A second category of reading behavior that should unquestionably be corrected is exhibited by students who read everything in exactly the same way. They start at the beginning, read every line at the same speed, and progress to the end of the passage—no matter what they are reading or what their purpose is for reading. McDonald (1965) found that most students exhibit this behavior even when they are instructed to read for different purposes and are given materials that differ in content, difficulty, and style.

There is general agreement among experts that when a reader is fluent, this kind of inflexibility is a definite handicap. There is a little less agreement as to what one is teaching students to do when one teaches them to vary the reading rate.

SWITCHING FROM ONE PROCESS TO ANOTHER

Some experimental evidence indicates that people vary the rate at which they read difficult and easy sections of texts (Rankin, 1970), and several investigators suggest that students can be taught to vary their rate in response to the purposes set for reading (Samuels and Dahl, 1975). Others (Sticht et al., 1974; Carver, 1981), however, argue that fluent adult readers read at a fairly constant rate of speed. What *appears* to be very fast reading and very slow reading is accounted for by the fact that the accomplished reader engages in different processes. The process the reader chooses depends on the content, difficulty, and style of the reading material and the purpose for reading it.

Scanning. Scanning is the process by which one seeks to find specific words or kinds of information. A person wishing to know Tolstoy's wife's name might scan an encyclopedia entry on Tolstoy looking only for names, stop when she finds one, go ahead if it is a male name, stop and read if it is a female name, go ahead as soon as she discovers whose name it is, or stop finally if she discovers it is Tolstoy's wife's name. In this process the person is looking at words but is making no attempt to make sense of them unless they meet the criterion—"a name." An accomplished reader scans to answer questions like "In what year did Elizabeth I ascend the throne?" and "Where is Harvard University located?"

Skimming. Skimming is a process whereby a person goes quickly through a text looking for titles, subtitles, headings, key words, topic sentences, summary statements, and so on, to get the gist of what information the passage contains.

Striving for Understanding. Striving for understanding is a process whereby a reader attempts to read a very difficult passage by hypothesizing the meanings of words, phrases, and sentences and checking to see if the hypothesized meaning is consistent with what he or she does understand about the passage or know about the topic.

Memorizing. Memorizing is a process whereby one attempts to increase the proba-

bility of verbatim recall by rereading, reciting, recalling, and reviewing.

ADVANTAGES AND DISADVANTAGES OF CHANGING RATE

Accomplished readers know when to skim or scan material; they appear to read very fast when they do this because they can answer questions about material on which they have spent very little time. (This, incidentally, is what speed reading courses teach people to do.) At the other end of the continuum, accomplished readers know when to stop and strive to understand a very difficult passage or attempt to memorize material. When they do this they appear to read very slowly because of the great amount of time they spend on the material.

It follows that to teach flexibility, one ought not encourage students to slow down or speed up their normal reading process. Instead, one ought to teach students to engage in processes that are considerably different from normal reading and to teach students to know when these processes are appropriate.

Specific suggestions for teaching these processes will not be addressed in this chapter, but the reader will find several citations in For Further Reading and Discussion for books on study skills. Further discussion of these processes and suggestions for teaching them can be found in these sources.

Increasing Rate and Flexibility: Two Different Goals

Increasing rate of reading and increasing flexibility of rate of reading are two different goals in teaching reading. The average rate of reading for normal reading has not been clearly established, and reading rate is often limited by other factors such as fluency. One should not attempt to increase a student's rate of reading if the student is not a fluent reader. However, slow reading is sometimes the result of habit or lack of motivation to read faster. This kind of problem can and should be addressed.

Flexibility of rate means that the student can speed up or slow down in response to the purpose and/or the difficulty of the material. Although readers may exhibit some difference in rate during normal reading, dramatic differences in time spent on passages are probably due to shifts to other processes such as scanning, skimming, striving for understanding, and memorizing. Students should be taught these skills, and they should be taught when these skills are appropriate in terms of their purpose and the difficulty of the text.

TEACHING COMPREHENSION AS READING TO LEARN

Reading enters into the teaching of school subjects such as history, science, and mathematics in two ways. First, teachers must help students learn to read materials that are appropriate to subject matter areas. This activity is usually referred to as *teaching reading in the content areas*. Second, teachers must help students to use reading as a tool in the effort to learn subject matter. This activity is usually referred to as *teaching study skills*.

Teaching Reading in the Content Areas

Each subject area presents unique demands on the reader's reading comprehension

skills. Subjects present specialized and technical vocabularies and unique text formats such as equations, maps, charts, graphs, and tables. When one engages in teaching students to cope with these special demands of content areas, one is teaching *reading*. It is in this sense that all teachers are teachers of reading, and it is for this reason that reading specialists are often called upon by content area teachers to help in the teaching of reading.

To the extent that the characteristics of all texts written in English overlap (and that is to a great extent), the techniques for teaching comprehension presented in this chapter apply to all subjects. For example, a directed reading lesson for a chapter in a science or social studies textbook written in straight prose follows the same steps and relies on the same principles as the directed reading lesson described earlier in this chapter. But since subject areas present unique challenges, special considerations for teaching comprehension are necessary.

VOCABULARY

A heavy load of new vocabulary is one of the greatest challenges in content area reading. An elementary school science teacher says "Although we do a lot of 'action learning'—experiments, demonstrations, model building, field trips and the like—I often think of my job as teaching vocabulary almost exclusively. You go to the zoo to teach the meanings of the words *vertebrate, fish, reptile, bird,* and *mammal*. You time kids as they run up a flight of stairs to teach the meaning of *weight, velocity,* and *horsepower*. When it comes down to it, there is a word for each concept, and my job is to teach the meanings of those words."

Teaching vocabulary in the content areas often means teaching the content area plus word recognition. All the word recognition skills, phonics, structure, and context come into play. Structure is often particularly useful in teaching vocabulary in content areas, since much technical and specialized vocabulary is consciously invented words. The meanings of affixes and roots are often aids to learning to recognize and remember the meanings of these words.

Teacher's guides to content area textbooks often designate subject matter vocabulary for each chapter or lesson. Lists of technical words and terms are often useful aids in preparing lessons in reading in the content areas. One such list is the *EDL Core Vocabularies in Reading, Mathematics, Science and Social Studies* (Taylor et al., 1979).

INFORMATION IN GRAPHIC, DIAGRAMMATIC, AND PICTORIAL FORM

There are many ways to present information in graphic, diagrammatic, and pictorial form in print media. With the addition of audiovisual media and particularly with the combination of interactive computers and television displays, the possibilities become seemingly endless.

In print media one finds bar graphs, line graphs, tables, time lines, flow charts, diagrams of hierarchical relationships, pictorial step-by-step direction, political cartoons, timetables, and maps. Of course, this list does not exhaust the possibilities. Furthermore, each of these categories has many variations. For example, different maps may show political boundaries, roads, air routes, distribution of crops, rainfall, minerals, and so on.

In preparing to teach any text, the teacher should be sensitive to the format in which information is presented and be aware that information that is easily, almost unconsciously, obtained from "graphics" by an experienced reader may be inaccessible to some students. Teaching students to interpret such material

may occur during the preparation, question/discussion, or skills development stages of a directed reading lesson. Teacher's guides that accompany content area textbooks often offer suggestions as to when and how to teach students to interpret graphic materials in the text.

Teaching Study Skills

Students are faced with numerous tasks that require them to read, comprehend, remember, and express what they have read. Requiring students to answer questions, or to discuss the content, or to express their feelings about a text immediately after reading is usually considered teaching or testing comprehension. Many such activities are discussed in this chapter and in Chapter 8.

However, many tasks require the student to remember and express ideas from texts that were read on the previous day, or within the past week or semester. Furthermore, tasks often require students to solve problems or answer questions that were not directly addressed in the material that was read. They are asked to analyze ideas and discuss the ways in which these ideas are related. They are asked to read several sources and synthesize what they have read in answering a question or presenting an argument. And they are asked to compare and evaluate materials they have read. This list of tasks required of readers follows Bloom's taxonomy of intellectual abilities (Bloom et al., 1956).

These tasks have two ingredients that the typical comprehension lesson does not have. The student's performance demonstrates that he or she has remembered over a period of time what he or she has read and that he or she has the ability to select and organize what he or she has read for a coherent presentation.

Commonplace tasks that make these demands are preparing oral and written reports and writing essay examinations. The skills demonstrated are referred to as *study skills.*

♦ Although teaching study skills is often presented as something that comes after teaching comprehension, you must not get the idea that the processes of reading, comprehending, remembering, and organizing are separate processes performed in that order. Organizing materials is often suggested as a first step to remembering. In fact, the discussions of schema in Chapter 8 and of story maps in this chapter indicate that sensing the organization of written material is a first step in comprehension.

Study skills include techniques for (1) finding information, (2) interpreting information, (3) recording information, (4) recalling information.

LOCATING INFORMATION

Library Skills. Using the card catalog is an important library skill. This skill encompasses alphabetizing, using guide words and letters, and understanding the concepts of title, author, and topic as well as understanding how to locate books shelved by the Dewey Decimal System or the Library of Congress Classification system.

A second library skill is using standard indexes to find information, such as the *Reader's Guide to Periodical Literature* and *The Short Story Index.* Using such guides requires all the skills needed in using the card catalog plus knowledge of which index to use to find the particular information one seeks.

A third library skill is using standard reference works, such as encyclopedias, atlases, dictionaries, and almanacs. Using these sources makes particular demands on a student's knowledge of using key words to find information, of which source to use, and on a

student's ability to scan texts to find particular information.

Book Use Skills. Book use skills for locating information include knowledge of how to use the table of contents, index, chapter titles, and subheadings within a text. Book use skills also include knowledge of what one can expect to find in a preface, an appendix, or a bibliography. Teaching students to cite the source of information properly includes teaching them to find the title, author (or editor), publisher, and the place and date of publication.

INTERPRETING INFORMATION

Study skills depend on comprehension of what is read; therefore, if one embarks on a program of "teaching study skills," a component of that program will naturally include techniques for "teaching comprehension" and "teaching reading in the content areas."

RECORDING INFORMATION

Underlining, outlining, taking notes, recording the relationship of ideas in flow charts or diagrams, and summarizing are all ways of organizing information so that it can be put to use by readers. Students need to learn when each technique is appropriate, as well as how to accomplish each technique.

RECALLING INFORMATION

Study is frequently associated with test taking. Test taking always demands that students remember what they have learned, and it often demands that they have reorganized what they have learned. Verbatim memorization is practically never desirable for several reasons. One is that well-constructed tests demand that students demonstrate their *understanding* of the subject matter. It is possible for a person to memorize language verbatim that he or she does not understand.

To demonstrate one's understanding of a topic, one should be able to distinguish main ideas and important facts from details. One should also be able to organize the information in a text to answer a question or to solve a problem that was not precisely addressed in the text. Techniques such as note taking, outlining, and so on, are often suggested as first steps in aiding recall.

A FORMULA FOR EFFECTIVE STUDY: SQ3R

After a great deal of experience in guiding college students in formulating successful study habits, Robinson (1970, originally published in 1961) presented what he found to be a sound systematic approach to study. The approach involves five steps:

1. *Survey.* Read chapter title, subtitles, and headings; read topic and summary sentences and introductory and summary paragraphs.
2. *Question.* Formulate questions based on chapter titles, subtitles, paragraph headings, and main ideas discovered in step 1.
3. *Read.* Seek answers to the questions developed in Step 2.
4. *Recite.* Answer questions orally or silently to check on recall of the content and ability to express the content.
5. *Review.* Go over material that presented difficulties in Step 4.

Robinson originally referred to this process by the formula Survey QRRR. It is currently referred to by the more abbreviated formula SQ3R.

The Reading Teacher's Responsibility

The skills a student must master in reading in the content areas and in study skills have been enumerated in this section. Many of these skills appear in social studies, science, written and oral language arts, and other school subjects. Familiarity with content area reading and study skills will make elementary school teachers aware of the many opportunities to reinforce reading skills while they are teaching other subjects and to reinforce content area skills while they are teaching reading.

Teachers who specialize in teaching reading will be expected to teach reading in the content areas and study skills as part of the reading curriculum beyond the primary grades, and they will be called upon by subject matter teachers for help in teaching these skills. These topics may be pursued in greater depth by following the suggestions in "For Further Reading and Discussion" at the end of this chapter.

SUMMARY

Durkin's observations in classrooms led her to conclude that there is practically no teaching of comprehension in reading classes. That may be true, or it may be that Durkin's definition of reading comprehension is too narrow. Teachers do not seem to be conscious of teaching reading comprehension as an isolated activity. They think of many activities involving language and meaning as teaching comprehension.

Four assumptions about teaching comprehension of language structure were examined in this chapter. The first assumption is that comprehension of language structure can be taught directly. The second assumption is that comprehension of language structure can be taught indirectly through rich and varied language experiences. The third assumption is that comprehension can be taught through general metalinguistic awareness. The fourth assumption is that comprehension can be taught through metalinguistic awareness of particular structures.

Strategies for teaching the comprehension of stories are suggested for three of the four stages of a directed reading lesson. At the preparation stage the children are supplied with information they must bring to the story for comprehension to take place, and vocabulary that may be new to the readers is introduced. Since knowledge of concepts and of word meanings is so intimately related, these two activities are often intermingled. A purpose for reading is also suggested to guide the reading and to aid in comprehension.

Questioning during the question/discussion stage of the directed reading lesson can be a method of teaching comprehension. Comprehension is presumably enhanced through questioning if the questions are derived from a structure that is believed to occur repeatedly from story to story. Repeated experiences with answering questions that reflect a story map (or schema) or a skills by level of comprehension framework will result in the student internalizing that schema or framework and using it for comprehension and recall of future stories. The two structures suggested for generating questions for teaching comprehension reflect the often-found contrast between the bottom-up concept of reading (reflected in the skills by level of comprehension framework) and the top-down concept of reading (reflected in the story map framework.)

Both frameworks play down the value of literal, factual questions. However, literal, factual questions should not be taboo. They serve the very practical purpose of ensuring that students read the text. Otherwise students sometimes learn that they can participate fully in the lesson without having read the text.

There is merit in hoping to induce a comprehension framework in a reader's mind by repeatedly leading that reader through a particular framework. There is further merit in the teacher's being more explicit in telling students what he or she hopes to accomplish through the questioning strategy. With younger students, the teacher can state the rationale for the questions as he or she proceeds. Older students might be introduced to the concept of the story map or skills by level of comprehension framework and asked to create questions based on those frameworks or to evaluate questions in terms of how they fit those frameworks.

The content of a particular selection restricts the kind of comprehension skills that are addressed in the earlier stages of a directed reading lesson. Comprehension skills that are only touched on in the selection are often singled out for attention during the skills development stage. Lessons found in the skills development stage tend to be the kind one finds in workbooks and other materials designed specifically to "teach comprehension." These lessons tend to focus on comprehension of language structures and on subskills described in the well-known taxonomies.

It is a well-established fact that word knowledge, or vocabulary, is intimately related to comprehension. It is also a well-established fact that learning the meaning of a word is a many-faceted process. According to Vygotsky, the study of word knowledge involves not only the development of thought in an individual, but also the historical growth of consciousness in the human race.

Words are defined through their correct use in sentences, by use of synonyms, antonyms, classification, examples, comparisons, and descriptions. Word definition and usage is complicated by presence of connotation, denotation, nuances, invented "insider's" meanings, historical changes, sarcasm, irony, humor, and narrowing of meanings.

Because of the profound relationship between the development of word meaning and thought and because of the great complexity of defining words and the many processes that affect word meanings, there is a nearly endless variety of lessons and activities designed for teaching vocabulary. Words in a selection are often introduced during the preparation stage of a directed reading lesson. Words appearing in selections are often used as the basis for lessons in word histories, word structure, the use of figurative language, jargon, and so on. Through these lessons, new words that are not in the selection are often introduced.

Lessons designed to increase word knowledge often appear as activities separate from directed reading lessons. Semantic feature analysis is a vehicle for students to learn relationships between words in terms of class, examples of a class, common properties of a class, and particular properties of examples. Lessons built on words having the same morphemes help students to use word structure as a word learning tool.

When students become fluent readers, rate or speed of reading should be given some attention. There is no established "average rate" for readers at any level of reading proficiency. Furthermore, the relationship between speed and comprehension is not straightforward. It is simply not true that in all groups, faster readers comprehend better than slower readers. However, there are undoubtedly students who would profit from speeding up their reading. Bright students who read remarkably more slowly than their classmates make up one group of such students.

Mechanical pacers are suggested by some

experts for their motivational value. However, mechanical pacers are expensive and cumbersome. Timed reading of easy material followed by comprehension tests may demonstrate to students who read unnecessarily slowly that they *can* read faster and still comprehend.

Good readers do not engage in the same reading process for every text and for every purpose. It has been proposed that proficient readers speed up and slow down the rate at which they read, depending on the difficulty of the text and their purpose for reading the text. A more current and probably more correct notion is that good readers do not engage in the same process with every text and for every purpose. Depending on their purpose and the difficulty of the text, readers skim, scan, read, strive for understanding, and memorize. Rather than teaching students to read faster and slower, students should be taught how and when to engage in these different processes.

All the strategies for teaching comprehension can and should be used in teaching reading in the content areas. However, reading in each of the content areas presents its own unique challenges to the reader. Content areas have specialized vocabularies. Information is often presented in graphic, diagrammatic, and pictorial forms. Students must learn to "read" these graphic displays, just as they must learn to read printed texts.

The content areas place special demands on the student's study skills. Study skills include: (1) learning how to locate information through using the card catalog, standard indexes, standard reference works, and books; (2) learning how to record information in useful ways, such as underlining, outlining, note taking, and summarizing; and (3) techniques for committing information to memory or recalling information. Since so much of a student's time is spent in studying textbooks in preparation for examinations, the study skills curriculum gives special attention to this process. The SQ3R formula (survey, question, read, recite, review) is often recommended as a guide to effective study.

Many elementary school teachers teach content areas as well as reading; they will find themselves teaching reading during content area classes and teaching content area skills and study skills during the reading period. Teachers who specialize in teaching reading will often be called upon by content area teachers for help in teaching reading and study skills.

FOR FURTHER READING AND DISCUSSION

1. Two frameworks for deriving questions about stories were presented in this chapter. The story map was suggested by Beck and her associates. The skills by level of comprehension framework was suggested by Ruddell. You may want to read the original sources on which this discussion was based.

Beck, I. L., M. G. McKeown, E. S. McCaslin, and A. M. Burkes. *Instructional Dimensions That May Affect Reading Comprehension: Examples from Two Commercial Reading Programs.* Pittsburgh: Learning Research and Development Center, University of Pittsburgh, 1979. ERIC Document 197322.

Ruddell, R. B. Developing comprehension abilities: Implications from research for an instructional framework. In S. J. Samuels (ed.), *What Research Has to Say about Reading Instruction.* Newark, DE: International Reading Association, 1978, 109–20.

Choose a story and generate questions using both frameworks. How are your lists of questions similar? How are they different? Which set do you prefer? Why? Do you think you could teach upper-grade children about these frameworks so they could generate their own questions from them or judge the fitness of questions you generate in light of these schemes?

2. Obtain teacher's manuals for two basal reading series at the same grade level. Look up "Comprehension" in the index of skills or lessons. Examine the lessons. Compare the basals. Questions like the following may be a useful basis for comparison.

1. What does the approach to comprehension of sentence meaning seem to be—direct teaching, a rich and varied language experience, or metalinguistic awareness of particular structures?

2. What seems to be the rationale for the questions suggested for the question/discussion stage of the directed reading lesson?

This activity may be more instructive if you choose one basal from the list of phonics-emphasis basals and one basal from among the eclectic basals listed in Chapter 7.

3. The following citations are of books that treat study skills in general—that is, reading rate, flexibility, reading in the content areas, and study skills.

Askov, E. N., and K. Kamm. *Study Skills in the Content Areas.* Boston: Allyn and Bacon, 1982.

Deese, J., and E. K. Deese. *How to Study.* New York: McGraw-Hill, 1979.

Rubin, D. *Reading and Learning Power.* New York: Macmillan, 1980.

Schmelzer, R. V., W. L. Christen, and W. G. Browning. *Reading and Study Skills.* Rehoboth, MA: Twin Oaks Publishers, 1980.

The following citations are devoted to particular topics concerning reading rate, reading in the content areas, and study skills.

Fry, E. *Skimming and Scanning.* Providence, RI: Jamestown Publishers, 1978.

McGraw Hill Basic Skills System: Tools for Learning Success.

This is a series of books under the editorship of Alton Raygor. The following titles are relevant to reading rate, reading in the content areas, and study skills.

Effective Rates
Library and Reference Skills
Main Idea in Science
Problem Solving
Skimming and Scanning
Study Skills
Study Type Reading
Underlining
Vocabulary Skills

Groups of students might form to investigate methods of teaching these skills. The investigations may result in comparing approaches or demonstrating techniques suggested by these authors.

REFERENCES

Adler, M. J. *How to Read a Book.* New York: Simon and Schuster, 1940.

Anderson, R. C., and W. B. Biddle, On asking people questions about what they are reading. In G. Bower (ed.), *Psychology of Learning and Motivation,* Vol. 9. New York: Academic Press, 1975.

Athey, I. Syntax, semantics and reading. In J. T. Guthrie, *Cognition, Curriculum and Comprehension.* Newark, DE: International Reading Association, 1977, 71–98.

Beck, I. L. Comprehension during the acquisition of decoding skills. In J. T. Guthrie, *Cognition, Curriculum and Comprehension.* Newark, DE: International Reading Association, 1977, 113–156.

————, M. G. McKeown, E. S. McCaslin, and A. M. Burkes. *Instructional Dimensions That May Affect Reading Comprehension: Examples from Two Commercial Reading Programs.* Pittsburgh: Learning Research and Development Center, University of Pittsburgh, 1979. ERIC Document 197322.

Bloom, B. S., M. D. Engelhart, E. J. Furst, W. H. Hill, and D. R. Krathwhol. *Taxonomy of Educational Objectives. The Classification of Educational Goals. Handbook I: Cognitive Domain.* New York: David McKay, 1956.

Bormuth, J. R. An operational definition of comprehension instruction. In K. S. Goodman and J. T. Fleming (eds.), *Psycholinguistics and the Teaching of Reading.* Newark, DE: International Reading Association, 1969, 48–60.

————, J. Manning, J. Carr, and D. Pearson. Children's comprehension of between- and within-sentence syntactic structures. *Journal of Educational Psychology,* 61 (1970): 349–57.

Bortnick, R., and G. S. Lopardo. An instructional application of the cloze procedure. *Journal of Reading* (January 1973): 296–300.

Brand, M. Wine on the desert. In S. Dunning, E. Katterjohn, and O. S. Niles. *Thrust.* Glenview, IL: Scott, Foresman, 1969, 332–40.

Carver, R. P. *Reading Comprehension and Reading Theory.* Springfield, IL: Charles C. Thomas, 1981.

Chomsky, C. S. *The Acquisition of Syntax in Children from 5 to 10.* Cambridge, MA: MIT Press, 1969.

Clymer, T. (senior author). *Reading 720. Level 7.* Lexington, MA: Ginn, 1976.

Collins, A., and M. Quillian. Retrieval time from semantic memory. *Journal of Verbal Learning and Verbal Behavior,* 8 (1969): 240–47.

Davis, F. B. Fundamental factors of comprehension in reading. *Psychometrika,* 9 (1944): 185–97.

Dewey, J. *How We Think.* Boston: D. C. Heath, 1933.

Dunning, S., E. Katterjohn, and O. S. Niles. *Thrust.* Glenview, IL: Scott, Foresman, 1969.

Durkin, D. What classroom observations reveal about reading instruction. *Reading Research Quarterly,* 14 (1979): 481–533.

Durr, W. K. (senior author). *The Houghton Mifflin Reading Series, Level J.* Boston: Houghton Mifflin, 1976a.

———— (senior author). *The Houghton Mifflin Reading Series, Level G.* Boston: Houghton Mifflin, 1976b.

Durr, W. K., V. O. Windley, and A. A. McCourt. *Teacher's Guide for Kaleidoscope: The Houghton Mifflin Readers, Level 10.* Boston: Houghton Mifflin, 1971a.

————. *Kaleidoscope: The Houghton Mifflin Readers, Level 10.* Boston: Houghton Mifflin, 1971b.

Finn, P. J. Illiterates who can read. In *The Scotsman* (Edinburgh, Scotland, daily newspaper). February 19, 1980.

Foster, R. J. *Celebration of Discipline.* New York: Harper & Row, 1978.

Frase, L. T. Purpose in reading. In J. T. Guthrie (ed.), *Cognition, Curriculum and Comprehension.* Newark, DE: International Reading Association, 1977, 42–64.

Froese, V., and S. Kurushima. The effects of sentence expansion practice on the reading comprehension and writing ability of third-graders. In M. L. Kamil and A. J. Moe (eds.), *Reading Research: Studies and Applications. Twenty Eighth Yearbook of the National Reading Conference.* Clemson, SC: National Reading Conference, 1979, 95–99.

Fry, E. B. *Reading Instruction for Classroom and Clinic.* New York: McGraw-Hill, 1972.

Greenberg, M., D. McAndrew, and M. Melerski. *Getting It Together: A Sentence Combining Workbook* (edited by C. Cooper and adapted by T. Callaghan and M. Sullivan). Mimeographed. Department of Instruction, State University of New York at Buffalo, 1975.

Guzak, F. J. Teacher questioning and reading. *The Reading Teacher,* 21 (1967): 227–34.

Harris, A. J., and E. R. Sipay. *How to Increase Reading Ability,* 7th ed. New York: Longman, 1980.

Herr, S. E. *Learning Activities for Reading.* Dubuque, IA: William C. Brown, 1977.

Hodges, C. A. Commentary: Toward a broader definition of reading comprehension. *Reading Research Quarterly,* 15 (1980): 299–306.

Hunt, K. W. *Grammatical Structures Written At Three Grade Levels.* Urbana, IL: NCTE, 1965.

Johnson, D. D., and P. D. Pearson. *Teaching Reading Vocabulary.* New York: Holt, Rinehart and Winston, 1978.

Jongsma, E. *The Cloze Procedure as a Teaching Technique.* Newark, DE: International Reading Association, 1971.

Kibby, M. W. Intersentential processes in reading comprehension. *Journal of Reading Behavior,* 12 (1980): 299–312.

Kingston, A. J., and W. W. Weaver. *Feasibility of Cloze Techniques for Teaching and Evaluating Culturally Disadvantaged Beginning Readers.* Athens: Research and Development Center in Early Education Stimulation, University of Georgia, 1970.

Martin, R. W. Transformational grammar, cloze, and performance in college freshmen. Unpublished doctoral dissertation, Syracuse University, 1968.

McCarthy, M. A World out of joint. *The Observer,* London (October 14, 1979): 35.

McDonald, A. S. Research for the classroom: Rate and flexibility. *Journal of Reading,* 8 (1965): 187–91.

Meichenbaum, D. *Cognitive Behavior Modification.* New York: Plenum Press, 1977.

————.Teaching thinking: A cognitive behavioral perspective. Mimeographed. Waterloo, Ontario: University of Waterloo, 1980.

Mellon, J. C. *Transformational Sentence Combining: A Method for Enhancing the Development of Syntactic Fluency in English Composition.* Urbana, IL: NCTE, 1969.

O'Hare, F. *Sentence Combining: Improving Student Writing without Formal Grammar Instruction.* Urbana, IL: NCTE, 1973.

Pearson, P. D., and K. Camperell. Comprehension of text structures. In J. T. Guthrie (ed.), *Comprehension and Teaching: Research Reviews.* Newark, DE: International Reading Association, 1981, 27–54.

Rankin, E. F. How flexibly do we read. *Journal of Reading Behavior,* 3 (1970): 34–38.

Robinson, F. P. *Effective Reading.* New York: Harper & Row, 1970.

————, *Effective Study.* New York: Harper & Row, 1961.

Ruddell, R. B. Developing comprehension abilities: Implications from research for an instructional framework. In S. J. Samuels (ed.), *What Research Has to Say about Reading Instruction.* Newark, DE: International Reading Association, 1978, 109–20.

————, and A. C. Williams. *A Research Investigation of a Literacy Teaching Model: Project DELTA.* Washington, DC: U.S. Department of Health, Education and Welfare, Office of Education, EDPA Project No. 005262, 1972.

Samuels, S. J., and P. R. Dahl. Establishing appropriate purpose for reading and its effect on flexibility of reading rate. *Journal of Educational Psychology,* 67 (1975): 38–43.

Shores, H. J., and K. L. Husband. Are fast readers the

best readers? *Elementary English*, 27 (1950): 52–57.

Singer, H., and I. H. Balow. Overcoming educational disadvantagedness. In J. T. Guthrie (ed.), *Comprehension and Teaching: Research Reviews.* Newark, DE: International Reading Association, 1981, 274–312.

Sticht, T. G., L. J. Beck, R. N. Hauke, G. M. Kleiman, and J. H. James. *Auding and Reading.* Alexandria, VA: Human Resources Research Organization, 1974.

Straw, S. B. The effects of sentence-combining and sentence-reduction instruction on measures of syntactic fluency, reading comprehension, and listening comprehension in fourth-grade students. Unpublished Ph.D. dissertation, University of Minnesota, 1978.

Taylor, S. E., et al. *EDL Core Vocabularies in Reading, Mathematics, Science and Social Studies.* New York: EDL/McGraw-Hill, 1979.

Vygotsky, L. S. *Thought and Language.* Cambridge, MA: MIT Press, 1962.

———. *Mind in Society.* Cambridge, MA: Harvard University Press, 1978.

Wilder, G. Five exemplary reading programs. In J. T. Guthrie, *Cognition, Curriculum and Comprehension.* Newark, DE: International Reading Association, 1977, 257–78.

INDIVIDUAL DIFFERENCES

FACTORS THAT INFLUENCE LEARNING TO READ

INTELLIGENCE

Measuring Intelligence

HISTORY OF IQ TESTING
THE "NORMAL" INTELLIGENCE TEST SCORE
AND ITS INTERPRETATION

The Use of IQ Test Scores in Teaching
Strategies

CARROLL'S MODEL OF SCHOOL LEARNING
MASTERY LEARNING
ASPECTS OF READING AND MASTERY
LEARNING

The Use of IQ Test Scores for Labeling People

IQ SCORES MAY CHANGE
IQ TESTS DO NOT MEASURE ALL KINDS OF
INTELLIGENT BEHAVIOR

The Use of IQ Test Scores to Explain Reading
Failure
The Use of IQ Test Scores to Evaluate Progress

VISUAL ACUITY: THE TEACHER'S ROLE

Symptoms of Vision Problems
Visual Problems and Reading

FARSIGHTEDNESS (HYPEROPIA)
ASTIGMATISM
BINOCULAR DIFFICULTIES

Referrals and Follow-up

AUDITORY ACUITY: THE TEACHER'S ROLE

Symptoms of Hearing Loss

Hearing Loss and Reading
Referrals and Follow-Up

NEUROLOGICAL AND EMOTIONAL FACTORS

Symptoms of Neurological and Emotional
Problems
Referrals and Follow-Up
Getting and Giving the Proper Advice

CULTURAL AND ECONOMIC FACTORS

Economic Status and Language Use

SUPERFICIALLY DIFFERENT
CHARACTERISTICS
CHARACTERISTICS UNIQUE TO
PARTICULAR GROUPS
CHARACTERISTICS ASSOCIATED WITH
ECONOMIC DEPRIVATION

Societal Characteristics Shared by the
Economically Disadvantaged
The Language of the School
Deprivation Theory

THE IDEA OF INFERIOR LANGUAGE
TWO VALUABLE CONTRIBUTIONS
EDUCATIONAL IMPLICATIONS

SUMMARY

FOR FURTHER READING AND DISCUSSION

REFERENCES

No two individuals are exactly alike. Some of the characteristics on which people differ may be relevant to their success in learning to read, and others may not be. The color of a person's eyes has no bearing on potential to learn to read; the quality of his or her eyesight may have.

Many characteristics have been investigated for possible relationships with success in learning to read. They have been classified in many different ways in books written for specialists in teaching reading and language to severely delayed students. Brown (1982), for example, reviews psychological, neurological, physiological, and sociological factors related to reading difficulties. Stauffer and others (1978) discuss intelligence, vision, learning, perceptual, and neurological factors. Harris and Sipay (1980) treat cognition factors, physical and physiological factors, and cultural factors. Bloom and Lahey (1978) identify "clinical syndromes": hearing impairment, childhood aphasia, mental retardation, and emotional disturbances (schizophrenia, psychosis, and autism) and "specific abilities" such as visual and auditory memory.

Some characteristics of individuals that appear to have an impact on learning to read are discussed rather extensively elsewhere in this book: Language development and visual and auditory perception, discrimination and memory are all discussed in Chapter 2; language development is discussed again in Chapters 8 and 9. Several more of these characteristics will be discussed in this chapter. There will be no attempt to present an exhaustive review of the literature; the discussions will be guided by the following objectives: (1) to familiarize classroom teachers with characteristics that affect learning to read so that they can make intelligent referrals to the appropriate specialist and intelligent judgments about whether the referrals are appropriately acted upon, and (2) to familiarize

readers with some controversies that surround the diagnosis and classification of these characteristics and their educational consequences so that they can discuss these matters intelligently with parents and other professionals.

INTELLIGENCE

Measuring Intelligence

Intelligence is the capacity for reasoning, understanding, and similar forms of mental activity. There is no doubt that people vary in this capacity, but *measuring* it is an enterprise fraught with questions, doubts, and pitfalls. We will first present a brief history (Ceprano, 1979) of the measurement of intelligence (IQ testing) in order to arrive at an understanding of what an IQ test score means and what it is believed to measure.

HISTORY OF IQ TESTING

Throughout history there have been references to the fact that some people are quicker to learn than others. The words *smart, quick, clever, brilliant, witty, keen,* and *bright,* on the one hand, and the words *slow, dull, dense,* and *stupid,* on the other, attest to the fact that such judgments are commonplace among even the least sophisticated people.

Binet's Work. Around the turn of the century, the French government became interested in setting up special schools for individuals who would not benefit from ordinary public schooling. Government officials were reluctant to ask teachers to identify slow learners or retarded children because they were afraid teachers would unconsciously (or perhaps consciously) so identify troublesome children and fail to identify truly slow children who were cooperative. So the government turned to Alfred Binet (1857–1911), a psychologists who had been studying individual differences and mental ability, to devise a test that would identify children who would not be likely to profit from regular schooling.

Binet experimented with test items ranging from simple tasks, such as pointing to one's own head, ear, and nose, to complex tasks, such as figuring out what time it would be if the large and small hands of a clock placed at five minutes to three were reversed—and then explaining why it would be impossible to reverse them exactly.

Experimenting with different questions and different-aged children, Binet created test items that could be answered by most 11-year-old children but not by most 9-year-old children; test items that could be answered by most 9-year-old children but not by most 7-year-old children, and so on. His first test consisted of several items that one would expect children to answer at ages 3 through 13.

The Concept of Mental Age. By asking questions calibrated according to Binet's method, one can determine where a child ceases to be able to answer. One can then speak of a child's *mental age* as the age associated with the most difficult questions the child was successful in answering. One could speak of a child as having a mental age of 7, for example, if he or she answered questions that 7-year-olds typically could answer, but failed to answer questions 8-, 9-, or 10-year-olds could typically answer. It would not matter whether the child was actually 5 or 15. His or her mental age would be determined from the highest level of questions answered correctly. Binet's test and the mental age that could be derived from it gave school authorities what they felt was a better guide for identifying children who needed special schooling than teacher's opinions on this matter.

The Concept of the Intelligence Quotient. By 1916 Binet's test had been translated into English and revised by Louis Terman (1877–1956) so that it could be used with an American population. Terman published the test under the title Stanford-Binet. Terman extended two of Binet's ideas. First, he devised his test so that each item was assigned a certain number of months' credit. By multiplying the number of items successfully answered by the number of months assigned to each item, a child's mental age culd be reported in terms of years and months. Second, knowing a child's mental age gives one no sense of whether the child is a fast or slow learner unless one knows the individual's actual age. Making judgments about a child's learning facility from mental age always *implied* a comparison of the individual's actual and mental age. Terman made this comparison explicit by expressing the relationship between mental age and chronological age (actual age) as a ratio or quotient. He called this relationship the *intelligence quotient,* or *IQ.*

A child who is 10 and has a mental age of 10 has an intelligence quotient of 100 because

$$\frac{\text{mental age}}{\text{chronological age}} \times 100$$
$$= \text{IQ} \quad \bigg| \quad \frac{10}{10} \times 100 = 100$$

A child who is 10 and has a mental age of 12 has an intelligence quotient of 120 because

$$\frac{\text{mental age}}{\text{chronological age}} \times 100$$
$$= \text{IQ} \quad \bigg| \quad \frac{12}{10} \times 100 = 120$$

A child who is 10 and has a mental age of 8 has an intelligence quotient of 80 because

$$\frac{\text{mental age}}{\text{chronological age}} \times 100$$

$$= IQ \ \left| \ \frac{8}{10} \times 100 = 80 \right.$$

As a result of advances in statistics and the study of the "normal distribution" of characteristics in a population, some test scores are converted to IQ scores through a slightly different arithmetic. But the rationale behind IQ scores remains nearly the same. An individual's performance in answering questions on a test is compared with the performance of large numbers of others who are very nearly the same age. If the individual's score equals the average score for others the same age, that person's IQ is determined to be 100. If the score is below the average score for others the same age, the IQ is determined to be below 100. If the individual's score is above the average for others the same age, the IQ is determined to be over 100. Just how much over or under 100 the IQ score is determined to be depends on how much higher (or lower) that person's score was compared to the average score for others the same age.

♦ It is ironic that the term *intelligence quotient* is used to refer to a score that is no longer derived from dividing mental age by chronological age and therefore is not a quotient. The term is at least half a misnomer. Whether this score is a measurement of "intelligence" or not will be taken up later in this chapter. If it is not, the term is entirely a misnomer.

An Interesting Sidelight: The Whole/ Part Controversy. Just as it is debated whether reading readiness, word recognition, and comprehension are better thought of as general, global affairs or whether they are better thought of as consisting of many separate parts that come together to make up the whole, there are two views of what is measured by an intelligence test.

One view is that intelligence tests measure a general factor and that in performing any intellectual task, a person calls on this general factor (or "G") plus knowledge or skill peculiar to the task. Therefore, people good at some things will tend to be good at most things simply because part of their performance on all tasks relies on their general intelligence. Charles Spearman (1863–1945), an English psychologist and a contemporary of Binet, is the best-known proponent of this global view of intelligence.

A second view is that intelligence is composed of separate and independent factors, such as spatial ability, numerical ability, verbal meaning, and inductive reasoning. In this view, a person could have ample spatial ability and limited capacity for inductive reasoning. This view of the nature of intelligence is known as the *primary mental abilities* theory. Its best-known proponent is the American psychologist L. L. Thurston (1887–1955).

THE "NORMAL" INTELLIGENCE TEST SCORE AND ITS INTERPRETATION

Because tests are never perfect and because people's test performance is never perfect, one cannot assume that if an IQ score is over 100, the person is a "fast learner," or if the IQ score is under 100, he or she is a "slow learner." Most experts consider IQ scores between 84 and 116 to be "normal." About 70 percent of the population falls into this range. About 15 percent falls above this range, and 15 percent falls below it.

IQ test scores indicate how much knowledge and skill relevant to school success an individual has acquired at a given point in time. There are two ways to interpret the idea that children who are the same age have acquired differing amounts of knowledge and skill that is relevant to school success.

The Potential Interpretation. One interpretation is that the children differ in potential to learn. The assumption is that all children have roughly the same experiences, but that some of the children learn a great deal from these experiences because they are good learners—have a great potential for learning. Others learn little from these experiences because they are poor learners—have less potential for learning.

The Rate of Learning Interpretation. If a child has acquired more knowledge and skill relevant to school success than the average child the same age, then one assumes the child's rate of learning has been faster than that of the average child. Conversely, if a child has acquired less knowledge and skill relevant to school success than the average child the same age, then one assumes the child's rate of learning has been slower than that of the average child.

IQ test scores yield an estimate of the rate of learning of past achievement. It is presumed that a measure of rate of past learning is a good predictor of rate of learning in the near future. Therefore, to the extent that one can trust IQ scores, one can expect children with low scores to learn less in the same amount of time than children with high scores, or for children with low scores to take more time to learn the same amount as children with high scores.

The Use of IQ Test Scores in Teaching Strategies

CARROLL'S MODEL OF SCHOOL LEARNING

Carroll (1963) proposed that school learning depends on five elements: (1) aptitude, (2) ability to understand instruction, (3) perseverance, (4) opportunity, and (5) quality of instruction. Carroll defined three of these five variables in terms of time:

— *Aptitude:* The amount of time needed to learn the task under optimal instructional conditions.
— *Perseverance:* The amount of time the learner is willing to engage actively in learning.
— *Opportunity:* The amount of time allowed for learning.

The ability to understand instruction is thought to be indicated by IQ test scores. Limitations on this ability show themselves in two ways. First, when the learner is left to infer for him or herself the concepts and relationships inherent in the material rather than having them carefully spelled out, limitations on the ability to understand instruction will cause a learning breakdown. This problem can be remedied by the teacher who understands what is to be learned, has a clear concept of how it is learned, and understands the importance of the learner being a conscious partner in the process. So some limitations imposed by ability to understand instruction can be overcome by quality of instruction.

The second limitation imposed by the ability to understand instruction occurs when instruction utilizes language beyond the grasp of the learner. Carroll is not referring here to poor quality of instruction; he is referring to the case in which one is attempting to teach concepts or relationships which require language that is simply beyond the grasp of the learner, even when those concepts or relationships are stated as simply, clearly, and explicitly as possible. When this limitation interferes with learning, one would expect the content of the lesson to be adjusted. MacGinitie (1969) stated it so well:

The teacher, knowing the eventual goals of education, should ask what and how this child is ready to learn. And the teacher should be aware of the fact that when a child is taught a little, he is then ready for a little more. (p. 399)

Carroll's model of school learning takes this ability, which is believed to be measured by IQ tests, into account, but he refers to it in an effort to promote successful learning and teaching, rather than as a method of explaining failure or classifying students.

MASTERY LEARNING

Bloom (1971) developed the concept of mastery learning. For skills that are sequential and limited in number, such as instant recognition of graded lists of sight words (Harris and Jacobson, 1972, or Fry, 1972, for example), Bloom proposed that there should be no relationship between aptitude and mastery if all students are given enough time to learn.

Bloom suggests that in a mastery learning situation, children who need extra help generally require only 10–15 percent more time to master the material. He suggests having children work in triplets or pairs on specific tasks, such as those related to errors made on tests (Alper, 1982).

Individual tutoring is also suggested as a way of eradicating differences in achievement. Ellison, Harris, and Barber (1968) reported that two fifteen-minute periods per day of tutoring of first-grade students improved the reading achievement of all the students. But it was most beneficial to slow learners, thereby closing the gap between children with high and low aptitude as measured by an IQ test.

In a recent study, Bloom also found that tutoring eradicates the relationship between aptitude and achievement. Bloom's tutors were not experienced teachers. He attributes their effectiveness to the one-to-one relationship in which instruction is tailored to the student and the tutor catches the pupil's misunderstandings immediately. (Note that tutoring permits optimal conditions for all five of Carroll's elements of school learning.) These studies reveal that the upper limits on an individual's capacity to learn are much higher than those approached by most students in most classrooms (Alper, 1982).

A half-century ago, Gates and Bond (1936) experimented with giving extra instruction to first-grade students whose reading achievement lagged behind that of their classmates. They concluded:

We think there is no ultimate justification for assuming that materials and methods of teaching must remain forever fixed as they are, waiting upon nature to change the child through maturity until he reaches a point at which he can proceed successfully.

ASPECTS OF READING AND MASTERY LEARNING

It is important to notice the qualifications Bloom places on the content of a mastery learning curriculum; the content must be sequential and limited in number. It is important to notice too that the mastery learning experiments mentioned here deal with primary reading instruction. Beginning reading instruction frequently deals with skills that are sequential and limited in number, such as basic sight word lists, the very reliable consonant letter-sound relationships, clues to vowel sounds, phonics relationships in words of more than one syllable, and so on.

One could argue that the outer aspects of reading receive the lion's share of attention at the initial stages of instruction and that these aspects of the process tend to be sequential and limited in number. One would expect, then, that much of the beginning reading curriculum would be conducive to mastery learning techniques.

However, there are inner aspects of reading as well—reading as a thought-getting process, reading as reasoning. These aspects do not lend themselves readily to sequencing schemes, although some hierarchical schemes for comprehension have been proposed (see Chapters 8 and 9). Furthermore, these aspects of reading are not limited in number. The skill and the knowledge necessary to master the inner aspects of reading are open-ended, and therefore they do not conform to the assumptions about the content of a mastery learning curriculum.

Singer (1977) has suggested that reading achievement can be considered under three headings: word recognition, word meaning, and reasoning-in-reading. He proposes that mastery of word recognition will be related to IQ scores only insofar as mastery will take some children more time than others. Furthermore, if goals in word meaning and reasoning-in-reading are kept within limits attainable by all members of a class, achievement in these areas will be related to IQ scores only insofar as mastery will take some children more time than others. But when goals of word meaning and reasoning-in-reading are established to tax the most able members of a class, achievement will differ and will be related to IQ test scores—and by implication to intelligence.

Soon after reading instruction begins, and especially in the middle and upper grades, the goals of the reading program shift from word recognition skills (skills amenable to mastery learning) to knowledge of word meaning and reasoning-in-reading skills. Students with a good record of success in school-related learning (and therefore high IQ test scores) do appear to have more facility with these kinds of learning tasks. Furthermore, lack of facility on these kinds of tasks does not appear to be remedied by simply increasing instruction time. But it makes better sense to work out learning objectives for an individual based on performance on learning tasks and to respond to that individual's limitations as they become apparent than to predict learning difficulties with an IQ score and risk a self-fulfilling prophecy.

The Use of IQ Test Scores for Labeling People

Throughout this chapter, the term *IQ score* has been used rather than *IQ*, and reference has been made to a person's *IQ score* rather than to a person's *IQ*. This may be considered a slightly unusual use of the word *score*, since a score usually refers to the number of items answered correctly on a test. However, to refer to a number derived from a test as an intelligence quotient or IQ seduces many people, even those who know better, into thinking that this number represents the "amount of intelligence" of the test taker in some straightforward and infallible way. This is a fallacious and dangerous assumption. We use the term *IQ score* as a repeated reminder that this number is ultimately derived from a test score; it is not some mystical quantity.

IQ SCORES MAY CHANGE

There are dangers inherent in interpreting IQ test scores as indicators of general brightness. In the first place, such interpretation implies more faith in the infallibility of the tests than is warranted by the facts. The same person may achieve different scores on IQ tests administered at different times in his or her life. Honzik and others (1948) report that one-third of one group of individuals changed more than 20 IQ points between ages 6 and 18. Since this range could move an individual from dull to average or average to bright (or vice-versa), one must conclude either that it is a fairly common occurence for an individual's "intelligence" to change dramatically over the school career, or that IQ test scores do not reveal true intelligence. In either case, identifying a person as one having low intelligence can have a devastating effect on that person's life. It is for this reason that schools are often reluctant to report IQ scores to parents or students and why attempts are sometimes made to ban IQ testing altogether (Green, 1975).

IQ TESTS DO NOT MEASURE ALL KINDS OF INTELLIGENT BEHAVIOR

A second reason why it is illegitimate to interpret IQ test scores as indicators of general brightness is that IQ tests, by design, do not attempt to measure all kinds of intelligent behavior. The original test devised by Binet had a particular purpose: to predict achievement in school. IQ tests are still devised and used for that purpose. If test makers discover that students who are successful in school tend to answer a particular item correctly and students who are unsuccessful in school tend to answer that particular item incorrectly, the item is kept in the test. If research shows that this is not true of an item, the item is removed from the test.

But many kinds of very useful knowledge have no apparent relevance to success in school. For a 10-year-old raised in Aspen, Colorado, to be able to step outside, listen to the crunch of the snow under his boot, and tell a tourist what kind of wax to put on his skis for that day is certainly useful knowledge, and it demonstrates a kind of intelligence. For a 12-year-old to test a batch of boiling fudge by dropping samples into cold water and to know precisely when to remove the fudge from the heat so it will not be soupy and will not crystallize is certainly useful knowledge and demonstrates a kind of intelligence. But since these kinds of skill and knowledge, and numerous others, have no apparent relevance to school success, there is no attempt to measure them on IQ tests.

People who believe that IQ tests identify (or are intended to identify) clever and slow-witted people are often simply ignorant of the facts. IQ test items are created to correlate with school success; the criterion for keeping an item is not whether the item appears to test some kind of "intelligence," but whether children who are successful in school answer it correctly and children who are unsuccessful in school answer it incorrectly.

The Use of IQ Test Scores to Explain Reading Failure

One use of IQ test scores is to justify poor performance, lack of progress, or plain failure on the part of a segment of the student population. This option is taken more often than one would hope, as evidenced by this kindergarten teacher's comments, quoted in Chapter 3.

It just appears that some can do it and some cannot. I don't think that it is the teaching that affects those that cannot do it, but some are just basically low-achievers. (Rist, 1970, p. 425)

It was argued in Chapter 2 that it is ill-advised to use readiness tests to determine whether or not a child is ready to learn to read; the best way to determine whether a child is ready to learn to read is by attempting to teach that child to read. The same line of reasoning applies to using IQ test scores to determine whether or not a child has the potential to succeed at any level of the reading program.

The most important question for a teacher to answer in regard to any child at any stage of learning to read is always: "What skill and knowledge does this child have and what skill and knowledge does he or she need next?" To answer this question, an assessment of the child's reading performance (Chapter 12) and knowledge of the reading curriculum are necessary. An IQ score does not help to answer this question.

Rosenthal and Jacobsen (1968) popularized a concept called "the self-fulfilling prophecy." They reported that when children were identified as having high intelligence, they were treated differently by teachers and achieved higher test scores than similar students who were not so identified. This study is often cited by critics of IQ testing who belive that the self-fulfilling prophecy works *against* students who score low on the tests. The danger is that if teachers are led to expect students to be dull and incapable, they expect less of the students and the students may put forth less effort.

The Use of IQ Test Scores to Evaluate Progress

IQ scores, however, are useful to the reading teacher to evaluate student progress. As an evaluator, a teacher may reasonably ask the question: "Does this child's reading progress reflect his or her potential?" To answer this question, an assessment of the child's performance and an estimate of the child's learning potential are necessary. The use of the IQ score as an estimate of potential has two legitimate applications. One has to do with students who are exceptionally slow learners; the other has to do with children who appear to have the potential to be exceptionally fast learners.

The original aim of the French government in 1904, to identify children who would not profit from usual classroom instruction, is still a valid aim and use for IQ tests. When teachers' observations or an IQ test administered in a classroom reveals a child who is suspected of being a very slow learner, the child is usually referred to a psychologist, who adminsters one or more individual IQ tests to determine whether the child qualified for special placement. Very slow learners may require more individual attention than it is possible to give in a regular classroom.

A child whose progress is average or slow is sometimes discovered to have a remarkably high IQ test score. Such discoveries may suggest that the child's performance may not be helped by additional time for learning, but that perhaps motivation or methods are at fault; special placement for such students is also sometimes indicated. This too is a legitimate use of IQ testing.

VISUAL ACUITY: THE TEACHER'S ROLE

Visual defects can seriously affect reading achievement, although specialists in severe reading problems agree that visual defects are not a major cause of reading failure (Brown,

1982; Stauffer et al., 1978, for example). The reason why vision is not a major cause of reading failure may be that most schools conduct routine screening procedures to detect vision defects and that the most common defects can be corrected with eyeglasses. However, some schools do not conduct screening procedures, or the procedures are sometimes inadequate; therefore, the classroom teacher sometimes detects symptoms of visual defects that are not discovered elsewhere.

Since problems of visual acuity are the province of specialists, the classroom teacher appears to have only two responsibilities in dealing with suspected problems:

1. To recognize symptoms of visual defects
2. To refer students with suspected defects to appropriate personnel for testing and/or referral to a specialist

However, sometimes "referral to appropriate personnel" means to recommend that the child be given a visual screening test, and such tests may not be adequate. Therefore, the classroom teacher should have some knowledge of the visual conditions that are associated with reading problems and of the kinds of examinations necessary to detect these conditions. With this knowledge, teachers can make an informed judgment about how well their referrals are acted upon.

Symptoms of Vision Problems

The following may be symptoms of vision problems (Fry, 1977; Stauffer and others, 1978):

1. Unusual appearance of the eyes
   a. Redness
   b. Tearing
   c. Bloodshot appearance
   d. Crustlike accumulation near the eye
2. Unusual habits
   a. Rapid blinking
   b. Twitching
   c. Facial contortions
   d. Holding a book unusually close
   e. Holding a book unusually far
   f. Avoiding tasks requiring near-point vision
   g. Having to get closer to chart or chalkboard
   h. Squinting
   i. Closing one eye
   j. Rubbing eyes
3. Complaints by the student
   a. Dizziness, fatigue, pain, or nausea after reading
   b. Distortion of what is seen

Visual Problems and Reading

FARSIGHTEDNESS (HYPEROPIA)

A farsighted person has difficulty focusing on objects at closer range. In order to focus on objects at close range, the person must exert muscular effort.

ASTIGMATISM

A person with astigmatism sees a blurred or distorted image because of irregularities in the lens of the eye.

BINOCULAR DIFFICULTIES

Binocular difficulties arise when both eyes do not focus on precisely the same object. This may result in blurred or double vision.

For a person who suffers from blurred, distorted, or double vision and has difficulty in focusing at near point, reading and most tasks associated with learning to read are likely to result in discomfort and fatigue. Therefore, children who suffer from these vision defects are likely to avoid reading and learning to read.

Referrals and Follow-Up

In the past, many schools relied on the Snellen Chart for visual screening. Subjects are placed 20 feet from the chart, which contains rows of letters of decreasing size. The subject is asked to read the rows, and his or her performance is compared with that of "normal" persons. A rating of 20/20 means the person is normal—he or she can see at 20 feet what a normal person can see at 20 feet.

The Snellen Chart is inadequate for identifying many vision defects that may cause reading problems. It is ironic that, in fact, the Snellen Chart is most effective in detecting nearsightedness, because nearsightedness, unless it is extreme, is not a source of reading difficulty. Moderately nearsighted people have no difficulty in focusing on printed materials at normal range. (Nearsighted children may have trouble focusing on the chalkboard or charts from a distance, however, and therefore there is an educational reason to have this condition corrected if it is discovered.)

If a teacher detects symptoms of a vision problem, he or she should refer the child to the appropriate school personnel (usually the school nurse) and inquire whether the child has been tested for visual acuity in each eye at near point and far point and for binocular coordination at near point and far point. This kind of examination can be done by a nurse or a reading clinician, but it requires an expensive device. Two such devices in wide use are the Keystone Vision Screening Test and the Ortho-rater. When adequate screening reveals a suspected vision defect, parents are requested to have the child given a professional examination.

AUDITORY ACUITY: THE TEACHER'S ROLE

There is a distinct probability that children who suffer from hearing loss will experience difficulty in learning to read. Some writers (Bond, Tinker, and Wasson, 1979) estimate that as many as 5 to 10 percent of our population has a hearing handicap.

Like problems in visual acuity, problems in hearing acuity are in the province of specialists. It is the responsibility of the classroom teacher to recognize symptoms of hearing loss and to refer students with suspected hearing loss to the appropriate school personnel for testing and/or referral to specialists.

Symptoms of Hearing Loss

The following may be symptoms of hearing loss:

1. Unusual appearance of the ear
   a. Inflammation
   b. Discharge
2. Unusual habits
   a. Inattention
   b. Frequent requests to have speech repeated
   c. Poor articulation; omitting or distorting sounds, particularly /s/, /z/, /ch/, /sh/, and /th/

d. Turning one ear toward speaker
3. Complaints by student
   a. Ringing in the ear
   b. Dizziness
   c. Inability to hear

Brown (1982) reports that children who experience hearing loss are often thought to be dull. He suggests that such children do not respond normally to things going on around them. When others do not realize these children cannot hear, they attribute the lack of response to dull-wittedness. Brown further observes that children who experience hearing loss are often thought to be remarkably good-natured. He suggests that, as a defense against being scolded for inattention, they smile and pretend to hear. This defense may give others the impression that the children are exceptionally serene.

Hearing Loss and Reading

Results of a hearing test are reported on two dimensions—frequency (or pitch) and intensity (loudness). Frequency is measured in cycles per second, and intensity is measured in decibels. A device called an audiometer is used to check a child's ability to hear tones at "normal" intensity. If a child fails to hear a tone, the intensity is increased to the point where he or she can hear it. The amount the intensity must be increased is recorded as a "decibel loss." A child with normal hearing is reported to have zero decibel loss.

The speech range of the human voice is between 100 and 4,000 cycles per second, and therefore this range is of particular interest to reading teachers. Children who experience significant loss in the frequency range of the human voice are likely to experience speech and reading difficulty. Losses among hearing-impaired children often occur in the high-frequency range of the human voice, which prevents them from hearing consonant sounds. This accounts for the poor articulation of children with severe hearing loss.

It is frequently recommended that, in teaching reading to children with hearing loss, a phonics approach be avoided in favor of a whole word approach, but there is no experimental evidence to support that advice.

Referrals and Follow-Up

Children suspected of having hearing loss should be referred to the appropriate school personnel for testing on an audiometer. Children who are found to have hearing loss of 15 to 20 decibels in the frequency range of the human voice should be referred to a hearing specialist for further evaluation.

Children with significant hearing loss present unique teaching-learning problems and are therefore often placed in special education classes or tutored in speech and reading by specialists. Such specialists ought to consult with and advise classroom teachers on ways to compensate for children's handicaps when part of a child's time is spent in regular classrooms.

NEUROLOGICAL AND EMOTIONAL FACTORS

Symptoms of Neurological and Emotional Problems

Some symptoms that may indicate neurological difficulties are (Creak et al., 1961):

1. Extreme difficulty in paying attention

2. Frequent distraction by unobtrusive stimuli

3. Problems of gross and fine motor co-ordination

4. Confusion in perception of stimuli

5. Inconsistent response to stimuli

6. Hyperactivity

Some symptoms that suggest emotional disturbances are (Creak et al., 1961):

1. Gross and sustained impairment of emotional relationships

2. Apparent unawareness of personal identity

3. Preoccupation with a few objects

4. Extreme reaction to any change in routine or environment

5. Excessive, diminished, or unpredictable responses to sensory stimulus

6. Illogical anxiety

7. Unaccounted-for dysfunction in body movements

8. Retardation of mental functioning

9. Loss of, lack of, late development of speech

Referrals and Follow-Up

When teachers suspect that a child is suffering from neurological or emotional impairment, referral should be made to the school psychologist. Psychologists are usually qualified to administer individual intelligence tests and tests of perception. Individual evaluation by a psychologist can be used to determine whether a neurological or psychiatric evaluation is indicated.

Getting and Giving the Proper Advice

The purpose of such evaluation is to give the teacher guidance on how teaching strategies should be altered to compensate for or to circumvent the neurological or emotional difficulties that appear to be interfering with learning. Unfortunately, such evaluations often result in classifying the child in terms of a clinical syndrome (mentally retarded, autistic, aphasic, neurologically impaired) and nothing more. Such classifications tell the teacher nothing about how to teach the child to read.

There is reason to believe that children classified in different categories have similar educational needs and that the same child may be classified in different ways by different clinicians. Bortner and Birch (1969) observed that children classified as emotionally disturbed and children classified as brain damaged showed very similar patterns of intellectual organization. These authors question the educational value of the two separate categories. Another study (Rosenthal, Eisenson, and Luckau, 1972) showed that the medical, psychological, and language evaluations were remarkably similar for children classified as hearing-impaired, aphasic, and experiencing a maturational lag. Kessler (1966) observed: "The same child may receive four or five different diagnoses, as successive clinics diagnose the case in terms of their special area of interest and experience" (p. 260).

The point is that a teacher who is prompted to refer a child for examination for suspected neurological or emotional impairment should not be satisfied if he or she is given only a label with which classify the child. The teacher should discover what reading skill the child possesses and determine what the child should learn next. The teacher should ask the specialist *how* the child's impairment interferes with learning to read and for suggestions for ways to teach the child that circumvent or overcome the child's impairment.

Making medical diagnoses and giving advice based on such diagnoses is unwise and unethical (and probably illegal) for a person who is not a medical doctor or a licensed member of a medically allied profession. Teachers who suspect that a child has a condition whose diagnosis and treatment is in the province of a specialist should refer the child to the appropriate school personnel. The teacher should describe the appearance, behavior, or complaints that led the teacher to suspect a problem. Teachers should *not* suggest (particularly to parents) that a child may have a severe hearing loss or brain damage or any other ailment that the teacher is not certified and licensed to diagnose.

CULTURAL AND ECONOMIC FACTORS

The relationship between reading failure and the economic status of the family of the child is well documented. One study of 11,000 7-year-olds (Kellmer-Pringle et al., 1966) found that one out of four children from poor families was classified as a poor reader, whereas fewer than one in ten children from wealthy families was classified as a poor reader. A study of 225 first-graders (Finn and Finn, 1978; Finn et al., 1979) found relationships between measures of both language and reading performance and the status of the occupation of the head of the child's household.

In these studies of young students, the relationship between economic status and measures of language and reading performance are clear—but they are not very strong. However, there is abundant literature to testify that as children become older, the relationship between economic status of the child's family and measures of reading and school-related language performance becomes stronger.

Economic Status and Language Use

Although no one denies that there is a relationship between the economic status and chances of success in learning to read, there is some disagreement as to the nature of this relationship. In this section, the proposition will be developed that economic deprivation affects the way one habitually uses language and that the way one habitually uses language affects one's chances of success in learning to read.

Smitherman (1980) proposes that the language of poor blacks has three kinds of characteristics: (1) characteristics that are only superficially different but that are shared by all speakers of English—including speakers of standard English; (2) characteristics that are unique to black English; and (3) characteristics that are associated with the language of economically deprived people.

These categories are useful in looking at the language of all economically deprived minorities and will be used here for that purpose. A difference between the analysis presented below and that of Smitherman, however, is that she refers in her third category to such matters as the imposition of the foreign language of colonial masters on subjugated peoples. In this discussion, the third category will refer instead to characteristics shared by the economically deprived that can be traced to cultural factors associated with poverty.

SUPERFICIALLY DIFFERENT CHARACTERISTICS

Phonology and Syntax. Some scholars have focused on the differences between dialects and standard English in terms of pronunciation and syntax and have explored the idea that it is these differences that are responsible for a disproportionate amount of reading failure among nonstandard speakers (Baratz and Shuy, 1969; Goodman, 1973; Wolfram, 1973).

For example, some black youngsters speak a dialect in which there is a tendency to simplify final consonant clusters. When such youngsters read phrases like "when I passed by" or "I looked for trouble," they pronounce the past tense verbs *passed* and *looked* as *pass* and *look*. That is, they do not pronounce the past tense morpheme that is heard in standard English. Labov (1970a) has shown that when black youngsters who speak such a dialect read sentences like sentence 1, many of them do not appear to understand that the sentence refers to the past rather than the present. One can tell how sentence 1 is interpreted by the way *read* is pronounced—to rhyme with *reed* (present tense) or *red* (past tense).

1. *When I passed by, I read the posters.*

Labov points out that such dialect differences may be the source of some confusion in learning to read, especially if a teacher is insensitive to the fact that words such as *pass* and *passed* may be homonyms to some students. However, after years of study, Labov maintains that this confusion is "not the inevitable result of deep-seated linguistic differences" and that differences in phonology between standard English and the dialect he was dealing with are superficial (1970a, p. 224).

Furthermore, there have been efforts to improve the success rate in learning to read among speakers of black English based on the idea that the phonology and syntax differences between black English and standard English were the cause of reading failure among black youngsters (Baratz, 1970). Special reading materials were created that conformed in wording and spelling to the syntax and phonology of black English. These experiments were not successful (Nolen, 1972;

Ramsey, 1972; Hall, Turner, and Russell, 1973), and their failure is further evidence that phonology and syntax differences are not the cause of reading failure among speakers of nonstandard dialects.

Educational Implications. Superficial differences in syntax and phonology do not appear to explain difficulties in learning to read in any direct way, but they may cause reading difficulties indirectly in two ways.

1. Teachers may view the child's language as inferior and unconsciously convey this attitude to the child. This may provoke feelings of alienation or hostility on the part of the child.
2. Because of the child's language characteristics, the teacher may identify the child as a member of a group that has little prestige in the community and therefore lower expectations for the child's success. As was pointed out earlier, this low expectation may become a self-fulfilling prophecy.

Labov (1970a) expressed this view over a decade ago, when he wrote:

In several years of work on nonstandard English (NNE) spoken by Negro children in the urban ghettos, we have observed a sharp contrast between their fluent and skillful use of oral language and their slow and erratic behavior in reading. The all-over pattern is one of reading failure rather than reading difficulty. The primary cause for this failure appears to be the conflict between the vernacular culture and the middle class culture of the schoolroom rather than any linguistic differences between their dialect and standard English. (p. 223)

More recently, Stubbs (1980) has pointed out: "One has to distinguish sharply between (a) the internal linguistic organization of a language variety, and (b) external social factors such as attitudes towards that variety in the community" (p. 150). The argument presented here is that the phonology and syntax (the internal linguistic organization) of nonstandard English dialects are not the cause of failure in learning to read. It is the attitudes of teachers toward children who speak a dialect and teachers' expectations of success for such children (external social factors) that may be the cause of failure in reading.

CHARACTERISTICS UNIQUE TO PARTICULAR GROUPS

Smitherman's (1980) examples of uniquely black English are among the most appealing, entertaining, and accurate examples to be found anywhere; other examples appear in Labov (1969, 1970) and Williams and Naremore (1969). For example, in commenting on the style of uniquely black oratory, Smitherman writes:

All emphasis is on process, movement, and creativity of the moment. The preacher says "y' all don wont to hear dat, so I'm gon leave it alone," and his audience shouts, "Naw, tell it Reverend, tell it!" and he does. (p. 166)

All cultures have their private in-group language forms that verge on art. There are individuals in all minority groups who possess a style and facility with language that is unique to the group; such facility is highly prized by members of the group. The Irish speak of having "the gift of gab," and to say someone "has kissed the Blarney Stone" is a high compliment. The quotes here from Smitherman and Labov attest to the value blacks place on verbal facility of a uniquely black variety. A fact that is sometimes overlooked is that privileged minorities have their unique language styles as well. One can recognize distinct styles such

as Marin County (California) or Boston Brahmin "dialects" among the most affluent classes in the country.

There is no reason to believe that the presence of such language forms has any effect whatever on success in learning to read. School failure is not related to racial or ethnic group membership: It is related to poverty (Williams and Naremore, 1969; Assam, 1981).

Educational Implications. Teachers who are aware that their students possess a heritage of oral language which gives them pleasure and pride have an opportunity to win their student's confidence and respect by acknowledging this unique and valuable aspect of the students' culture. Teachers can cultivate in themselves and in their classrooms the attitude that differences in language do not constitute deficits. In doing so, the teacher must get rid of the destructive notions that, because the language of a child's community is different, it is inferior.

A second and equally destructive notion is that, because the language of the child's community is vital, expressive, attractive, and creative, the language of the school—the standard language of the larger culture—is inferior or irrelevant to the child. This idea may lead to the notion that such classics as E. B. White's *Charlotte's Web* is irrelevant to a black inner-city youngster. Furthermore, since those aspects of language that are unique to minority groups tend to appear in oral rather than written language, this idea may lead to devaluation of the skill of reading.

By romanticizing the positive aspects of a minority culture, one can effectively rationalize shutting youngsters away from the wider culture; this may contribute to their continued isolation from the wider culture and the social, economic, and political benefits that access to the wider culture makes possible.

CHARACTERISTICS ASSOCIATED WITH ECONOMIC DEPRIVATION

There are numerous sources showing that communication between economically disadvantaged people tends to depend on previously shared meanings between speaker and listener—that is, that the language habitually used by economically disadvantaged people tends to be implicit and context-dependent (Bernstein, 1964; Bruck and Tucker, 1974; Dunn, 1980; Hess and Shipman, 1968; Smitherman, 1980; Williams and Naremore, 1969).

Implicit, Context-Dependent Language. *Implicit language* is language that implies meaning rather than stating it—usually because the speaker refers to or alludes to knowledge or opinions he or she assumes listeners share. *Context-dependent language* is language one would not understand unless one were present and knew the situation in which the language was uttered.

Explicit, Context-Independent Language. In contrast to implicit, context-dependent language, one finds explicit, context-independent language. Explicit, context-independent language is often employed when the speaker does not presume that the listener shares his or her meanings, beliefs, or opinions, and when the topic of the language is far removed (in terms of time, space, or abstraction) from the physical environment in which the language is used. In such cases, the speaker must spell out meanings precisely enough to make them understood, rather than alluding to shared meanings or to things present in the context.

Examples of these two kinds of language use are as follows: A schoolboy expressing his pleasure at the victory of the school football team to a fellow student may be implicit and context-dependent. In the right circumstances, the exclamation, "How about that!" may convey his meaning satisfactorily, because the listener shares his knowledge and opinions and the context tells the listener what is being referred to. On the other hand, a history teacher explaining the causes of the French Revolution would probably use language that is highly explicit and context-independent. She could not presume on shared knowledge, beliefs, or opinions or on the physical context to convey meaning.

All speakers of English are capable of using implicit, context-dependent language and explicit, context-independent language. It has been observed, however, that not everyone has as much occasion to use explicit, context-independent language and that people who are frequently called upon to use explicit, context-independent language tend to use it more habitually and have more facility with it. People who are infrequently called upon to use explicit, context-independent language tend to use it infrequently and to have less facility with it.

Certain characteristics appear in the cultures of all economically disadvantaged people, regardless of race or ethnicity, and these characteristics promote the habitual use of implicit, context-dependent language. They promote strong feelings of group solidarity and fail to foster feelings of individuality. Feelings of group solidarity further encourage the habit of using implicit, context-dependent language (Bernstein, 1967; Levitas, 1974; Finn, 1980).

Societal Characteristics Shared by the Economically Disadvantaged

Certain characteristics tend to appear in the culture of all economically underprivileged people, regardless of race or ethnicity. Four such characteristics are

1. Conformity is demanded.

2. Authority is vested in position.

3. There is a feeling of powerlessness.

4. The group is isolated from outsiders.

Numerous sources show that these characteristics are associated with lower-income families (Bronfenbrenner, 1958; Duvall, 1946; Hess and Shipman, 1968; Kohn, 1957; Sears, Maccoby, and Levin, 1957; Shatzman and Strauss, 1955). And there is a relationship between these societal characteristics and habits of language use.

Attitudes toward Conformity. Where conformity is expected, opinions are dictated by group consensus and there is no need to explain one's thoughts, beliefs, or behavior. Communication is frequently possible by alluding to shared opinions and beliefs, rather than by explicitly expressing these opinions and beliefs. Communication tends to be implicit and context-dependent. The dominant theme of such groups is solidarity rather than self-awareness and individuality (see Figure 10.1).

In groups where nonconformity is encouraged or at least permitted on a wide range of topics, opinions are frequently challenged. People are often reminded that what they know and believe is distinct from what others know and believe. In this situation, language becomes explicit, and the dominant theme becomes one of self-awareness, of individuation rather than solidarity (see Figure 10.2).

Attitudes toward Authority. Where authority is positional—that is, invested in roles—there is little need for explicit language to control youngsters or to arrive at group decisions. In communities where people appeal to reason to control youngsters and to arrive at group decisions, there is continuous need

FIGURE 10.1
THE RELATIONSHIP BETWEEN CONFORMITY, SOLIDARITY, AND HABITUAL USE OF IMPLICIT, CONTEXT-DEPENDENT LANGUAGE.

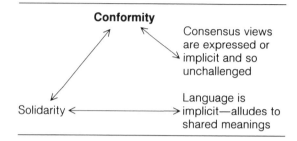

FIGURE 10.2
THE RELATIONSHIP BETWEEN NONCONFORMITY, INDIVIDUALITY, AND THE HABITUAL USE OF EXPLICIT, CONTEXT-INDEPENDENT LANGUAGE.

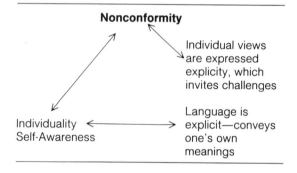

for explicit language. For example, "I want you in by 11 because the streets are dangerous after 11 and you've got to get up for school in the morning and you need your sleep."

Whether authority is positional or based on appeals to reason is not absolute; it is a matter of emphasis in different groups. There is very little difference between 11 and 11:15, and if the person in authority is challenged, she is likely to switch from an appeal to reason to an appeal to position and say: "I said 11, and that's that." On the other hand, in a culture where the parent says from the start "Be in by 11 because I told you to," the child and others involved are aware that this is to some extent a rational order. The difference is that in the one situation the reasons are made explicit, and in the other the reasons remain implicit.

Social pressure to accept positional authority discourages challenges to authority, leads to habitual use of implicit language, and creates or reinforces feelings of solidarity (see Figure 10.3). Social pressure on those in authority to make their reasons explicit invites challenges, leads to habitual use of explicit language, and creates or reinforces feelings of self-awareness and individuality (see Figure 10.4).

Feelings of Power. Where feelings of powerlessness are the dominant theme, there is little need to make plans, to express one's plans, or to convince others to follow one's plans. Attitudes toward political and economic forces are expressed in clichés: "You can't fight city hall." "These are hard times." "It's them or us!" "All politicians are the same." These clichés have practically no explicit, context-independent meaning; they allude to shared opinion and beliefs in particular contexts. They reinforce feelings of group solidarity (see Figure 10.5).

On the other hand, feelings of power lead to the use of explicit language. When one believes one has control over one's destiny, one analyzes political and economic forces, makes plans to affect those forces, and explicitly states those plans to convince others to follow. This, of course, invites challenges to one's analysis of the situation and to the wisdom of one's plans. This process encourages the use of explicit, context-independent language and reinforces feelings of individuality (see Figure 10.6).

FIGURE 10.3
THE RELATIONSHIP BETWEEN POSITIONAL AUTHORITY, SOLIDARITY, AND THE HABITUAL USE OF IMPLICIT, CONTEXT-DEPENDENT LANGUAGE.

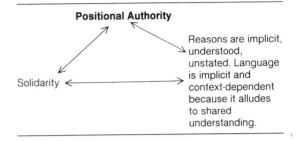

FIGURE 10.4
THE RELATIONSHIP BETWEEN AUTHORITY THAT APPEALS TO REASON, INDIVIDUALITY, AND THE HABITUAL USE OF EXPLICIT, CONTEXT-INDEPENDENT LANGUAGE.

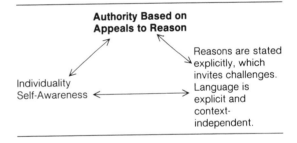

FIGURE 10.5
THE RELATIONSHIP BETWEEN FEELINGS OF POWERLESSNESS, SOLIDARITY, AND HABITUAL USE OF IMPLICIT, CONTEXT-DEPENDENT LANGUAGE.

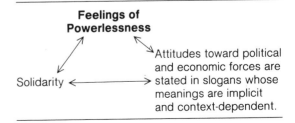

Isolation. A number of years ago, a group of sociologists (Schatzman and Strauss, 1955) went into a town in Arkansas after a devastating tornado. They interviewed people in the town and asked them to tell where they were and what they saw.

They found that the farmers and people with menial jobs around the town said things like, "Well it hit the Jones place and killed all of them and then it swung around down the creek and wrecked the church, but no one was in it." Business and professional people were apt to say, "Well the tornado first touched down three miles south of town. It hit the house of a family called Jones and killed them all—the parents and four teenaged children. It then swung east and wrecked the Congregational church."

One version of that story assumes that the listener knows where the Jones place is, who the Joneses were (how many is *all?*), where the creek lies, and what church is down the creek. The second version makes none of these assumptions. One version is implicit; it presumes the listener possesses knowledge that, in this case, the listener does not possess. The second version is explicit.

According to the study, the difference between the people who did these two kinds of reporting was the relative isolation of the people. People who are rarely in contact with others from outside their town, neighborhood, or place of work simply have no practice at talking to people who do not know where the Jones farm is or who the Joneses are, so they do not have practice at using language that does not rely on shared context or shared information.

Where individuals rarely have occasion to deal with strangers, they tend to rely on allusion to shared experience for communication; this encourages their use of implicit, context-dependent language and enhances their feelings of solidarity (see Figure 10.7). Where in-

FIGURE 10.6
THE RELATIONSHIP BETWEEN FEELINGS OF POWER, INDIVIDUALITY, AND HABITUAL USE OF EXPLICIT, CONTEXT-INDEPENDENT LANGUAGE.

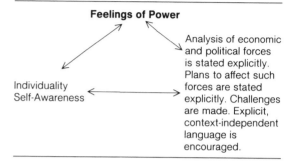

FIGURE 10.7
THE RELATIONSHIP BETWEEN ISOLATION, SOLIDARITY, AND HABITUAL USE OF IMPLICIT, CONTEXT-DEPENDENT LANGUAGE.

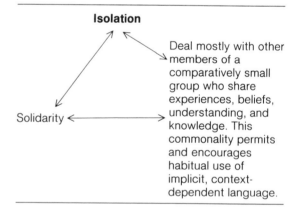

dividuals must communicate with strangers frequently, they learn they cannot rely on shared experiences; they cannot be sure of what the other person knows or thinks. This encourages the use of explicit, context-independent language and enhances their feelings of self-awareness and individuality (see Figure 10.8).

FIGURE 10.8
THE RELATIONSHIP BETWEEN FREQUENT CONTACT WITH STRANGERS, INDIVIDUALITY, AND THE HABITUAL USE OF EXPLICIT, CONTEXT-INDEPENDENT LANGUAGE.

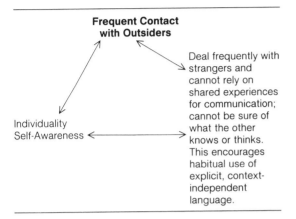

FIGURE 10.9
CHARACTERISTICS OF SOCIAL GROUPS, LANGUAGE, AND WRITTEN LANGUAGE.

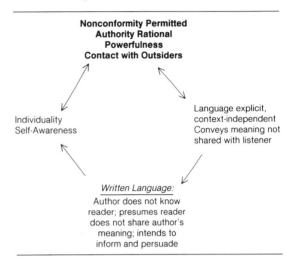

The Language of the School

The language of the school, particularly the written language of the school, is explicit and context-independent. Children who arrive in school and have had experience with explicit, context-independent language experience further development of the kinds of habits with which they have had some experience. Bernstein (1970, p. 29) refers to this as "an elaboration of social identity." That is, the language of the school reinforces and fosters further development of the language of the homes and validates the social characteristics that give rise to such language (see Figure 10.9).

Children who arrive in school and have habitually used language that is implicit and context-dependent experience a kind of culture shock. There is a discontinuity between the child's habitual mode of use of language and the language of the school. The school fails to validate the social characteristics that give rise to the child's habitual use of language and may even repudiate them: "Thus between the school and the community of the working class child there may exist a cultural discontinuity based upon two radically different systems of communication" (Bernstein, 1970, p. 29).

Deprivation Theory

THE IDEA OF INFERIOR LANGUAGE

The suggestion that the poor share certain characteristics of language that place their youngsters at a disadvantage in school has been the subject of some controversy. One seemingly obvious implication is that the children of the poor fail in school because they have been deprived of something necessary to intellectual development, and because they have been exposed to an inferior variety of language or not been exposed to enough language. Notorious versions of this proposal can be found in Bereiter and Engelmann (1966) and Jensen (1969).

This point of view was met with bitter opposition, notably from William Labov. In an incisive criticism of Bereiter and Engelmann (1966) and Jensen (1969), Labov (1970b; 1972a) asserts that Jensen's notion "is first drawn from Basil Bernstein's writings" (1970b, p. 156) and that Bereiter's views stem from Bereiter's interpretation of Bernstein.

As a result of Labov's very influential papers (1970b, 1972a) many people came to believe that Bernstein had proposed a "deprivation theory"—that Bernstein believed that the language of the poor is inferior and that the poor are intellectually inferior or illogical. Labov (1972b) later acknowledged that his discussion may have caused readers to misunderstand Bernstein's position, and he expressed the "hope that the unfortunate ambiguity in my article will not contribute to the misunderstanding of Bernstein's important ideas" (p. 45, 1972b). Nevertheless, many educators still believe that Labov attacked and discredited Bernstein's ideas regarding language use and school success.

As a matter of fact, Bernstein (1972) criticized deprivation theory, and he has stated repeatedly and explicitly that he does not believe people in lower economic brackets are linguistically deprived. In an essay published in 1973, he totally disavowed any responsibility for the ideas of Jensen and Bereiter and Engelmann and expressed dismay that his name had been associated with such ideas.

In fact, Bernstein never claimed that the poor *always* used an implicit, context-bound language and that the middle class *always* used an explicit, context-independent language. He always maintained that all people are capable of both kinds of language and all people engage in both kinds of language. His claim was that characteristics of a group (such as feelings of powerlessness or of power) are conducive to habits of using implicit or explicit language. Furthermore, although he claimed that children who habitually use implicit language are at a disadvantage in school, where explicit language is the typical medium of instruction, he never asserted that one variety of language is superior to the other.

TWO VALUABLE CONTRIBUTIONS

After a thorough analysis of the alleged conflict between the views of Labov and Bernstein, Stubbs (1980) summarizes—clearly, concisely, and correctly—as follows:

The two bodies of work are . . . not directly comparable in terms of either data or theory. Bernstein and Labov are, therefore, only "apparent protagonists" (Davies [ed.], 1977, p. 4) and have never discussed each other's work in any detail, although they have made brief and critical references to each other. A typically oversimplified reference is by Tough (1977, p. 31) who says: "There have been many criticisms of Bernstein's work, most notably by William Labov." This is inaccurate. (p. 156)

Bernstein and Labov have each made valuable contributions to the study of the language of children from economically underprivileged sectors of society. Each has made valuable suggestions regarding the probable causes of school failure among such children. It is most regrettable that the contributions of these two scholars are popularly believed to be at odds, particularly since this is an area where the need for solutions is so great.

EDUCATIONAL IMPLICATIONS

Three propositions have been developed here regarding language use. First, there is a tendency for some children habitually to use implicit, context-bound language and rarely to use explicit, context-independent language. Other children also use implicit, context-bound language, but they have considerable experience with using explicit, context-independent language as well.

The second proposition is that the medium of instruction in school, particularly the written language of the school, is explicit and context-independent. Therefore, habitual users of implicit, context-dependent language are at a disadvantage at the start. This disadvantage is magnified throughout their school careers as the language of the classroom and schoolbooks becomes more and more explicit and context-independent. On the other hand, children who have considerable experience with explicit, context-independent language are at an advantage from the start and continue to be at an advantage because they have only to continue to use explicit, context-independent language.

The third proposition developed here is that economic deprivation tends to encourage social group characteristics that foster group solidarity and the habitual use of implicit, context-dependent language, while economic security and privilege tends to encourage social group characteristics that foster individuality and a considerable amount of experience in using explicit, context-independent language.

We now examine these three propositions for the effect they might have on teacher's attitudes and teaching strategies.

Explaining Failure. If one accepts the first and second propositions, one might use them to explain the reading failure of some students and do nothing more. Research into the causes of reading failure has sometimes led to the invention of labels that explain failure rather than suggest methods of teaching children who are experiencing failure. Bloom and Lahey (1978) report that such labels can be important if they suggest *how* to teach children, but "unfortunately, the category label itself abstracts the information and too often decreases the understanding of the child" (p. 524).

Providing Experience with Explicit, Context-Independent Language. On the other hand, a person might accept the first and second propositions and attempt to remedy the possible cause of reading failure that the propositions suggest. The teacher can provide opportunities for students to learn to use explicit, context-independent language and to become aware of the necessity for such language by such activities as those suggested in Figure 10.10.

The teacher who accepts the connection between the habitual use of implicit, context-dependent language and social factors such as attitude toward authority and feelings of powerlessness can conduct his or her classroom in ways that promote the use of explicit and context-independent language.

It is quite revealing, almost astonishing, to read Harvey's (1980) descriptions of children's behavior and teachers' responses in classrooms composed of children from low-income families and classrooms composed of children from middle-income families and to compare them with child-rearing practices in low-income and middle-income homes as reported by Sears, Maccoby, and Levin (1957), for example. Many of the factors that encourage implicit, context-dependent language in homes are duplicated in low-income classrooms.

If teachers understand the culture that produces children who have little experience with explicit, context-independent language and adapt their classroom management strategies to it, they may be failing to add a dimension to the children's language experience that is necessary for success in reading. Levitas (1974) suggests that these strategies enable us to handle children rather than to teach them.

Teachers who accept the first and second propositions should be wary of adopting too simplistic a view of the third proposition. There is a *tendency* for habitual use of implicit, context-dependent language to be associated with poverty. That does not mean that all poor children will exhibit this trait nor that all financially secure children will have facility with explicit, context-independent language. Teachers should observe children's performance in dealing with explicit, context-independent language and plan teaching strategies based on these direct observations, rather than predict the child's performance from socio-economic data. Such predictions may easily become self-fulfilling prophecies.

FIGURE 10.10
EXERCISES TO ENCOURAGE THE USE OF EXPLICIT, CONTEXT-INDEPENDENT LANGUAGE.

Exercise 1

Write a shopping list for yourself.

Write a shopping list for a member of your family.

Write a shopping list for a classmate.

Write a shopping list for a visitor from China.

(As one addresses less familiar audiences, one must become more explicit.)

Do same with directions to find school from home, to find a particular shop in a shopping mall, and so on.

Exercise 2

Read about some event that happens in a setting. The setting is recreated in a model—a model town, room, building.
Tell the event to a person who is looking at the model, to a person who has seen model but is not looking at it, and to a person who has never seen model. Record and compare differences in language necessary.

SUMMARY

IQ tests were developed by Alfred Binet for the purpose of identifying children who would not profit from ordinary public schooling. Binet devised questions that could be answered by most 13-year-olds, but not by most 12-year-olds; questions that could be answered by most 12-year-olds, but not by most 11-year-olds; and so on. He then administered these items to children and took note of the most difficult items the subject was capable of answering. He referred to the age group associated with these items as the child's mental age. Terman introduced the idea of comparing mental age with chronological age. He referred to this comparison (mental age divided by chronological age) as an intelligence quotient. Currently, however, although the score is still called a *quotient,* it is no longer arrived at by division.

There are two theories about the nature of intelligence. Spearman is associated with the notion that intelligence is general quality, a global affair. Thurston is associated with the idea that intelligence is a collection of primary mental abilities and that an individual can possess one to a high degree and others to a lesser degree.

IQ tests are designed so that individuals who are successful in school will be successful on the tests. Items are tried out and if successful students answer them correctly and unsuccessful students answer them incorrectly, they are used in the tests. If this condition is not met, they are not used. As a result, IQ tests are designed to measure knowledge and skills that are relevant to school success.

There are two interpretations of what success on an IQ test means. One is that a person who does better than agemates has a better learning facility or potential; the second is that a person who does better than agemates learns more quickly than others. If one views IQ test scores solely as a measure of potential, one is apt to use a poor score as a way to explain failure. If one sees IQ test scores solely as a measure of rate of learning, one is apt to use IQ test scores as an indication of the amount of time a student will need to learn. Carroll's model of school learning takes both the time necessary for learning and the student's ability to understand instruction into account.

Bloom's mastery learning concept focuses on the idea that the essential difference between learners is the amount of time necessary to learn. His studies have shown that extra learning time and tutoring result in greater achievement than is often presumed to be possible for many students who are identified as having a limited potential. Mastery learning concepts are applied, however, to skills that are sequential and limited in number.

Singer has suggested that reading achievement can be considered under three headings: word recognition, word meaning, and reasoning-in-reading. Word recognition skills are to some extent sequential and limited in number. As a result, there should be no difference in the mastery of word recognition

skills (and, therefore, of much of the primary grade reading curriculum). Some students simply need longer, more frequent, or more personalized lessons. The same should be true when word meaning and reasoning-in-reading objectives are kept within a limited range. However, when these objectives become open-ended, it appears that longer or more frequent or more personalized lessons are not enough to bring all students to par with the most able students.

Although there is no question that IQ test scores frequently identify very able students and those who are not so able, the scores themselves should be treated very carefully. Individuals may earn different scores on different tests or at different times. And IQ tests are not designed to measure knowledge and skills that are not related to school success. A person may possess knowledge and skills that are valuable in many life situations and still earn a low score on an IQ test.

A frequently cited danger of the use of IQ test scores is that they are sometimes used to explain failure rather than to plan teaching strategies. Deciding from IQ scores who will be able to learn to read is very likely to promote self-fulfilling prophecies. IQ test scores play an important part in the decision to remove a child from a normal classroom and place him or her in a class for special students. The child's performance on an IQ test administered by a qualified psychologist is a valuable and necessary source of information in making this decision. IQ test scores may also be instrumental in discovering gifted students whose talents have gone unnoticed.

Defects of visual acuity can affect reading achievement. Although most schools conduct routine visual screening, this screening is sometimes inadequate. If a teacher suspects that a child is experiencing visual acuity problems, the teacher should refer the child to the school nurse or appropriate professional and follow up on the referral. An adequate examination involves tests for acuity and binocular coordination at near point and far point.

Defects of auditory acuity can affect reading achievement. Hearing loss frequently causes a child to be unable to distinguish between consonant sounds. Teachers should refer children whom they suspect of suffering from hearing loss to the appropriate school personnel and follow up on the referral. An adequate examination involves testing on an audiometer.

Neurological impairment and emotional disturbances may affect reading achievement. Children who exhibit symptoms that may be indicative of neurological impairment or emotional disturbance should be referred to a psychologist, who may in turn refer the child to a medical doctor. In following up such a referral, the teacher should be aware that classifying a child as autistic or mentally retarded or brain injured (to name a few classifications) is not the goal of the referral. The purpose of the referral is to discover *how* the child's condition interferes with learning so that teaching strategies can be devised to circumvent the child's difficulties.

Poverty undoubtedly has a negative influence on reading achievement. Three categories of characteristics associated with the language of economically oppressed minorities have been examined as possible causes of failure to learn to read. The most salient difference between standard English and the dialects of economically oppressed minorities are found in pronunciation and syntax. It has been suggested that pronunciation differences between standard English and the dialect of urban blacks may account for the disproportionate amount of failure among urban blacks. However, many researchers agree that the phonological and syntactic difference between standard English and nonstandard dialects are superficial and that the phonic generalizations

between nonstandard dialects and written English are no more irregular than the phonic generalizations between standard English and written English.

Although the syntax and phonology of the child's dialect probably does not interfere directly with learning to read, a teacher's attitude toward a child who speaks a nonstandard dialect can have a negative effect on the child's reading performance.

A second and not so obvious characteristic of all dialects—those spoken by the rich and powerful as well as those spoken by the poverty-stricken and powerless—is that each group has a private, in-group language form that verges on art. Since a version of this kind of prized oral language facility appears in all cultural groups, there appears to be no intrinsic connection between it and success in learning to read. Teachers who are aware of this kind of language form can enhance their rapport with students by acknowledging its value. On the other hand, disrespect for this kind of language may destroy rapport and interfere with students' ability to learn from the teacher.

There is a danger of overdoing one's appreciation for this kind of language; one can adopt the romantic notion that certain oral language forms of a particular group are so valuable and fragile that literacy may be either irrelevant or detrimental to the group. Maintaining a pluralistic society is a valuable goal, but it must be a pluralistic society in which each group has equal access to political and economic power. This can be accomplished only through working toward universal literacy while respecting the unique language forms of minorities.

The third characteristic of the language of poverty-stricken people arises from social structures that are typical of the homes and communities of the economically oppressed. Economically oppressed communities tend to insist more upon conformity; they tend to vest authority in position; they experience greater feelings of powerlessness; and they are more isolated from people who are not members of their group. These characteristics result in interpersonal relationships in which explicit, context-independent language is not frequently necessary for communication.

Among more affluent people, nonconformity is permitted to a greater degree; there is a greater tendency to appeal to reason in justifying authority; there is a greater feeling of power; and members of groups are more frequently brought into contact with outsiders. These characteristics result in interpersonal relationships in which explicit, context-independent language is frequently necessary for communication.

The language of the school, and especially the written language encountered in school, tends to be heavily explicit and context-independent. Children who are raised in homes where explicit, context-independent language is frequently used experience further development when they arrive in school. Children who are raised in homes where explicit, context-independent language is infrequently used experience discontinuity. Their experiences place them at a disadvantage when they arrive at school, and their disadvantage is exacerbated as the written language of the school takes on more and more the characteristics of institutional writing.

A widely known and very unfortunate controversy arose over the question of whether the language of economically oppressed people interferes with their learning to read. Labov looked at the phonology and syntax of black English and determined that these differences were superficial and are not responsible for the disproportionately high rate of school failure among blacks. Labov took note of the esthetic value of much of the language that is unique to black Americans and implored the education establishment to understand the culture of black Americans

and to acknowledge oral language art forms where they exist rather than disparage all deviations from standard English.

Bernstein compared the cultures of the English working class and middle class and the degree to which these cultures gave rise to the habitual use of explicit, context-independent language. He pointed out that children from working-class homes are likely to have a more limited experience with explicit, context-independent language than children from middle-class homes. However, this relationship is not absolute. Some working-class children may be quite facile with explicit, context-independent language, and some middle-class children may not be. Bernstein concluded, however, that on the basis of exposure to explicit, context-independent language, working-class English children are likely to enter school at a disadvantage.

Labov appears to have attacked Bernstein's position. There are many more people who know about Labov's apparent attack on Bernstein than there are people who understand the very valuable contributions that both men made to solving the problem of disproportionate school failure among children from economically oppressed families.

Limited experience in using explicit, context-independent language probably affects success in learning to read. A teacher can use this knowledge in two ways. He or she can *explain* the school failure of children in terms of their experience with explicit, context-independent language, or attempt to *remedy* that failure by (1) teaching lessons designed to give children additional experience with explicit, context-independent language, and (2) promoting a classroom atmosphere that permits nonconformity, where authority is based on reason, where children communicate with people outside their group. This latter remedy would presumably create a classroom community where explicit, context-independent language is necessary for communication.

FOR FURTHER READING AND DISCUSSION

1. If one views intelligence tests as truly measuring a child's aptitude for learning or the speed at which he or she learns, one presumes that all children have equal access to the kind of knowledge or skill the test measures. Since IQ tests are constructed to measure school-relevant learning and since all children are not raised in homes that have equal access to school-relevant learning, this assumption is obviously untrue. IQ tests are undoubtedly culturally biased. This important point has been made repeatedly in educational literature. The following citations present the issues and recommend different solutions to this problem.

Bersoff, D. Silk purses into sows' ears: The decline of psychological testing and a suggestion for its redemption. *American Psychologist*, 10 (1973): 892–99.

Charters, W. W. Social class and intelligence tests. In W. W. Charters and N. L. Gage (eds.), *The Social Psychology of Education.* Boston: Allyn and Bacon, 1963, 12–21.

Fishman, J. A., M. Deutsch, L. Kogan, R. North, and M. Whiteman. Guidelines for testing minority group children. In A. H. Passow, M. Goldberg, and A. J. Tannenbaum (eds.), *Education of the Disadvantaged.* New York: Holt, Rinehart and Winston, 1967, 155–169.

Kamin, L. J. Social and legal consequences of IQ tests as classification instruments: Some warnings from the past. *Journal of School Psychology*, 13 (1975): 317–23.

Rosenthal, R., and L. Jacobson. Teacher expectations for the disadvantaged. *Scientific American* (April 1968): 19–23.

In light of these readings, do you think IQ tests ought to be given routinely to all students and become part of their records? Do you think IQ test scores should be routinely given to classroom teachers?

Do you think IQ testing should be abandoned entirely? If so, how would you protect the rights of a child who is being removed from a classroom where regular instruction is given? What would your grading and promotion policy be—that fifth-graders who cannot read from the fifth-grade reader get an F on their report cards? Do such children remain in fifth grade year after year until they can read from the fifth-grade reader?

2. One of the most widely known controversies in educational literature is the apparent dispute between William Labov and Basil Bernstein. In the following articles (the second article is based on and very similar to the first), Labov appears to accuse Bernstein of saying that the language of economically disadvantaged people is an inferior language.

Labov, W. The logic of nonstandard English. In F. Williams (ed.), *Language and Poverty: Perspectives on a Theme.* Chicago: Markham, 1970, 153–89.

Labov, W. Academic ignorance and black intelligence. *Atlantic Monthly* (June 1972): 59–67.

In the following chapter, Bernstein charges Labov with criticizing him for something he never wrote or even believed.

Bernstein, B. A brief account of the theory of codes. In H. P. Dreitzel (ed.), *Childhood and Socialization.* New York: Macmillan, 1973, 213–39.

In the following letter, Labov expresses the hope that the ambiguity of his article will not contribute to the misunderstanding of Bernstein's important ideas.

Labov, W. Letter to the editor. *Atlantic Monthly* (November 1972): 45.

In the following chapter, Michael Stubbs discusses the literature concerning the relationship between language, economic deprivation, and school success.

Stubbs, M. Initial literacy and explanations of educational failure. In M. Stubbs, *Language and Literacy.* London: Routledge and Kegan Paul, 1980, 139–59.

Read these citations and reflect on the following questions:

1. What is your position on the question of whether characteristics of the language of economically disadvantaged people interfere with learning to read?
2. If you believe there are characteristics of the language of economically disadvantaged people that interfere with learning to read, what is the nature of these characteristics, and what do you think a teacher ought to do with knowledge of these characteristics?

REFERENCES

Alper, M. All our children can learn. *The University of Chicago Magazine* (Summer 1982): 2–9 and 30.

Assam, Ann P. A comparison of written English of native Canadian and immigrant West Indian students in Canada. Unpublished Ph.D. dissertation, State University of New York at Buffalo, 1981.

Baratz, J. C. Beginning readers for speakers of divergent dialects. In J. A. Figurel (ed.), *Reading Goals for the Disadvantaged.* Newark, DE: International Reading Association, 1970, 77–83.

————, and R. W. Shuy (eds.). *Teaching Black Children to Read.* Washington, DC: Center for Applied Linguistics, 1969.

Bereiter, C., and S. Engelmann. *Teaching Disadvantaged Children in the Preschool.* Englewood Cliffs, NJ: Prentice-Hall, 1966.

Bernstein, B. Elaborated and restricted codes: Their social origin and some consequences. In J. J. Gumperz and D. Hymes (eds.), *The Ethnography of Communication.* Menasha, WI: American Anthropological Association, 1964, 55–69.

————. Open schools, open society? *New Society,* 14 (1967): 351–53.

————. A sociolinguistic approach to socialization: With some reference to educability. In F. Williams (ed.), *Language and Poverty: Perspectives on a Theme.* Chicago: Markham, 1970, 25–61.

————. Education cannot compensate for society. In D. Rubenstein and C. Stoneman (eds.), *Evolution of the Comprehensive School.* London: Routledge and Kegan Paul, 1972, 61–66.

————. A brief account of the theory of codes. In H. P. Dreitzel (ed.), *Childhood and Socialization.* New York: Macmillan, 1973, 213–39.

Bloom, B. S. Mastery learning and its implications for curriculum development. In E. W. Eisner (ed.), *Confronting Curriculum Reform.* Boston: Little, Brown, 1971.

Bloom, L., and M. Lahey. *Language Development and Language Disorders.* New York: Wiley, 1978.

Bond, G. L., M. A. Tinker, and B. B. Wasson. *Reading Difficulties: Their Diagnosis and Correction,* 4th ed. Englewood Cliffs, NJ: Prentice-Hall, 1979.

Bortner, M., and H. G. Birch. Patterns of intellectual ability in emotionally disturbed and brain-damaged children. *Journal of Special Education,* 3 (1969): 351–69.

Bronfenbrenner, U. Socialization and class through time and space. In E. E. Maccoby et al., *Readings in Social Psychology.* London: Methuen, 1958, 400–24.

Brown, D. A. *Reading Diagnosis and Remediation.* Englewood Cliffs, NJ: Prentice-Hall, 1982.

Bruck, M., and R. Tucker. Social class differences in the acquisition of school language. *Merrill Palmer Quarterly* (1974): 205–19.

Carroll, J. B. A model of school learning. *Teachers College Record,* 64 (1963): 723–33.

Ceprano, M. Notes on various views of intelligence. Mimeographed. Buffalo: Department of Learning and Instruction, State University of New York, 1979.

Creak, M., et al. Schizophrenic syndrome in childhood. *Cerebral Palsy Bulletin.* 3 (1961): 501–4.

Davies, A. *Language and Learning in Early Education.* London: Heinemann, 1977.

Dunn, J. Playing in speech. In L. Michaels and C. Ricks (eds.), *The State of the Language.* Berkeley: University of California Press, 1980, 202–12.

Duvall, E. M. Conceptions of parenthood. *American Journal of Sociology,* 52 (1946–47): 190–92.

Ellison, D. G., P. Harris, and L. Barber. A field test of programmed and directed tutoring. *Reading Research Quarterly* (1968): 307–68.

Finn, M. E., and P. J. Finn. The development of linguistic and cognitive abstractions in children of different social backgrounds. Paper presented at New England Educational Research Organization, Sturbridge, MA, 1978. Mimeographed, State University of New York at Buffalo.

Finn, P. J. *Failure in Learning to Read.* Edinburgh, Scotland: Worker's Education Association, 1980.

—————, M. E. Finn, and E. Friedland. Assessment of children's oral language development and reading achievement. Paper presented at Second Annual Conference on Child Language, Boston University, 1979. Mimeographed, State University of New York at Buffalo.

Fry, E. B. *Reading Instruction for Classroom and Clinic.* New York: McGraw-Hill, 1972.

—————. *Elementary Reading Instruction.* New York: McGraw-Hill, 1977.

Gates, A. I., and G. L. Bond. Reading readiness: A study of factors determining success and failure in beginning reading. *Teachers College Record,* 37 (1936): 678–85.

Goodman, K. S. Dialect barriers to reading comprehension. In J. S. DeStephano (ed.), *Language, Society, and Education: A Profile of Black English.* Worthington, OH: Charles A. Jones, 1973, 265–75.

Green, R. Tips on educational testing: What teachers and parents should know. *Phi Delta Kappan,* 1957 (October 1975): 89–92.

Hall, V. C., R. R. Turner, and W. Russell. Ability of children from four subcultures and two grade levels to imitate and comprehend crucial aspects of standard English. *Journal of Educational Psychology,* 64 (1973): 147–158.

Harris, A. J., and M. D. Jacobson. *Basic Elementary Reading Vocabularies.* New York: Macmillan, 1972.

Harris, A. J., and E. R. Sipay. *How to Increase Reading Ability,* 7th ed. New York: David McKay, 1980.

Harvey, M. R. Public school treatment of low-income children: Education for passivity. *Urban Education,* 15 (1980): 279–323.

Hess, R. D., and V. Shipman. Maternal influences upon early learning. In R. D. Hess and R. M. Bear (eds.), *Early Education.* Chicago: Aldine, 1968, 91–103.

Honzik, M. P., J MacFarlane, and L. Allen. The stability of mental test performance between two and eighteen years.

Jensen, A. R. How much can we boost IQ and scholastic achievement? *Harvard Educational Review,* 39 (1969): 1–123.

Kellmer-Pringle, M. L., N. R. Butler, and R. Davie. *11,000 Seven Year Olds.* London: Longmans, 1966.

Kessler, J. *Psychopathology in Childhood.* Englewood Cliffs, NJ: Prentice-Hall, 1966.

Kohn, M. L. Social class and parental values. Paper read at the annual meeting of the American sociological society, Washington, DC, August 27–29, 1957.

Labov, W. *The Study of Nonstandard English.* Washington, DC: Center for Applied Linguistics, 1969.

—————. The reading of the -ed suffix. In H. Levin, and J. P. Williams, *Basic Studies in Reading.* New York: Basic Books, 1970a, 222–45.

—————. The logic of nonstandard English. In F. Williams (ed.), *Language and Poverty: Perspectives on a Theme.* Chicago: Markham, 1970b, 153–89.

—————. Academic ignorance and black intelligence. *Atlantic Monthly* (June 1972a): 59–67.

—————. Letter to the editor. *Atlantic Monthly* (November 1972b): 45.

Levitas, M. *Marxist Perspectives in the Sociology of Education.* London: Routledge and Kegan Paul, 1974.

MacGinitie, W. N. Evaluating readiness for learning to read: A critical review and evaluation of research. *Reading Research Quarterly,* 4 (1969): 396–410.

Nolen, P. A. Reading nonstandard dialect materials: A study at grades two and four. *Child Development,* 43 (1972): 1092–97.

Ramsey, I. A comparison of first grade Negro dialect speakers' comprehension of standard English and Negro dialect. *Elementary English,* 49 (1972): 688–96.

Rist, R. C. Student social class and teacher expectation. *Harvard Educational Review,* 40 (1970): 411–51.

Rosenthal, R., and L. Jacobson. Teacher expectations for the disadvantaged. *Scientific American* (April 1968): 19–23.

Rosenthal, W., J. Eisenson, and J. A. Luckau. A statistical test of the validity of diagnostic categories used in childhood language disorders: Implications for assessment procedures. *Papers and Reports in Child Language Development,* 4 (1972): 121–43. Palo Alto, CA: Stanford University Press.

Schatzman, L., and A. Strauss. Social class and modes of communication. *American Journal of Sociology,* 60 (1955): 329–39.

Sears, R. R., E. Maccoby, and H. Levin. *Patterns of Child Rearing.* Evanston, IL: Row, Peterson, 1957.

Singer, H. IQ is and is not related to reading. In S. F. Wanat (ed.), *Linguistics and Reading Series: 1.*

Arlington, VA: Center for Applied Linguistics, 1977, 43–55.

Smitherman, G. White English in blackface, or who do I be? In L. Michaels and C. Ricks, *The State of the Language.* Berkeley: University of California Press, 1980, 158–68.

Stauffer, R. G., J. C. Abrams, and J. J. Pikulski. *Diagnosis, Correction and Prevention of Reading Disabilities.* New York: Harper & Row, 1978.

Stubbs, M. *Language and Literacy: The Sociolinguistics of Reading and Writing.* London: Routledge and Kegan Paul, 1980.

Tough, J. *The Development of Meaning.* London: Allen and Unwin, 1977.

Williams, F., and R. Naremore. On the functional analysis of social class differences in modes of speech. *Speech Monographs,* 36 (1969): 77–102.

Wolfram, W. Sociolinguistic alternatives in teaching reading to nonstandard speakers. In J. S. DeStephano (ed.), *Language, Society and Education: A Profile in Black English.* Worthington, OH: Charles A. Jones, 1973, 291–311.

CHAPTER 11

ORGANIZATION FOR INSTRUCTION AND READING PROGRAMS

REASONS FOR GROUPING

Activities That Require Small Groups
Student Characteristics

INDIVIDUAL DIFFERENCES
ACHIEVEMENT LEVELS
SKILL DEFICITS
INTERESTS

ORGANIZATION FOR INSTRUCTION WITHIN THE
CLASSROOM

Three-Group Plan Using Basal Reader

GROUPING BY GRADE LEVEL
TEMPORARY GROUPING BY NEEDS
TEMPORARY GROUPING BY INTERESTS
MOVEMENT BETWEEN GROUPS
NAMING GROUPS
REGULAR WHOLE CLASS READING
   ACTIVITIES
INDEPENDENT WORK
AN ECLECTIC APPROACH

Individualized Instruction: Holistic Approach

THE INDIVIDUALIZED READING PROGRAM

Individual Instruction: Atomistic Approaches

PROGRAMMED READING INSTRUCTION
SKILLS MANAGEMENT SYSTEMS
PROGRAMMED INSTRUCTION AND SKILLS
   MANAGEMENT SYSTEMS: ASSUMPTIONS

ORGANIZATION PROBLEMS

Learning How a Program Works
The Danger of Busywork

The Quality of Teacher-Student Interaction
Threats to the Teacher's Leadership Role
Advice to the Beginning Teacher

SCHOOLWIDE ARRANGEMENTS TO NARROW
INDIVIDUAL DIFFERENCES

Classroom Assignment Strategies

CHILDREN WITH SPECIAL NEEDS
HOMOGENEOUS CLASSROOMS
HOMOGENEOUS READING CLASSES

Advantages of Narrowing the Range of
   Achievement
Problems

FLEXIBILITY
THE MYTH OF HOMOGENEITY
TRACKING
OBSCURING THE RESPONSIBILITY FOR
   READING INSTRUCTION

COMPETING IDEALS: OBLITERATING VERSUS
ACCENTUATING DIFFERENCES IN ACHIEVEMENT

SUMMARY

FOR FURTHER READING AND DISCUSSION

REFERENCES

One of the greatest challenges a beginning teacher faces is classroom management. One of the greatest complications of classroom management is the practice of having different children doing different things at the same time. This practice has a particularly long tradition in teaching reading.

If a principal walked into a room and found the entire class engaged in the same activity—listening to the teacher, doing the same written assignment, engaging in a discussion—he or she would probably not find that remarkable unless it were a reading lesson. Then the principal might ask why the children were not working individually or in groups and whether most of the instruction was not done with individuals or in groups. Of course, the teacher might have a perfectly good reason why the children were working together as an entire class. The point is that the tradition of children working in groups during reading lessons is so well established that one expects to find it.

the person doing the oral reading is involved in the primary purpose of the lesson. It makes sense, then, to do oral reading individually (ideally) or in small groups so that the children engaged are fully involved as much of the time as possible.

On the other hand, if a written lesson is assigned to give students practice in a skill they have presumably learned, one would expect them to work individually. But there is no reason for them to work on that lesson at the same time. Some of them may be engaged with the teacher in an activity that calls for a small group. This is one reason for the traditional appearance of groups during reading instruction.

But if the nature of the lessons were the only factor calling for grouping, children could be assigned to groups arbitrarily. One could take any six children for an activity calling for a small group. The only concern would be that every child be included in *some* group covering the activity in question. But that is not the case; other factors must be considered.

REASONS FOR GROUPING

Activities That Require Small Groups

Large groups are undesirable for some reading activities. Whereas the teacher might read to the class while each child listens, in some activities a child is engaged only while he or she is performing. The teacher may, for example, have individual children read orally to evaluate the children's use of context for word recognition or their pronunciation or phrasing or expression. One likes to think that the other children are profiting by ''following'' the oral reading in their own books, but only

Student Characteristics

INDIVIDUAL DIFFERENCES

There are discussions in Chapters 2 and 10 of ways children differ from one another that are relevant to reading instruction. Before reading instruction begins, one will find differences in performance on tasks designed to measure visual and auditory discrimination (Figures 2.1 and 2.2) and the other areas of reading readiness described in Chapter 2. Before instruction begins and while it proceeds, one will find differences in the cognitive, physical, and sociological characteristics described in Chapter 10. These differences often give rise to small group instruction. It makes sense, for example, to arrange it so that slow learners receive additional instruction in small groups.

ACHIEVEMENT LEVELS

Whatever the approach to reading instruction, one will find differences in how much individuals have learned almost as soon as instruction begins. If one uses a phonic-linguistic approach (described in Chapter 2), one will discover that on the third or fourth day some children know the names of the letters taught thus far and recognize words that begin with the sound they were taught to associate with the letters. Other children know the names of the letters, but do not recognize words that begin with the sound they were taught to associate with the letters. Still other children do not know the names of the letters that have been taught. And, of course, some children will know some letter names (but not all) and will recognize some words that begin with the sounds they were taught to associate with the letters (but not all).

If one uses a language experience approach like that described in Chapter 2, one will soon have children with dozens of words in their "word banks" and who have begun to work on phonic relationships. At the same time, there will be children in the class who have few or no words in their word banks.

By the middle grades, it is not unusual to find children who compare with seventh-graders and children who compare with third-graders on standardized tests of reading achievement in the same classroom. Some of the instruction and materials designed to challenge the children with the highest reading achievement scores will be too difficult for many children in the class, and some of the reading instruction and materials designed to develop the reading skills of the children with the very lowest achievement scores will be of little value to many of the children in the class. Thus, differences in levels of achievement give rise to grouping for instruction in reading in the typical classroom.

SKILL DEFICITS

At early stages, most members of a class may be progressing satisfactorily with a given program, but the teacher will notice that not all individuals have mastered all the skills presented. Children who demonstrate roughly the same level of achievement differ in terms of individual skills. One or two children may not know the names of all the letters. Others may not recognize the recommended sight words for their level. Another child may not use context to aid in word recognition. Two or three children may have particular problems with oral reading; a few may rely too heavily on phonics; others may fail to grasp main ideas.

Children who demonstrate the same general achievement level are often divided into groups for instruction in specific skills that are lacking or underdeveloped, considering their general level of ability.

INTERESTS

An important component of effective instruction is to enlist the students' desire to learn. One way to get children to want to learn to read is by incorporating reading instruction into activities children are already interested in. A short time ago one might have thought that girls could be motivated to learn to read through reading recipes and romance novels, that boys could be interested in learning to read through reading automobile repair manuals and westerns, and that inner-city black children would be inspired to learn to read by the works of Langston Hughes and Richard Wright.

Fortunately, such stereotyping is no longer fashionable; but the principle behind these assumptions is still valid. If students see learning to read as something that will satisfy an immediate need, they are apt to learn to read. As a result, individual reading in the school or classroom library is encouraged and groups are formed around common interests such as sports, hobbies, or careers. Therefore, individual interests give rise to forming groups for reading instruction.

ORGANIZATION FOR INSTRUCTION WITHIN THE CLASSROOM

Different grouping practices are suggested by several reading approaches and programs.

Three-Group Plan Using Basal Readers

The most widely used strategy for teaching reading in this country is to use a basal reading program (with or without supplementary materials and techniques) and a three-group plan. Figure 11.1 shows one week of such a plan for a first-grade class. Figure 11.2 shows one week of such a plan for a fifth-grade class. Through commenting on these plans and suggesting ways they could be elaborated upon, we will present an overview of common practices for grouping and the reasons for these practices.

GROUPING BY GRADE LEVEL

These plans are based on the assumption that different achievement levels exist in classrooms, and that by grouping children by achievement level, one minimizes the risk that children will be asked to perform tasks that are too difficult or too easy for them and therefore a waste of time and effort.

In the first-grade plan (Figure 11.1), the groups were presumably formed as the children moved at differing rates through the pre-primers (usually three or four books), the primer, and finally grade 1 levels. In the fifth-grade plans (Figure 11.2), one presumes that the children in the groups are capable of mastering the reading tasks included at different levels of the basal reading series.

In most classrooms, this would mean that the middle group was using the grade-level reader designed for the grade, while the low group was using a lower-level reader and the high group was using a higher-level reader. For example, in a fifth grade, one might find the low, middle, and high groups using third-, fifth-, and sixth-grade readers. However, it is not unusual to find that the high group is using the grade-level reader while the middle group is using a lower-level and the lower group is using an even lower level. In such a fifth-grade classroom, the three groups might be using second-, third-, and fifth-grade readers. Depending on the diversity of achievement levels of the groups, any graduated sequence of grade-level readers is possible.

Number of Groups. Classes are most often divided into three groups for reading instruction, but three is more of a practical number than an ideal number. Beginning teachers are often adivised to start with two groups; one wants to gain experience in teaching groups while being responsible for the entire class, but attempting to maintain more than two groups at the start may be too ambitious.

One plan is to divide the class into children who can perform satisfactorily with on-

FIGURE 11.1
THREE-GROUP PLAN FOR SECOND HALF OF FIRST GRADE.

Pre-Primer Group	Primer Group	First Reader Group
9:10– Work independently on 9:40 teacher-made letter and word discrimination practice.	*Teacher conducts* lesson preparing for new story. Follows suggestions in teacher's guide for basal reader.	Silent reading of materials selected by pupils.
9:40– *Teacher conducts* lesson 10:10 preparing for a new story. Follows suggestions in teacher's guide for basal reader.	Nonreading activity (Work independently on addition facts.)	Nonreading activity (Work independently on addition facts.)
10:10– Cut pictures from 10:40 magazines for an initial consonant sound word file.	Work independently on duplicated worksheets: Using letter-sound associations and context clues to recognize words.	*Teacher directs* lesson to check comprehension of last story. Selected oral reading.
10:40– 11:10	Recess	
11:10– *Teacher directs* the whole class in developing an experience story about the school bake sale. 11:40 Students practice reading the experience story.		

FIGURE 11.2
THREE-GROUP PLAN FOR FIFTH GRADE.

Red Book Group	Blue Book Group	Green Book Group
9:55– *Teacher conducts* 10:15 discussion and oral reading of story read on previous day.	Silent reading of story introduced on previous day.	Silent reading and written comprehension check of materials from supplementary program (self-corrected).
10:15– Workbook exercises 10:35 related to story.	*Teacher conducts* discussion and oral reading of story.	Plan dramatization of story with group chairperson or teacher aide.
10:35– Independent reading period. 10:55 *Teacher conducts* individual conferences and works with a group of students who have a common oral reading problem.		

grade materials and those who cannot. Materials are chosen at the average achievement level for the low group and at on-grade achievement levels for the high group. Soon the teacher can begin to plan individual or small group activities for the least able children in the low group and for the most able in the high group.

These groups can meet during periods when the whole class in engaged in an activity at which children can work independently of the teacher, such as in the whole class activity from 10:35 to 10:55 in Figure 11.2. Once the class is functioning well in two groups and the children have learned to work together in groups and to work independently without the teacher's guidance, a permanent third group can be formed for the least able or most able students.

At the center of a busy, productive classroom there must be a competent, stable, and steadfast presence: a teacher who enables children to learn and function securely in a setting where there is considerable activity and opportunity for distraction. Classroom organization schemes that are beyond the teacher's competence to manage threaten the teacher's ability to ensure security. That is why more than three permanent groups is the exception. This tension between the practical limitation on the number of groups the teachers can manage and the desirability of forming many groups for many reasons leads to the next observation about the plans in Figures 11.1 and 11.2: Namely, permanent groups and special purpose groups exist simultaneously.

TEMPORARY GROUPING BY NEEDS

Membership in a permanent group should afford each child consistent instruction that is challenging but not too difficult. But there are many reasons to form special purpose groups that will last for a short time. In a fifth grade,

for example, one may discover three children in the low group who do not recognize the Dolch Basic Sight Vocabulary. These three children might be paired with three other children for practice in recognizing basic sight words on flash cards. Or two children from the middle group and one child from the high group may do oral reading very rapidly and substitute words that sound like words in the text, but which do not make sense. This group might meet with the teacher or with an aide to practice oral reading for meaning, reading with expression, and becoming aware of the role of context in word recognition.

As soon as a child accomplishes the goal for which such a group is created, the child is no longer a part of that group. As soon as all the children in the group have accomplished the goal of the group, the group no longer exists.

TEMPORARY GROUPING BY INTERESTS

Children with different levels of achievement and different skills strenghts can comprise groups based on common interest. Children interested in a common topic might find books written at levels each child can read and come together to discuss their books or write reports on their topics. For example, as a result of a social studies unit some children in the class might become interested in finding out what it must have been like to be a child in colonial America. Children with varying levels of reading achievement might read from biographies of people who lived in colonial America and construct a list of differences under the headings *clothing, food, education, work* and so on.

MOVEMENT BETWEEN GROUPS

A point that is not obvious from Figure 11.1 and 11.2 but that is fundamental to the assumption on which grouping for reading instruction is based is that teachers should always be alert for indications that a student should be moved from one group to another.

Initially, groups are formed on the best information available, such as test scores or the teacher's evaluation of one or two oral reading performances. A child's performance from day to day in reading lessons sometimes indicates that he or she has been placed in the wrong group. Long-term observation of a child in learning situations is a more valid measure of achievement than test scores or other assessment procedures, and teachers should not hesitate to move students from group to group as a result of such observations. A student's pace of achievement may pick up or slacken off as well. This too can be the cause of a change in group assigment.

NAMING GROUPS

Because of the time-honored practice of forming groups around basal reader levels, publishers of basal readers do not spell out the grade levels on textbooks or accompanying materials. This is done to avoid embarrassing children who are assigned to a reading level below their grade. Although even the youngest students know almost immediately which groups are doing the most advanced and least advanced work, there is no reason for them to know the precise level of material each group is using.

This leads to the question of what one should name the groups. Calling them "high, middle, and low" or "ones, twos, and threes" or "As, Bs, and Cs" to reflect their actual order is a constant and unnecessary reminder of their rank-order. Reversing the order (calling the lowest group "highs" or "ones" or "As") does not deceive anyone. Calling them by the color of their book or the name of their book clearly identifies the groups in a neutral and matter-of-fact way.

REGULAR WHOLE CLASS READING ACTIVITIES

There are two reasons why whole class reading lessons should occur regularly. One reason is that the teacher does not want to lose sight of the value of a learning community. Separating children who know more from children who know less and separating children who lack a skill from children who have that skill prevents children from learning from one another.

The second reason why whole class activities occur regularly is that some activities will benefit everyone in the class and there is nothing about the activity that makes a large group inefficient. In a seventh-grade class, for example, a teacher may conduct a lesson on Latin roots and their meanings with the entire class. Students might read and discuss a weekly current events magazine as an entire class in fifth grade. A first-grade teacher may conduct a lesson on telling when word pairs begin with the same or different sounds with the entire class. A teacher may read passages from books to the entire class in preparation for selecting books for individual reading. When such activities will benefit everyone in a classroom, there is nothing to be gained by repeating the activity two or three times in small groups.

INDEPENDENT WORK

One of the most striking facts revealed by Figures 11.1 and 11.2 is that when teachers group children for reading instruction, children are expected to work independently of the teacher more often than they are expected to be engaged in a lesson conducted by the teacher. This kind of independent activity takes two forms: Children work together as a group on some project or lesson, or they work individually at silent reading, work sheets, workbook pages, and so on. Both kinds of activities take a great deal of planning on the part of the teacher and a great deal of understanding and cooperation on the part of the students.

AN ECLECTIC APPROACH

The traditional three-group plans shown in Figures 11.1 and 11.2 are typically used with basal readers. It has been pointed out earlier in this book that most widely used basal reading series are eclectic—that is, they draw on both the empiricist and rationalist traditions. Therefore, within the traditional three-group plan where a basal reader is the core of the program, one is not surprised to find a teacher doing an experience story (a holistic, top-down approach) and working on letter recognition using flash cards (an atomistic, bottom-up approach) on the same day.

Teachers who adopt such an approach do not feel compelled to draw phonics lessons out of children's individual successes with experience stories, as they would if they adhered dogmatically to a top-down philosophy. On the other hand, teachers do not feel obligated to avoid words having letter-sound correspondences that have not been mastered in isolation, as they would if they adhered dogmatically to a bottom-up philosophy.

Teachers using eclectic approaches view the assumptions underlying empirical and rationalistic approaches as complementary rather than contradictory. They see the experience story and the phonics lesson as two ways of entering into the process of learning to read. While purists insist on working from the bottom up or from the top down, the eclectic teacher concentrates on filling in the middle—from both directions.

Individualized Instruction: Holistic Approach

Some teaching strategies that emphasize individualized instruction have been dis-

cussed previously in this book. In mastery learning, for example, it is presumed that some children will require more instruction and practice than others, and provisions are made for enough instruction and practice on an individual basis. Individualized instruction of this kind should be and usually is a part of the grouping for instruction plans exemplified in Figures 11.1 and 11.2. There are other approaches to teaching reading in which individualized instruction is the dominant or exclusive approach. Three such approaches are described here.

Although organizational plans that emphasize teaching and learning in groups tend to be eclectic, plans that emphasize individual instruction tend to rely on rigidly rationalist *or* on rigidly empiricist assumptions. As a result, individualized reading programs fall into two categories: (1) programs based on the rationalist assumption that learning to read is a holistic process in which learners will acquire different skills in different order in essentially a top-down fashion, and (2) programs based on the empiricist assumption that learning to read is an atomistic process in which students will learn approximately the same skills in the same order, but at different rates of speed, in essentially a bottom-up fashion.

An individualized instruction program based on rationalist assumptions and several based on empiricist assumptions are discussed in the following sections.

THE INDIVIDUALIZED READING PROGRAM

How the Program Works. The individualized reading program as articulated by Veatch (1978) incorporates the language experience approach into a wider program. Soon after children have begun to learn to read what they themselves have written (or have taken part in writing), they are encouraged to investigate books and choose books to read. The teacher meets with children individually to see what kind of progress they have made and where they are encountering difficulties. The teacher then plans and carries out instruction.

If more than one child is having the same problems, the instruction is carried out in groups. Some groups meet regularly with the teacher for direct instruction, other groups work independently. The nature of what needs to be learned determines whether the children receive direct instruction or work independently. An occasional time for "sharing" enables children to come together as a whole class. A six-step plan for an individualized reading program is shown in Figure 11.3.

The Underlying Rationalist Assumptions.

Veatch (1978) argues the merits of this program in terms of how well it provides for twenty assumptions she makes about learning to read (Figure 11.4). These assumptions reflect "the profoundly revolutionary character of the instruction program" (p. 8). Assumptions 1, 2, 3, and 6 relate to the language experience aspect of the program. The remainder of the assumptions relate to the part of the program built on reading individually chosen books.

The assumptions on which the individualized reading program relies are rationalist assumptions. Reading is viewed as a holistic enterprise. The teacher makes instruction decisions for each child based on that child's performance in working with whole stories. One presumes the child will find a book he or she can understand in a general way. Problem areas or separate skills where instruction is needed are discovered within the framework of the child's total understanding. The order in which the child will learn skills is not thought to be predetermined. One expects the child to play an active part in discovering how to read and in identifying his or her own problem areas.

♦ It would be worthwhile to review the models of reading readiness based on rationalist assumptions in Chapter 2 and compare them with the assumptions and techniques of the individual reading program.

Exceptional Demands of the Program.

The individualized reading program presents five exceptional demands:

1. Because one does not expect to teach all skills to every child, or to teach skills in the same order to every child, the teacher must possess extraordinary diagnostic skill and knowledge of the reading and learning process to determine what the child knows, what the child needs to learn, and how to teach what the child needs to learn.

   This is too often not the case. Harris and Sipay (1975) state flatly: "Diagnostic skills have not been given much attention in teacher-education programs, and the present level of diagnostic proficiency among classroom teachers leaves much to be desired" (p. 116). Levine (1982) suggests that many teachers do not know how to select reading skills to improve performance. Reviewers of literature on "open schools," schools based on many of the same assumptions as individualized reading programs and therefore schools where such programs are likely to be adopted, are often cirtical of a too-casual approach to teaching reading (Kozal, 1972; Southgate, 1973).

2. Because each child is working on his or her own project and individual conferences are at the heart of the program, classroom management becomes a central issue. Students must know how to work on their own, and they must work independently enough so the teacher can engage in conferences without interruption.

FIGURE 11.3
A SIX-STEP PLAN FOR AN INDIVIDUALIZED READING PROGRAM.
(Following Veatch, 1978, pp. 17–20.)

I. Selecting
Child chooses materials on two criteria
   A. He likes it
      and
   B. He can read it

II. Planning—child decides
   A. To read the book for himself. When finished he goes back to step 1
      or
   B. To prepare this book for an individual conference with the teacher

III. Independent work
   A. Reads
   B. Proceeds with preparation for individual conference such as
      1. Intensive study to retell story to teacher
      2. Develop a report to share with class
      3. Polish a skill from another curriculum area, such as writing a composition based on the story

IV. Individual conference: An intensive, individual session on a one-to-one basis with the teacher. Teacher keeps detailed records of each conference. Instruction is based on these records.

V. Organization of groups. Based on observations made in individual conferences, teacher forms groups.
   A. Groups for instructional purposes based on specific clear-cut needs that require continuing direct instruction from the teacher
   B. Groups for independent work based on specific clear-cut needs that do not require continuing direct instruction from the teacher

VI. Sharing follow-up and evaluation
   1. Children tell about the book they read—preferably during time allotted in addition to the regular reading period.
   2. Children complete workbook pages and similar materials chosen by the teacher to meet the needs of individuals and groups.
   3. During individual conferences, children receive immediate evaluation of their progress. Reports to parents of student progress are based on records kept by the teacher.

As each child completes the six-step plan, he returns to step I to begin the cycle anew.

3. Because each child is working individually and at the same time children are grouped for instruction, extensive and accurate records must be kept on each child.

4. Because conferences are far less satisfactory when teacher has not read the books the child has read, successful teachers must be familiar with dozens and dozens of books.

5. Because the method is based on a child's ability to do a great deal of reading from a great number of books, a large classroom library is necessary.

Individual Reading Program Packages. Publishers of educational materials have produced packages of books and materials that help solve some of the problems posed by using the individual reading program (see Figure 11.5). One can purchase sets of approximately fifty to one hundred books with additional materials designed to make the programs manageable. These materials may include summaries of books, vocabulary lists, comprehension checks, outlines for structuring individualized conferences, suggestions for forming skills instruction groups, suggestions for individual and group projects based on interests related to individual books, and forms for keeping records of students' progress and needs. Books in these packages are usually similar in level of difficulty.

FIGURE 11.4
TWENTY ASSUMPTIONS UNDERLYING THE INDIVIDUAL READING PROGRAM.
(From Veatch, 1978, pp. 7–8.)

1. Reading must be taught as part of all of the other language arts.

2. Spelling is as important in learning to read as it is in learning to write.

3. Reading and spelling are but two sides of the same coin.

4. Children learn to read better and faster when they are free to pace their own growth, seeking help when necessary.

5. The act of reading must center upon the child, with the materials used of secondary importance.

6. Children's own language is a valuable source material for reading instruction.

7. Individual differences are met by teaching individuals one by one.

8. Classroom efficiency is enhanced when groups are organized upon an identified need, problem, difficulty, or interest.

9. There is no established rank order of reading materials.

10. There is a series of progressions or developmental stages that can be recognized and provided for with a variety of materials.

11. Reading growth results when a pupil commits himself to a piece of material.

12. As reading is a personal act, the choice of material is an expression of self.

13. The human factor of personal commitment of the pupil will enhance reading growth when matched by the ability of the teacher to change and adapt procedures on the spot.

14. Not all skills need be taught to every child, nor in identical sequence to more than one child.

15. Progress may be steadily cumulative, but it may also be apparent in great leaps and bounds.

16. Skills are gained during the act of reading and not before it.

17. There is no clearly established sequence of skills for all children.

18. There is no single piece of material that meets the needs of every pupil in any given class.

19. While silent reading is central, oral reading is placed in a prominent position with a purpose.

20. The love of books and reading is encouraged when loved books are read.

♦ It would be a valuable exercise to examine a program like The Random House Reading Program (Figure 11.5) and to compare it to the six-step plan (Figure 11.3) and the twenty assumptions (Figure 11.4) presented by Veatch (1978) and to discuss ways these packages might alleviate the five problems inherent in an individualized reading program cited in the last section. Three individualized reading programs are listed under "For Further Reading and Discussion" at the end of this chapter.

Notice that as these packages become more structured and detailed, the "open-ended" flavor of this approach gives way to more controlled and predetermined choices of both reading materials and learning objectives. It might be useful to think about and discuss with your classmates which of Veatch's twenty assumptions might possibly be vi-

olated by highly structured and detailed packages and how teachers might use these packages in such a way as to maintain the spirit of the individualized reading program and reap the benefits of the aids offered in these packages as well.

Individual Instruction: Atomistic Approaches

PROGRAMMED READING INSTRUCTION

Linear Programmed Instruction. Figure 11.6 shows a page from *Programmed Reading* (Buchanan and Sullivan, Associates, 1973), which is a widely recognized reading series

FIGURE 11.5
THE RANDOM HOUSE READING PROGRAM.

based on principles of programmed instruction. Programmed instruction is based on the premise that learning can be divided into small units and organized into a sequence so that when a student learns the sequence, he or she will have learned the whole concept or skill.

Typically, each bit of instruction is presented in a frame. The frame presents instruction and a question (or questions). In a paper and pencil program, the answers are available to the student: The student reads the instructions, answers the question(s), and checks his or her answer(s). If the answer is wrong, the student presumably reflects on why that answer was wrong and why the correct answer was right. He or she then proceeds to the next frame. Because the learner proceeds from frame to frame in a fixed order, such programs are called *linear programs.*

Although linear programmed instruction such as *Programmed Reading* clearly qualifies as reading instruction engaged in by individuals independently of the teacher, there is some question as to whether it qualifies as individualized reading instruction. Children with varying degrees of achievement may start at different points in such a program and some children will proceed from frame to frame faster than others, but there is no provision for tailoring the skills, methods, and materials to fit the needs and interests of individual children.

Branching Programmed Instruction. Computers make it possible to add another dimension to programmed instruction. Rather than moving relentlessly from frame to frame, the computer makes it possible to present the "next" frame if the child answers the ques-

FIGURE 11.6
A PAGE FROM A PROGRAM BASED ON PRINCIPLES OF LINEAR PROGRAMMED INSTRUCTION. (From C. D. Buchanan and Sullivan *Programmed Reading*, Book 6, 3rd ed. Webster McGraw-Hill, 1973.) The student covers the answers in the left column with a card which he slides down to expose each answer after he has decided the answer to the question.

tion(s) correctly for a given frame or to present an alternative frame if the child answers the question(s) incorrectly. Figure 11.7 shows part of a branching lesson designed to review the recognition and meaning of prefixes.

The capability for branching opens enormous possibilities for programming instruction. A pretest can be presented and frames can be selected and sequenced on the basis of wrong answers on the pretest. A wrong answer on any frame can call up remedial lessons. A series of correct responses on the remedial lessons can return the learner to the original flow of frames.

The Motivation Factor. At a recent convention where electronic aids to classroom instruction were on display, a salesperson described the computer as "an electronic workbook." Although that remark was meant to be a selling point, perhaps it should be taken as a warning.

Conceptualizing and implementing branching instructional programs for the computer calls for a great deal of ingenuity. The program designer must construct pretests to uncover problems, design series of frames to teach whatever is necessary to overcome the problems, and design alternate frames to be presented when wrong answers are given. While programming the computer—complete with graphics in full color—is fascinating work, sitting at a terminal typing in short answers to questions that can be only right or wrong may be far less interesting. As the novelty of video games and home computers wears off, what appears to be a highly motivating activity may become far less motivating.

Beginning in the middle grades, it may be useful to share the work of analyzing the reading process into steps and constructing lessons and mastery tests related to these steps with students. Students ought to be brought into instruction design and programming as early as possible in their learning careers. They will not only share in the fun; they may learn more.

Because computers have been introduced into a large number of classrooms only recently, we can only speculate as to whether or not they will result in more rapid learning and higher levels of accomplishment. This will undoubtedly be a tremendously active area of research and development for some time.

SKILLS MANAGEMENT SYSTEMS

How the Systems Work. Skills management systems are based on four premises: (1) that it is useful to think of the reading curriculum as a series of skills, (2) that the skills can be divided into small sequential steps, (3) that through testing, one can determine which steps a child has mastered and which steps are beyond the child's present achievement level, and (4) that through careful management of instruction, no child is asked to work on skill steps that he or she has mastered or that are beyond his or her present achievement level.

Skills management systems are constructed in the following way:

1. Reading experts analyze the process into elements or cognitive skill categories, such as word recognition, vocabulary, comprehension, and study skills.
2. These elements are divided and subdivided until skills are identified that represent small sequential steps.
3. These steps are translated into behavioral objectives stated in a way that specifies the student behavior which signifies mastery of the skill.
4. Tests are devised that will determine whether the child has mastered the skill.
5. Materials are found or created that teach each skill.

FIGURE 11.7
AN EXAMPLE OF A COMPUTERIZED BRANCHING PROGRAM DESIGNED TO REVIEW THE RECOGNITION AND MEANINGS OF COMMON PREFIXES.

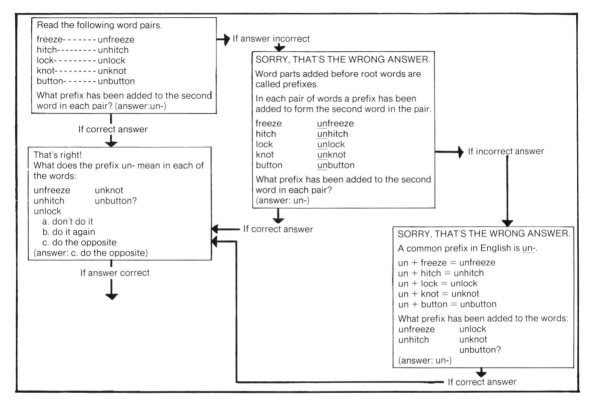

6. Methods of keeping records are devised, forms for keeping records are produced, and a management system is created.

7. Lists of objectives, tests of objectives, materials for teaching objectives (or references to places where such materials can be found), record forms, and a manual describing how the whole system is to be operated are published.

The most widely recognized skills management system is the *Wisconsin Design for Reading Skill Development* (Otto and Askov, 1973). This program consists of six "program elements": word attack, comprehension, study skills, self-directed reading, interpretive reading, and creative reading. Figure 11.8 shows a portion of the skills (there are approximately 300 skills in all six elements) in the word attack element. Figure 11.9 shows a criterion reference test for recognizing root words. Figure 11.10 shows the teacher's resource file for teaching to the behavioral objective concerning the variant sounds associated with the letters *c, s,* and *g.* Presumably the teacher has access to a well-supplied materials center where he or she can find the les-

FIGURE 11.8
FOUR LEVELS OF WORD ATTACK SKILLS IN THE WISCONSIN DESIGN FOR READING SKILL DEVELOPMENT.

LEVEL A:	LEVEL C:
Rhyming words	Sight vocabulary
Rhyming phrases	Consonant variants
Shapes	Consonant blends
Letters, numbers	Long vowels
Words, phrases	Vowel $a + r, a + l, a + w$
Colors	Diphthongs
Initial consonants	Long and short *oo*
All A skills	Middle vowel
	Two vowels separated
LEVEL B:	Two vowels together
Sight vocabulary	Final vowel
Left-right sequence	Consonant digraphs
Beginning consonants	Base words
Ending consonants	Plurals
Consonant blends	Homonyms
Rhyming elements	Synonyms, antonyms
Short vowels	Independent application
Consonant digraphs	Multiple meanings
Compound words	All C skills
Contractions	
Base words	**LEVEL D:**
Plurals	Sight vocabulary
Possessives	Consonant blends
All B skills	Silent letters
	Syllabication
	Accent
	Unaccented schwa
	Possessives
	All D skills

FIGURE 11.9
CRITERION-REFERENCED TEST FOR RECOGNIZING ROOT WORDS FROM THE WISCONSIN DESIGN FOR READING SKILL DEVELOPMENT.

1. fished
   Ⓐ fi <u>shed</u>
   Ⓑ fish ed
   Ⓒ f <u>ish</u> ed

2. jumps
   Ⓐ jum ps
   Ⓑ jump s
   Ⓒ <u>jum</u> ps

3. running
   Ⓐ ru nning
   Ⓑ run <u>ning</u>
   Ⓒ <u>run</u> ning

4. that's
   Ⓐ <u>that</u> 's
   Ⓑ t <u>hat</u> 's
   Ⓒ th <u>at</u> 's

5. going
   Ⓐ <u>go</u> ing
   Ⓑ <u>goin</u> g
   Ⓒ go <u>ing</u>

6. washer
   Ⓐ <u>was</u> her
   Ⓑ was <u>her</u>
   Ⓒ <u>wash</u> er

sons listed on the resource file to use with the student who has failed the criterion referenced test on that particular skill.

Two other skills management systems are the *Fountain Valley Teacher Support System in Reading* (1971) and the *Prescriptive Reading Inventory* (1972). Although these two programs are based on the same premises and constructed in the same way as the *Wisconsin Design for Reading Skill Development,* each has unique features. *The Fountain Valley Teacher*

Support System in Reading includes self-scoring tests and taperecorded test directions designed to free the teacher of the burden of administering and grading the numerous tests necessary in implementing a skills management system. *The Prescriptive Reading Inventory* features machine-scorable tests whose results can be stored in a computer bank. The computer is programmed to supply the teacher with sta-

FIGURE 11.10
PART OF THE TEACHER'S RESOURCE FILE FOR WORD ATTACK LEVEL C FROM THE WISCONSIN DESIGN FOR READING SKILL DEVELOPMENT.

the Wisconsin Design for Reading Skill Development
Teacher's Resource File: Word Attack

Word Attack—Level C
Skill 2: Consonants and Their Variant Sounds

Objective

Given words containing variant sounds of *c, s,* and *g* (e.g., *cake-city, sit-trees, go-giant*), the child indicates whether the underlined letters in given pairs of words have the same or different sounds.

Printed Materials

Allyn and Bacon, *Arrivals and Departures*, teacher's ed. (1968), pp. 60-61, 174, 192, 330.

Allyn and Bacon, *Believe and Make-Believe*, teacher's ed. (1968), p. 59.

Allyn and Bacon, *Fields and Fences*, teacher's ed. (1968), p. 298.

Allyn and Bacon, *Finding the Way*, teacher's ed. (1968), pp. 100, 102-103, 234.

Allyn and Bacon, *Letters and Syllables*, teacher's ed. (1971), pp. 31-36, T12.

Allyn and Bacon, *Magic Windows*, teacher's ed. (1968), pp. 119, 270, 281.

Allyn and Bacon, *Open Gates*, teacher's ed. (1969), pp. 116, 138-139.

Allyn and Bacon, *Our School*, teacher's ed. (1968), p. 129.

Allyn and Bacon, *Story Caravan*, teacher's ed. (1968), pp. 80, 149.

Allyn and Bacon, *Syllables and Words*, teacher's ed. (1971), pp. T7, T9, 12, 85-88.

Allyn and Bacon, *Town and Country*, teacher's ed. (1968), pp. 52-54, 175-176, 236, 271, 282.

American Book, *And So You Go! Be On the Go! Can You?*, Workbook, teacher's ed. (1968), pp. 35, 71-72.

American Book, *Can You?*, teacher's ed. (1968), p. 52a.

American Book, *Days and Ways*, teacher's ed. (1968), pp. 27a, 27b, 36a, 48b, 71a, 87a, 143a, 151a, 176, 181, 188.

American Book, *Days and Ways*, Workbook, teacher's ed. (1968), pp. 9, 19, 37, 44.

American Book, *Each and All*, teacher's ed. (1968), pp. 62a, 62b, 174, 220.

American Book, *Far and Away*, teacher's ed. (1968), pp. 57a, 57b, 73, 213, 222, 229.

American Book, *Far and Away*, Workbook, teacher's ed. (1968), p. 74.

American Book, *Gold and Silver*, teacher's ed. (1968), pp. 112, 133, 157.

American Book, *Gold and Silver*, Workbook, teacher's ed. (1968), p. 68.

American Book, *High and Wide*, teacher's ed. (1968), pp. 50, 67, 164, 164b, 235.

American Book, *Ideas and Images*, teacher's ed. (1968), pp. 172, 268.

American Book, *Kings and Things*, teacher's ed. (1971), p. 25.

American Book, *Launchings and Landings*, teacher's ed. (1968), p. 71b.

American Book, *Pattern Resources: Phonics Kit A* (1970), nos. 31, 65, 66.

American Book, *Pattern Resources: Phonics Kit C* (1970), nos. 177, 179, 183, 185.

American Education Publications, *Phonics and Word Power, Program 1: Book B* (1965), pp. 19-20.

American Education Publications, *Phonics and Word Power, Program 2: Book C* (1964), p. 6.

American Education Publications, *Phonics and Word Power, Program 3: Book A* (1964), pp. 6, 7.

American Education Publications, *Reading Success Series, Scores 1-6*, teacher's guide (1969), pp. 23, 24.

Benefic, *Reading Laboratory* (1966), Kit 405, card 6.

Continental Press, *Adventures in Wordland E* (1960), pp. 26-27.

Continental Press, *Phonics and Word-Analysis Skills, Grade 3: Part 1* (1968), p. 14.

Continental Press, *Phonics and Word-Analysis Skills, Grade 4: Part 1* (1968), p. 2.

Continental Press, *Phonics and Word-Analysis Skills, Grade 4: Part 2* (1968), p. 2.

Continental Press, *Phonics and Word-Analysis Skills, Grade 5: Part 2* (1969), p. 6.

Economy, *Keys to Independence in Reading*, Grade 4, teacher's manual (1964), pp. 49, 121.

Economy, *Phonetic Keys to Reading*, Grade 1, teacher's manual (1967), pp. 50-51, 70, 109.

Economy, *Phonetic Keys to Reading*, Grade 2, teacher's manual (1967), pp. 24-25, 27-28, 29, 66-72, 75, 130-133.

Economy, *Phonetic Keys to Reading*, Grade 3, teacher's manual (1967), pp. 67, 69, 105-106, 119.

Ginn, *All Sorts of Things*, teacher's ed. (1969), pp. 62, 64, 75, 77, 81-82, 186, 209, 210-211, 226, 314-315, 324.

tus reports on individual students and class grouping reports that identify students who need instruction in each skill category.

Through administering tests and keeping records, the teacher can determine which skill each child has mastered and which skill each child needs to work on. Groups can be formed and materials selected to teach each skill.

The typical instruction cycle for a skills management system is depicted in Figure 11.11. The groups formed in a skills management system are similar to the temporary groups formed on the basis of skills deficits in the more traditional grouping exemplified in Figures 11.1 and 11.2. A child may be included in one group of children for a word attack lesson, another group for a comprehension lesson, and a third for an interpretive reading lesson.

Some Exceptional Demands. Although skills management systems enumerate and order skills to some extent, there are sometimes many skills at the same level in a skill element. For example, on the Wisconsin Design Word Attack Profile (Figure 11.8), there are eighteen word attack skills included in level C. It is not suggested that skill 1 must be mastered before skill 2, or even that children master all of level A before level B. Wayne Otto, the principal author of the system, offers the following advice:

Be realistic in selecting an order for teaching the chosen skills. By their very nature, lists of specific reading skills are ordered. However, one should keep in mind that relatively little is known about skill hierarchies. So don't become overly concerned about such matters as whether you should teach consonants or vowels as a first step in decoding. Obviously, most children will need both if they are to become fluent decoders. Although some beginning readers may be able to

FIGURE 11.11
TYPICAL INSTRUCTION CYCLE FOR A SKILLS MANAGEMENT SYSTEM.

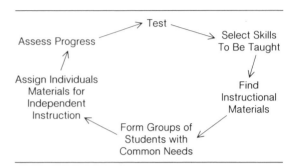

grasp the "abstractness" of short vowels quickly and to discriminate among their sounds, others may have difficulty. If you find this, shift gears and adjust instruction accordingly. Don't be locked into one instructional sequence if it fails to work with your students.

On the other hand, skipping blithely from one sequence to another can cause great confusion and even fatal gaps in skill development. Many programs for skill development assume competence in skills introduced earlier in the sequence. Later skills are taught as though the earlier skills were necessary prerequisites. Therefore, if the students do not have these skills, the skills introduced later may be made more difficult to learn.

No one sequence has been validated. Choose one that makes sense to you, and modify the sequence carefully if it doesn't work for you. (Otto et al. 1979, p. 55)

In skills management systems, recordkeeping becomes one of the teacher's greatest concerns. The teacher must administer and score tests, assign materials, and keep track of a wealth of materials. All this demands keeping records. The demand for excessive recordkeeping is often cited as a near-insurmountable problem in using this approach. Carner (1973) reports: "Some teachers who initially embraced the systems approach later were inclined to feel trapped by it. The amount of testing, observational note taking and general bookkeeping has, in some cases, approached the point of absurdity" (p. 1).

Schmidt (1982) reported on a large school system where a skills management approach was employed in which there was a test for each of 525 skills taught in grades kindergarten through 8. He estimated that a teacher with a class of thirty or thirty-five students might administer, grade, and record scores for between 2,000 and 3,000 tests in a single year. The teachers' union in this district negotiated a reduction in the number of reading skills (and therefore in the recordkeeping related to these skills) to 273—half the original number. Schmidt commented drolly: "There was not more than a flicker of scientific interest in the fact that the number of 'essential' reading skills could be reduced by half through the collective bargaining process" (p. 39).

Publishers of skills management systems have attempted to alleviate the burden of recordkeeping through mechanized and even computerized test-scoring and recordkeeping systems. Advocates of skills management systems claim there could be a beneficial tradeoff for the amount of time and energy invested in recordkeeping, since testing sometimes reveals that skills have already been mastered and do not need to be taught (Otto et al., 1979).

tradition and its interest in the outer aspects of reading (letter names, phonics, word recognition), its emphasis on parts (phonics, word structure, separation of comprehension skills), its assumption that mastery of parts leads to the complicated activity known as reading (bottom-up strategy), and its focus on a predetermined, proper sequence of steps in presenting the program to a reader who is assumed to be relatively passive—waiting for the appropriate stimulus to evoke the appropriate response.

Linear programmed instruction takes this presumption to an extreme. There is no variation in the order in which skills are presented, or the method and materials used to present the skills. Branching programmed instruction permits flexibility, but the assumption that reading instruction can be conceived of as separate skills that can be specified and put in a hierarchical sequence is still central to branching programmed instruction.

Skills management systems rely heavily on the assumption that reading and instruction should be conceived as separate skills that can be learned in small steps, but there is more flexibility in ordering the skills and in the materials and methods employed in teaching the skills. Once a teacher decides what skill to teach, there are dozens of sources of materials and methods suggested in the teacher's resource file, and there is no strong suggestion that any one skill at a given level must be taught before another. In fact, a lack of criteria for ordering skills instruction and for selecting instructional materials is sometimes cited as a weakness of skills management systems.

PROGRAMMED INSTRUCTION AND SKILLS-MANAGEMENT SYSTEMS: ASSUMPTIONS

Programmed instruction and skills management systems are based on the empiricist

♦ It would be worthwhile to review the models of reading readiness based on empiricist assumptions in Chapter 2 and compare them with the assumptions and techniques of the programmed instruction and skills management systems.

ORGANIZATION PROBLEMS

Learning How a Program Works

Teachers may encounter a variety of difficulties simply because they assume that classroom procedures are self-evident, when indeed they are not. For example, a teacher who decides to use the *Random House Reading Program* may look the program over, put the materials out, and start the class using them with instructions such as: "Everyone choose a book and answer the questions on the Survey Card and the Vocabulary Card." Such a procedure will almost surely result in chaos.

The teacher's guide for *The Random House Reading Program* suggests that the program be introduced in several lessons over several days. Lessons include: (1) introducing the program, (2) learning about book cards, and (3) learning how to check one's own answers and keep records.

The lesson for learning about book cards takes up seven pages of the teacher's guide and includes directions on how to use the answer sheet, directions on when to answer the questions on the cards, where to put one's answers, what the purpose of each card is, and how or when to sign up for a conference. How to correct answers and record scores are not taken up until the next lesson. Another lesson is suggested for use several days later to teach the children how to use the skills exercises included in the program.

This kind of detail is typical of lessons for the use of basal reading programs, "packaged" individualized reading programs, programmed instruction, and skills management systems. Such lessons are necessary for the orderly and efficient management of a classroom—but in fact, they are not all the instruction necessary.

In each classroom local rules must be established. Children must learn when they are included in a group receiving direct instruction from the teacher. They must learn how to conduct themselves when they are assigned to work independently or when they are members of a group working independently of the teacher. Children must know what they are supposed to do, where to find materials they will need, what to do with their work when they have finished, whether or not to correct their own work, to whom to go for help, and what to do when they are finished. A variety of problems arise when teachers do not realize how much a student has to understand to make any plan work.

Time on Task Is Diminished. Berliner (1981) describes the "learning student" as one who "works on an academic task that is designed to result in increased knowledge or skills" (p. 218). Assuming that the teacher has planned tasks designed to increase knowledge and skill for all the children, those children who do not know what to do or how to do it are not learning students. They are students whose time is being wasted.

Tranquility of the Classroom Is Diminished. Children who do not know what they are supposed to be doing are likely to engage in behavior that is aimless or disruptive— more often because they are bored than because of malicious intent.

The Teacher's Attention Is Diverted. The benefit of small group and individual instruction is that children are given access to the most scarce commodity in the classroom, the teacher's undivided attention. If the teacher is interrupted by children asking for directions or by disruptive behavior in the classroom, the whole reason for small group instruction and individual conferences is defeated.

In observing classrooms, Harvey (1980) found that in low-achieving classrooms the teachers were frequently interrupted while they were teaching small groups by students who were supposed to be working independently. In the high-achieving classrooms she observed, teachers working with small groups were rarely interrupted by students not in the group: Students working independently understood what they were supposed to be doing, and they understood that the teacher would not tolerate interruption.

The Danger of Busywork

A well-known and often lamented hazard of grouping for instruction is that children who are working independently are sometimes given activities designed to keep them busy rather than activities designed to teach them or give them practice in some newly acquired skill.

One reason this happens is that teachers are attempting to satisfy demands that sometimes come into conflict. They want to choose the best activity to teach the children what they need to learn next, but if a teacher works with groups, some activities must be ones that can be done independently. And sometimes a compromise must be struck between what is the best activity and what can be done without the guidance of the teacher. There are two ways to help ensure that the compromise will result in activities that will teach what the children need to learn next.

Using Teacher's Aides and Student Chairpersons.   One is to use a student or teacher's aide as a stand-in for the teacher in

a group working independently. This will permit a wider choice of activities for groups working independently. Notice that in Figure 11.2 in the second time slot the high group is scheduled to plan a dramatization of a story with a student chairperson or teacher's aide.

However, one should not entertain the notion that groups of students will work together productively because the teacher tells them to or appoints a chairperson. Galton and Simon (1980) suggest that both social and intellectual skills are necessary for groups to work independently of the teacher.

Of primary importance is the children's capacity to challenge each other's contributions, to raise questions and also to reason. These are intellectual skills which can be learned, but of course, they will (or may) not be learned unless teachers regard them as important. Then, for the maintenance of self-sustaining groups, the tasks set need to be structured so as to demand co-operative working, and relevant resources must be provided (Worthington, 1974). Finally, there are certain social skills, for instance a degree of tolerance of each other's idiosyncrasies, a willingness to listen to each other and a certain level of responsible behavior in the absence of an adult; in short, the skills needed to work co-operatively with others on a common task. Such skills, and they are complex, need to be learned, and so taught. (p. 207)

Choosing Materials and Activities from a Coherent Program.   The second way to ensure that independent work is not busywork is to follow suggestions for independent activities from coherent, sequential programs rather than to sample helter-skelter from spirit-duplicated worksheets, workbook pages, and boxes of reading activities. Basal readers and coherent, sequential supplemental reading programs often suggest whole class activities, small group activities, and activities to be done independently.

If these activities are sometimes uninspired, they are at least usually consistent with both the long-term and short-term aims of the reading program. Students working at the appropriate achievement level of such a program are likely to find the suggested independent activities relevant to their small group and whole group lessons and challenging as well.

The Quality of Teacher-Student Interaction

British primary schools have had a longer tradition of individualization of instruction, and nearly exclusive use of individualized instruction is much more frequently found in British schools than in schools in the United States. An important factor in the trend toward individualization of instruction in Great Britain was the Plowden Report (1967), which recommended that primary school children should be involved in more discovery learning (or what the British call "enquiry-based learning") and that the proportion of higher-order cognitive statements and questions on the part of teachers should be increased. The Plowden Report stated that these objectives could best be accomplished by an increase in individualization of instruction and in students working together and learning from one another in small groups.

However, a study of fifty-eight classrooms in nineteen schools over a five-year period (1975–1980) casts doubt on both the question of whether the recommendations of the Plowden Report have been implemented and the assumptions of the report (Galton and Simon, 1980). Two observations regarding the entire sample of classrooms were that (1) "Group-

ing appears to be an organizational or managerial device, rather than a technique for promoting enquiry-based learning using collaborative methods. There was, in fact, little cooperative group work in evidence in our sample" (p. 34), and (2) that "the teacher-pupil interaction process does not appear to have a cognitive content; our data indicate that it is largely managerial or instructional in content, having the function of keeping things moving and assisting individual pupils with the completion of their tasks. Paradoxically, there are more questions and statements of higher cognitive order by the teacher in the whole class situation than in the individualized or group situation" (p. 34). Some of the implications of this study are that teachers should be trained in methods that involve whole classes of students with different levels of ability and in techniques for managing the whole class as a unit.

Whole class and group instruction is *direct* instruction. Ideally, every child is involved with the teacher to some extent, although no child is extensively involved with the teacher. Teachers addressing whole classes or groups may spend more of their time concerned with cognitive, subject-oriented matters, such as letter-sound correspondences or word meanings or comprehension. Whole class instruction and group instruction focuses on characteristics that children have in common rather than on characteristics that differentiate them from one another. Individual instruction forecloses on the opportunity of students to learn from one another and detracts from a sense of community.

There are advantages that are unique to both individualized instruction and group instruction. When teachers use either kind of instruction, they ought to consider not only the advantages they are getting, but the benefits they are forgoing, and attempt to balance the two.

Threats to the Teacher's Leadership Role

Reading programs that emphasize individualization of instruction run the risk of minimizing the role of the teacher as leader, decision maker, and model. The empiricist's preoccupation with identifying minute subskills can lead to individualized teaching plans in which children are expected to teach themselves by working through step-by-step instructional materials. In such a scheme, the teacher may be reduced to paper grader, recordkeeper, and manager of materials. There is little opportunity for the teacher to arouse and nourish a child's curiosity and provide a rich and challenging intellectual environment.

On the other hand, the rationalist assumption that the human mind is an active seeker and organizer of stimuli leads to a fascination with discovery learning. This notion can lead to the assumption that planned learning is somehow undesirable. The teacher may be seen as a classroom manager presiding over largely unplanned discoveries on the part of students. This attitude certainly threatens the teacher's role as leader, planner, and model.

However, the importance of the teacher as leader, planner, and model has been repeatedly reasserted by rationalists, especially those who view language learning primarily as a social process. Dewey (1933), who is often accused of having favored teachers assuming a nondirective role in the classroom, wrote:

In some schools the tendency to minimize the place of the teacher takes the form of supposing that it is an arbitrary imposition for the teacher to propose the line of work to be followed or to arrange the situation within which problems and topics arise. It is held that, out of due respect for the mental freedom of those taught, all suggestions are to come from them. Especially has this idea been applied in some kindergartens and primary grades. The result is often that described in the story of a young child who, on arriving at school, said to the teacher: "Do we have to do today what we want to do?" The alternative to proposals by the teacher is that the suggestions of things to do come from chance, from casual contacts, from what the child saw on his way to school, what he did yesterday, what he sees the next child doing, etc. Since the purpose to be carried out must come, directly or indirectly, from somewhere in the environment, denial to the teacher of the power to propose it merely substitutes accidental contact with some other person or scene for the intelligent planning of the very individual who, if he has a right to be a teacher at all, has the best knowldege of the needs and possibilities of the memebers of the group of which he is a part.

Two of the central themes in Vygotsky's (1962, 1978) views on education and learning are that learning occurs in the zone of proximal development (see Chapter 1) and that the development of "higher functions" are social and cultural in nature. Both themes emphasize the teacher's role as a leader, planner, and model.

The concept of the zone of proximal development supposes that one can specify what is to be learned and that there is an order in what is to be learned, and that the teacher's task is to discover which concepts and tasks the child can deal with only in colloboration with a knowledgeable and skillful adult (a teacher). This presupposes that the reading teacher understands the concepts and tasks involved in reading and how they are ordered.

Second, Vygotsky views learning reading as social and cultural in nature. He sees learning as occuring when a child deals with concepts and accomplishes tasks in partnership with knowledgeable and skillful adults. Once again, the teacher's role as leader and model is crucial. Those who view language learning as a social process do not support a haphazard curriculum where disocvering "what the teacher wants to have discovered" is seen as a bad thing (Kamii, 1973, p. 200).

Advice to the Beginning Teacher

In classrooms one practically never finds a single pattern of organization that does not incorporate some features of other patterns of organization. The basic three-group approach presented in Figures 11.1 and 11.2 is, by design, capable of incorporating each of the organizational patterns and methods discussed in this chapter. Teachers might assign programmed materials to an individual or a group formed to work on a common skill deficit. Groups formed on achievement levels might be given mastery tests from a skills management system and assigned to individual work or to skills deficit instruction groups on the basis of such tests. And an individual reading program may be employed one day a week—or as the mainstay of the program for the group of students whose achievement scores are well above grade level.

On the other hand, each of the individualized approaches described in this chapter recommends group teaching for students who are identified as having common instructional needs. The question for the beginning teacher is whether to start with grouping and work toward individualization where it is indicated, or to start with an individualized program and incorporate group teaching as it is indicated.

If one were to advise beginning teachers to start with an individualized approach, one could legitimately suggest that the teacher choose an individualized reading program or a programmed instruction or skills manage-

ment system based on that teacher's empiricist or rationalist sympathies. However, we do not suggest that a beginning teacher start with an individualized approach, for the following reasons:

Difficulty. The individualized reading program and the skills management system both require knowledge of the reading and learning process and skill in classroom management that one can expect to find only in experienced teachers. Inexperienced teachers who tackle such programs as the mainstay of their reading program run the risk of being overwhelmed by recordkeeping and problems that arise when students find themselves in a classroom where leadership is uncertain and where their responsibilities and prerogatives are unclear.

Boredom. Programmed instruction, on the other hand, is a very easy program for a new teacher to manage. The teacher need only administer the appropriate tests, start each student at the appropriate level in the program, and check on progress from time to time. However, here there are *no* high-level cognitive interactions between teacher and student. Although the content of the program may change, the *procedure* engaged in by the student is the same—frame after frame. Whether those frames are presented on a page or a television screen, monotony must surely ensue, probably much sooner for gregarious, extroverted, highly verbal students than for others. When skills management systems are employed by teachers who are overwhelmed by the details, similar drudgery may result for students, who are given test after test, worksheet after worksheet, workbook page after workbook page.

Learning from Others. Where the class size and energy and expertise of the teacher allow for it, individualized programs employ group teaching and learning so that students can learn from one another, experience membership in a learning community, and become aware of their common characteristics and strengths. However, in a classroom with more than twenty-five students and/or with an inexperienced teacher, individual approaches sometimes do not get beyond their individualized aspects. In such instances, these approaches fail to utilize the social forces that facilitate learning and are therefore not recommended as the sole approach for the beginning teacher.

Although the basic three-group plan shown in Figures 11.1 and 11.2 also requires a great deal of knowledge on the part of the teacher and taxes the beginning teacher's managerial and organizational skills, its flexibility and eclectic nature permit the beginning teacher to start with an organization that is realistic but gives experience in whole class, small group, and individual instruction. As the teacher gains knowledge and experience, he or she can incorporate an individualized reading program approach or a skills management approach and eventually emphasize one of these approaches.

In order to get the best out of small group and individualized instruction, students need to learn a great deal about the mechanics of the program, what they are supposed to be learning, how they are supposed to learn it, and what their responsibilities are to themselves, their small group, and the entire class. In describing teaching styles, Galton and Simon (1980) single out one teacher whom they obviously admire: "As pupils acquired the desired learning habits, the original formal structure was deliberately relaxed, with the pupils taking increased responsibility for planning their own work on an individualized basis" (p. 38).

When teachers are new, one might apply the principle observed here to both teacher and students: As the pupils acquire the desired learning habits and as the teacher acquires more knowledge of the reading and the learning process and acquires the necessary organizational and managerial skills, the original formal structure is deliberately relaxed, with pupils taking an increasing responsibility in consultation with the teacher for their own learning on an individualized basis.

SCHOOLWIDE ARRANGEMENTS TO NARROW INDIVIDUAL DIFFERENCES

Classroom Assignment Strategies

CHILDREN WITH SPECIAL NEEDS

Some children are not placed in regular classrooms or are removed from regular classrooms because they have needs the classroom teacher is not trained to meet or because the regular classroom is not thought to be the best place to meet their needs. Children who score exceptionally low on achievement tests in reading or children who are observed by teachers to exhibit extraordinary difficulty in learning are sometimes placed in special classrooms or removed from regular classrooms for reading instruction.

There are also comparatively rare cases of children who have been diagnosed as schizophrenic or autistic or who are blind or profoundly deaf. Such children are often assigned to special classrooms with teachers prepared to meet their needs, or they are assigned to special reading teachers when they are members of regular classrooms.

HOMOGENEOUS CLASSROOMS

In larger schools, where there is more than one classroom for each grade, students are sometimes assigned to classrooms on the basis of scores on standardized tests. For example, if there are sixty third-graders, they may be ranked from high to low on the basis of standardized reading test scores. The twenty children with the highest scores are assigned to one classroom, the next twenty to a second classroom, and the next twenty to a third classroom.

HOMOGENEOUS READING CLASSES

A variation on homogeneous classroom assignment is to have an entire school have reading during the same time period and to have children leave their regular classroom and report to a reading classroom for instruction. This permits one to group by achievement scores across grade level as well as within grade.

For example, in a school that has kindergarten through grade 6, with approximately thirty children per grade, the ninety children in grades 1, 2, and 3 are ranked from high to low on the basis of a standardized reading test. The thirty children with the highest scores are assigned to one classroom, the next thirty to a second classroom, and the next thirty to a third classroom. The same procedure is followed in assigning students to reading classes in grades 4, 5, and 6.

Advantages of Narrowing the Range of Achievement

Narrowing the range of achievement within reading classes through schoolwide arrangements may permit more whole class in-struction and may require fewer groups based on achievement within classrooms. Each classroom may still have a range of achievement scores, but it may be necessary to use only two levels of a program rather than three. Or using three levels may more truly accommodate the range of levels than when these efforts are not made.

When there is a reduced demand for grouping to accommodate different levels of achievement, teachers can devote their energy and organizational skills to grouping for activities that demand small groups for efficiency and to grouping children on the basis of needs and interests.

Problems

FLEXIBILITY

One of the great dangers of all grouping is that children may not be moved from group to group based on performance and need as readily as one would hope. The processes that impede easy movement from group to group within a classroom are exaggerated when the school administration must be involved in the transfer.

THE MYTH OF HOMOGENEITY

Children with the same score on an achievement test may have very different strengths and weaknesses in areas measured by the achievement tests. Children who have the same number of correct responses on a test have not necessarily responded correctly to the same items. Furthermore, there is no reason to believe that children with the same scores on an achievement test are at all similar in areas not measured by the test. Where students are grouped by achievement, teachers sometimes adopt the false notion that the children are the same in every way, and efforts at grouping on needs and interest are diminshed rather than increased.

TRACKING

Segregating high achievers from low achievers may have some very undesirable effects. Being placed in low achievement groups has been shown to have a negative effect on children's self-esteem (Esposito, 1973). Furthermore, identifying children as slow learners and then segregating them from other students may contribute to a self-fulfilling prophecy. This problem is made worse by the fact that school failure is related to economic status. It has been suggested that grouping by achievement segregates economically disadvantaged children and contributes to segregation within society based on income (McDermott, 1977).

THE IRONIC EFFECTS OF ONE EFFORT TO HELP CHILDREN SUFFERING FROM POVERTY

In 1978, a researcher was observing in a classroom in a city where the schools had been integrated through busing. The school was located near a public housing project populated by black families having incomes below the poverty line. To achieve racial balance, white students were bused in from more affluent areas of the city.

There were several federally funded programs in the school for students who were both poverty-stricken and had achieved below grade level in reading and arithmetic. These children were removed from the classroom for "extra" instruction. As a result, of this class of twenty-seven students, there were only twenty students left in the classroom. It was the more able and economically advantaged students who were "left behind" with a very hard-working teacher.

Since the observer did not follow the children who left the room, she could not comment on the quality of the experience they had with their special teachers; but she noted that the federal funds directed at improving the performance of poor chil-

dren had in fact created a superior learning environment for the economically advantaged children in this classroom (M. E. Finn, 1978).

OBSCURING RESPONSIBILITY FOR READING INSTRUCTION

Several of the schoolwide plans to group children by ability involve removing a child from the regular classroom for reading instruction. Therefore, for most of the day the child is in a classroom with a teacher who is not his or her reading teacher. This encourages the teacher who has the major responsibility for the child to feel that he or she is not responsible for the child's reading performance.

This may be a particularly bad situation when low achievers are removed from their classrooms to work with remedial reading teachers alone or in small groups. The children's classroom teacher may feel he or she is not responsible for their reading performance, but at the same time the remedial reading teacher may see as many as sixty students during a week and feel that he or she is supplying *extra* instruction and that the classroom teacher bears the primary responsibility for reading performance. This difficulty was cited as one of several reasons why federal programs to improve the education of inner-city school children have met with limited success (Levine, 1982).

COMPETING IDEALS: OBLITERATING VERSUS ACCENTUATING DIFFERENCES IN ACHIEVEMENT

Two quite contrary aims of individualization and grouping for instruction have been discussed in Chapter 10 and in this chapter. On the one hand, in the section on mastery learning in Chapter 10, the idea was expressed that if the objectives of a reading program were sequential skills that are limited in number, one should be able to keep all the children in the class at the same level of achievement by providing extra time and instruction for children who require it. It is implied that the purpose of grouping and individualized instruction is to obliterate differences in achievement that arise as a result of differences in aptitude and previous achievement.

In this chapter the idea has been expressed repeatedly that the purpose of individualization is to avoid giving the most able students learning tasks they have already mastered and thereby to accelerate their progress and to avoid giving the least able students learning tasks beyond their level of achievement. Since the very able and the least able are presumed to have different rates of learning, and since the time devoted to learning is presumed to be the same for both groups, it would follow that differences in achievement will be accentuated through individualized instruction.

This aim of individualized instruction is reflected in many textbooks on reading instruction. For example, Farr and Roser (1979) say that "Given appropriate instruction, the range of differences within each classroom should broaden as time goes by" (p. 371). Stauffer, Abrams, and Pikulsky (1978) say, "Every teacher knows, too, that 'good teaching increases individual differences'" (p. 358).

It has been pointed out before that achievement levels are related to social, cultural, and economic differences in children. McDermott (1977) states flatly:

Almost invariably, such problems [school failure] arise when a group in power educates the children from a minority group. The picture is quite uniform. Indian children throughout North and South America fail, Mexican children in American Anglo schools fail, African children in Western colonial schools fail, Oriental Jews
in European Israeli schools fail, black children in American schools fail, and so on. (p. 176)

When considered in this context, the question of whether the differentiating instruction results in diminishing differences in achievement or increasing differences in achievement takes on social, economic, and political implications.

It is clear that if either of these ideals is pursued exclusively, it will be to the detriment of either the most able or the least able students. Teachers who understand the tension between these ideals are in a better position to accommodate the needs of all their students than teachers who, through lack of reflection, see both ideals as desirable and do not see that they are contradictory.

SUMMARY

There are two reasons why grouping is a common practice in teaching reading. (1) Some of the lessons that are necessary or desirable in teaching reading cannot be conducted efficiently with groups as large as the whole class. (2) Students differ in many respects; appropriate objectives, methods and materials for some students may be inappropriate for others. Some differences that are considered in grouping for reading instruction are rate of learning, auditory and visual acuity, reading achievement, skills deficits, and interests.

Figures 11.1 and 11.2 are examples of the most widely used organizational plans for teaching reading. Permanent groups are based primarily on general achievement levels; temporary groups are formed on the basis of skills deficits and special interests. When such plans are successful, movement between groups is easily accomplished, and temporary groups are easily established and dissolved. Whole class activities and independent activities are regularly occurring features of this plan.

Usually, a basal reading series provides the mainstay of the program for the three-group plan. Such programs are usually eclectic—that is, they rely on empiricist assumptions for some lessons and rationalist assumptions for others; they do not dogmatically insist on one set of assumptions or dogmatically reject one set of assumptions.

Individualized instruction is used to some extent in the basic three-group classroom organization; however, some organizational plans are based primarily on individual instruction. In the individualized reading program, students choose books that interest them. In conferences with the teacher, their skills are assessed and they are assigned to groups for instruction or are assigned individual work. The whole class comes together regularly for sharing. The individualized reading program is based on rationalist, top-down notions of how one learns to read. This approach demands extraordinary skills in diagnosis of difficulties, lesson planning, and classroom management. An extensive classroom library is necessary, and the teacher must be familiar with dozens of books.

Several "packaged" individual reading programs are available that represent a compromise between a completely open-ended program and the more structured methods typical of classrooms where basal reading programs are the mainstay of the program.

Programmed instruction is based on empiricist, bottom-up notions dealing with specified skills in a specified order. In linear programmed instruction, the student progresses from frame to frame, answering questions, correcting the answers, and presumably learning one fact or skill after another which add up to proficient reading. This may be categorized

more accurately as independent rather than individualized instruction because every child covers every step. In branching programmed instruction, each child does not cover every frame. On the basis of answers to test questions and success in answering in the frames as they are presented, the student progresses to frames deemed appropriate to him or her as an individual. Computerized branching programmed instruction will no doubt receive a great deal of attention in the near future.

In skills management systems, the reading process is divided into elements that are in turn divided into skills and subskills categorized by order of difficulty. Tests are devised to determine whether a student has mastered each skill at each level. Through administering these tests, learning objectives are determined for the individual. Students are brought into groups for instruction based on common learning objectives. Lessons are planned for groups using a resource file. This approach demands extraordinary skill in classroom management. It requires a prodigious amount of test administration, correcting, and record-keeping.

All attempts to individualize or to group for instruction result in a situation where individual students must work without the immediate supervision and guidance of the teacher. This means that a great deal of attention must be given to establishing orderly, efficient, and effective classroom procedures and teaching students to operate within them. Failure to do this leads to disorder and an inefficient learning environment.

While teachers are working with small groups or individuals, students outside the teacher's immediate supervision must be kept occupied. Unfortunately, this often leads to assigning tasks (often in the form of spirit duplicate sheets or workbook pages) for the purpose of keeping students busy rather than to accomplish any clearly thought-out learning objective. The use of teacher's aides or student leaders gives the teacher a wider choice of activities to assign to students working independently. However, teacher's aides and students must be trained to work in groups. Choosing materials for individuals and groups working independently of the teacher from a coherent program reduces the danger that children will be assigned tasks whose primary objective is to keep them busy.

Although it is frequently assumed that individual instruction results in a higher quality of teacher-student interaction, this is not necessarily the case. Teacher-student interaction in some individual instruction programs tends to center around what page the child should "do" next and where he should put his answer sheet. Teachers sometimes engage in more questions and statements of a higher order when addressing the whole class than when addressing either individuals or small groups.

It is often assumed that working in small groups permits children to learn from one another in ways that are not possible in large groups. However, small groups are often treated no differently than large groups, and students are offered no opportunities for learning that are notably different from those offered in large groups. Students need to be taught how to generate learning objectives and pursue them cooperatively in small groups.

Individualized programs based on rationalist, top-down assumptions sometimes become so focused on the discovery aspects of learning that the teacher's role *as teacher* is neglected. The teacher is the one person in the learning community who presumably understands the whole process and is aware of the long-term objectives. Therefore, the teacher should exercise leadership and direct the objectives and curriculum from day to day. In fact, progressive educators such as Dewey and advocates of the rationalist model of learning and teaching such as Vygotsky stress the role of the teacher as leader and decision maker in the classroom.

Individualized programs based on empiricist, bottom-up assumptions can reduce the role of the teacher to one of manager and recordkeeper. The goal expressed by authors of such programs is, however, to free the teacher and help him or her manage instruction so that he or she is able to *teach* individuals or small groups precisely what they need to learn.

Because of the demands of programs that emphasize individual instruction, it is probably advisable for beginning teachers to work toward a standard three-group approach and to incorporate an individualized program into their repertoire, if they are so inclined, as they gain skill and experience.

Schoolwide arrangements designed to narrow the range of differences within reading classes include: (1) setting up special classes for students who have extremely low learning aptitudes or severe physical difficulties such as deafness or blindness; (2) assigning children to classrooms on the basis of reading scores; or (3) grouping children across grade levels by reading achievement scores during a special time slot designated for reading instruction. The obvious advantage of such schemes is that when there is a narrower range of achievement in a class, the teacher stands a better chance of being able to cater to individual needs.

Negative aspects of schoolwide grouping by achievement levels include: (1) the increased difficulty of changing a child's group assignment; (2) the inclination of some teachers to feel there is *less* necessity to attend to individual needs when a classroom is "homogeneously" grouped; (3) segregation of high achievers from low achievers; and (4) the perception of many classroom teachers that if a child is taught by another teacher, the child's reading performance is not the classroom teacher's responsibility.

Individualized instruction may lead to narrowing the achievement gap between students in a classroom if efforts are directed toward improving the achievement of the poorest performers. On the other hand, individualized instruction can increase the range of achievement if the most able students are segregated from poorer students and given every resource for further improvement. Teachers sometimes strive for both goals without reflecting on the contradiction between them. Since achievement is related to the economic status of the family of the child, where the schools concentrate their resources becomes a question with social and political ramifications.

FOR FURTHER READING AND DISCUSSION

Choose a particular grade level. Examine the following programs at that grade level and answer the questions following the citations.

These kinds of materials are often not found in the regular collections of college or university libraries. You may find them in Resource Centers in university and college libraries, education departments in colleges and universities, or school districts.

Basal Readers

Choose one eclectic basal reader and one phonics-emphasis basal reader from the list in Chapter 7.

Programmed Instruction

Buchanan, C. D., and Sullivan Associates, *Programmed Reading.* St. Louis: Webster Division of McGraw-Hill, 1973.

Individualized Reading Programs

Barrett, F. L., D. Holdaway, and P. Lynch. *The Three I's Program.* Richmond Hill, Ontario: Scholastic-TAB Publications, 1983.

Cochran, E., D. Coleman, A. Cortright, D. Forman, and E. Reid. *Random House Reading Program.* New York: Random House, 1970.

Lynch, P. *Individual Reading from Scholastic.* New York: Scholastic, 1969.

Skills Management Systems

Prescriptive Reading Inventory. Monterey, CA: CTB/McGraw-Hill, 1972.

Fountain Valley Teacher Support System In Reading. Fountain Valley, CA: Richard L. Zweig Associates, 1971.

Otto, W., and E. Askov. *The Wisconsin Design for Reading Skill Development.* Madison, WI: Learning Multi-Systems, Inc. 1973.

Questions for Discussion

1. What are the assumptions—empiricist, rationalist, or eclectic?

2. How much attention is given to whole group, small group, and individualized instruction?

3. What provisions are made for low achievers? For high achievers?

4. If you were an experienced teacher with unlimited resources, which would you choose?

5. If you were an inexperienced teacher or a teacher with limited resources, which program would you choose?

6. If your choice of program is different for the two previous questions, what considerations led to these different choices?
   a. What would you want to learn as you moved from one program to the other?
   b. What kind of resources would you want to pursue?

REFERENCES

Berliner, D. C. Academic learning time and reading achievement. In J. T. Guthrie (ed.), *Comprehension and Teaching: Research Reviews.* Newark, DE: International Reading Association, 1981, 203–226.

Buchanan, C. D., and Sullivan Associates. *Programmed Reading, Book 6,* 3rd ed. St. Louis: Webster Division of McGraw-Hill, 1973.

Carner, R. L. Reading forum. *Reading News,* 2 (August 1973).

Cochran, E., D. Coleman, A. Cortright, D. Forman, and E. Reid. *Random House Reading Progam.* New York: Random House, 1970.

Dewey, J. *How We Think.* Boston: D. C. Heath, 1933.

Esposito, D. Homogeneous and heterogeneous ability grouping: Principal findings and implications for evaluating and designing more effective educational environments. *Review of Educational Research,* 43 (Spring 1973): 163–79.

Farr, R., and N. Roser. *Teaching a Child to Read.* New York: Harcourt Brace Jovanovich, 1979.

Finn, M. E. Personal communication. 1978.

Fountain Valley Teacher Support System In Reading. Fountain Valley, CA: Richard L. Zweig Associates, 1971.

Galton, M., and B. Simon. Effective teaching in the primary classroom. In M. Galton and B. Simon (eds.), *Progress and Performance in the Primary Classroom.* London: Routledge and Kegan Paul, 1980, 179–212.

Harris, A. J., and E. R. Sipay. *How to Increase Reading Ability,* 6th ed. New York: David McKay, 1975.

Harvey, M. R. Public school treatment of low-income children: Education for passivity. *Urban Education,* 15 (October 1980): 279–323.

Kamii, C. Pedagogical principles derived from Piaget's theory: Relevance from educational practice. In M. Schwebel and J. Ralph, *Piaget in the Classroom.* New York: Basic Books, 1973.

Kozol, J. *Free Schools,* rev. ed. New York: Bantam Books, 1972.

Levine, D. U. Successful approaches for improving academic achievement in inner-city elementary schools. *Phi Delta Kappan* (April 1982): 523–526.

McDermott, R. P. The ethnography of speaking and reading. In R. W. Shuy (ed.), *Linguistic Theory: What Can It Say About Reading.* Newark, DE: International Reading Association, 1977.

Otto, W., and E. Askov. *The Wisconsin Design for Reading Skill Development.* Madison, WI: Learning Multi-Systems, 1973.

Otto, W., R. Rude, and D. L. Spiegel. *How to Teach Reading.* Reading, MA: Addison-Wesley, 1979.

Plowden Report. *Children and Their Primary Schools.* Report of the Central Advisory Council for Education in England. London: HMSO, 1967.

Prescriptive Reading Inventory. Monterey, CA: CTB/McGraw-Hill, 1972.

Schmidt, G. N. Chicago mastery reading: A case against a skills-based reading curriculum. *Learning* (November 1982): 37–40.

Simon, B., and M. Galton. Research in the primary classroom. In M. Galton and B. Simon (eds.), *Progress and Performance in the Primary Classroom.* London: Routledge and Kegan Paul, 1980, 5–42.

Southgate, V. Language arts in informal British primary schools. *The Reading Teacher,* 26 (January 1973): 367–373.

Stauffer, R. G., J. C. Abrams, and J. J. Pikulski, *Diagnosis. Correction, and Prevention of Reading Disabilities.* New York: Harper & Row, 1978.

Veatch, J. *Reading in the Elementary School.* 2nd ed. New York: John Wiley & Sons, 1978.

Vygotsky, L. S. *Mind in Society.* Cambridge, MA: Harvard University Press, 1978.

———. *Thought and Language.* Cambridge, MA: MIT Press, 1962.

Worthington, F. A theoretical and empirical study of small group work in schools. Unpublished Ph.D. thesis, University of Leicester (England), 1974.

CHAPTER 12

ASSESSMENT OF READING ACHIEVEMENT AND TEACHING READING

CHARACTERISTICS ALL TESTS MUST POSSESS

Validity
Reliability

EVALUATING PUBLISHERS' CLAIMS

ASSESSMENT METHODS DETERMINED BY PURPOSE

STANDARDIZED READING ACHIEVEMENT TESTS

Characteristics of Standardized Reading
Achievement Tests

PUBLISHED
STANDARDIZED ADMINISTRATION
PROCEDURES
NORM-REFERENCED
GROUP ADMINISTERED
SURVEY FORMAT

Individually Administered Tests

FORMATIVE EVALUATION

The Informal Reading Inventory

HOW AN INFORMAL READING INVENTORY
WORKS
FUNCTIONAL LEVELS OF READING

CREATING AN INFORMAL READING
INVENTORY
ADMINISTERING AN INFORMAL READING
INVENTORY
DETERMINING FUNCTIONAL LEVELS
DISCOVERING DIFFICULTIES
IMPORTANCE OF THE TEACHER'S SKILL
STRENGTHS AND WEAKNESSES
STEPS TOWARD PROFICIENCY

Standardized Individual Diagnostic Tests

DURRELL ANALYSIS OF READING
DIFFICULTIES
OTHER STANDARDIZED INDIVIDUAL TESTS

Standardized Group Diagnostic Tests
Criterion-Referenced Testing

THE EMPIRICIST TRADITION
THE RATIONALIST TRADITION
TWO ASSUMPTIONS OF CRITERION-
REFERENCED TESTING

Standardized Achievement Tests and
Formative Evaluation

SUMMARY

FOR FURTHER READING AND DISCUSSION

REFERENCES

This chapter is on assessment, but the reader may be aware that assessment has been discussed repeatedly in this book in connection with other topics. The question of readiness (Chapter 2) is a question of assessment. A teacher decides when a child is ready to learn to read by assessing the child in terms of some concept of what learning to read entails. The chapters on word recognition (Chapters 3–7) and comprehension (Chapters 8–9) addressed questions of what one teaches when one teaches reading and how one teaches reading. But the interplay between what the child needs to know and do and what he or she does know and can do repeatedly returned the discussion to assessing the child in terms of some concept of what reading entails.

The intellectual, perceptual, neurological, and emotional differences that may have a bearing on how one should teach a child to read were discussed in Chapter 10. Here again the discussion turned to assessment. It was pointed out, in fact, that there is an enormous amount of activity among researchers and teachers devoted to assessing students in terms of these differences and not enough devoted to discovering how to teach exceptional children to read. Finally, in the discussion of reading programs and grouping for instruction in Chapter 11, the question is always one of defining what the process of learning to read entails and what the best way to help students acquire that process is. The next step is to assess each student's progress so that instruction will result in growth for each individual.

The need to assess reading achievement appears in every phase of teaching reading. In this chapter we will focus on the things teachers should know about assessment and discuss some of the problems we face when we attempt to test achievement and to interpret the results of achievement tests.

CHARACTERISTICS ALL TESTS MUST POSSESS

Validity

In Chapter 2 we cautioned against assuming that one knows what a test measures because of the test name. If a test is named a reading test, it is no guarantee that it is a test of reading. For example, many people are not convinced that the ability to look at a list of words and say them is a test of reading, although that is precisely what some "tests of reading" consist of (the reading test of the Wide Range Achievement Test, for example). If one is convinced that a test measures what its authors claim it measures, the test is said to be *valid*.

Face Validity. A reasonable way for a person to determine validity is to obtain a copy of the test, look at it (perhaps administer it to a child or take it oneself), and decide whether one believes the test is a valid measure of what it is alleged to measure. To argue that reasonable and informed people would be convinced of a test's validity by this procedure is to argue that the test has *face validity*. However, face validity is a somewhat subjective concept. Reasonable and informed people are liable to disagree on whether a test is valid.

Content Validity. Test publishers often attempt to establish the validity of a test with reasoned arguments. For example, authors may describe how the items on a test were derived from objectives stated in reading curriculum guides published by state departments of education and city school districts. Or authors may attempt to show that items on their test are related to objectives stated in basal reading series and other published reading programs. Such arguments attempt to establish *content validity.*

Concurrent Validity. Authors sometimes show that students who score high (or low) on their test also score high (or low) on other tests that are widely acknowledged to be valid measures of reading ability. Or they ask teachers to rate students as good readers or poor readers. If the students identified as good readers obtain high scores and the students identified as poor readers obtain poor scores on a test, the test author may use this fact to convince users that the test is a valid measure of reading achievement. This kind of argument is referred to as evidence of *concurrent validity.*

Other techniques have been devised to establish validity; the reader may want to refer to the discussion of *predictive validity* in Chapter 2.

Reliability

If a fifth-grade student took a twelve-item test in the morning and answered eight questions correctly, what would one guess the student's score would be if she took the test in the afternoon of the same day? It seems reasonable that she would score 8. She may, however, have made some mistakes on one or both tests, and she may have made some lucky guesses. Therefore, one might guess that the student would score *around* 8. This guess is based on the assumption that the test is a *reliable* measure of a skill the child possesses to some degree, and that the degree to which the child possesses the skill will not change significantly over a short time. In the language of testing, one would say the test is *reliable.*

On the other hand, one would be very surprised if the student scored 8 on one performance and 3 (or 12) on the other. If one could presume that the student made a serious effort on both attempts and that the conditions under which the test was taken were the same, one would conclude that something was very wrong. The test does not appear to be a reliable measure of what it is thought to measure. In the language of testing, one would say the test is *unreliable.* There is no point in giving such a test, because one cannot trust the score. Administering an unreliable test is worse than pointless because people tend to put great faith (or *reliance*) in test scores.

Test-Retest Reliability. Of course, one cannot assume that a test is reliable or unreliable on the basis of the performance of one child. Tests are administered to many students on two separate occasions, not too distant in time, and the results are examined for evidence that each student's score remains approximately the same. Because other influences (mistakes, luck, effort) enter into test scores, one cannot expect a perfect match.

A statistical procedure known as *correlation* is done on the results of the two tests. If the students' scores remain approximately the same, the *correlation coefficient* will be high. (Positive correlations can vary from .00 to .99.) If the students' scores fluctuate a great deal, the correlation coefficient will be very low. This procedure is known as *test-retest reliability,* and it is expressed in terms of a correlation coefficient. Experts agree that test-retest reliability of less than .80 is cause for serious concern (Diederich, 1974, for example).

There are other aspects of testing where reliability is an important factor. Three additional kinds of reliability are often established for standardized tests.

Internal Consistency or Split-Half Reliability. If a test has many items, one presumes that every item is about as valid and about as reliable as every other; that is, one presumes the test is internally consistent as a measuring instrument. This is called *internal-consistency reliability* or *split-half reliability*. "Split-half" refers to the statistical technique used to establish internal-consistency reliability.

Alternate Form Reliability. Standardized tests are often published in two or more equivalent forms. For example, the Gates-MacGinitie Reading Test, Level A, appears in two forms, 1 and 2. A student should earn the same derived scores (grade equivalent score, percentile, and so on) on one form of a standardized test as he or she would earn if he or she took an equivalent form. This is *alternate-form reliability.*

Inter-Rater Reliability. Two or more persons grading the same test should arrive at the same score. This is called *inter-rater reliability.* Inter-rater reliability is rarely an issue in standardized testing because standardized tests are typically multiple-choice, machine-scorable tests. Inter-rater reliability becomes an issue in assessment procedures that rely on observation of behaviors which are less rigidly controlled than responses on multiple-choice, paper and pencil tests.

EVALUATING PUBLISHERS' CLAIMS

One expects that the authors of published tests will attempt to establish the validity and reliability of the test and report the data in the user's manual. The data are often missing. When they are missing, one suspects that the data, if reported, would not establish the test's validity and reliability. Sometimes these data are supplied, but if properly interpreted, fail to establish the test's validity and reliability.

Since this is a very technical and specialized field, it is advisable to look at reviews of tests by experts to determine whether the test is satisfactory in terms of validity and reliability. A standard reference for reviews is Buros' *Mental Measurements Yearbook* (1978). Salvia and Ysseldyke (1981) is another valuable source for reviews of standardized tests of reading achievement.

ASSESSMENT METHODS DETERMINED BY PURPOSE

There are many purposes for evaluating students, and there are many ways of conducting assessments. The method of assessment should be chosen to fit the purpose. Three kinds of questions lead to assessment: teachers' questions, parents' questions, and questions asked by school officials and public policymakers. One way of determining the purpose of assessment is to determine what question is being asked and who is asking it.

Teachers' Questions. When a teacher engages in assessment as part of teaching strategy, the relevant question is, "What does the child know, and what can he or she do?" The teacher wants the answer to this question to be able to answer the next question: "What does the child need to learn next?"

The kind of assessment that follows from teachers' questions has often been called *diagnostic* assessment or *formative evaluation* (Bloom et al., 1971). This kind of assessment will be taken up in the second half of this chapter.

Parents' Questions. Although parents are often interested in formative evaluation and the questions that lead to it, they are usually interested in a further question: "What does my child know, or how does he or she perform *in comparison with what the teacher expects?*"

The teacher's expectations of the child depend on (a) the child's individual characteristics, (b) the child's general achievement in reading as compared with others in the grade, and (c) the child's progress in achieving the learning objectives that grow out of diagnostic assessment. Assessment of children's individual characteristics was taken up in Chapter 10. Assessment of children's general reading achievement and diagnostic assessment are taken up in this chapter.

Policymakers' and School Administrators' Questions. Those elected to school boards, education departments, legislative bodies, and so on, are responsible to the general public for money spent on education, and they are responsible to their constituents for the education of their children. Such individuals ask the question, "How well are the students in my charge (or the students among my constituents) learning to read?" This question does not seek information on what children know in an absolute sense; it seeks an evaluation in a comparative sense: "What do these children know compared to others the same age or in the same grade?"

School administrators and supervisors are sometimes interested in the same information for the same reasons. They are also often interested in individual students' reading achievement for purposes of placing students in classes, whether regular classes or special classes. But the question once again is not what individuals know in an absolute sense, but what individuals know in comparison to other children. This kind of question is best addressed by what are known as standardized tests of reading achievement.

In a sense, the assessment yielded by standardized tests of reading achievement is the least interesting and the least useful to teachers. It does not determine precisely what a child knows, what a child needs to learn next, nor how to teach a child what he or she needs to learn next. However, many concepts and issues essential to proper assessment are most easily introduced in connection with standardized tests of reading achievement.

STANDARDIZED READING ACHIEVEMENT TESTS

Interest in educational measurement in the last half-century has given rise to an enormous technology of test construction and interpretation. This technology has produced reading achievement tests that possess the following characteristics: They are published, standardized, norm-referenced, group administered, survey tests of reading. These characteristics are defined and discussed below.

♦ Several widely used standardized group survey tests of reading achievement are the Gates-MacGinitie Reading Tests, the Metropolitan Reading Tests, and the reading sections from the California Achievement Tests and the Iowa Test of Basic Skills. It would be useful to obtain copies of one or more of these tests together with the manuals for administering and interpreting the scores and to examine them in terms of the characteristics described here.

Characteristics of Standardized Reading Achievement Tests

PUBLISHED

Standardized group survey tests are published—that is, they are not teacher-made tests. Several of the characteristics of these tests demand technical and financial resources that prohibit their construction by individual teachers.

STANDARDIZED ADMINISTRATION PROCEDURES

Directions are explicit, clear, and workable. Typically the administration procedures are field-tested in an effort to ensure that every child taking the test will take it under as nearly the same conditions as every other child. Answer sheets are supplied so that every child will record answers in the same way.

The directions are *read* by the teacher from the manual, and limitations on the amount and kind of help the teacher can offer are delineated. The amount of time permitted in taking the test is explicitly stated. Suggestions are offered to ensure that the test will be administered in a well-lighted, comfortable, distraction-free setting.

NORM-REFERENCED

In the course of preparing these tests for publication, they are given to large numbers of students who are chosen to represent the kinds of students for whom the test is designed; that is, if the test is designed to be used throughout the nation for pupils in grades 4, 5, and 6, it is administered to large numbers of students throughout the nation in grades 4, 5, and 6 before the test is published. These students are chosen to represent all children in this category—rich and poor; boys and girls; urban, suburban, and rural; high, medium, and low ability; white, black, Chicano. This group is referred to as the *normative group.*

Statistics are gathered to describe the test performance of the normative group. Based on

these data, tables are provided with the tests that enable a teacher to interpret a child's score on the test in terms of how it compares with the scores of children in the normative group. For example, one may discover that a score of 46 correct on the test compares with the average score of the children in the normative sample who are in the fifth month of fourth grade. One would interpret the child's score as a *grade-equivalent score* of 4.5 (fourth grade, fifth month). All scores possible on the test can be converted to a grade equivalent score using the tables in the user's manual accompanying the test.

Using the same procedure, tables are often devised and published that enable one to convert scores to *age-equivalent scores.* If a child's age-equivalent score is 9.1, for example, it means that the score that child made on the test compares with the average score of children in the normative sample who were 9 years, 1 month old.

Using statistical descriptions of the test performance of the normative sample, tables of *percentile equivalents* are often provided also. If a child is in sixth grade, for example, and his or her score places him or her in the 86th percentile, it means that of all sixth-graders represented by the normative group, one would expect 85 percent to score below that child and 14 percent to score above.

Students' performance can be compared to the performance of the normative group in other ways. The concepts of *standard score* and *stanine* are often used for this purpose. Readers who are interested will find references in the For Further Reading section at the end of this chapter that explain these concepts fully.

Grade-equivalent scores, age-equivalent scores, percentile rankings, and standard scores are all called *derived scores;* that is, the number correct (called the *observed* or the *raw* score) is converted to a score that compares an individual's test performance with the performance of the normative group. Such tests are called *norm-referenced tests.*

When a test is said to be *standardized,* one presumes that it is both norm-referenced and that the administration procedures are explicit, clear, and workable. The rules and conditions under which the test is administered must match the rules and conditions under which the normative group took the test; otherwise comparison between a child's score and the scores of the normative group are meaningless.

GROUP ADMINISTERED

These tests are designed to be administered in groups. They are sometimes referred to as pencil and paper tests because the child's responses are recorded by that child individually with a pencil (as opposed to an oral response or gesture that would require individual attention by the person administering the test).

SURVEY FORMAT

These tests usually yield a single derived score (grade equivalent, age equivalent, or percentile). This score is interpreted as an estimate of the child's global reading ability; for this reason, the tests are referred to as *survey* tests.

Many survey tests do have separate vocabulary and comprehension tests that yield separate scores. Some yield other subtest scores, such as speed of reading. Although publishers sometimes suggest that these tests are useful in formative or diagnostic evaluation, there is little support for this claim.

Individually Administered Tests

For the purposes of comparing a group of students to a normative group (the kind of as-

sessment policymakers and administrators frequently wish to have), carefully administered standardized group survey tests of reading are perfectly adequate. However, when the purpose of an achievement test is to place students in classes, particularly special classes, the results of a standardized group survey test should be verified by an individually administered reading achievement test. Some state regulations require that certain placement decisions be based on individually administered tests.

Two well-known individually administered reading achievement tests are the reading subtests of the Peabody Individual Achievement Test and the Wide Range Achievement Test. Salvia and Ysseldyke (1981) find the standardization of the Wide Range Achievement Test to be inadequate and are not satisfied with the validity or reliability data reported in the 1978 manual (p. 176). These authors also believe that the reading subtests of the Peabody Individual Achievement Test are not reliable enough for making important educational decisions (p. 174). However, these tests are often used to verify the results of more reliable group-administered standardized reading achievement tests—particularly when individualized testing is required by law.

When the purpose of testing is to compare students' (or a student's) performance with the performance of other students, standardized reading achievement tests are appropriate. Standardized achievement tests are the product of many years of highly technical development.

In choosing a standardized test of reading achievement, one should check the user's manual for evidence that the normative group is appropriate for the children (or child) to be tested and for evidence that the test is valid and reliable. It is advisable to read reviews written by experts as well.

FORMATIVE EVALUATION

Teachers typically engage in assessment to find out precisely what a child knows and what the child can do. The purpose of such assessment is to enable the teacher to decide what to teach next. This has been described as formative evaluation. Standardized tests of reading achievement are not designed for this. Three kinds of assessment procedures that have been developed for this purpose are the informal reading inventory, diagnostic tests, and criterion-referenced tests.

The Informal Reading Inventory

A 1923 textbook entitled *The Teaching of Reading* (Wheat, 1923) offers the following advice:

Upon taking charge of the instruction in reading of a grade or group of grades, the teacher should proceed immediately to the task of determining the standing of each pupil in the subject. The teacher should know first of all how well each pupil can read orally and how well silently. The reading periods of the first week of school may very well be spent in giving tests in the two kinds of reading, though the pupils do not need to be made aware of the fact that they are being "tested." The work of testing may proceed as follows:

In oral reading: *For the pupils of each grade choose three paragraphs for oral reading—one from their reader of two years ago, one from last year's reader, and one from their reader of this year. The first paragraph should ve bery easy; the second, easy; and the third, of average difficulty. Test the pupils individually in a quiet place where they will be free from distraction and where the remainder of the pupils to be tested*

will not hear the reading. When everything is in readiness show the first paragraph to the pupil and say: "I should like you to read this paragraph for me. If you should find some hard words, read them as best you can without help and continue reading. Begin when I say 'Begin.'" Hand him the book and say "Begin." When the pupil has finished show him the next paragraph, and so on. Keep a record of the time taken to read each paragraph and of the number and kinds of errors. (Wheat, 1923, quoted in Beldin, 1970)

Wheat's sound advice, however, raises many questions, some of which are left unanswered. How does one choose the passages? How long should the passages be? How does one decide how well a pupil can read orally and silently? Is one oral reading error permissible? Two? Three? What is an oral reading error? How does one test silent reading? What is the point of noting the amount of time it takes to read a passage? Given today's wide range of reading ability within a classroom, is testing materials from "their reader of two years ago" and then "last year's reader" enough? Should every child start the test on the same level when the teacher has evidence that some students have much more ability than others?

Perhaps the most basic questions are these: What is meant by a pupil's "standing"? What does one look for in terms of strengths and weaknesses? By what criteria does one determine a pupil's standing? And finally, what does one do with the information gathered in this process?

Some of the most illustrious people in the field of teaching reading in the past half-century (Edward L. Thorndike, 1934; Arthur Gates, 1936; Emmett Betts, 1936; and Donald Durrell, 1937) have experimented with, written about, and made recommendations about this process, which Durrell (1940) called "the best basis for planning instruction" (p. 18).

This process has come to be known as the *informal reading inventory*. More recent contributors to the discussion are Powell (1969 and 1978), Sipay (1964), Johnson and Kress (1965), Pikulski (1974), and Brown (1982).

HOW AN INFORMAL READING INVENTORY WORKS

In an informal reading inventory, the student reads a passage like the one in Figure 12.1 orally and answers comprehension questions about it. Next the student reads a second passage (about the same length and about equally as difficult) silently and answers comprehension questions about that passage. Based on the student's performance, the teacher (a) decides whether the passages are too easy, too difficult, or exactly right for instruction; and (b) records observations that will be used in planning the student's instructional program.

If the passages are determined to be too easy, the student repeats the process on two passages that are more difficult. The process continues until the student encounters passages that are too difficult. At that point, the teacher *reads the passage to the child* and asks questions about the passage. Based on the child's performance, the teacher decides whether or not the child understands the passage when it is read to him or her. If the student does understand the passage, a more difficult passage is read. This process continues until the child encounters a passage that he or she does not understand when it is read to him or her. When this process is completed, the teacher, based on these observations, determines what are known as the *functional levels of reading* for the child.

An informal reading inventory has two purposes. One is to determine a child's independent level, instructional level, frustration level, and capacity level. The second purpose

is to observe and record what may be causing the child difficulties and how the child attempts to overcome problems when he or she encounters them. When the teacher accomplishes these two purposes, he or she is ready to plan effective instruction.

FUNCTIONAL LEVELS OF READING

The Independent Level. The independent reading level is the level at which the child can read the material with virtually no oral reading errors and with near perfect comprehension.

The Instructional Level. The instructional reading level is the level at which the child is challenged by the material; he or she makes some oral reading errors and has less than perfect comprehension. However, with the aid of a teacher and directed reading lessons (see Chapter 9), the child should be able to cope satisfactorily with the material, and his or her reading skills should improve since they are being challenged.

• The term *instructional reading level* has been used in teaching reading to mean precisely what Vygotsky describes in broader areas of learning. It is the zone of proximal development in reading. It is that level of difficulty where the individual cannot quite cope unaided, but where he or she can cope in cooperation with others who are more accomplished (usually teachers) in performing the task. It is in the zone of proximal development that learning takes place.

Frustration Level. The frustration level is the level at which the child encounters numerous difficulties in oral reading and comprehension falls off to near zero. The child simply cannot read the material—with or without help.

FIGURE 12.1
A TYPICAL PASSAGE FOR USE IN AN INFORMAL READING INVENTORY. (From *Down Singing River,* Betts Basic Readers, American Book (1958) pp. 201, 202.)

The Young Newsboy

Almost everyone knew big Bill,
who worked on the morning newspaper.

"We like the way he writes," many people
would say. "A news story by Big Bill is
always the best in the Garden City News."

Almost no one knew Little Bill.
He wanted to follow in his father's footsteps.
Little Bill wanted to write for the paper,
too, when he grew up.

First, Little Bill wanted
to be a newsboy for the Garden City News.

For a long time Big Bill had told him,
"You are still too young."

201

At last Big Bill said, "I guess you are old enough to carry papers. I was a newsboy, too, when I was young. In the morning I'll be glad to show you how to be one. Get up early."

Next morning Little Bill dressed very early. Big Bill was the one to oversleep.

Still, daylight had not come when they both left for the office. On the way they met the milkman. Little Bill wanted to call, "Hello."

His father said, "Above all, a newsboy must not make any noise. He must not let the neighbors say he woke them up too early."

The Capacity Level. The highest level of material the child understands when the passage is *read to him or her* is known as the *capacity level.* The four levels of reading ability are shown from a student's point of view and from a teacher's point of view in Figure 12.2.

Defining Level. It is customary for those writing about the informal reading inventory to stipulate that this procedure can be based on various kinds of instructional materials. However, this procedure is so intimately related to the use of basal readers, both historically and in current practice, that one presumes the materials come from basal readers unless otherwise stated.

Therefore, when one says that a child's instructional level is third grade and his or her frustration level is fifth grade, one is referring to the child's performance on passages taken from a third-grade reader and a fifth-grade reader from some basal reading series—usually the basal reading series used for reading instruction in the child's classroom.

The term "level" gives one a rough indication of the difficulty of the reading passages used to observe the student's performance. It is a *rough* indication, however, because by some measures some basal reading series are more difficult than others (Bernard and De-Gracie, 1976), and the difficulty of the reading material may change from selection to selection within the same text. The imprecision of the meaning of terms used in assessment is regrettable but to a large extent unavoidable. Educators who lose sight of this imprecision are apt to make unwise educational decisions.

The problem of measuring the precise difficulty of a passage has occupied some of the best-known scholars in the field of reading research and education (Spache, 1953 and 1974; Dale and Chall, 1948; Chall, 1957; Fry, 1968; Klare, 1963, 1976; Bormuth, 1968). Various formulas have been developed that combine some measure of word difficulty and some measure of the difficulty of syntax. These formulas arrive at a measure of difficulty expressed as a grade-equivalent score. The cloze procedure has also been used to estimate the readability of passages (Bormuth, 1968, 1975; Froese, 1975).

♦ There are many absorbing issues connected with readability—its validity, its reliability, its usefulness, its cost (in terms of teacher time and effort) to benefit ratio are some. This topic is treated in For Further Reading at the end of this chapter. It is a very useful topic to pursue, because consideration of the issues involved leads one to consider very basic questions about reading, the reading process, and teaching reading.

CREATING AN INFORMAL READING INVENTORY

Choosing Representative Passages. Two passages are chosen from each level—one for oral reading and one for silent reading. When basal readers are carefully constructed, as most of them are, passages become progressively more difficult from the beginning to the end of each book. To find representative passages, it makes sense to select them from near the middle of the book. It is advisable to choose two passages from the same selection, since comparisons will be made between oral reading and silent reading performance. If passages are taken from the same selection for the two trials, there is less chance that differences in the topic of the passages or in the author's style are responsible for differences in performance.

♦ The meanings of the words *passage* and *selection* can easily be confused. In this book, *selection* refers to whole stories, poems, or essays that appear in basal readers or literature anthologies. *Passage* refers to a portion of connected text taken from a book. It is usually longer than a sentence, but does not include a whole selection.

FIGURE 12.2
FUNCTIONAL LEVELS OF READING FROM A TEACHER'S POINT OF VIEW AND FROM A CHILD'S POINT OF VIEW. (Adapted from Betts, 1957, p. 448.)

Functional Levels of Reading

From a Child's Point of View	From a Teacher's Point of View
Independent level	Independent level
I can read by myself without help, and can understand what I read, I can pronounce almost every word. I feel comfortable and enjoy reading. I read for fun and to find out things. I can give reports on what I have read.	This is the level of supplementary and independent reading. Child should be able to read the book at home or school without aid. The material should cause no difficulty and have high interest value.
Instructional level	Instructional level
I understand what I am taught from the readers and other books and can get honors in the tests. I can pronounce 95 out of 100 words. I don't fidget, read with my lips, or point as I read, but I feel at ease.	This is the teaching level. The reading material must be challenging and not too difficult.
Frustration level	Frustration level
I don't understand half of what I read and I feel worried and unhappy. Sometimes I can't stand still as I read and I'd like to point with my fingers and read with my lips. Often I can't pay attention. I should not read on this step often, for my reading will not improve.	This level is to be avoided. It is the lowest level of readability at which a child is unable to understand. The material is too difficult and frustrates the pupil.
Capacity level	Capacity level
I understand what is being read to me but I would be unable to read the story myself. I can listen to radio stories and other programs and lessons, understand them, and enjoy them. I can give oral reports on what I have heard.	This is the hearing level—the highest level of readability at which a child is able to understand when listening to someone read or talk. Pupil must understand the selection and be able to express himself accurately. No verbalism. Adequate background of experience.

One wants the passages to be typical of the reading levels they represent and the student's performance to be typical of his or her usual performance. Therefore, one would rule out passages that have peculiar features, such as foreign words like *très bien* or unusual names like *Quiqueg;* one would also rule out passages that could not be understood without knowledge of some little-known fact, such as that Theodore Roosevelt was sworn into the office of president in Buffalo, New York.

Length of Passages. The length of the passages chosen for an informal reading inventory should reflect both the characteristics of the texts at various levels and the kind of reading tasks children in various grades are accustomed to. An entire selection in a primer may be less than fifty words long, and during a typical reading lesson children are asked to read very short portions at one time. For an informal inventory, one wants to observe as much reading performance as possible, so the minimum length of passages chosen at the preprimer and primer level is twenty-five words. The minimum at first grade is fifty words.

Beyond primary grades, selections in basal readers become much longer, and students are asked to read several pages at a time in normal reading assignments. At third grade level and above, 100 words is considered a bare minimum for an informal inventory. At this point the time needed to administer the test becomes a limiting factor. One would probably not want to choose passages as long as 200 words at any level because of time considerations.

If passages do not represent the difficulty of the basal level, or if they are atypical, or if the length of the passage creates an unusual reading task for the student, the procedure is not valid—that is, the procedure does not test what it is purported to test.

Writing Comprehension Questions. About ten comprehension questions are written to accompany each passage chosen for an informal reading inventory. Since passages through the second-grade level tend to be very short, fewer comprehension questions (five to eight) are written to accompany these passages.

Guidelines for creating comprehension questions to accompany passages reflect the same concerns as those expressed in Chapters 8 and 9. Teachers are advised to ask only a few literal-factual questions about the passage (one-third such questions are sometimes rec-

ommended). The remaining questions should call for such skills as recalling sequences, stating main ideas, and perceiving cause and effect and should reflect higher levels of comprehension such as interpretation and application of knowledge gained through reading the passage. Ruddell's (1978) skills by level of comprehension framework (see Figure 9.11) is a handy guide for generating and classifying questions. Each question is labeled in terms of the level of comprehension it is designed to test (see Figure 12.3, for example).

Preparing Materials. During the procedure, the student reads from the books where the passages appear. This permits the teacher to observe a child very closely and carefully while the child is reading from the materials normally used in instruction. The size of page and type and the art work and graphics are all present and unchanged.

After passages are selected, they are typed out onto a sheet with the questions, identifying information, and other information that will be useful in recording observations and interpreting the results. This permits the examiner to write on his or her copy of the inventory as the procedure unfolds. Figure 12.3 is a typical teacher's copy of one level of an informal reading inventory.

ADMINISTERING AN INFORMAL READING INVENTORY

Where to Begin. One wants to begin an informal reading inventory at a level where the child will encounter no problems; however, since this is an individualized procedure, the amount of time expended becomes a crucial issue. Starting every child at the preprimer levels will undoubtedly waste much valuable time.

FIGURE 12.3
TEACHER'S COPY OF A PASSAGE PREPARED FOR AN INFORMAL READING INVENTORY.

Second-Grade Reader Level

Passage

The Young Newsboy

Almost everyone knew Big Bill, who worked on the morning newspaper. "We like the way he writes," many people would say. "A news story by Big Bill is always the best in the Garden City News."

Almost no one knew Little Bill. He wanted to follow in his father's footsteps. Little Bill wanted to write for the paper, too, when he grew up.

First, Little Bill wanted to be a newsboy for the *Garden City News.* For a long time Big Bill had told him, "You are still too young."

At last Big Bill said, "I guess you are old enough to carry papers. I was a newsboy, too, when I was young. In the morning I'll be glad to show you how to be one. Get up early."

Next morning Little Bill dressed very early. Big Bill was the one to oversleep. Still, daylight had not come when they both left for the office. On the way they met the milkman. Little Bill wanted to call, "Hello."

His father said, "Above all, a newsboy must not make any noise. He must not let the neighbors say he woke them up too early."

(From *Down Singing River,* Betts Basic Readers, American Book Company [1958] pages 201–202.)

Comprehension Questions

1. Who is Big Bill? (factual)

2. What do people like about him? (factual)

3. Who is Little Bill? (inference)

4. The story says Little Bill wants to "follow in his father's footsteps." What does that mean? (interpretive)

5. What does this expression tell us about this story? Why did the author use it? (applicative)

6. In what way does Little Bill start to be like his father? (interpretive)

7. What time did Little Bill and Bill go out in the morning? Why? (inference)

8. Do you think Little Bill will change his mind about what he wants to be by the time he is grown up? Explain why you think so. (applicative)

Word recognition errors _____
% word recognition errors _____
Number of words = 193
% per error = .52%
Word recognition in oral reading
    4 errors = 98%
    10 errors = 95%
    20 errors = 90%
Comprehension questions incorrect _____
% comprehension questions incorrect _____
Number of comprehension questions = 8
% per incorrect answer = 12.5%
Comprehension score
    1 error = 88% (independent level)
    2 errors = 75% (instructional level)
    4 errors = 50% (frustration level)

(From an unpublished informal reading inventory constructed by Carol Kelly. The Reading Center, State University of New York at Buffalo [1983].)

This passage could be used for silent reading or it could be read to the child for a measure of his reading capacity. In either case, the word recognition errors would be ignored.

Teachers usually have some evidence of how well a child reads from the child's records. Grade-equivalent scores on a standardized reading achievement test may be useful in determining at what level one should begin to administer an informal inventory. However, several studies indicate that standardized tests overestimate a child's instructional level by at least one year (Sipay, 1964). Teachers are advised to begin an informal reading inventory with materials at least two years below a child's grade-equivalent score on a standardized test.

Evaluating the oral reading of the first passage chosen will reveal any gross miscalculations. At this stage, as at every stage in this procedure, good judgment on the part of the teacher is indispensable.

How to Proceed.   The child is presented with the book containing the first oral reading passage. After he or she has found the passage (usually marked with a bookmark), he or she is told to read the passage aloud and to read it carefully because he or she will be asked questions about it.

Recording Oral Reading Performance. As the child reads, the examiner records the child's performance. Two kinds of notations are made: In one, errors in oral reading (that is, inaccurate renderings of the text as it is printed) are recorded. Such inaccuracies are omitted words, inserted words, substituted words, transposed words, and mispronounced words. If a child stays on a word for as long as five seconds without attempting to pronounce it, the examiner supplies the word and records that the word was supplied. Notations for recording these categories of oral reading inaccuracy are found in Figure 12.4.

♦ Kenneth Goodman (1967 and 1969; also Goodman and Goodman, 1977) has made valuable obser-

FIGURE 12.4
SYMBOLS USED TO RECORD ORAL READING ERRORS.

1. *Omission of a word or group of words.* Circle the omitted word or group of words. Example:
   They fly passengers, freight, and mail from one city to another.

2. *Insertion of a word or group of words.* Place an insert mark and write the word(s) above the point at which they were added. Example:
   clear
   The∧sky was bright blue.

3. *Substitution of one meaningful word or several for others.* Example:
   sat on
   A boy had a wagon.

4. *Inverting or changing word order.* Example:
   He ran rapidly there.

5. *Mispronunciation.* Such an error is marked by drawing a straight line under the entire word and writing the pupil's pronunciation phonetically.
   fratific
   Example: traffic

6. *Aid.* When the pupil hesitates for *five seconds* without making any audible effort to pronounce the word, or *ten seconds* if he appears to be trying to pronounce it, the examiner pronounces the word. The error is marked by an underlined bracket.
   Example: [geologists]

(Adapted from the *Gray Oral Reading Tests, Manual of Directions for Administering, Scoring and Interpretation,* by William S. Gray, Bobbs-Merrill, 1967, pp. 5–6.)

vations about the causes of oral reading inaccuracy and the insights such inaccuracies may give researchers into reading and language processes (see Chapter 8). Goodman referred to oral reading inaccuracies as "miscues" rather than "errors," and for a time it seemed the term *miscue* would replace *error* in discussions of oral reading performance.

However, in an informal reading inventory, inaccuracies are interpreted as evidence of difficulty with reading the text—not as evidence of properly functioning reading-language processes. Therefore, the term *error* seems to express more clearly and directly what is being observed, and the term *error* is used in this discussion.

A second kind of notation made during oral reading is designed to record flaws in the quality of the reading. Repeating words, ignoring punctuation marks, word by word (rather than fluent) reading, and pointing with a finger, for example, are observed and recorded. Such observations are useful in planning a child's program but are not taken into consideration in establishing functional levels of reading for the child. Notations for recording observations about the quality of the oral reading performance are found in Figure 12.5.

Oral Reading Comprehension. After the child has finished reading the oral reading passage, he or she closes the book and the examiner reads the questions in order. Correct answers are recorded with a check mark after the question. Incorrect or doubtful answers are written on the teacher's copy, as these answers may be useful in determining the child's weaknesses in comprehension.

Silent Reading. The child is directed to read the passage chosen for silent reading. The examiner observes the child during silent reading and takes note of such habits as lip movement, finger pointing, and looking back and rereading. Such observations may be useful in planning the child's program.

Silent Reading Comprehension. After the child has finished reading the silent reading passage, he or she closes the book, and the comprehension questions for the passage are

FIGURE 12.5

METHODS OF RECORDING FLAWS IN QUALITY OF ORAL READING THAT ARE NOT COUNTED AS ORAL READING ERRORS IN DETERMINING FUNCTOINAL LEVELS.

Symbols, explanations, and examples of flaws in quality of oral reading.
1. *Repetition.* Wavy line under the word(s). Example:
    The boy ran away.
2. *Ignoring punctuation.* Punctuation mark is *X'd* out. Example:
    Wendy looked at the boys and girls. She looked at the toys, too.
3. *Lack of fluency.* Vertical lines where pauses occur. Example:
    Wendy|looked|at|the|boys and girls.

A checklist approach to recording flaws in the quality of oral reading

OBSERVATIONS
(Check statement and circle each part)

_____ Word-by-word reading

_____ Poor phrasing

_____ Lack of expression

_____ Monotonous tone

_____ Pitch too high or low; voice too loud, too

     soft, or strained

_____ Poor enunciation

_____ Disregard of punctuation

_____ Overuse of phonics

_____ Little or no method of word analysis

_____ Unawareness of errors

_____ Head movement

_____ Finger pointing

_____ Loss of place

(From *Examiner's Record Booklet for the Gray Oral Reading Test.* Indianapolis: Bobbs-Merrill, 1963, p. 1.)

asked, answered, and recorded in the same manner as the oral reading comprehension questions.

Oral Rereading. After the silent reading comprehension questions have been asked and answered, the child may be asked to open the book once again to the silent reading passage, to find the answer to an additional question, and to read orally that portion of the text that answers the question. The examiner notes the child's performance in rereading a portion of the passage which he or she has just read silently. The examiner also observes the child's behavior in looking for particular information. Such observations may be useful in planning the child's reading program. This is an optional phase of the inventory; the child's performance is not considered in establishing functional levels of reading.

DETERMINING FUNCTIONAL LEVELS

Two criteria are considered in determining a student's functional level: the word recognition score in oral reading and the comprehension scores.

Word Recognition Errors in Oral Reading. The word recognition score in oral reading is determined by the number of reading inaccuracies (see Figure 12.4) per 100 words in the test passage. Since passages are rarely exactly 100 words, the percent per error is calculated based on the number of words in the passage:

$$\frac{1}{\text{number of words in the passage}} \times 100$$
$$= \% \text{ per error}$$

If a passage contains 100 words, 1 percent is deducted from 100 percent for each error in determining the word recognition in oral reading score. If a passage contains 50 words, 2 percent is deducted from 100 percent for each error in determining the word recognition in oral reading score.

The crucial percentages in determining the functional levels are 98, 95, and 90 percent. Therefore, the number of oral reading errors that result in these crucial percentages is sometimes calculated and recorded on the teacher's copy of the oral reading passage, as in Figure 12.3. Percentages based on different total numbers of words in passages are presented in Figure 12.6.

FIGURE 12.6
CALCULATIONS OF NUMBER OF ORAL READING ERRORS FOR DETERMINING FUNCTIONAL READING LEVELS BASED ON THE NUMBER OF WORDS IN A PASSAGE.

Number of words = 193
% per error = .52%
Word recognition in oral reading
    4 errors = 98%
    10 errors = 95%
    20 errors = 90%

Number of words = 105
% per error = 1%
Word recognition in oral reading
    2 errors = 98%
    5 errors = 95%
    10 errors = 90%

Number of words = 173
% per error = .58%
Word recognition in oral reading
    3 errors = 98%
    9 errors = 95%
    17 errors = 90%

Comprehension Score. The comprehension score is determined by the number of comprehension questions answered correctly and expressed as a percent. The crucial percentages for comprehension in determining the functional level are 90, 75, and 50 percent. Since the number of questions varies as a function of the length of the passage, the number of correct answers that result in these crucial percentages is sometimes calculated and recorded on the teacher's copy of the oral reading *and* silent reading passages, as in Figure 12.3. Percentages based on different numbers of questions are presented in Figure 12.7.

Quantitative Criteria. Figure 12.8 shows the criteria widely accepted in determining functional levels of reading. Unfortunately, an individual student's performance rarely fits these criteria precisely, and examiners have to rely on other observations to estimate the child's functional levels.

For example, an examiner estimated the functional levels of a fourth-grade child whose scores are reported in Figure 12.9 to be:

— Independent level—second grade
— Instructional level—third grade
— Frustration level—fourth grade

Although the word recognition score at third grade is below the instructional level, the comprehension scores at the third-grade level are at the instructional level. The examiner took the seriousness of the word recognition

errors at the third-grade level into account and determined that the third-grade passage would be appropriate for instruction.

DISCOVERING DIFFICULTIES

The second and equally important purpose of the informal reading inventory is to

FIGURE 12.7
CALCULATION OF NUMBER OF COMPREHENSION QUESTIONS ANSWERED INCORRECTLY FOR DETERMINING FUNCTIONAL READING LEVELS BASED ON THE NUMBER OF COMPREHENSION QUESTIONS.

Number of comprehension questions = 10
% per correct answer = 10%
      1 error = 90%
      2 errors = 80%
      5 errors = 50%

Number of comprehension questions = 8
% per correct answer = 12½%
      1 error = 87%
      2 errors = 75%
      4 errors = 50%

Number of comprehension questions = 5
% per correct answer = 20%
      0 errors = 100%
      1 error = 80%
      2 errors = 60%

FIGURE 12.8
CRITERIA FOR DETERMINING FUNCTIONAL LEVELS OF READING.

Functional Reading Level	Percent Word Recognition in Oral Reading	Percent Comprehension Questions Answered Correctly
Independent level	98%	90%
Instructional level	95	75
Frustration level	90	50
Capacity level		75

FIGURE 12.9
INFORMAL READING INVENTORY SCORES FOR A FOURTH-GRADE PUPIL.

Grade level of Passage	Percent Word Recognition in Oral Reading	Percent Oral Reading Comprehension	Percent Silent Reading Comprehension
2	99%	90%	90%
3	90	80	80
4	90	70	60

discover and classify possible causes of reading difficulties. Betts (1957) suggests a "detailed form" (pp. 472–474) to be used by inexperienced examiners to record observations that will presumably determine the strategies that will be used in teaching the child to read. Figure 12.10 presents a list of behaviors to be noted during oral reading and silent reading that follows the Betts list very closely.

The reader may notice that this list is very much like the lists of behaviors one is urged to take note of during the individual conference phase of an individualized reading program (see Chapter 11). The same observation made about the individualized reading program can be made about the diagnostic and remedial aspect of the informal reading inventory: The teacher must possess excellent diagnostic skills and knowledge of the reading and learning processes to determine what the child knows, what skills the child possesses, what the child needs to know, and how to teach the child what he or she needs to learn.

IMPORTANCE OF THE TEACHER'S SKILL

In 1957, Betts expressed the belief that "as standards for the professional preparation of teachers and school psychologists are raised, professional competency should become less serious as a limitation of these techniques [the Informal Reading Inventory]" (p. 471).

However, current writers continue to lament the fact that "the present level of diagnostic proficiency among classroom teachers leaves much to be desired" (Harris and Sipay, 1980) and that "informal reading evaluation is only as good as the person conducting the evaluation . . . the effectiveness of the technique is dependent on the skill of the examiner" (Pikulski, 1978, p. 102). There is in fact startling research evidence (Vinsonhaler et al., 1983) that teachers' diagnoses of causes of reading problems are very unreliable. Different teachers observing the same student tend to identify different causes of failure and recommend different instructional programs.

STRENGTHS AND WEAKNESSES

Because of the many advantages of the informal reading inventory, teachers are encouraged to make the effort to acquire the knowledge and skill necessary to master the technique. The chief advantages of the technique derive from its informality and the fact that the child is tested on materials that are used in instruction and that the procedures used are typical of instruction. This direct link between test and teaching enables the teacher to incorporate observations directly into lessons for the individual. It enables the student

FIGURE 12.10

SUGGESTED LIST OF BEHAVIORS TO BE NOTED DURING ORAL READING AND SILENT READING IN AN INFORMAL READING INVENTORY. (From Betts, 1957, pp. 472–74.)

Difficulties Observed During Oral Reading	Difficulties Observed During Silent Reading	Difficulties Observed Throughout the Procedure
Comprehension Inability to state main idea Inaccurate recall of details Inaccurate recall of sequence of ideas Faulty inferences	*Comprehension* Inability to state main idea Inaccurate recall of details Inaccurate recall of sequence of ideas Faulty inferences	*General Reaction Time* Overly slow Too fast (at expense of accuracy and correctness)
Rate Reads slowly Reads slowly and haltingly Reads too fast	*Rate* Reads slowly Reads too fast	*Emotional Reactions* Indifferent Shy Fearful Aggressive Sullen Rebellious Overconfident
Voice Control High pitch Too loud Too soft Breathing irregular	*Vocalization* Silent lip movement Whispering Low vocal utterance Reads audibly	*Speech Characteristics* Stutters Lisps Immature articulation
Rhythm Word-by-word reading Unable to anticipate meaning Ignores punctuation Hesitates Skips lines	*Finger Pointing*	
Word Recognition Meaningful substitutions Meaningless substitutions Repetitions Insertions Omissions Reverses letters Reverses words Reverses word sequence Overdependence on picture clues Lack of emphasis on meaning Confusion of short vowels Overdependence on initial clues Overdependence on final clues Confusion of initial consonants Confusion of final consonants	*Head Movement* *Tension Movements* Hands Feet Legs Body *Posture* Book too close Book too far Book at an angle *Visual Inefficiency* Frowns Squints Blinks Rubs eyes Shades eyes Covers one eye Complains that print blurs Complains that print doubles	

to see the relevance of the testing experience to his or her learning experiences.

Ironically, these advantages all contribute to the vulnerability of the procedure. A poorly constructed informal reading inventory, like any poorly constructed test, is likely to produce erroneous assessment decisions. An inexperienced or unskilled examiner may fail properly to record a child's performance or may misinterpret a child's performance and arrive at poor instructional decisions.

STEPS TOWARD PROFICIENCY

Using Published Inventories as a Base. One way to eliminate the disadvan-tages of poorly constructed informal reading inventories is to use one of the several *published* reading inventories. Several are shown in Figure 12.11. The advantage of these inventories is that the authors and publishers have had the time and resources to make sure that the passages fairly and accurately represent the level of reading they are supposed to represent and that the comprehension questions assess the skill and level of comprehension they are supposed to assess. Such inventories also offer aids to examiners such as oral reading scoring guides and student record sheets to aid in recording and analyzing performance (see Figure 12.12).

The problem with these inventories is that they lose one of the primary advantages of the

FIGURE 12.11
PUBLISHED READING INVENTORIES.

informal reading inventory: The passages the child is tested on are not in the materials that will be used for instruction. Therefore, the direct link between the test and the placement of the child at his or her instructional level *in the materials used in instruction* is lost, and the direct link between the difficulties discovered during testing and the difficulties the child will encounter in the materials used for instruction is lost.

A helpful first step to creating an informal reading inventory would be to examine a published inventory and evaluate it in terms of the characteristics discussed here: appropriateness of the reading passages, quality of the comprehension questions, usefulness of the recording forms, and criteria for establishing functional levels. Such an exercise would help the beginner to become aware of the many details that must be attended to in creating an informal reading inventory. This exercise might become the basis of a useful class activity.

Learning Diagnostic Skills. A second approach to overcoming the susceptibility of the informal reading inventory to misuse and misinterpretation is to concentrate on the diagnostic skills of the persons administering the inventories (Della-Piana et al., 1970). Since one can only begin to acquire diagnostic skills by reading about them, the reader is urged to acquire these skills through learning to adminster one of the published inventories, preferably with the guidance and supervision of a reading specialist.

One way to become proficient in recording oral reading performance is to:

1. Audio- or video-tape several children reading passages orally and answering the questions from a published reading inventory.

2. Follow the procedures in the test manual. Record, score, and interpret the oral reading performance of the children. Replay the tape as necessary to record the children's performances accurately.

3. Repeat this procedure until you are able to administer, score, and interpret the test *without* replaying the tape.

4. Compare your assessment of oral reading errors, comprehension question performance, and assessment of difficulties with others (the class instructor or other students) who have carried out this procedure on the same recorded reading performance. You will no doubt discover many discrepancies at first. Some can be resolved through replaying the recording; others may be resolved through discussion that will clear up misconceptions relating to terminology or concepts.

This exercise will serve three purposes.

1. It will enable you to learn and practice the skills necessary to administer and record an oral reading performance with some degree of confidence.

2. It will enable you to learn and practice the skills necessary to administer a large and important part of an informal reading inventory with some degree of confidence.

3. It will give you a realistic sense of the value of the process. You will discover that the process reveals a great deal about the student's reading, but that knowledgeable and skillful examiners will not always agree on how to interpret the results. This may help you to see the wisdom of keeping your assessment and instructional decisions tentative and remaining alert while teaching the child for evidence that the decisions were correct (or incorrect).

FIGURE 12.12
EXAMPLE OF A SUMMARY SHEET FOR AN INDIVIDUAL READING INVENTORY.

Individual Reading Inventory Summary

NAME _____   DATE _____
GRADE _____   AGE _____
SOURCE OF PASSAGES _____

Level	% Word recognition in oral reading	% Comprehension in oral reading	% Comprehension in silent reading	% Comprehension in listening (capacity)
Primer				
First				
Second				
Third				
Fourth				
Fifth				
Sixth				
Seventh				
Eighth				
Ninth				

Functional reading levels: Skills needed:

Independent _____

Instructional _____

Frustration _____

Capacity _____

Comments:

Standardized Individual Diagnostic Tests

DURRELL ANALYSIS OF READING DIFFICULTIES (1980)

The Durrell Analysis of Reading Difficulties Test is an individually administered test of oral reading, silent reading, listening comprehension, word recognition, and word analysis. It is designed for use with children whose reading ability falls within the range of nonreader through sixth grade. Optional subtests include tests of letter knowledge, hearing sounds in words, visual memory of words, phonic spelling of words, spelling, and handwriting.

Although grade-equivalent norms are provided, the authors state that the test is "designed primarily for observing faulty habits and weaknesses in reading which are pertinent to planning a 'remedial program.'" In keeping with their aims, the authors have included numerous checklists designed to alert the examiner to behaviors that may be important in making instructional decisions. The authors believe that observing the behaviors included on these checklists is more important than grade-equivalent scores. This is undoubtedly true. Salvia and Ysseldyke (1981) assert that becuase there are no data in the manual about the normative sample, reliability, or validity, the grade-equivalent scores should not be used in any event.

The Durrell Analysis enables the examiner to observe the reader in a wide variety of reading and reading-related activities, and the checklists guide the examiner's observations. For these reasons, this test is useful for learning to use diagnostic techniques. It is desirable to learn and practice administering the test under the guidance of a reading specialist and to compare notes with other examiners observing the same student's performance.

Experienced users of the Durrell Analysis of Reading Difficulty rarely use all the subtests. Some experts (Pikulski, 1978) claim that the considerable time necessary to administer the Durrell Analysis of Reading Difficulties would be better spent using informal techniques. What is suggested here is that gaining proficiency on the Durrell will enhance one's informal diagnostic skills, whether or not one continues to use the Durrell after learning these skills.

OTHER STANDARDIZED INDIVIDUAL TESTS

Those specializing in diagnosis of reading disabilities will want to become familiar with other standardized individual diagnostic tests, such as the Gray Oral Reading Test, the Gilmore Oral Reading Test, the Spache Diagnostic Reading Scales, and the Gates-McKillop Reading Diagnostic Tests.

◆ Assessment techniques that are designed to discover precisely what a child knows, what a child can do, and what a child needs to learn have come to be referred to as *diagnostic* tests or techniques. The word *diagnostic* was of course borrowed from medicine. The use of this term in education is in some ways unfortunate because (in the minds of most people, at least) diagnosis in medicine is a precise science. When teachers borrow the terminology of medicine, they sometimes assume an arrogance that results from having precise and useful knowledge that is shared by very few. This kind of arrogance is unwarranted. More important, it is destructive. The usefulness of diagnostic techniques in teaching reading depends on the knowledge, skill, intelligence, and open-mindedness of the person doing the assessment. Arrogance does not replace any of these qualities. Arrogance can neutralize these qualities even when they are present.

Standardized Group Diagnostic Tests

Standardized group diagnostic tests are paper and pencil tests administered to groups of students, but the tests attempt to measure progress in individual skill areas in reading rather than to measure reading achievement in a general sense, as survey tests of reading achievement do. The Stanford Diagnostic Reading Test, for example, has subtests in auditory vocabulary, auditory discrimination, phonetic analysis, structural analysis, word reading, reading comprehension, and rate. (Although not all subtests appear on all four levels of the test, which covers grades 1 through 12.) Another battery of tests, The Silent Reading Diagnostic Tests, are designed for pupils whose reading skills range from grades 2 through 6. It has subtests in recognizing words in isolation, recognizing words in context, identifying root words, separating words into syllables, applying syllabication rules, blending sounds, distinguishing beginning sounds, distinguishing ending sounds, and distinguishing vowel and consonant sounds.

The advantage of group diagnostic tests is that many tests can be administered at once. However, although the results may help the teacher pinpoint *areas* of weakness in students' reading skill, a teacher cannot plan a program for a child without knowing which items the student failed to answer correctly. These tests also fail to give the teacher the opportunity to observe the child while taking the test. For these reasons, group diagnostic tests are a poor third choice when compared to informal reading inventories or individually administered standardized diagnostic tests.

♦ The assessment techniques for determining specific reading difficulties (diagnostic techniques) that have been reviewed here can be classified as coming under the empiricist or the rationalist sphere of influence, just as reading methods can be so classified. The informal reading inventory has many characteristics of the rationalist sphere. The procedure begins with a holistic reading performance. From this performance, individual skills are identified and may be isolated for teaching. It is a holistic, top-down approach to assessment and is based on many of the same assumptions as the eclectic basal reading and the individualized reading program approaches.

The standardized group diagnostic tests described here reflect the empiricist assumptions. Subskills are tested individually. This is an atomistic, bottom-up approach to assessment, and it is based on many of the same assumptions as the programmed instruction and the skills management approaches.

Criterion-Referenced Testing

THE EMPIRICIST TRADITION

A review of the seven steps taken in creating a skills management system (Chapter 11) will remind the reader that mastery tests are at the heart of the program. Skills management systems are based on assumptions that have been repeatedly related to the empiricist sphere of influence in teaching reading. The assumptions are that the reading process can be analyzed into small, sequential skills; that the presence or absence of these skills can be measured; and that teaching reading is essentially the process of discovering where the student is in mastery of the skill sequence and teaching the next skill in the sequence. Tests associated with skills management systems are often criterion-referenced tests.

The term *criterion-referenced test* was first used by Glaser (1963) to identify tests that measure mastery of content. Glaser argued that important instructional decisions cannot be made on the basis of how a child's performance compares with a normative sample (as determined by standardized achievement tests) or even on the basis of whether a child's current performance exceeds past performance (as can be determined through diagnostic tests). Important instructional decisions are made on the basis of how well a child has mastered some content (skill, knowledge, and so on).

Criterion-referenced tests usually consist of items that repeatedly measure the same category of skill or knowledge. The child must answer nearly every item correctly to pass the test. In other words, the child's performance must meet a standard or *criterion* set so high that meeting it demonstrates mastery of the category.

For example, if one wanted to know if a student knew and could employ the VCCV rule for dividing two-syllable words into syllables (see Chapter 4), one might give the child a test like the one in Figure 12.13. Notice that mastery is ten out of twelve, or over 80 percent correct responses. Another way of saying this is that the criterion for passing this test is ten correct, or over 80 percent correct.

♦ *Criterion* is the seldom heard but correct singular form of the more commonly heard word *criteria.*

FIGURE 12.13
A CRITERION-REFERENCED TEST OF DIVIDING TWO-SYLLABLE WORDS CONFORMING TO THE VCCV RULE.

Directions: Draw a line between the two syllables in the following words.

1. af/ter	7. bounty
2. blizzard	8. argue
3. account	9. totter
4. under	10. motley
5. boulder	11. gambol
6. alley	12. segment

Score _____ (mastery = 10 correct)

Criteria is often used incorrectly as a singular noun. For example, the sentence "What is your criteria?" is not strictly standard usage. "What are your criteria?" or "What is your criterion?" is more acceptable.

THE RATIONALIST TRADITION

Although criterion-referenced tests are frequently associated with skills management systems, they are useful in other approaches to reading as well. A teacher using an individualized reading program may observe that a child does not use phonetic analysis in attempting to recognize unfamiliar words. The teacher may embark on a word analysis program with the child and use criterion-referenced tests such as the one in Figure 12.13. This would not violate the principles of the individualized reading program.

Similarly, criterion-referenced tests are frequently used with basal readers. In the skills development phase of a directed reading lesson (see Chapter 9), and in small groups formed around needs (see Chapter 11), instruction is often based on the assumption that the reading process can be analyzed into small skills which can be taught sequentially. Under these conditions, criterion-referenced tests are appropriate and frequently used.

TWO ASSUMPTIONS OF CRITERION-REFERENCED TESTING

There are two assumptions inherent in the concept of criterion-referenced testing. The first is that the test writer can specify the content the test covers. The writer can itemize the units of content (called the *domain*) and create an item to test each unit of the content. The second assumption is that (a) the test includes every item that is possible to test the content, or (b) that it contains a representative sample of all the items that are possible.

An Easy Case: An Extraordinarily Limited Domain.   For example, it is easy to produce a criterion-referenced test of recognizing and naming upper- and lower-case letters. One simply prints the twenty-six upper-case letters on cards and the twenty-six lower-case letters on cards and presents them to the student one at a time. The student says the name of each letter presented. One could set the criterion at 100 percent.

The domain of letter recognition is unusually easy to specify. The alphabet is a small, limited set. Even here, the test of letter recognition is rather long—fifty-two items. One might want to shuffle the cards and present the subject with twenty-five letters randomly chosen. One might presume that a child who performed with 100 percent accuracy on this set would perform with 100 percent accuracy on the entire set.

A More Difficult Case: A Domain That Can Be Defined but Not Listed.   In testing even seemingly simple concepts, the domain often becomes so large that it is not practical to list every item of content. For example, if one wanted to test the child's mastery of the VCCV rule for dividing two-syllable words (as in Figure 12.13), the domain might be defined as all two-syllable words where the rule applies and that the child would be likely to encounter. Certainly, one cannot practically enumerate all such words. Even if it were practical, one would not want to test the child on every word in the domain. In order to satisfy the assumptions of criterion-referenced testing, one needs only to present a representative sample of all the words in the domain.

As one proceeds through the reading curriculum from letter recognition to syllabication rules, recognizing words in context, vocabulary knowledge, and finally comprehension skills, it becomes progressively more difficult

to satisfy the assumption that the test measures all instances of a given domain or that it presents an unbiased sample of a domain. It is for this reason that criterion-referenced tests tend to concentrate on atomistic reading skills where the domain is easily defined (if not easily listed or itemized).

When the Domain Cannot Be Listed and Is Difficult to Define.   Several researchers have proposed systems of writing comprehension test items that will produce an unbiased sample of all the comprehension questions that could be written over a given passage (Bormuth, 1970; Finn, 1975; Roid and Haladyna, 1982). However, people who write so-called criterion-referenced tests of such things as comprehension or recognizing words in context often fail to specify the domain or to establish that the test is a representative sample of the domain. The only characteristic of such tests that leads them to be called criterion-referenced is that a passing (or criterion) score is supplied by the test writer.

Standardized Achievement Tests and Formative Evaluation

Most of the information teachers need about student achievement is properly obtained through diagnostic techniques or criterion-referenced tests. Although authors of standardized achievement tests frequently make an effort to show how their tests might be useful in identifying reading difficulties, these tests were not designed for and are not useful for this purpose.

Standardized achievement tests may contribute to formative evaluation, but the contribution is indirect. First, standardized test scores and analysis of an individual's errors may give a teacher some leads on where to start informal assessment. Second, standardized survey test results offer teachers a valuable touchstone for the conclusions they draw from informal procedures. Although grade-equivalent scores earned on standardized survey tests tend to be higher than the instructional level arrived at in an informal reading inventory (Sipay, 1964), standardized scores at wide variance from the results of an informal assessment should provoke further investigation.

SUMMARY

Two qualities all tests must possess are validity and reliability. If a test has validity, it measures what it is designed to measure. Some methods of establishing validity are face validity, content validity, concurrent validity, and predictive validity. If a tests is reliable, it measures some skill or knowledge that is relatively stable and (1) it yields approximately the same measure from one testing session to the next (test-retest reliability), (2) one set of items on the test yields about the same measure as another set of items (split-half reliability, (3) one form of the test yields the same measure as another form of the test (alternate-form reliability), and (4) one person scoring the test will arrive at the same score as another (inter-rater reliability). Since the procedures used to establish validity and reliability are beyond the technical skills of many teachers, in choosing tests it is advisable to be guided by reviews published by experts.

Tests should be administered to gain specific information. Questions of what a child knows so as to decide what to teach that child next are answered through evaluation proce-

dures such as informal reading inventories, diagnostic tests, and criterion-referenced tests. Questions of what the child knows as compared to what one would expect the child to know are answered through evaluation of the child's individual characteristics (Chapter 10), plus an evaluation of the child's achievement compared to that of others in the age group or grade in school. The latter depends on standardized norm-referenced achievement tests. Questions of how groups of students are performing compared to others of the same age or in the same grade are most often asked by school administrators and policymakers. These questions tend to be answered exclusively through standardized norm-referenced tests.

Published standardized tests of reading achievement are the product of years of test-making technology. They are standardized in the sense that the directions and conditions under which they are taken by students and graded by administrators are uniform from setting to setting. These tests are norm-referenced. They are administered to large numbers of students who represent a carefully described population called the *normative group*. Through statistical procedures, scores earned by students taking the test are converted to scores that indicate the relative standing of the child as compared to the normative group. Grade-equivalent scores, age-equivalent scores, and percentiles are all derived scores of this kind.

Most standardized tests are survey tests. The score they yield is a global estimate of a person's reading achievement—or a *survey* of skills. They are often designed to be administered in groups. Standardized, norm-referenced achievement tests designed to be administered individually are also available. They are usually used to verify the results of group achievement tests when these tests are used to place students in other than normal classrooms.

Assessment that is done as part of instruction or that is carried out to determine teaching strategies is called formative evaluation. Three kinds of formative evaluation are the informal reading inventory, diagnostic testing, and criterion-referenced testing.

The informal reading inventory is a technique in which the student is asked to read a series of passages of increasing difficulty orally and silently. Through observing the child's word recognition errors in oral reading and performance on comprehension questions, the examiner determines the child's independent, instructional, and frustration levels of reading. Through performance on comprehension questions on passages read to the child, a capacity level is also determined. The "levels" are determined by the level of the basal reader where the passages used in the procedure are found. This definition of the difficulty of passages is imprecise. More precise measures of passage difficulty have been attempted through formulas known as *readability formulas*.

Creating an informal reading inventory involves choosing passages at each level that are representative and that are of the appropriate length. Comprehension questions are written and teacher's copies of the materials are prepared with the passages, questions, and scoring and evaluating aids.

Administering an informal reading inventory involves recording oral reading performance, administering the oral reading comprehension test questions, the silent reading passage, and the silent reading comprehension questions. Through a combination of evaluating the errors in oral reading and the answers to the comprehension questions, levels are determined. This aids the teacher in determining the level of materials to use in instruction. Teaching strategies are determined through observations made while the student is engaged in the informal reading inventory.

Because the informal reading inventory is teacher-made, teacher-administered and teacher-evaluated, the procedure is very susceptible to problems of validity and reliability. It is suggested that experience with published reading inventories may help in both constructing and learning to administer an informal reading inventory.

Standardized individual diagnostic tests are also used in formative evaluation. Although these tend to be norm-referenced tests, norm referencing is not very useful for formative evaluation. Parts (subtests) of these tests are often used to get information on particular reading skills. At such times, the norms cannot be legitimately used. It is sometimes useful for teachers to administer standardized individual diagnostic tests to observe the student engaging in a wide variety of reading tasks. This experience may help the teacher to become aware of behaviors relevant to making instructional decisions.

Criterion-referenced tests are appropriate where the content to be tested can be specified or itemized so that the test can measure every item of content or cover a representative sample. One can then infer the percentage of the content the student has mastered from the percentage of items correct on the test performance. When these conditions are met, one can set the criterion score near 100 percent. When the criterion is met, one infers that the student has mastered the content measured by the test.

With some aspects of reading instruction, the domain is fairly easy to itemize (such as recognizing and naming the letters of the alphabet). In other aspects of reading instruction, the domain can be defined more readily than it can be itemized (such as applying the VCCV rule to two-syllable words). However, in areas such as comprehension, the domain to be tested becomes very difficult to define. In such cases, tests are sometimes inappropriately referred to as criterion-referenced simply because a criterion score is prescribed.

Standardized reading achievement tests are not directly useful in formative evaluation.

They may be indirectly useful for suggesting where to start formative evaluation procedures, and they may serve as a second source of information to verify the accuracy of informal evaluation.

FOR FURTHER READING AND DISCUSSION

1. The following publications are Reading Inventories. Obtain one or two of them and practice administering them to classmates.

Bader, L. A. *Bader Reading and Language Inventory.* New York: Macmillan, 1983.

Brown, D. A. *Reading Diagnosis and Remediation.* Englewood Cliffs, NJ: Prentice Hall, 1982, 316–63.

Johns, J. L. *Basic Reading Inventory Pre-primer— Grade Eight.* Dubuque, IA: Kendall/Hunt, 1978.

————. *Advanced Reading Inventory Grade Seven Through College.* Dubuque, IA: William C. Brown, 1981.

Rinsky, L. A., and E. de Fossard. *The Contemporary Classroom Reading Inventory.* Dubuque, IA: Gorsuch Scarisbreck, 1980.

Silvaroli, N. *Classroom Reading Inventory,* 3rd ed. Dubuque, IA: William C. Brown, 1976.

Sucher, F., and R. A. Allred. *Reading Placement Inventory.* Oklahoma City: The Economy Company, 1973.

Woods, M. L., and A. J. Moe. *Analytical Reading Inventory.* Columbus, OH: Charles E. Merrill, 1977.

Create your own informal reading inventory using one of the basal reading series listed in Chapter 7. Discuss the problems you encounter in (a) finding passages to represent the level of the basal readers and (b) writing comprehension questions.

Compare your efforts with one or more of the published reading inventories listed above.

2. One of the most complex problems of reading assessment is attempting to determine the level of difficulty of the reading passages used in the assessment procedure. The level of reading difficulty of a text is known as *readability.* George Klare has written several masterful reviews of the literature related to research in readability, as cited below. Read one of these reviews and discuss the assumptions that readability formulas appear to rest upon; that is, what, according to the creators of readability formulas, makes texts difficult to read? Do you agree with this assumption? Do you think other aspects contribute to difficulty? What are they? Do you think they can be measured?

Klare, G. R. *The Measurement of Readability.* Ames: Iowa State University Press, 1963.

————. Assessing readability. *Reading Research Quarterly,* 10 (1974), 62–102.

————. A second look at validity of readability formulas. *Journal of Reading Behavior,* 8 (1976): 129–52.

3. The legitimate use of standardized tests of reading achievement depends on the user's understanding of the concepts of (a) identifying a normative group or population, (b) choosing a representative sample from the normative population, and (c) the normal curve. The following chapters present these ideas clearly.

Salvia, J., and J. E. Ysseldyke. *Assessment in Special and Remedial Education*, 2nd ed. Boston: Houghton Mifflin, 1981. Chapter 4, Descriptive Statistics (pp. 41–64); Chapter 5, Quantification of Test Performance (pp. 65–76); Chapter 8, Norms (pp. 114–127).

What are some of the dangers of misusing standardized reading achievement tests? You may want to relate the problems of IQ testing to the problems of interpreting standardized tests of reading achievement by referring to Chapter 10, For Further Reading and Discussion.

REFERENCES

Beldin, H. O. Informal reading testing: Historical review and review of the research. In W. K. Durr (ed.), *Reading Difficulties: Diagnosis, Correction, and Remediation*. Newark, DE: International Reading Association, 1970, 67–84.

Bernard, D. P., and J. DeGracie. Vocabulary analysis of new primary reading series. *The Reading Teacher*, 30 (1976): 177–80.

Betts, E. A. *The Prevention and Correction of Reading Difficulties*. Evanston, IL: Row, Peterson, 1936.

——————. *Foundations of Reading Instruction*. New York: American Book, 1957.

Bloom, B., S. Hastings, and G. Madaus. *Handbook of Formative and Summative Evaluation of Student Learning*. New York: McGraw-Hill, 1971.

Bormuth, J. R. The cloze readability procedure. In J. R. Bormuth (ed.), *Readability in 1968*. Champaign, IL: National Council of Teachers of English, 1968, 40–47.

——————. *On the Theory of Achievement Test Items*. Chicago: University of Chicago Press, 1970.

——————. The cloze procedure: Literacy in the classroom. In W. D. Page (ed.), *Help for the Reading Teacher: New Directions in Research*. Urbana, IL: National Conference on Research in English, 1975, 60–89.

Brown, D. A. *Reading Diagnosis and Remediation*. Englewood Cliffs, NJ: Prentice-Hall, 1982.

Buros, O. K. (ed.). *The Eighth Mental Measurements Yearbook*, Vols. I and II. Highland Park, NJ: Gryphon Press, 1978.

Chall, J. S. Readability: An appraisal of research and application. *Bureau of Educational Research Monographs* (1957).

Dale E., and J. S. Chall. A formula for predicting readability. *Educational Research Bulletin*, 27 (1948): 11–20, 28.

Della-Piana, G., B. J. Jensen, and E. Murdock. new directions for informal reading assessment. In W. K. Durr, *Reading Difficulties: Diagnosis, Correction and Remediation*. Newark, DE: International Reading Association, 1970.

Diederich, P. B. *Measuring Growth in English*. Urbana, IL: National Council of Teachers of English, 1974.

Durrell, D. Individual differences and their implications with respect to instruction in reading. In *Teaching of Reading a Second Report, The 36th Yearbook of the National Society for the Study of Education*. Bloomington, IL: Public School Publishing, 1937, 325–56.

——————. *Improvement of Basic Reading Abilities*. Yonkers-on-Hudson, NY: World, 1940.

Finn, P. J. A question writing algorithm. *Journal of Reading Behavior* (1975): 341–67.

Froese, V. Cloze readability versus the Dale-Chall formula. In B. S. Schulwitz (ed.), *Teachers Tangibles Techniques: Comprehension of Content in Reading*. Newark, DE: International Reading Association, 1975, 23–31.

Fry, E. A. A readability formula that saves time. *Journal of Reading*, 11 (April 1968): 513–16.

Gates, A. I. *Improvement of Reading*. New York: Macmillan, 1936.

Glaser, R. Instructional technology and the measurement of learning outcomes: Some questions. *American Psychologist*, 18 (1963): 519–21.

Goodman, K. S. Reading: A psycholinguistic guessing game. *Journal of the Reading Specialist*, 6 (1967): 126–35.

——————. Analysis of reading miscues: Applied psycholinguistics. *Reading Research Quarterly*, 5 (1969): 9–30.

——————, and Y. M. Goodman. Learning about psycholinguistic processes by analyzing oral reading. *Harvard Educational Review*, 47 (1977): 317–33.

Harris, A. J., and E. S. Sipay. *How to Increase Reading Ability*, 7th ed. New York: David McKay, 1980.

Johnson, M. S., and R. A. Kress. *Informal Reading Inventories,* Reading Aids Series. Newark, DE: International Reading Association, 1965.

Klare, G. R. *The Measurement of Readability.* Ames: Iowa State University Press, 1963.

——————. Assessing readability. *Reading Research Quarterly,* 10 (1974): 62–102.

——————. A second look at validity of readability formulas. *Journal of Reading Behavior,* 8 (1976): 129–52.

Pikulski, J. A critical review: Informal reading inventories. *The Reading Teacher,* 28 (1974): 141–51.

——————. Approaches to evaluating reading. In R. G. Stauffer, J. C. Abrams, and J. J. Pikulski, *Diagnosis, Correction, and Prevention of Reading Disabilities.* New York: Harper & Row, 1978, 53–103.

Powell, W. R. Reappraising the criteria for interpreting informal inventories. In D. DeBoer (ed.), *Reading Evaluation,* 1968 Proceedings, 13, part 4. Newark, DE: International Reading Association, 1969.

——————. Measuring reading performance. ERIC clearing house on reading and communication skills, National Council of Teachers of English, ED 155 589, 1978.

Roid, G. H., and T. M. Haladyna. *A Technology for Test-Item Writing.* New York: Academic Press, 1982.

Ruddell, R. B. Developing comprehension abilities: Implications from research for an instructional framework. In S. J. Samuels (ed.), *What Research Has to Say About Reading Instruction.* Newark, DE: International Reading Association, 1978, 109–20.

Salvia, J., and J. E. Ysseldyke. *Assessment in Special and Remedial Education,* 2nd ed. Boston: Houghton Mifflin, 1981.

Sipay, E. R. A comparison of standardized reading scores and functional reading levels. *The Reading Teacher,* 17 (1964): 265–68.

Spache, G. D. A new readability formula for primary-grade reading materials. *Elementary School Journal,* 53 (1953): 410–13.

Thorndike, E. L. Improving the ability to read. *Teachers College Record,* 36 (November 1934): 123–44.

Vinsonhaler, J. F., A. B. Weinshank, C. C. Wagner, and R. M. Polin. Diagnosing children with educational reading problems: Characteristics of reading and learning disabilities specialists, and classroom teachers. *Reading Research Quarterly,* 18 (Winter 1983): 134–64.

Wheat, H. G. *The Teaching of Reading.* Boston: Ginn, 1923.

NAME INDEX

Abrams, J. C., 259, 288, 292, 325
Adelman, H., 48, 60
Adler, M. J., 204, 225
Allen, C., 152
Allen R. V., 152
Allred, R. A., 323
Almy, M., 59
Alper, M., 234, 257
Ames, W. S., 133
Anderson, R. C., 157, 160, 161, 163, 173, 183, 199, 225
Applebee, A. N., 183
Arthur, G. A., 59
Artley, A. S., 134
Ashton-Warner, S., 65, 66, 84
Askov, E. N., 224, 275, 291, 292
Assam, A., 257
Athey, I., 165, 183, 194, 225
Atkinson, R. C., 152
Austin, M. C., 136, 143, 153

Bader, L. A., 323
Bailey, M. H., 98, 104
Balow, I. H., 190, 227
Baratz, J., 243, 257
Barnhart, C. L., 11, 25, 84, 178, 183
Barr, R., 39, 60
Barrett, F. L., 291
Barrett, T. C., 38, 39, 60, 172, 181
Bartlett, F. C., 183
Beck, I. L., 178, 183, 197–200, 202, 204, 205, 224, 225, 227
Beilin, H., 147, 153
Beldin, H. O., 300, 324
Bereiter, C., 250, 257
Berger, N., 177, 183
Berliner, D. C., 77, 84, 280, 292
Bernard, D. P., 304, 324
Bernstein, B., 20, 21, 25, 245, 249, 250, 255, 256, 257
Bersoff, D., 256
Betts, E. A., 300, 307, 312, 324
Biddle, W. B., 199, 225

Binet, A., 230, 231, 236, 252
Birch, H. G., 241, 257
Black, J. B., 183
Blakey, J., 85, 152
Bloom, B. S., 172, 183, 219, 225, 234, 253, 257, 296, 324
Bloom, L., 230, 251, 257
Bloomfield, L., 6, 25, 81, 84, 183
Blumenthal, A. L., 6, 13, 25
Bond, G. L., 39, 60, 234, 239, 257, 258
Bormuth, J. R., 156, 157, 165, 183, 190, 193, 225, 304, 320, 324
Bortner, M., 241, 257
Bortnick, R., 192, 225
Botvin, G. J., 148, 153
Bougere, M. B., 53, 60
Bower, G. H., 163, 183, 225
Brady, M. E., 174, 185
Brainerd, C. J., 15, 25, 40, 60, 143, 153
Brand, M., 205, 225
Bransford, J. D., 158, 159, 160, 174, 183, 184
Braun, C., 78, 84
Brittain, M. M., 53, 60
Bronfenbrenner, U., 246, 257
Brown, D. A., 230, 237, 240, 257, 301, 323, 324
Brown, R., 109, 123
Browning, W. G., 224
Bruck, M., 245, 257
Bruner, J., 59
Bryan, Q., 39, 60
Buchanan, C. D., 291, 292
Buhler, K., 160
Burke, C. L., 163, 184
Burkes, A. M., 183, 224
Burmeister, L. E., 100, 104
Buros, O. K., 296, 324
Butler, N. R., 258

Calfee, R. C., 50, 60
Callaghan, T., 226
Camperell, K., 192, 226
Carducci-Bolchazy, M., 43, 60
Carner, R. L., 279, 292

Carr, J., 157, 183, 225
Carroll, J. B., 73, 84, 92, 101, 233, 234, 253, 257
Carver, R. P., 197, 216, 225
Cazden, C. B., 48, 52, 60
Ceprano, M., 230, 257
Chall, J. S., 39, 60, 143, 153, 304, 324
Chapman, C. A., 170, 184
Charters, W. W., 256
Chase, W. G., 184
Cherry, C., 8, 25
Chomsky, C. S., 193, 225
Chomsky, N., 12, 13, 16, 25, 141, 150
Christen, W. L., 224
Clark, M. M., 50, 60, 64, 84
Cleland, D. L., 143, 153
Clymer, T., 38, 60, 98, 104, 172, 178, 181, 184,
    201, 225
Cochran, E., 291, 292
Cole, M., 19, 25
Coleman, D., 291, 292
Collins, A., 225
Cook-Gumperz, J., 55, 60
Cooper, C., 226
Copperman, P., 88, 105
Cortright, A., 291, 292
Cowen, S., 143, 153
Cramer, R. L., 48, 60
Creak, M., 240, 241, 257
Cromer, W., 170, 184
Cunningham, P. M., 104, 119, 123
Cutts, W. G., 60

Dahl, P. R., 216, 226
Dale, E., 304, 324
Davie, R., 258
Davies, A., 250, 257
Davies, P., 73, 84, 92
Davis, F. B., 168, 173, 182, 184, 202, 207
DeBoer, D., 325
DeGracie, J., 304, 324
DeHirsh, K., 39, 53, 55, 60
DeSaussure, F., 6
DeStaphano, J. S., 258, 259
Deese, J., 224
Deese, E. K., 224
Deighton, L. C., 134

Della-Piana, G., 312, 324
Deutch, M., 256
Dewey, J., 200–203, 225, 283, 290, 292
Diedrich, P. B., 295, 324
Dolch, E. W., 73, 84
Downins, J., 142, 153
Dreitzel, H. P., 256, 257
Duckworth, E., 72, 84
Dunn, J., 245, 257
Dunning, S., 210, 211, 225
Durkin, D., 49, 59, 60, 84, 113, 121, 123, 147, 149,
    153, 188, 189, 199, 202, 221, 225
Durr, W. K., 191, 197, 199, 225
Durrell, D. D., 38, 39, 60, 61, 300, 324
Duval, E. M., 246, 257
Dykstra, R., 39, 60, 143, 153

Ehri, L. C., 64, 68, 73, 84
Eisenson, J., 241, 258
Eisner, E. W., 257
Elliot, G., 85, 152
Ellison, D. G., 234, 257
Emans, R., 98, 104, 105
Engelhart, M. D., 183, 225
Engelmann, S., 250, 257
Esposito, D., 287, 292

Farr, R., 88, 105, 147, 153, 288, 292
Fay, L., 105
Feldman, M. J., 163, 184
Feldman, S., 39, 61
Feshbach, S., 48, 60
Figurel, J. A., 257
Finn, M. E., 242, 257, 258, 287, 292
Finn, P. J., 55, 60, 204, 226, 245, 257, 320, 324
Fishman, J. A., 256
Flake, E., 85, 152
Fleming, C. W., 39, 61
Fleming, J. T., 183, 225
Flesch, R., 142, 153
Flood, J., 24, 51, 54, 61
Forman, D., 291, 292
Foster, R. J., 204, 226
Francis, W. N., 73, 85
Franks, J. J., 158, 183
Frase, L. T., 199, 226

Freebody, P., 173, 183
Freedle, R. O., 185
Friedland, E., 258
Fries, C. C., 81, 85
Froese, V., 192, 226, 304, 324
Fry, E. B., 55, 56, 60, 74, 83, 85, 143, 153, 225, 226, 234, 238, 258, 304, 324
Furst, E. J., 183, 225
Furth, H. G., 56, 60

Gage, N. L., 256
Galton, M., 281, 282, 285, 292
Gates, A. I., 41, 59, 60, 165, 184, 234, 258, 296, 300, 324
Gavel, S. R., 39, 60
Glaser, R., 318, 324
Glenn, C. G., 162, 185
Goetz, E. T., 183
Gold, L., 153
Goldberg, M., 256
Goodman, K. S., 9, 25, 163, 165, 182, 183, 184, 225, 243, 258, 308, 324
Goodman, Y., 163, 165, 182, 184, 308
Goody, J., 179, 184
Gray, W. S., 76, 81, 85, 308
Green, R., 236, 258
Greenberg, M., 193, 194, 226
Griffin, P., 177, 184
Griffiths, N., 60
Gumperz, J. J., 257
Guthrie, J. T., 84, 183, 184, 185, 225, 226, 227, 292
Guzak, F. J., 202, 226

Haladyna, T. M., 320, 325
Hall, R. A., 11, 25
Hall, V. C., 243, 258
Halliday, M. A. K., 2, 15, 16, 21, 25
Hammill, D., 44, 60
Hammond, W. D., 143, 153
Hanna, J., 105
Hanna, R. P., 89, 105
Harris, A. J., 44, 60, 73, 76, 85, 143, 153, 213, 226, 230, 234, 258, 269, 292, 312, 324
Harris, P., 257
Hartley, R. N., 76, 85

Hartman, T., 72, 85
Harvey, M. R., 251, 258, 281, 292
Hastings, J., 324
Hauke, R. N., 227
Havighurst, R., 59
Hay, K. G., 191, 192
Hayes, R. B., 143, 153
Henderson, E. H., 64, 85
Hensen, D. M., 152
Herr, S. E., 210, 226
Hess, R. D., 59, 245, 246, 258
Hildreth, G. H., 38, 60
Hill, W. H., 183, 225
Hodges, C. A., 188, 189, 202, 226
Hodges, R., 105
Holdaway, D., 291
Holden, M. H., 50, 60, 68, 85
Holmes, M., 59
Honzik, M. P., 236, 258
Hopkins, C. J., 84
Horn, E., 84
Huey, E. B., 81, 85, 168, 184
Hughes, L., 263
Hunt, J. M., 59
Hunt, K. W., 192, 226
Husband, K. L., 216, 226
Huttenlocher, J., 68, 85
Hymes, D., 257

Jackson, A., 200
Jacobson, L., 61, 237, 256, 258
Jacobson, M. D., 73, 85, 234, 258
James, H., 227
Jansky, J., 39, 55, 60
Jensen, A. R., 250, 258
Jensen, B. J., 324
Johns, J. L., 323
Johnson, D. D., 72, 84, 85, 165, 184, 207, 210, 211
Johnson, M. K., 158, 159, 160, 162, 174, 184
Johnson, M. S., 301, 325
Jongsma, E., 191, 192, 226

Kamii, C., 284, 292
Kamil, M. L., 226
Kamin, L. J., 256
Kamm, K., 224

Kant, I., 161, 184
Katterjohn, E., 225
Keats, E. J., 51, 60
Kellmer-Pringle, M. L., 242, 258
Kelly, C., 307
Kemp-Smith, N., 184
Kennedy, D. K., 177, 184
Kessler, J., 241, 258
Kibby, M. W., 39, 60, 207, 226
Kingston, A. J., 191, 226
Kintsch, W., 185
Kirk, S. A., 41, 61
Kirk, W., 41, 61
Kittell, J. E., 191
Klare, G. R., 304, 323, 325
Kleiman, G. M., 227
Klein, H. A., 185
Kogan, L., 256
Kohn, M. L., 246, 258
Koppenhaver, A. H., 59
Kozal, J., 269, 292
Krathwohl, D. R., 183, 225
Kress, R. A., 301, 325
Kucera, H., 85
Kurushima, S., 192, 226

LaBerge, D., 177, 182, 184, 185
Labov, W., 114, 123, 243, 244, 250, 255, 256, 258
Lahey, M., 230, 251, 257
Langford, W. S., 55, 60
Lapp, D., 24, 51, 54, 61
Lee, D. M., 25, 37, 48, 61
Lennon, R. T., 168, 169, 182, 184, 202
Lesgold, A. M., 177, 182, 184
Levin, H., 153, 246, 251, 258
Levine, D. U., 269, 287, 292
Levitas, M., 20, 25, 55, 61, 258
Loban, W. D., 39, 53, 61
Lopardo, G. S., 192, 225
Luckau, J. A., 241, 258
Luria, A. R., 19, 21, 23, 25
Lynch, P., 291

MacGinitie, W. H., 30, 40, 41, 44, 50, 59, 60, 61, 68, 85, 234, 258
Maccoby, E. E., 257, 258

Madaus, G., 324
Mandler, J. M., 162, 163, 184
Mann, H., 81
Manning, J., 183, 225
Martin, R. W., 191, 226
Matthews, M. M., 81, 85, 88, 105
Mazurkiewicz, A. J., 152
McAndrew, D., 193, 194, 226
McCarthy, J., 61
McCarthy, M., 204, 226
McCaslin, E. S., 183, 224, 225
McCourt, A. A., 225
McCracken, G., 45, 61
McCollough, C. M., 134
McDermott, R. P., 55, 61, 76, 85, 287, 288, 292
McDonald, A. S., 226
McGauvran, M. E., 60
McKeown, M. G., 183, 224
Mehan, H., 55, 61
Meichenbaum, D., 205, 226
Melerski, M., 193, 194, 226
Mellon, J. C., 192, 226
Merritt, J. E., 184
Michaels, L., 257, 259
Midwinter, E., 55, 61
Miller, G. A., 8, 25
Milner, E., 59
Moe, A. J., 72, 84, 85, 226, 323
Monroe, M., 54, 61
Morgan, W., 39, 61
Morphett, M. V., 59
Morris, D., 64, 85
Morrison, C., 136, 143, 153
Murdock, E., 324
Murphy, H. A., 38, 61, 72, 84, 85
Murray, F. B., 148, 153

Naremore, R., 244, 259
Negley, H., 105
Nezworski, T., 163, 185
Niles, O. S., 225
Nolen, P. A., 243, 258
North, R., 256

O'Hare, F., 192, 226
Ollila, L. O., 59

Osburn, W. J., 119, 122, 123
Otto, W., 24, 275, 278, 279, 291, 292

Paradis, E. E., 44, 61
Passow, A. H., 256
Pearson, P. D., 157, 165, 183, 184, 192, 207, 210, 211, 225, 226
Perfetti, C. A., 177, 182, 184
Piaget, J., 13, 14, 15, 16, 17, 19, 40
Pike, K., 6
Pikulski, J. J., 259, 288, 292, 301, 312, 317, 325
Polin, R. M., 325
Premack, D., 185
Pryzwansky, W. B., 44, 61

Quillian, M., 225

Ralph, J., 292
Ramsey, I., 243, 258
Randall, D., 85
Rankin, E. F., 216, 226
Reid, E., 291, 292
Resnick, L. B., 184
Reynolds, R. E., 183
Richman, B., 73, 84, 92
Ricks, C., 257, 259
Rinsky, L. A., 323
Rinsland, H. D., 123
Rist, R. C., 76, 77, 85, 237, 258
Robinson, F. P., 221, 226
Robinson, H. A., 54, 61
Robinson, H. M., 39, 54, 184
Roid, G. H., 320, 325
Rosenthal, R., 61, 237, 256, 258
Rosenthal, W., 241, 258
Roser, N., 147, 153, 288, 292
Rubenstein, D., 257
Rubin, J. B., 25, 37, 48, 61
Rubin, D., 224
Ruddell, R. B., 75, 85, 143, 153, 202, 203, 204, 206, 224, 226, 306, 324
Rude, R., 24, 292
Rumelhart, D. E., 162, 163, 185
Rupley, W., 51, 61
Rush, R. T., 84, 85

Russell, D. H., 142, 153
Russell, W., 142, 243, 258
Rutledge, L., 85

Salvia, J., 296, 299, 317, 323, 324, 325
Samuels, S. J., 78, 85, 177, 182, 184, 185, 224, 226
Santostefano, S., 78, 85
Sawicki, F., 85, 152
Schallert, D. L., 183
Schatzman, L., 248, 258
Schmeizer, R. V., 224
Schmidt, G. N., 279, 292
Schneyer, J. W., 143, 153
Schweibel, M., 292
Scribner, S., 19, 25
Sears, R. R., 246, 251, 258
Seibert, L. C., 134
Serwer, B. L., 153
Sharp, R., 55, 61
Shatzman, L., 246, 258
Shaw, F., 59
Sheldon, W. D., 143, 153
Sherk, J. K., 84
Shipman, V. C., 59, 245, 246, 258
Shores, H. J., 216, 226
Shuy, R. W., 101, 105, 184, 243, 257, 292
Silvaroli, N., 39, 61, 323
Silverberg, N., 39, 61
Simon, B., 281, 282, 285, 292
Simons, H. D., 157, 185
Singer, H., 190, 227, 235, 253, 258
Sipay, E. R., 76, 85, 213, 226, 230, 258, 269, 292, 301, 308, 312, 321, 324, 325
Skinner, B. F., 9, 12, 13, 25
Sloan, G., 68, 85
Smith, F., 9, 25, 75, 85, 163, 182, 185
Smitherman, G., 242, 244, 245, 259
Soffietti, J. P., 81, 85
Southgate, V., 269, 292
Spache, E. B., 61
Spache, G. D., 39, 61, 136, 153, 305, 325
Spearman, C., 232, 252
Spearritt, D., 168, 182, 185
Spiegel, D., 24, 292
Stauffer, R. G., 25, 44, 54, 56, 61, 143, 152, 153, 230, 238, 259, 288, 292, 325
Stein, N. L., 162, 163, 185

Stewart, P., 126
Sticht, T. G., 197, 216, 227
Stoneman, C., 257
Stotsky, S. L., 121
Strauss, A., 246, 248, 258
Straw, S. B., 192, 227
Stubbs, M., 179, 180, 183, 185, 243, 250, 256, 259
Sucher, F., 323
Sullivan, M., 226
Swift, M., 59

Tannenbaum, A. J., 256
Taylor, S. E., 219, 227
Terman, L. M., 173, 185, 231, 252
Thorndike, E. L., 73, 85, 122, 165, 185, 300, 325
Thorndike, R. L., 168, 185
Thorndyke, P., 162, 185
Thurston, L. L., 168, 181, 182, 185, 232, 252
Tiedt, I., 51, 61
Tinker, M. A., 239, 257
Tough, J., 250, 259
Trabasso, T., 170, 185
Tucker, R., 245, 257
Tuinman, J. J., 174, 185
Turner, R. R., 243, 258
Turner, T. J., 183

Veatch, J., 66, 85, 152, 268, 269, 270, 271, 292
Venezky, R. L., 50, 60
Vilscek, E. C., 143, 153
Vinsonhaler, J. F., 312, 325
Vygotsky, L. S., 16, 17, 18, 19, 21, 23, 25, 42, 61, 198, 200, 202, 205, 207, 222, 227, 283, 290, 292

Wachs, H., 56, 60
Wagner, C. C., 325
Walcutt, C., 45, 61
Wardaugh, R., 98, 105
Washburne, C., 59
Wasson, B. B., 239, 251
Watt, I., 179, 184
Weaver, P. A., 184
Weaver, W. W., 191, 226
Weener, P., 177, 184
Weikart, D. P., 143, 153
Weiner, M., 39, 61
Weinshank, A. B., 325
Weintraub, S., 39, 61
Whaley, J. F., 162, 183, 185
Wheat, H. G., 300, 325
White, E. B., 203, 244
Whiteman, M., 256
Wiederbolt, J. L., 60
Wilder, G., 189, 190, 227
Williams, A. C., 202, 226
Williams, F., 244, 245, 256, 257, 259
Williams, J. P., 153, 258
Wilson, F. T., 39, 61
Wimmer, H., 170, 185
Windley, V. O., 192, 225
Wolfram, W., 243, 259
Woods, M. L., 323
Worthington, F. A., 281, 292
Wray, M., 88, 105
Wright, R., 263
Wuest, R. C., 143, 153
Wundt, W., 5, 13

Ysseldyke, J. E., 296, 299, 317, 323, 324, 325

SUBJECT INDEX

Ability grouping, 285
Accent and suffixes, 119
Accent, 99
Academic learning time, 77
Advanced Reading Inventory, 323
Advice to teacher, 284
Affixes, 108, 111
    compared to syllables, 122
Age-equivalent score, 298, 321
Alphabet knowledge, 31, 48, 57
Analytical Reading Inventory, 323
Aphasia, 230
Apperception, 5
Approaches:
    analytic, 140, 151
    atomistic, 5, 36, 48, 53, 56, 57
    bottom-up, 4, 6, 22, 121, 122, 268, 289, 318
    holistic, 5, 36, 48, 54, 56, 57, 158
    language experience, 44, 45, 73, 87, 152
    linguistic, 81, 83
    synthetic, 140, 150
    top-down, 4, 6, 22, 121, 268, 289
Aptitude, 233
Assessment, 294
    language development, 53
    oral reading, 313
    purposes of, 296
    school readiness, 24
Associations, 5, 9
Astigmatism, 238
Attention of students, 75, 83
Audiometer, 240
Auditory acuity, 239, 254
Auditory discrimination, 30, 36, 41, 43, 48, 57, 114, 150, 262
Auditory memory, 48, 57, 230
Augmented alphabet, 152

Bader Reading and Language Inventory, 323
Basal readers, 72, 82, 136, 151, 264, 268, 289, 291
    contrasted, 138, 141
    defined, 70
    phonics emphasis and eclectic, 136, 150
    whole word method, 70, 72, 73

Basic Reading Inventory, 323
Basic vocabulary lists, 73
Behaviorism, 9, 11, 12, 13, 15, 23
Binocular vision, 238
Black English, 10, 243
Bottom-up approach, 4, 6, 22, 121, 222, 268, 289, 318
Bound morphemes, 111

California Achievement Tests, 297
Capacity reading level, 304, 305
Carroll, Davies and Richmond Word List, 73
Carroll's Model of Learning, 233, 253
Choosing:
    materials, 281, 290
    tests, 299
Classroom Reading Inventory, 323
Classroom:
    management, 262, 284, 289
    organization, 264, 280
    society, 19
Cloze technique, 191, 207
Cognition, 2, 13, 15, 19, 230
Cognitive development, 14, 15, 16, 20, 23
Cognitive psychology, 3, 6, 13, 15, 23
Communication theory, 7, 8, 11
Compare/contrast strategy for word recognition, 104
Compound words defined, 113
Comprehension defined, 156, 165
Comprehension and:
    cloze, 191
    decoding, 176
    factor analysis, 166, 181
    hierarchical subskills, 169, 171
    holistic semantic events, 158
    knowledge of context, 159
    knowledge of language, 156
    knowledge of the world, 158
    listening, 176
    measurement, 166
    metalinguistic awareness, 222
    miscues, 163
    oral language, 35, 57, 174, 177

Comprehension and: (*cont.*)
 psycholinguistic model, 163
 retelling stories, 163
 schema, 160
 sentence combining, 192
 subskills, 166, 181, 182
 syntax, 156
 vocabulary knowledge, 173, 175, 181
Comprehension instruction defined, 188
Comprehension questions, 157, 306
Computer assisted instruction, 152
Concept of "word," 64
Concepts about Print Test, 50
Concepts related to print, 49
Concurrent validity, 295
Consonant blends, 93, 103
Consonant defined, 90, 102
Consonant digraphs, 93, 102
Contemporary Classroom Reading Inventory, 323
Content area reading, 218, 223, 225
Content validity, 294
Context, 83, 126, 141, 150
Context:
 classifying clues, 133
 linguistic, 128
 physical, 127
 pictures, 128
Criterion-referenced tests, 318, 319, 321, 322
Cross-cultural research, 19
Cultural bias, 256
Cultural factors, 230, 242
Cultural isolation, 248, 255

Decoding, 4
 comprehension, 176, 182
Deductive method, 144, 151
 and empiricism, 145, 148
Derivational suffixes, 109, 110, 111, 113, 116, 120
Diagnosis, 230, 312
Diagnosis and school readiness, 56
Diagnosis, other than reading difficulties, 241
Diagnostic teaching, 42
Diagnostic tests, 321
Dialect, 10, 115, 244
Digraphs, 93
Directed reading lesson, 93, 196, 222
Dolch Basic Sight Vocabulary, 73, 74

Dolch Picture Words, 74, 78, 79
Durrell Analysis of Reading Difficultues, 317

Eclectic approach, 151, 268
Eclectic basal readers, 136
Economic deprivation, 245
Economic factors, 242, 254, 265
Egocentric speech, 14, 17
Elaborated code, 20, 21, 23
Emotional disturbances, 230
Emotional factors, 240, 254, 294
Empiricism, 4, 7, 12, 23
 and the deductive method, 145, 148
 and word structure, 119
Empiricist tradition, 5, 6, 9, 11, 22, 24, 36, 150, 268, 279, 318
English root words, 109, 113
Etymological elements, 121
Evaluating tests, 296
Experience story approach, 72
Explaining failure, 55, 236, 251, 253, 255
Explicit, context-independent language, 21, 22, 24, 245, 249, 251, 255

Face validity, 294
Factor analysis and comprehension, 166, 168
Failure and IQ, 236
Formative evaluation, 322
Farsightedness, 238
Flexibility of reading rate, 212, 216
Fluency, 212, 213
Formative evaluation, 300, 320
Fountain Valley Teacher Support System in Reading, 276
Free morphemes, 111
Frequency and learning, 5, 6, 9, 11
Frustration reading level, 301, 305, 311
Fry Instant Words, 74
Functional reading levels, 301, 305, 310

Gates-MacGinitie Reading Test, 297
Gates-McKillop Reading Diagnostic Test, 317
Gilmore Oral Reading Test, 317
Grade-equivalent scores, 298, 321
Gray Oral Reading Test, 317

Group diagnostic tests, 318
Grouping for instruction, 262–267, 282, 288

Harris and Jacobson Word List, 73
Harrison Jacobson Core Words, 74
Head Start, 59
Hearing loss, 240
Homogeneous grouping, 286

IQ testing and interpretation, 230, 231, 235, 252, 256
Implicit, context-dependent language, 21, 24, 245, 250, 251
Increasing rate and flexibility, 217
Increasing rate, 217
Independent learning, 267
Independent reading level, 301, 305, 311
Individual differences, 229, 262
Individuality, 251
Individualized instruction, 268, 290
Individualized Reading Program, 152, 268, 270, 269, 290, 291
Individually administered tests, 299
Inductive method, 144, 147, 148, 151
Inflectional suffixes, 109, 111, 113, 116, 120
Informal Reading Inventory, 300–303, 307, 313, 316, 321, 323
Inner speech, 14
Instant Words, 83
Institutional written language, 178, 182
Instruction, vocabulary of, 50, 58
Instructional reading level, 301, 305
Integration of word recognition techniques, 131
Intellectual factors , 294
Intelligence, 230
Interest, 65
Interpreting graphics, 219
Iowa Test of Basic Skills, 297
Irregular inflectional systems, 110, 111

Key vocabulary, 65, 82
Kucera and Francis Word List, 73

Language codes, 20
Language development, 13–15, 39, 230
    assessment of, 53
Language differences:
    deficit theory, 244
    deprivation theory, 249
Language experience approach, 44, 65, 82, 152
Language functions, 16
Language learning, 15
Language of school, 249, 255
Language use, 3, 242
Language, study of, 2, 3, 5, 7
Large group instruction, 22
Learning and social group, 72
Learning theory, 9
Letter name knowledge, 33, 39
Letter names, 36, 48
Letter-sound correspondence, 11, 33, 36, 48, 150
Library skills, 220
Linguistic approach, 11, 81, 82, 83
Linguistic readers, 11, 153
Linguistics, 2–4, 11, 12, 15, 23
Listening comprehension, 176, 181
Literacy, 28, 57
Literal questions, 204

Main idea, 209
Mastery learning, 234–235, 253
Maturation, 14, 15, 23, 40
Meaning, 6, 11, 17
Measurement, 4
Mechanical pacers, 223
Mental Measurement Yearbook, 296
Mental age, 231, 252
Mental development, 13
Mental retardation, 230
Metacognition, 205
Metalinguistic awareness, 191
Metropolitan Reading Test, 297
Modeling using context, 130
Morphemes, 120
    bound and free defined, 108, 111
Morphology, 110, 120
Motivation, 274

Nativism, 12, 13, 15, 16, 23
Neurological factors, 230, 240, 254, 294
Nonstandard English, 244
Norm-referenced test, 298–299, 321
Normal curve, 323
Normative group, 298, 321, 323

Operant conditioning, 9, 10, 14
Oral and written language, 177, 182
Oral language, 35, 39, 57
Oral reading, 3
    assessment, 313
    comprehension, 309
    errors, 308, 310
    miscues, 308
    performance, 308
Organization for instruction, 264

Paired associate learning, 82
Paragraphs identifying meaning, 208
Percentile scores, 298, 321
Perception, 5, 6, 28
Perceptual factors, 294
Permissiveness, 10
Personality traits, 28
Philosophy, 2, 4
Phonetics, 88, 102
Phonic-linguistic method, 45–47
Phonics emphasis basal readers, 136
    and empiricism, 151
Phonics, 4, 83, 87, 102, 133, 140, 150
    attitude toward, 90
    criteria for teaching, 90, 92, 103
    defined, 88
    timing instruction, 92
Phonology, 2–4, 102, 242–243
Physiological factors, 230
Picture interpretation, 219
Pictures, use of, 78, 83
Plowden Report, 282
Potential for learning, 233, 237, 253
Poverty, 242, 254
Powerlessness, 247, 254
Predictive validity, 38, 39, 295
Prefixes, 108, 111, 117
    active and absorbed, 121
Prescriptive Reading Inventory, 276

Primary mental abilities, 232
Programmed Reading, 272
Programmed instruction, 152, 291
    branching, 272–274
    linear, 271, 272
Psycholinguistic model, 8, 164, 165, 181
Psycholinguistics, 2, 11, 12, 13, 15, 23, 180
Psychological characteristics, 28
Psychological factors, 229
Psychological perspective, 22, 24
Psychosis, 230
Published reading inventories, 314
Purpose for reading, 198
Purpose of assessment, 296

Questions,
    skills by level of comprehension framework,
        202
    story map framework, 200
    teaching using context, 130, 133

Random House Reading Program, 271, 272, 280
Rate of reading, 212, 213
Rationalist tradition, 4–8, 12–13, 15–16, 22–24,
    119, 147–148, 150, 268, 319
Readability formulas, 304, 322, 323
Reading Placement Inventory, 323
Reading pacers, 216
Reading rate, 225
Reading readiness, 18, 28, 39, 41, 43–44, 51, 262,
    294
    assumptions, 30
    atomistic approach, 36, 48, 53, 57
    empiricist tradition, 36, 48, 53, 57
    history, 58, 59
    holistic approach, 36, 48, 57
    parents' role, 59
    prereading curriculum, 58
    purpose, 37
    rationalist tradition, 37, 48, 54, 57
    school readiness, 58
    tests of, 30, 37
Reading, defined, 2
Record keeping, 270, 275, 279, 284
Referrals, 241
Reinforcement, 9

Reliability, 295, 321, 322
Remedies for failure, 255
Restricted code, 20, 21, 23
Root words, 108, 109, 111, 120, 215

Scanning, 217, 223
Schema, 160, 180, 183, 222
Schizophrenia, 230
School readiness, 55
Scientific concepts, 18
Segregating students by ability, 40, 287
Self-awareness, 246
Self-fulfilling prophesy, 41, 235, 237, 252
Semantic feature analysis, 211, 223
Semantic network, 210
Semantics, 2, 3, 181
Sentence,
    combining, 192, 207
    comprehension, 199, 207
Silent Reading Diagnostic Tests, 318
Silent letters, 94, 103
Silent reading assessment, 313
Silent reading, 205, 309
Skills by levels of comprehension framework, 202,
    203, 222, 224
Skills development, 206
Skills management systems, 274, 278, 289, 291
Skimming, 217, 223
Small group instruction, 22
Socialized speech, 14, 17
Social,
    aspects of learning, 283, 284, 285
    characteristics of learners, 28
    competence, 55
    implications of grouping, 288, 291
    interaction, 15–18
    skills, 56
    status, 28, 55
Society of classroom, 29, 55
Sociological factors, 230
Sociological perspective, 21–24
Sociology, 2, 3
Solidarity, 246, 247, 251
Spache Diagnostic Reading Scales, 317
Spelling and suffixes, 114, 118, 120
Spontaneous concept, 18
SQ3R, 221, 224
Standardized individual diagnostic tests, 317, 322

Standardized reading achievement tests, 297
Stanford Diagnostic Reading Test, 318
Stimulus-response theory, 9, 14
Story grammar, 161–162, 180
Story map framework, 200, 222, 224
Stress, 99, 103
Structural analysis, 107
Student's attention, 83
    attitude, 90
    interest, 90, 94, 112
Study skills, 219, 223–225
Subskills theory:
    and comprehension, 166, 182
    and reading readiness, 41
Suffixes, 109, 111, 214
    accent, 119
    defined, 108
    dialect, 114
    spelling, 118, 120
Survey tests, 299, 321
Syllabication, 97, 133
Syllables, 96, 103
    compared to affixes, 122
Synonymous sentences, 157
Syntax, 2, 242–243
Synthetic approach, 150

Taxonomy of educational objectives, 172
Teacher's attitude, 244, 254
    expectations, 41
    referrals, 230, 239
    responsibility, 224, 291
    role, 18, 143, 152, 283
    skill in diagnosis, 312, 315
Teacher-student interaction, 282, 290
Teaching:
    approaches contrasted, 141
    approaches, research, 142
    as test of readiness, 44
    example lessons, 136–137, 139, 145–146
    inductive and deductive method, 144, 147–148
    synthetic and analytic methods, 140
Test-retest reliability, 295
Thorndike and Lorge Word List, 73
Time on task, 280
Top-down approach, 4, 6, 22, 121, 268, 289
Transformational grammar, 12, 23, 157,
    180

Validity, 38, 39, 294, 321, 322
Visual acuity, 237, 253
Visual discrimination, 29–32, 36, 39, 41, 43, 45,
    48, 57, 150, 262
Visual memory, 45, 48, 57, 230
Vocabulary, 35, 39, 207, 218, 223
    and comprehension, 173–175
    and morphemes, 211
    and semantic features, 211
    and semantic network, 210
Vocabulary of reading instruction, 50
Vowel defined, 90, 102

Whole word approach, 3, 63
    basal readers, 70, 72, 73
    experience story, 72
    frequency, 68, 71–72
    function words, 68–69, 72
    interest, 65, 71
    key vocabulary, 65, 72
    key word approach, 73
    language experience approach, 65,
        73
    linguistic approach, 81
    paired associate learning, 65

practice, 79
principles for teaching, 75
reasons for using, 80
selecting words, 71
words in environment, 67
Wide Range Achievement Test, 294
Wisconsin Design for Reading Skills Development,
    275–277
Withholding instruction, 40, 54
Word bank, 45
Word frequency lists, 73, 83–84
    uses of, 74
Word learning, 34, 57
Word meaning, 64, 207, 209
Word recognition errors, 310
Word structure, 83
    bottom-up approach, 121
    empiricism, 119
    rationalism, 119
    top-down approach, 121
Written and oral language, 182–183
    contrasted, 177

Zone of proximal development, 17–18, 42, 200,
    283

About the Author

Patrick Finn was born in Chicago in 1935. He was educated at St. Leo Grammar School, Calumet High School, Chicago Teachers College, and the University of Chicago. His fascination with language began in the seventh grade under the tutelage of Sister Catherine Ann Muldoon. He was fortunate enough to have a number of teachers who fostered this interest; among them were John Carter, Virginia McDavid, John Bormuth, Rebecca Barr, David McNeill, and Victor Yngve.

Finn has taught grades 6–10 in Chicago, Ft. Greeley, Alaska, and Norridge, Illinois. He has taught at Rutgers University and presently teaches at the State University of New York at Buffalo. He has taught reading courses at the undergraduate and graduate levels and teaches courses in language arts and language acquisition as well.

In 1962 Finn married Mary Groshong, a fellow teacher at Ridgewood High School. His interest in the philosophy, sociology, and history of education grew out of his association with his wife, who has published papers in these areas. They have two children, Molly and Amy.

Finn teaches and writes from September through June and manages a family-owned inn at Point Chautauqua, New York, during July and August.